The Lion
Companion to

Christian
Art

In Memoriam
John Higgitt

The Lion
Companion to
Christian
Art

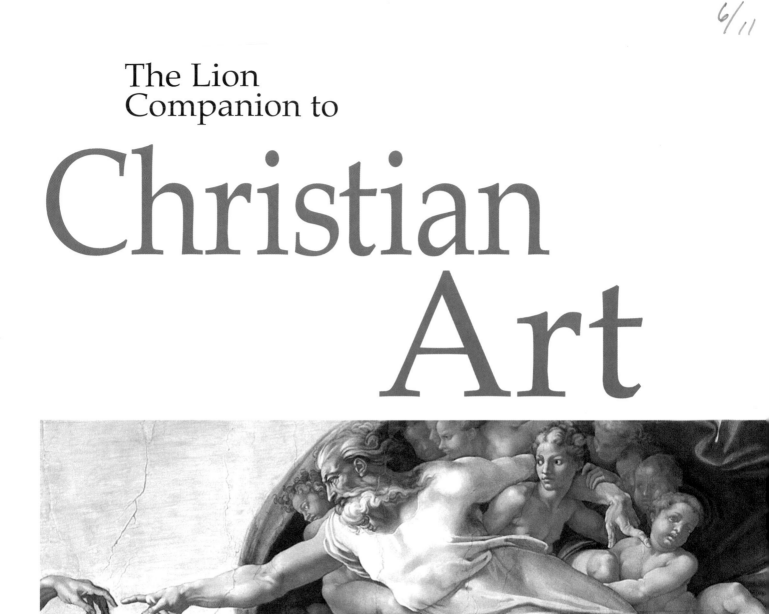

Michelle P. Brown

LION

A Lion Book
an imprint of
Lion Hudson plc
Wilkinson House, Jordan Hill Road,
Oxford OX2 8DR, England
www.lionhudson.com
UK ISBN 978 0 7459 5177 5
US ISBN 978 0 8254 7826 0

First edition 2008
10 9 8 7 6 5 4 3 2 1

Acknowledgements

Scripture quotations are from the New Revised
Standard Version published by HarperCollins Publishers,
copyright © 1989 by the Division of Christian Education
of the National Council of the Churches of Christ in the USA,
and are used by permission. All rights reserved.

A catalogue record for this book is available
from the British Library

Typeset in 10/16 Book Antiqua
Printed and bound in Hong Kong

Distributed by:
UK: Marston Book Services Ltd, PO Box 269, Abingdon, Oxon
OX14 4YN
USA: Trafalgar Square Publishing, 814 N Franklin Street,
Chicago, IL 60610
USA Christian Market: Kregel Publications, PO Box 2607, Grand
Rapids, Michigan 49501

List of Contributors

Dr Victoria Avery, Department of Art History, University of Warwick, UK

Emily D. Bilski, Hebrew University, Jerusalem, Israel

Professor Sheila S. Blair and Professor Jonathan M. Bloom, Boston College and Virginia Commonwealth University, USA

Professor Iole Carlettini, Faculty of Letters and Philosophy, Università di Chieti-Pescara, Italy

Professor Daniela Gallavotti Cavallero, Department of Art History, Università degli Studi della Tuscia, Italy

Meryl Doney, Curator, Hayward Gallery, London, UK

Dr Mark Evans, Senior Curator of Paintings, Victoria and Albert Museum, London, UK

Dr Peter Forsaith, Curator of the Methodist Art Collection, Oxford Brookes University, Oxford, UK

Donald Jackson, The Scriptorium, Hendre, Monmouthshire, UK

Professor Herbert L. Kessler, Department of the History of Art, Johns Hopkins University, Baltimore, USA

Dr Griffith Mann, Keeper, Walter's Art Museum, Baltimore, USA

Professor Nancy Netzer, Director, McMullen Museum, Boston College, Massachusetts, USA

Revd Regan O'Callaghan, St John Bethnal Green, London, UK

Professor Virginia Raguin, College of the Holy Cross, Worcester, Massachusetts, USA

Dr James Romaine, Professor of Art History, The Graduate Center of the City University of New York, New York, USA

Professor Conrad Rudolph, University of California, Santa Barbara, USA

Contents

Introduction

What is Christian Art?

A survey of Christian art will perforce embrace much of the history of art in the West, and in parts of the Middle East, Africa, Asia, the Americas and Australasia, from Antiquity to the present. It is, of course, but one strand in the complex interwoven fabric of world culture and history, and one that in large part reflects the cultural amalgam of Europe and the far-off lands colonized by its peoples. For, despite its Middle Eastern origins, Christianity became appropriated as the social norm of faith within these territories, from the time that it became the state religion of the Roman empire – following decrees by Theodosius I in the 380s CE – until the rise of secularism in the wake of the World Wars of the twentieth century. Much of the art produced therein reflected Christian themes and agendas, sometimes overly conflated with those of the secular sphere. Art in the service of the kingdom of God was frequently employed in pursuit of the aims of worldly kingdoms; but it might also challenge them, just as art, advertising, film, broadcasting and publishing still sometimes do today. And yet, such public contexts for art have been counter-balanced by its role in stimulating private contemplation and an emotional, intellectual and experiential response from the individual. Beauty lifts and inspires the beholder and can thus serve the agendas of both culture and faith. And yet art, religious or otherwise, is not always beautiful.

Christian art can be religious when it serves the needs of the religion and conveys its teachings through recognizable symbols and images; it can be spiritual when, like non-faith-specific art, it helps us to access a dimension of being and of meaning that transcends the purely physical and material; and it can be sacred when it enshrines values that are universally considered sacrosanct and sublime.

The didactic role of art in Christianity – in exploring and commenting upon its meaning, inspiring devotion, and providing a focus for contemplation and prayer –

has stimulated a rich Christian cultural heritage and has contributed to the development of art in general. But other considerations have also periodically surfaced, including misgivings concerning idolatry related to the veneration of iconic images, and unease concerning the commissioning of expensive artworks when Christ advocated the use of wealth to alleviate the misery of the poor. Iconoclasm and evangelical puritanism, verging on philistinism, have resulted at one extreme, while excessively grandiose acts of artistic patronage – aimed more at the glorification of the individual and the office than that of God – have featured on the other. The gaudy or gruesome images of popular piety, which have more to do with folklore and superstition than aesthetics, also feature in Christian art, for it has a function beyond those of 'fine' art. For art associated with faith also has a practical purpose – which is to enable the viewer, and often the maker, to draw closer to God. Such functional images are also part of the story of Christian art, even if they are not usually considered part of the 'history of art'.

Many theologians have written on art, from the times of Gregory the Great and John of Damascus onwards, exploring the shared vocabulary that is often used by those who have experienced spiritual insight through the medium of art: Balthasar, Karl Barth, Hans Küng, Jacques Maritain, Paul Tillich and, more recently, Michael Austin, Margaret Barker, David Brown, David Tracy and Rowan Williams, to name but a few. This book does not seek to do likewise, but rather attempts to trace the meaningful convergence of art, Christian beliefs and social context throughout the course of history. This is a massive, not to say foolhardy, undertaking and some materials and issues will inevitably have received insufficient coverage, or have been inadvertently excluded, for which I crave the reader's forgiveness and forbearance.

Attempting to define 'Christian' art

What then is 'Christian' art? Is it art produced by practising Christians? If so, this would omit the inspirational ecclesiastical stained glass by the Jewish artist Chagall, the paintings of beautiful swan-necked Madonnas by the alchemist Parmigianino, the vapid Virgins of the avowed atheist Perugino, and the sensual figures of saints and sinners by Caravaggio, an artist steeped in the dark side of sex, violence and crime.

Is it art made for a specifically Christian audience or as the sacred art of the Christian faith, used to reinforce its scriptures and rituals in places of worship? If so, do Bill Viola's video installations, which incorporate aspects of Christian philosophy and art into a broader web of cultural references, have nothing to say to the Christian viewer simply because they were not aimed specifically at them? This was surely not

13

Michelangelo's embodiment
of the connection between
the human and the divine
during the moment of
creation, *God creating Adam*,
1508–12; Sistine Chapel
ceiling, Vatican.

13

13

INTRODUCTION

the intention of their makers. If Christian art was solely for the consumption of the faithful, then its power to evangelize or to contribute to the dialogue of interfaith by conveying shared human experience would be negated – let alone the higher goals of art as a universal mode of communication and empathization and as a means of seeking truth and an ultimate reality. The sacred enclave at the heart of Jerusalem itself demonstrates the dangers of any such claims to exclusivity, conflating as it does the sites of the sacrifice of Abraham, the Judaic Temple, which also witnessed much of Christ's public ministry, and the Prophet Muhammad's Night Journey and Ascension, commemorated by the Dome of the Rock. Struggles for control of this holy place have occasioned much conflict across the ages, and sadly this continues still, while it nonetheless remains a sacred symbol to all.

Is 'Christian' art only art that relates biblical narrative or overtly appertains to Christian themes, symbols and iconographies? If so, this would preclude a spiritual response from Christians to non-faith-specific works such as the powerful, organic interlocking forms of the sculpture *Mother and Child* by the humanist Henry Moore. It would likewise negate Christian subscription to Picasso's supremely eloquent protest against the obscenity of war – *Guernica*.

No simple definition evidently suffices, and in the present work a broad approach is adopted which crosses boundaries in order to explore how art has reflected and stimulated a response to the teachings of Christ and to Christian thought and experience across the ages – and how it speaks to us still, helping us to understand, to challenge, to perceive and to grow. As Maritain pointed out, art, like music, can make things 'more than they are' and penetrates beyond the acts of seeing and experiencing to a deeper level of perception. In letting go of the artwork and allowing it to be itself, the artist implicitly acknowledges the power of creation to make a thing become more than it is – a peeling away of the layers of the onion to reveal both its complexity and the regenerative simplicity of its core, akin to the traditional roles of exegesis and hermeneutics. For if the human urge to create can be seen as part of a perpetual quest to draw closer to the ultimate creative force that Christians, like so many others, know as 'God', then giving birth to art – as to children and ideas – is a powerful expression of that impulse. As Archbishop Rowan Williams writes in his book *Grace and Necessity*[1], art is 'bound to show what is in some sense real; it shows something other than its own labour of creation'. Like prayer, it offers a potential route to connection with the Creator, as Michelangelo recognized when he conceived that electrifying iconic image that hovers upon the ceiling of the Sistine Chapel, embodying the moment of creation and the prefiguring of reconciliation, when the outstretched fingertips of God and Adam, the Divine and the human, are about to touch.

14

1

The Art of the Earliest Christians

Judaic and Graeco-Roman Roots

15

The Middle East was the cradle of monotheistic religion, from the time
that the Pharaoh Akhenaten (1353/36–1351/34 BCE) withdrew from Luxor
in the second millennium BCE to found Amarna, a city devoted to the worship
of one god, symbolized by the sun – the Aten. This led to the development
of the Abrahamic faiths, Judaism, Christianity and Islam, which subscribe
to belief in one god whose divine will is revealed to and realized through
a common ancestor, Abraham, and his descendants. Many other religions
also began in this part of the world, including Zoroastrianism, Mithraism
and Gnosticism, and the pantheons of deities of the ancient Egyptians and the
Greeks also took shape there. Not surprisingly, aspects of such earlier beliefs
and art continued to be reflected in the monotheistic religions, as did those of
the Romans, the Celtic and Germanic peoples of Europe, and the less
structured animism and nature-cults of rural communities. Likewise, the
influence of other great world religions can sometimes be detected within
their thought and its visual expression; for example, the symbolic patterns of
Buddhist prayer mandalas are recalled in the geometric painted wall panels of
the Coptic church at Bawit (now in the Louvre) and in the carpet-pages of the
Lindisfarne Gospels from Anglo-Saxon Northumbria.

Some iconographies (images imbued with meaning) were accordingly adapted
from earlier art for Christian use, such as the Good Shepherd with a lamb borne
upon his shoulders, an antique Roman pastoral motif which was appropriated to
represent Christ. Likewise, the head of a youthful hero framed by a sunburst or
nimbus might be taken to represent a historical figure such as Alexander the Great,
the sun god Apollo, or Christ. Such ambiguity could enable overt signalling of
adherence to the Christian faith without provoking official reprisals during times
of persecution, for the interpretation lay in the mind of the beholder.

Good Shepherd with knapsack, a marble sculpture of early fourth-century date in which a traditional classical image of the rural idyll is reinterpreted as Christ the pastor. Mariotti Collection, Pio Christian Museum, Vatican, Rome.

THE ART OF THE EARLIEST CHRISTIANS

Judaism and the Aniconic Tradition

One religion that did not exert as great an artistic influence upon the early visual symbolism of Christianity as might be expected was that from which its scriptures were descended – Judaism. For such imagery did not enjoy great favour within a religion concerned with the implications of idolatry contained in a commandment given to Moses and his people by the Lord in Exodus, 'You shall not make for yourself an idol, whether in the form of anything that is in the heaven above, or that is on the earth beneath, or that is in the water under the earth' (Exodus 20:4). The question of whether it was permissible to depict the divine would preoccupy Judaic, Christian and Islamic religious authorities throughout succeeding centuries, as we shall see. Consequently, at the time of the destruction of the Second Temple in Jerusalem by the Roman General (and later Emperor) Titus (70 CE), Jewish sacred art was minimal and figural images were eschewed. However, the Hellenistic Jewish communities of the Diaspora absorbed the artistic conventions of the Graeco-Roman societies within which they lived and increasingly adopted plant, animal and figural motifs, and by Late Antiquity human figures were widely depicted in the synagogues of Palestine (although Judaism would soon deny the power of images). Synagogues were often adorned with depictions of the Temple implements, such as the seven-branched candlestick (the Menorah), the ritual ram's horn (shofar) and the ark containing the Torah scroll, and might also house images of scenes from the Hebrew Bible. There is a particularly striking mosaic floor in the main aisle of the synagogue at Hammat Tiberias in Palestine in which the Ark of the Torah, the implements of the Judaic faith and the lions of Judah are depicted alongside a roundel bearing the signs of the zodiac around a central depiction of the sun, Helios, shown as a youthful deity with a sunburst halo. Such iconographies would all soon be adopted and adapted by Early Christians.

The early artistic traditions of Judaic, Christian and other faith groups living within the Roman empire all absorbed and reflected those of society in general, and consequently share certain motifs and ornamental repertoires. In third-century Roman Dura Europos (modern Qalat es Salihiye) on the Euphrates, between Aleppo and Baghdad, mainstream temples to Roman gods, those dedicated to local deities, Jewish synagogues and Christian churches were all decorated in similar fashion, the synagogue housing some forty to fifty panels illustrating scenes from the Hebrew Bible. Accordingly, it would be difficult from the symbolism and style of the imagery alone to determine the faith-specific context of the mosaic gracing the floor of the main hall of the synagogue at Hamman Lif (Naro), with its vine-scroll tendrils framing animals, birds and baskets of fruit, its dolphins and other

fish swimming in a river flanked by palm trees framing a *cantharus* (chalice), upon which perch two peacocks and from which springs the fountain of life.

Jews and Christians both tended to eschew statuary, owing to its particular associations with the brazen images worshipped by the Israelites and condemned by Moses, and also because of its extensive use in the cults of pagan Graeco-Roman deities. Other images were less obviously contentious, however. The use of icons (Greek *eikōn*) by some Christians can be traced back as far as the second century –

Judaic mosaic floor depicting the Tabernacle and Temple instruments and signs of the zodiac, from the main aisle of the synagogue at Hammat Tiberias (Palestine).

THE ART OF THE EARLIEST CHRISTIANS

panel paintings of saints and even of Christ, based upon images of pagan heroes whose status was signalled by the triumphal halo or nimbus, a ring of light framing the head (with painted panels of nimbed military deities surviving from Egypt and Syria). During the fourth century Eusebius wrote disapprovingly of them: 'I have examined images of his apostles Paul and Peter, and indeed of Christ himself, preserved in colour paintings; which is understandable, since the ancients used to honour saviours freely in this way following their pagan custom'.[1] In a letter to the sister of Constantine he states further that 'these are excluded from churches all over the world'.[2] He also confiscated a painting of Christ and St Paul, depicted as philosophers, which a woman brought to him – although he did not destroy it but kept it in his own home, probably recognizing that it was not images themselves that represented an idolatrous threat, but the way in which people regarded them during their prayers: was the icon the subject or the object of devotion? Public pagan cult figures tended to take the form of statues, while domestic deities and the ancestors and emperors (the *lauraton*) venerated in the home were often painted. Despite the misgivings of the Church Fathers, Christians continued to feel the need for images as a focus for contemplation and the icon was destined to play a major role in the development of Christian devotional art, especially within the Orthodox Churches.

Early Christian Symbolism

Nonetheless, the periodic attempts by the Roman authorities to suppress the subversive Christian cult meant that overt signs of faith had to be avoided. Christians therefore tended to signal their belief by clandestine symbols. The most popular of these was the fish, a creature imbued with sacred significance since ancient times, the Greek term for which – *ichthus* – formed an acrostic, its letters being expanded to form the phrase '*Iēsous Christos Theou Huios Sōtēr*, Jesus Christ Son of God our Saviour'. (Its meaning was expounded by Tertullian during the early third century in his *De baptismo*.) This symbol was used because of its connection with the apostolic role as fishers of men, with the feeding of the five thousand, with the Eucharistic feast, and with Old Testament episodes interpreted as prophesies relating to Christ, such as Jonah and the whale – Jonah's sojourn in the great fish's stomach presaging Christ's entombment and resurrection. Another favored symbol was the chi-rho – an X with a P superimposed upon it, based on the Greek letters *chi*, 'X', and *rho*, 'P' – a contraction of the Greek word *Christos*, 'the Anointed One'. From this derived the chrismon, a symbol resembling a cross with a hook to the right of its upper arm. Others included the marigold, symbolic of rebirth in the ancient world; the lamb, the *Agnus Dei*, the sacrificial victim; the dove, symbol of peace, which came to symbolize the Holy Spirit; the peacock, whose flesh was thought not to putrefy, making it an ideal symbol of resurrection; the *cantharus* or wine-chalice, signifying the cup of salvation – the chalice used at the Last Supper; the Eucharistic vine-scroll (adapted from the Graeco-Roman symbolism of Dionysius, and often inhabited by the birds and beasts of creation which it sustains), and the Tree of Life.

The earliest Christians would have been found among the circle of the apostles, their followers and the early faith communities that they founded. Their beliefs would have been disseminated to those who came into contact with travellers bringing news of novel Eastern cults. Some would themselves have been merchants, or their servants, based in busy provincial trading outposts, such as Oxyrhynchus, or metropolitan centres, such as Antioch, Alexandria and Rome. The Christian message contained hope for the poor and the oppressed and was eagerly embraced by them, but the very nature of their circumstances precluded their leaving much in the way of material possessions, let alone artistic expressions of their faith. Artefacts found across the Roman empire carry such motifs and may betoken Christian ownership, but this was, of necessity, discreet. Many of these are portable articles, such as strap ends, rings and pottery lamps, which were easily stolen or lost during travel, and their find-spots do not necessarily reflect the geographical spread of Christian belief. There are also, however, more static Christian artefacts related to places of worship, such as mosaics, architectural decoration and inscriptions, funerary monuments, and a series of shallow lead tanks bearing chi-rhos, identified as possible baptismal tanks or containers for holy water. For many baptisms were of adults and the usual rite was one of affusion, in which holy water was poured over the catechumen's head as they stood within a baptismal pool or foot tank, rather than by immersion.

The Spread of the Mystery Religions

The essential basis of religious observance under Roman imperial rule was materialism and the desire for individual physical and financial well-being. Emperor worship and the pantheon of gods mirrored these limited human concerns. During the third century the urban and military classes began to adopt Christianity in greater numbers, as one of a number of exotic belief systems that caught on as social and political instability led people to search for more spiritual, mystical meanings to life. People looked to the afterlife to compensate for the shortcomings of the present and sought a super-hero to secure their salvation. Mithraism was one of several mystical religions that gained popularity at this time, all of which were of Eastern derivation and involved complex ritual practices and a belief in an afterlife. These have become collectively termed the 'mystery religions'. Mithras, the bull-slayer, was a Persian deity descended from the Indian and Iranian gods of light – the Mitra-Varuna of the Vedas and the Mazda of Zoroaster – who upon passing into Europe acquired an astrological connotation. He was either depicted wrestling with a bull, its shed blood ensuring the fertility of creation, or as a winged, lion-headed deity, enclosed in a serpent's coils and covered with zodiacal symbols. He was sometimes equated with Aion, god of Time, believed by many to be the Creator, and the symbolic blood-letting of the cult led to it sometimes being confused in the public consciousness with Christianity. The invincibility of the sun and the strict moral code demanded of the soldier of the faith ensured its appeal to the military, by whose agency it spread around the empire from the first century CE. The venues for their mystic ceremonies, or *mithraeums*, might be found as far afield as Carrawburgh on Hadrian's Wall in northern Britain.

Another popular cult was that of Isis, mother of the god Horus, who together with her husband, Osiris, formed an influential trinity of deities from ancient Egypt. She is often depicted enthroned, suckling or holding Horus, in an iconic pose later adopted by Christian artists when depicting Mary and Christ. When the Christian Copts occupied the ancient Egyptian temples they did not redecorate, but rather relabelled and reinterpreted some of the ancient iconography they found there. Eclipsing the other Egyptian goddesses, Isis became equated by the Greeks with Aphrodite and was the goddess of fertility and of the dead. She was termed by the Romans the 'star of the sea' (a forerunner of the Marian epiphet 'stella maris') and patroness of travellers – the cult of Isis was carried to northern Europe by sailors, soldiers and slaves. The third of the great mystery cults that swept across the empire during the third century was Christianity.

Christianity and the Roman Status Quo

Christian teaching was radical and socially transforming and, fearing for the political status quo, the Roman authorities resorted to censorship, persecution and state-sponsored genocide in an attempt to eradicate it. Following Nero's initial lead in the generation following Christ's death, systematic persecutions were implemented under the emperors Septimius Severus in the early third century, Decius and Valerian in the mid-third century and Diocletian in the early fourth century. Many Early Christians died for their faith; many more lived for it, moulding their lives to the image of Christ's teaching. They would probably have felt little need to express this in the conventional artistic trappings of pagan religions.

The practice of the Christian religion became easier, however, following the edicts of religious toleration that followed the victory of Emperor Constantine in 312 CE, vouchsafed by his vision of the cross. Christianity became the official state religion of the Roman empire during the late fourth century, and by the time that the empire began to fragment, during the early fifth century, most Roman citizens would probably have given their religion as 'Christian' without actively practising it or living out its doctrines – as many people do today – while in rural areas pagan practices remained entrenched. As had been the case for millennia the new religion probably merged, for many people, with pre-existing beliefs. Some prehistoric and Romano-Celtic shrines continued in use; others were abandoned or destroyed, while others were replaced by Christian churches, ensuring continuity of worship reinterpreted in the light of the revelation of the New Testament. In north-western Europe a proximity to nature developed into a distinctive appreciation of its value as a visible manifestation of God's bounty and beauty, while, as elsewhere, the plethora of minor deities whose role was to intercede for the daily needs of humankind was gradually replaced by a myriad of local and international saints who assumed their functions. Thus Sts Cosmas and Damian, the Christian twin physicians, usurped the traditional healing roles of the Greek Hippocrates, and the Roman god Mars and the Celtic goddess Brigid metamorphosed into the Christian saint and founder of Kildare.

Foxes Have Holes: Early Christian Places of Assembly and Burial

Prior to the fourth century most Christian communities were forced to meet clandestinely, in discreet house churches, coming together for acts of worship and fellowship in private homes, sometimes in concealed rooms. Other relatively safe meeting places were the houses of the dead – the underground warrens of passages lined with sepulchral niches known as the catacombs – although their use by Christians is now thought to be more an extension of existing Roman burial practices than the clandestine meetings of an underground sect during times of persecution. Particularly important Christian catacombs have been discovered in Rome and Thessaloniki. Some individual chambers and gathering places used for Christian meetings and worship are adorned with particularly fine painted frescoes and ceilings depicting *canthari*, peacocks, birds, fish (including the popular dolphin motif), vine-scrolls and chi-rho symbols. Other frescoes portray fishing scenes, such as the miraculous catch of fish, or fishers of men, and feasting scenes that could simultaneously represent funerary meals – the *agape* or feast of love, celebrated by pagans as a symbol of reunion with their dear departed and by Christians in recollection of the Last Supper, source of the Eucharistic feast. This feast was also observed in Arab communities and perpetuated within early Islam. A fine depiction of such a meal was chosen to commemorate those who rested (for the Early Christians sometimes referred to their tombs as 'sleeping places' where they awaited the resurrection) in a fourth-century Christian tomb (the Tomb of the Banquet) at Constanza in Romania. The broken sherds of tableware used in funerary feasts (recalled in the survival of the Irish wake) can be found in many such tombs, where they were eaten to celebrate the passage of the soul. The frescoes adorning the remarkable North African necropoli such as Tipasa, and the catacombs of Rome and Thessaloniki, where Constantine constructed an important harbour, include still-life paintings of fruit, flowers, fish, prepared meat and other foodstuffs, recalling the ostentatious display of urban plenty likewise celebrated in seventeenth-century Dutch 'flower-paintings' and other still-life subjects – the cornucopia of the pagan Elysian Fields transplanted in the Christian paradise. By the late fourth century such feasting was deemed to have escalated to unseemly levels by church authorities and was banned by St Ambrose. The wealth of many Early Christian townsfolk of the third to fifth centuries is also demonstrated by the jewellery and other grave-goods with which they were buried, until such practices fell out of favour in the fifth century.

Other catacomb frescoes depict scenes from the antique repertoire, imbued with Christian meaning, such as the third-century vault mosaic of Christ as *Sol Invictus* ('the sun triumphant') in the necropolis beneath the Vatican, as well as a range of biblical and apocryphal scenes: Adam and Eve; Abraham's Sacrifice; Daniel in the Lions' Den (based on images of conflict in the arena); Noah's Ark; the Hebrews in the Furnace; Jonah and the Whale; Susannah and the Elders; the Adoration of the Magi; the Baptism of Christ; the Marriage at Cana; the Raising of Lazarus; miracles of healing and the loaves and fishes. Occasionally saints, such as St Thecla, were depicted: although Christian burials initially lay among those of their pagan contemporaries in cemeteries and catacombs, from the third century they might be grouped around the shrine (*martyrium*) of a leader or saint in areas specified by the church; and from the eighth century they were placed inside churches or their precincts, the altars of which were often sited above a saint's tomb. During the Early Middle Ages altars had to contain relics, perpetuating the association of many of the earliest Christian churches with the remains of those who laid the foundations of the Early Christian church.

One such important Early Christian place of assembly and burial was the Catacomb of Priscilla in Rome, with two levels of galleries named after the senatorial family Priscilla of the Acilii. Unusually, it grew up on the site of an abandoned stone quarry at what is now 430 Via Salaria. Here lie Aquila and Priscilla, titulars of the church on the Aventine hill (a couple often mentioned by the apostle Paul), and their contemporaries Sts Prassede and Pudenziana, daughters of Pudens, to whom two further important early churches were dedicated. Other saintly burials included those of Sts Felix and Philip, and many popes, the earliest being Marcellinus (296–304 CE), were also interred there – presumably attracted by the significance of these early saints. One of the earliest decorated chambers, of second-century date, is the Capella greca or cubiculum of the fractio panis, with its central table and wall benches where the agape may have been celebrated. It is adorned with stucco (plasterwork), painted faux marble panels and architectural decoration of 'Pompeian' style, Greek inscriptions, and frescoes of biblical episodes, such as the Adoration of the Magi (symbol of the foundation of the church), the oldest known image of the Virgin and Child, and a splendid depiction of the Eucharistic feast. Nearby is the slightly later cubiculum of the Velati. Its frescoes,

Deceased Christian man at prayer, wearing a prayer stole resembling those of Judaic tradition, flanked by scenes of his marriage and grieving widow and child; third century. Chamber of the Velati, Catacomb of Priscilla, Rome.

23

Sarcophagus in which a prominent Roman Christian, Junius Bassus, was interred, fourth century. St Peter's Treasury, Rome.

from the second half of the third century, depict scenes from the life of the deceased. He appears with his hands raised in the orans attitude of prayer (a gesture of supplication and worship in which the hands are raised, palm up, either side of the head, rather than clasped together in the Medieval gesture of homage), and with a scarf resembling a Jewish prayer shawl covering his head. He is flanked by scenes depicting his marriage and by his grieving widow nursing their child, recalling the Virgin and Child. The painting style is loose and impressionistic and powerfully conveys the emotion of the scene. At his feet is the signature of the antiquary Antonio Bosio (1575–1629) who first discovered and studied the Roman catacombs, bringing them to the attention of the public.

Some wealthier Christians chose to be buried in sarcophagi of stone, wood or lead, a fashion which became popular in Roman territory from the second to the fifth centuries CE, with the transition from cremation to inhumation as the normal form of burial. Rome, Ravenna and Arles have yielded particularly plentiful and fine examples. Most are simply marked with the Christian symbols already discussed, and those of Jews with the Menorah, but some carry figural scenes of antique fashion resembling those of their pagan peers. A particularly ostentatious fourth-century example is that which contained the remains of Junius Bassus, found beneath St Peter's in Rome. Its antique colonnades contain naturalistic, classicizing figures depicting: (upper register) the '*Traditio legis*' (the handing of authority from Christ to Sts Peter and Paul), the sacrifice of Abraham, the capture of Peter, the arrest of Christ, Christ before Pilate; and (lower register) Job, Adam and Eve, the entry into Jerusalem, Daniel in the lion's den, St Paul led to his martyrdom. This iconographic scheme goes to some lengths to associate the martyrdom of the fathers of the Roman Church with the Passion of Christ and its prophecy within the Old Testament. Another fine sarcophagus in Rome, carved in porphyry to emphasize the imperial status and depicting a battle scene, is thought to have contained the mortal remains of St Helena, mother of the first Christian emperor, Constantine, for whom it may originally have been intended.

2

In the Sign of the Cross

Constantine and the Entry of Christianity into the Social Mainstream

It was an image of the cross, victoriously framed above Apollo's symbol, the sun, and thereby emphasizing Christ's triumph over the invincible – seen in a vision on the eve of his bid for imperial supremacy at the Battle of the Milvian Bridge in 312 CE – that was reported to have ensured the triumph of Emperor Constantine and to have furthered the process of rendering Christianity socially and politically acceptable. Constantine may have not accepted baptism until he lay on his deathbed in 337 CE, but from the time that he came to power he became an active promoter of the Christian cause, and a massive head of Constantine from the Basilica Nova in Rome shows him with large eyes staring as if into eternity, still inspired by his vision. In 313 CE the Edict of Milan accorded toleration of worship to all in the Western empire, ending the persecution of Christians that had characterized Diocletian's reign – a benefit that was extended to its Eastern counterpart in 324 CE along with Constantine's rule, following his defeat of his colleague the Eastern emperor Licinius. In order to consolidate and symbolize the union of the two parts he founded a new Rome on the site of an ancient Greek town named Byzantium, bridging the Bosphorus and the East/West divide. This he renamed after himself – Constantinople, a city that would become the focal point of artistic production in the Orthodox Eastern Church.

The 'Publication' of Christian Scripture

By 332 CE Constantine had founded a number of churches in his new capital and wrote to Eusebius, Bishop of Caesarea, the chronicler of the age, requesting that he

Head of Constantine, the emperor who first accorded religious toleration to Christians, fourth century. Basilica Nova, Rome.

commission fifty copies of Christian scripture to be placed within them. For all churches required books, in order to perform their increasingly complex liturgies and from which biblical lessons could be read. The books that Eusebius supplied – thereby beginning the 'publication' of Christian scripture – were probably undecorated like the Codex Sinaiticus, the earliest complete Christian Bible to have survived, copied in Greek probably in Caesarea during the fourth century. Nonetheless, like this imposing volume they would have marked a new departure in the treatment of sacred text. The codex, or book form as we know it – as opposed to the scroll, which had been the major vehicle for literary texts during Antiquity – had been used since the first century but remained a cheap, alternative form of publication which had only really achieved popularity among Early Christian communities. They favoured it for its affordability and ease of manufacture. Most Early Christian codices consisted merely of a single gathering of folded papyrus leaves (like those excavated at Oxyrhynchus in Egypt); the Gospels, epistles and other texts they carried served simply as the working manuals of humble faith communities. They were also readily portable and concealable during times of persecution and were well suited to the cross-referencing of texts. Simple papyrus scrolls and codices were also used by a sect known as the Gnostics who mixed elements from several religions, including Christianity, and combined them with caballistic magic and mysticism. One of their early texts, a third- to fourth-century scroll from Egypt,[1] is decorated with a drawing of a ring-headed ankh cross – ancient Egyptian symbol of life, perpetuated not only in Gnostic but also in Christian circles, where it was known as the *crux ansata* (Latin for 'cross with a handle').

The codex finally came out into the open, along with Christian worship, during the fourth century, and the biblical pandects (or 'all receivers', a term used of complete bibles) that began to appear sporadically (for they were always a costly exception and a symbolic statement of the unity of the biblical texts) from that time onwards were expensive tomes, written in large, formal uncial script (a formal, rounded book-hand) on finely prepared parchment. The stage of the page was set to receive the trappings of decoration as the sacred codex gradually came to be recognized, along with the cross, as the ultimate symbol of faith.

Foundations of the Byzantine Church

Constantine's patronage brought a new set of artistic opportunities and challenges to the Christian faith. He wanted to clarify what exactly the new faith that he and his subjects were embracing consisted of, and he also wished to foster unity throughout what he conceived of as the Christian *oikoumenē* (or ecumen – the universal Christian fellowship). Accordingly, he began to convene international church councils, such as the first international ecumenical council at Nicaea in 325 CE, attended by representatives from the early churches in order to discuss shared ritual and belief, to establish a canonically defined body of scripture, to determine orthodoxy and to reject heretical thought. This process would contribute to the establishment of a number of regional churches that stood outside or on the fringes of orthodoxy and Byzantine hegemony: Syriac, Armenian, Georgian, Coptic,

Ethiopic and Nubian. Each of these would develop its own Christian culture, using their own written vernacular languages, scripts and styles of art to reinforce their identities (see Chapter 4).

Constantine's mother, St Helena (c. 250–330 CE), was dispatched on an embassy to tour the holy places mentioned in the Gospels, perhaps as a means of promoting the authority of the emergent Byzantine Church and empire. Local guides were quick to avail themselves of her patronage and to show her sites traditionally associated with biblical events. Like her son before her, Helena is said to have received a vision, revealing the burial place of the gallows upon which Christ was crucified – the relic of the 'True Cross', which she excavated and retrieved. Helena had converted to Christianity in 312 CE, while in her sixties, and was renowned for her modest dress, her charitable works and her pilgrimage to the Holy Land where she died. The finding, or 'invention', of the True Cross is usually dated to 335 CE and the association with Helena may be apocryphal. Her role was first ascribed to her by St Ambrose, but the earliest reference to the discovery is given by Cyril of Jerusalem, who wrote in 346 CE that the 'saving wood of the Cross was found at Jerusalem in the time of Constantine and that it was disturbed fragment by fragment from this spot'. The cross, an ignominious and feared instrument of torture, had not previously been venerated as a symbol of Christian faith, but from this time onwards it began its rise to a position of crucial significance.

The recollection of Constantine's links with Britain may have played a part in the region's subsequent role, from the seventh century, in elevating the cross to its place as the foremost symbol of Christianity and eternal life. A monastery was quickly established on the site, and at the spot that Helena identified as Calvary Constantine built the Church of the Holy Sepulchre, with the mound of Golgotha and a structure containing what was believed to be the tomb of Christ at its core. Others included those on the Mount of Olives and at Bethlehem, overlying the site of Christ's birth. Not forgetting the foundations of his power, he also constructed major churches in Rome, including St Peter's, the Lateran and the Church of Christ Saviour. Constantinople gained his Hagia Eirene, and the Church of the Holy Wisdom (Hagia Sophia, later rebuilt by Justinian) and the Church of the Holy Apostles, both constructed by his son, Constantius II, while Jerusalem was given the 'new' Church of the Theotokos (the Nea). In Thessaloniki the Rotunda constructed by Galerius was converted into a church around this time and its dome adorned with mosaics of a celestial throng of beautiful angels. Its massive basilican Acheiropoietos, one of the oldest churches still in Christian use, also dates from the fourth or fifth centuries, as do the large church of St Demetrius and little St George's, with its fine mosaic of Christ in Majesty and the evangelist symbols.

The Emergence of Early Christian Art

Such foundations, along with the palaces favoured by Constantine, including those in Constantinople, Trier and Paderborn with their accompanying churches, received lavish adornment and stimulated the production of art with Christian themes. Accounts of his gifts, long since destroyed – no doubt melted down for their bullion value – include a lamb made of 30 lb (13.6 kg) of gold, pouring water into the font in the baptistery at the Lateran, flanked by five-foot (1.5 m-) tall figures of Christ and John the Baptist, weighing in at 170 lb (77 kg) and 125 lb (57 kg) respectively – Christ being the heavyweight. While at St Peter's (the Vatican) the altar of gold and silver sported 400 jewels. Constantine's churches could rival any pagan temple.

The decoration of these, and of other churches that sprang up around the Mediterranean, perpetuated many themes from Antiquity. Nilotic scenes in which crocodiles, palm trees and other flora and fauna, stemming from ancient Egypt, continue to appear, are carved upon the ceiling beams in the nave of the church of St Catherine on Mount Sinai, where they summon up the concept of Eden through the fertile plenty of the River Nile. Depictions of the four seasons as human personifications, found adorning the floors of many a Roman villa around the empire, can also be seen in the mosaic floor of the church at Petra. Images from the calendar illustrating the labours of the months (harvesting and the like), which likewise enliven the floors of the Villa of the Falconer at Argos, were adopted by the Early Christians and perpetuated throughout the Middle Ages, continuing to appear in the calendar pages of Late Medieval liturgical manuscripts. Alongside them often occur the signs of the zodiac and celestial personifications. For the passing of time and the movement of the heavenly bodies were not considered antipathetic to Christian teaching. Rather, they were viewed as part of the mechanism by which God's will was enacted through creation – *influxus stellarum*, or the influence of the stars, being the agent of cosmic will, as any Medieval Christian theologian would have told you, and as Shakespeare acknowledged with his 'star-crossed lovers'.

Elsewhere within the Roman empire, even in the most remote provinces such as Britannia, the practice of the Christian faith grew and became socially acceptable. House churches that had previously operated in secret began to convene openly and many new ones were formed. To take the case of provincial Britain, at Lullingstone Villa in Kent the cellar nymphaeum was sealed up and replaced by two ground-floor rooms, cut off from the house itself and with an external entrance to permit general access – a domestic shrine had given way to a public church attached to a private home. On the west wall was a large painted frieze of six figures in late-Roman Eastern-style dress, their hands raised in the *orans* position of prayer still observed in many Eastern churches and used as part of the Islamic sequence of prayer. They may depict the members of the Christian family that commissioned them, those who ministered there (some of the clothing perhaps representing early vestments), or favourite saints. The colourful patterned fabrics and personal ornaments are decidedly Eastern in character, reflecting the influence of Constantine's court and presaging the style of Early Medieval Byzantine art. On another wall was painted a large chi-rho symbol, flanked by the Greek characters 'Alpha' and 'Omega' – 'I am Alpha and Omega, the beginning and the ending, saith the Lord, which is, and which was, and which is to come' (Revelation 1:8) – set within a victor's laurel wreath with doves, symbols of peace and of the Holy Spirit, perching upon it. This symbol is contained within a classical triumphal arch, these layers of meaning all reinforcing belief in Christ's victory over death and his role as

the eternal *Logos*, the Word: 'In the beginning was the Word, and the Word was with God and the Word was God' (John 1:1).

The precious fragments of painted plaster from Lullingstone have been painstakingly reconstructed at the British Museum, where another of the most important examples of Early Christian art is also to be seen, a fourth-century mosaic from the Villa of Hinton St Mary in Dorset. In its central roundel is a youthful, clean-shaven bust of Christ wearing Roman draped clothing, with a chi-rho behind his head serving as a nimbus, flanked by two pomegranates symbolizing eternal life. This was proudly displayed in the main reception room and is the first extant depiction of Christ from Britain and one of the earliest from the entire western Roman empire. Other elements of the iconography of this mosaic accord with classical imagery but may have been given Christian interpretations, such as the four corner heads – traditionally the winds, but here perhaps denoting

Fourth-century fresco depicting Early Christians in the 'orans' attitude of prayer, from a room that had been a pagan nymphaeum but which was adapted to form a Christian house church during the fourth century at Lullingstone Villa, Kent. British Museum.

31

the evangelists – and Bellerophon spearing the Chimaera, which here may represent the triumph of good over evil, later transformed into the Christian iconography of St Michael and, later, St George, spearing the dragon. The mosaic at the Villa of Frampton (Dorset) likewise combines Christian and pagan imagery, featuring a chi-rho, a *cantharus*, dolphins, a rider spearing a lioness, and Bacchic imagery perhaps adapted with reference to the Eucharist. It adorned what was probably the dining room, a room suitable not only for daily meals but also for the Christian *agape*.

More ambiguous in their subject matter are the mosaics from Littlecote Villa, Wiltshire, found in a religious building with three apses and a bath suite that stood apart from the house itself. They portray *canthari*, marine life and panthers. The latter was a symbol of Christ in the Early Christian text of the *Physiologus* or 'Marvels of the East' – one of the sources of the Medieval bestiary, which discussed the mythical inhabitants, flora and fauna of Africa and Asia and imbued them with Christian allegorical symbolism. Alongside these images are depictions of Orpheus in his guise as Apollo, both seen as Christ-like saviour-gods. This may be another case of Christians adapting pagan imagery, just as Celtic deities had become associated with those of Classical Antiquity over the course of the preceding four hundred years (for example, the temple of Sulis Minerva in Bath). Alternatively, this iconography might even signal a fourth-century pagan householder's rebellion against what was becoming the Christian norm following its adoption as the state religion.

Twilight of the Roman Empire

By the beginning of the fifth century the empire was imploding. In Italy, Gaul and Iberia the bishops stepped into part of the power vacuum left as the empire contracted and was transformed by the pressure of external attack and the migration of the 'barbarian' peoples from beyond its *limes* (frontiers) – as economic migrants or as local conquerors and settlers. During the late fourth and fifth centuries numerous hoards of precious metalwork were buried to protect them from raiders and several are thought perhaps to represent assemblages of church plate. Three such hoards from late Roman Britain are: the late fourth-century Water Newton Hoard, which includes Christian dedication inscriptions and metal leaves inscribed with crosses; the Hoxne Hoard; and the Traprain Law Treasure, an assembly of silver, some of it secular and some Christian church plate, such as a rare silver-gilt jug embossed with Old and New Testament scenes (the Fall, Moses, Adoration of the Magi) – the booty of Britons who raided the beleaguered neighbouring Roman province during the early fifth century and carried their spoils off to their hill-fort near Edinburgh.

Many continental towns continued to function as cathedral cities, sustained by local markets and episcopal administration. In Britain the decay of many towns, a primarily agrarian economy and an inclination towards rural places of worship meant that many of the settlements and structures that embodied the contribution of the Romans gradually fell into ruin, their remains being eulogized by their Anglo-Saxons successors as 'the work of giants' in the tenth-century Old English poem, 'The Ruin'. Yet, even here, the memory of the Roman Period, which had witnessed the beginnings of Christianity in Britain, lingered on and would resurface time and again in the art and culture of the successor states and their rulers who saw themselves as the heirs of Rome. Meanwhile Constantine, who had first been declared emperor in York in 306 CE, lay entombed in far-off Constantinople in the church that he had built to commemorate the disciples of Christ – presenting himself to posterity as the heir to both the imperial and the apostolic dignity through the symbolism of his foundation and its art.

33

3

Martyrs and Mosaics

The Early Churches of Italy

Of all the early centres of the Christian faith, Rome, heart of the empire that dominated the Late Antique world, has yielded the most visual and archaeological evidence of the lives and worship of Early Christians. The city, where the apostle Peter was martyred in 64 CE, already had a large Jewish element among its traders, who were probably among the first to receive the Christian teaching (Acts recounts that there were 'strangers of Rome' present when the apostles first preached in Jerusalem). This may have contributed to Claudius's expulsion of the Jews from Rome in 50 CE. They soon returned after his death, and it is probably from this time on that a rift between Jews and Christians began to widen as the latter admitted a torrent of Gentile converts. There was already a well-organized Christian community in the city when the apostle Paul arrived in 61 CE. These Early Christians were drawn largely from the poorer sectors of society – keyworkers, slaves, entertainers, traders and the like – but leading members of society, including the niece of Emperor Diocletian, Flavia Domitilla (who was accordingly exiled), were also professing their faith by the end of the century and forming house churches. By the fourth century there were twenty-five such *tituli* (the forerunners of parishes) in Rome; the names of their founders, many of whom were acclaimed as saints, were preserved in the dedications of the churches that grew on their sites. Traces remain of some of these early house churches and the burial places of their members, but others are lost, some possibly convening within apartments on upper floors (as some synagogues still do today, for example, in the Venetian ghetto).

Early Christian Basilicas

During the more tolerant fourth century, Christian basilicas, modelled upon Roman civil buildings, began to be constructed. Constantine's own Roman foundations included St Peter's (the Vatican), the Church of Christ Saviour, and the Lateran, which he built on the site of the barracks of his personal guard. Constructed around 313–14 CE, along with Rome's first baptistery and the residence of the Bishop of Rome (which was to become the papacy), the Lateran was originally dedicated to the Saviour, but was later rededicated to Sts John the Baptist and John the Divine by Gregory the Great. The proportions of the original basilica are reflected in Borromini's Baroque rebuild, and its baptistery, with its accompanying atrium and entrance chapels, are of Early Christian date and retain their marble and mosaic decoration, including the Mystical Lamb (*Agnus Dei*) of the book of Revelation, representing Christ, the sacrificial victim. The *scrinium* also contains a sixth- to seventh-century fresco of St Augustine.

In 321–29 CE Constantine constructed an even larger basilica on the site of the tomb of St Peter, within a necropolis situated close to the circus of Gaius and Nero, where the apostle is said to have been martyred. The monumental bronze pine cone from the fountain in the basilica's courtyard, and the bronze peacocks that topped the canopy over it – all symbols of renewal and eternal life – are preserved in the nearby Vatican Museum. The saint's funerary monument in the apse was surmounted by four

A depiction of the fourth-century Constantinian tomb of St Peter, Rome, on the ivory Pola casket from Pula, Croatia, c. 430 CE. Archaeological Museum, Venice.

barley-twist columns (still preserved in St Peter's), recalling those that surrounded the Tabernacle in the Temple in Jerusalem – a motif that would recur throughout Christian art. Gregory the Great later raised the presbytery and constructed an altar above the tomb, beneath the canopy. But a depiction of the tomb of St Peter as it appeared under Constantine survives on the ivory Pola casket in Venice, carved around 430 CE as a memento of the holy sites of Rome, and found in Pula, Croatia.

Also of early fourth century date were San Lorenzo, Santi Marcellino e Petri and the basilica of San Sebastiano, overlying catacombs from the first century onwards, which would have greeted pilgrims as they entered Rome from Porta San Sebastiano. One of the most extensive Early Christian ecclesiastical enclaves was Sant' Agnese fuori le Mura. It was built by Constantine's daughter, Constantia, while she was living as a widow in Rome (338–50 CE), on an imperial estate overlying a complex of Christian catacombs dating from the second century onwards and incorporating the *martyrium* of St Agnes, martyred during Decius's persecutions in the third century. A *sacellum* (shrine/altar) was constructed over Agnes's tomb at the same time as the now ruined Constantinian basilica and baptistery, and was replaced by the grand current basilica constructed by Pope Honorius (625–38 CE). Constantia's own mausoleum also stands within this impressive complex. At the centre of this imposing circular edifice stood the porphyry sarcophagus of Constantia (now in the Pio Clementine Museum, Vatican), beneath a dome decorated with mosaics depicting a scene of youths of pagan origin harvesting grapes, which had assumed a Christian interpretation deriving from John 15:1–17, in which Christ compares himself to the vine and his disciples to its branches.

Another church outside the walls, which probably originally dated from the Constantinian period, is San Paolo fuori le Mura. Lying above the tomb of St Paul, it attracted the patronage of the papacy; it was redecorated with frescoes and stuccowork by Leo I (440–61 CE) and Paul's tomb was enhanced by Pope Gregory the Great (590–604 CE). Damaged by fire in the nineteenth century, the present building is largely reconstructed. Pope Sixtus III (432–40 CE) is credited with building the grandiose basilica of Santa Maria Maggiore atop the Esquiline Hill. Beneath the windows of the nave are stucco niches framing mosaics illustrating scenes from the Old Testament (Genesis, Exodus, Numbers and Joshua), which are the original decorative scheme. Further mosaics on the triumphal arch into the apse were added slightly later by Sixtus III, announced by his dedicatory inscription, 'Built by Sixtus the Bishop for the people of God'. Its scenes from Christ's Nativity and Infancy celebrate *Theotokos* ('the one who bore God' or 'Mother of God'), an important validation of the concept of Mary's divine motherhood, as recently endorsed by the Council of Ephesus in 431 CE. Santa Maria Maggiore therefore

37

retains one of the earliest and most extensive series of Early Christian mosaics – the art-form popularized throughout the classical world now applied increasingly not only to floors but also to walls and domes, enhancing the liturgical space and elucidating the Word.

On the crest of another of Rome's hills, the Aventine, stands the austere brick profile of the basilica of Santa Sabina, restored to its Early Christian appearance. It

Mosaic depicting Joshua leading the Israelites across the River Jordan (above) and sending spies to Jericho (below), illustrating Joshua 1–3, fifth century. Nave of Santa Maria Maggiore, Rome.

was built by a Dalmatian priest, Peter of Illyria, during the second quarter of the fifth century. Most of its interior decoration has perished, save the mosaic dedication inscription in the nave, which reads:

> 'When Celestine had the supreme apostolic dignity and shone through all the world
>   as the first of Bishops
> This marvel was created by a priest of Rome, a native of Illyria
> Peter, a man worthy of this name for his nourishment from birth was in the wake of Christ
> Rich for the poor, poor for himself
> Having shunned the good things of the present life
> He well deserves to hope for the gift of the future life.'

Panel depicting the crucifixion, with Christ between the two thieves, fifth century. From the wooden doors to Santa Sabina, Rome.

This is flanked by female figures representing Synagogue, holding the book of the Old Testament, and Ecclesia, holding the New Testament – symbolizing the church's

origins in East and West and the triumph of the new dispensation over the old. Originally Sts Peter and Paul and the evangelists stood above. Fragments of the cladding of the nave walls remain, with architectural motifs, curtains and victory trophies all executed in *opus sectile* (a sort of stone jigsaw in which the forms of the design were composed of shaped pieces of marble). But perhaps the most remarkable survival is the original wooden door that gives entry to the nave. Made of cedar or cypress (biblical plants) it is carved on both sides: the back depicts plants taken from illustrations to the first-century treatise on herbal medicine by the Alexandrian physician Dioscorides, and the front is decorated with a vine scroll, inhabited by beasts, which twines around panels containing scenes from the lives of Moses, Elijah and Christ – illustrating St Augustine's renowned comparison of the Law, the Prophets and the Gospels. The influence of illumination from the Christian Orient (from manuscripts such as the somewhat later Syriac Rabbula Gospels of 586 CE) has been suggested, but little from that early has survived. The scenes include the earliest sculptural representation of the crucifixion in which Christ is shown triumphant upon the cross, bearded, without a nimbus, and set between the two thieves against a row of buildings. This is framed and stands alone. Other scenes in registers illustrate miracles related in John's Gospel, such as the healing of the blind man, the miracle of the loaves and fishes, and the marriage at Cana. These recall ivory carvings and Italian manuscript illumination, such as the Augustine Gospels, made probably in Rome in the late fifth century and thought to have been taken to England by St Augustine of Canterbury in his mission to convert the pagan Anglo-Saxons in 597 CE. Such themes would recur on Anglo-Saxon sculptures over the next three centuries (such as the Reculver and Ruthwell crosses), and the Illyrian connection would later be celebrated in the doors of Split Cathedral (Illyria in modern Croatia) carved by Master Buvina in 1214. Both Augustine and Pope Gregory the Great, who dispatched his mission, were well acquainted with Santa Sabina and its doors, and it was probably these narrative depictions that Gregory had in mind when he wrote to the iconoclast Bishop Serenus of Marseilles, around 600 CE, urging restraint on the grounds that:

> *'It is one thing to adore a picture, another to learn what is to be adored through the history told by the picture. What Scripture presents to readers, a picture presents to the gaze of the unlearned. For in it even the ignorant see what they ought to follow, in it the illiterate read.'*

This influential statement prepared the way for subsequent pictorial narrative in Western art.

Mosaics in Early Christian Rome

One of the greatest contributions of Early Medieval Rome to this pictorial tradition was its use of splendid mosaics, which perpetuated the classical tradition. Two important examples occur in civil buildings of Constantine's era, which were subsequently converted into churches. One is Santa Pudenziana, formed from a bath-house basilica and a second-century private house around 387–98 CE in a poorer part of town in the *subiura*. The book held by Christ in its apsidal mosaic is inscribed with the name of Pudens, friend of the apostles, who turned his home into a house church (*titulus*) which may have lain on the site. A lost inscription on the

Heavily restored apsidal mosaic depicting Christ in Majesty with the apostles and evangelist symbols flanking the *Crux Gemmata*, symbol of the resurrection, early fifth century. Santa Pudenziana, Rome.

mosaic naming its patrons dates it to the time of Pope Innocent I (401–417 CE). It was heavily restored from the sixteenth to the nineteenth centuries and only the head of St Peter is thought to be original, although the overall composition is thought to preserve that of the fifth century. It depicts Christ in Majesty, surrounded by the apostles, adapted from imperial iconography and scenes of Christ teaching, with two women representing Synagogue and Ecclesia. The Mystical Lamb and the dove of the Holy Spirit also once appeared. Behind the figures is a cityscape – perhaps denoting the holy places of Palestine – and at the centre, behind Christ and raised up on a mound, is the *Crux Gemmata*, the jewelled cross of the resurrection, set against a colourful, atmospheric bank of clouds from which emerge the busts of the four winged evangelist symbols, arranged in the Western order: Matthew's man; Mark's lion; Luke's calf or bull; and John's eagle. Elements of this iconography would become recurrent themes in Medieval Christian art, no doubt transmitted via centuries of derivative images upon pilgrimage souvenirs.

Another Constantinian civil building, this time in a prominent location on the edge of the Forum, was converted into the church of Santi Cosma e Damiano under Pope Felix IV (526–30 CE), by simply adding a stunning mosaic to its apse. Once again partially restored during the sixteenth and seventeenth centuries, it nonetheless appears much as it would originally have done. Christ, bearded, nimbed, holding the scroll of the Law and clad in golden robes, stands upon a ladder-like mound of dramatic clouds of fiery red, yellow, white and blue, set against a dark blue sky. This vision effectively conflates the ascension, the second coming and judgement: '…they shall see the Son of Man coming in the clouds of heaven with power and great glory' (Matthew 24:30). Below, in a paradisiacal landscape through which runs the Jordan, the river of redemption, stand the figures of Sts Cosmas and Damian: twin physicians, who hold their martyrs' crowns in draped hands and are presented to the Saviour by Sts Peter and Paul. Behind them stand the donor, Felix IV, and St Theodore, holding palms symbolizing resurrection. On a frieze below is the Mystical Lamb – Christ – flanked by twelve sheep representing the apostles. On the triumphal arch above, added under Sergius I (687–701 CE), is an even more symbolic representation of the apocalypse, drawn from the Revelation of John (chapter 4 verse 5). On a *clipeus* (shield) is the jewelled throne on which stand the Mystical Lamb and the cross. The seven seals lie upon the footrest, flanked by seven jewelled lamps of fire, four angels and the evangelist symbols. Beneath these, the twenty-four elders, clad in white robes, lift crowns in their veiled hands.

Elements of both these iconographic schemes recur in the church of Santa Prassede, which is close to that of her sister, Santa Pudenziana. This contains a splendid apse mosaic depicting Christ receiving the crown from his Father, attended by Sts Peter, Paul, Prassede, Pudenziana and the patron, Pope Paschal I (817–24 CE), whose square halo indicates that he was still alive at the time. It also contains the Chapel of St Zeno, constructed by Pope Paschal I in honour of his mother Theodora to house the relics of Sts Zeno and Valentine and the pillar to which Christ was tied during the flagellation. The interior of the chapel is encrusted with mosaics, like a little jewel casket, rough set in Byzantine fashion to better reflect the light. Angels support its vault and roundels contain busts of the Pope, his mother, the Virgin and the saints. Zeno was himself from Byzantium and, along with the Exarchate of Ravenna, was responsible for introducing significant eastern artistic, liturgical and devotional influences to Rome and the West.

Other Roman churches contain important early frescoes, notably Santa Maria Antiqua in the Forum with its solemn rows of saints, and San Clemente, which is a remarkable multi-tiered set of churches, now excavated, the lowest levels of which go back to the earliest Christian era. San Clemente incorporates a *mithraeum* and the house of Flavius Clemens, whose house church became that of St Clement – whose fourth-century *Acta* recount his work as a missionary, following exile to the Crimea under Trajan. This led the Roman authorities to tie him to an anchor (his symbol) and toss him into the sea, which subsequently revealed an island with his splendid tomb. These events are illustrated by late eleventh-century frescoes in the Early Christian lower church that underlies its beautiful Medieval successor. One scene depicts the Mass of St Clement attended by the donor, Bonone de Rapiza, his wife, Maria Macellaria, and their children; their generosity is recorded in an inscription which is one of the earliest uses of the Italian vernacular. Other early frescoes there include an enthroned Virgin and Child, depicted frontally in Byzantine fashion and with Mary wearing an elaborate bejewelled Eastern headdress.

Many of Rome's other churches might be mentioned here. Elsewhere in Italy, important remains of Early Christian churches are to be found in Milan, the alternative residence of the western Roman emperor. Here the marble-clad remains of the baptistery pool in which St Ambrose baptized St Augustine still lie beneath the Medieval Duomo; the fourth-century edifice of San Lorenzo Maggiore has been successively restored; and the significant suburban Medieval monastery of Sant' Ambrogio contains Early Christian mosaics decorating a martyrium above the tomb of San Vittore. Important centres such as the patriarchate of Aquileia, a strategic north Italian port and sometime imperial residence, and Naples, would once likewise have contained notable examples of Early Christian art and architecture. Vestiges still remain at Aquileia, incorporated into the later cathedral and excavated at the Fondo Tullio. In Brescia the imposing basilica of San Salvatore survives, along with some of the treasures that would once have graced it, such as the magnificent

RIGHT: Mosaic depicting the Virgin and angels with Pope Paschal I, whose square halo shows that he was still alive when he commissioned the image during the early ninth century for Santa Prassede, Rome.

43

MARTYRS AND MOSAICS

An early depiction of a liturgical celebration, the Mass of St Clement attended by donors; late eleventh-century fresco. Lower Church of San Clemente, Rome.

sixth-century purple gospelbook, the Codex Brixianus. At Albenga in Liguria mosaics of the second quarter of the fifth century adorn the vault of the baptistery, depicting a triple (Trinitarian) chi-rho on a starry celestial blue background denoting the descendants of Abraham, flanked by twelve doves representing the apostles and with two lambs standing either side of the cross. Usually lambs symbolize the apostles, but here they may represent the holy cities of Jerusalem and Bethlehem from which processions of lambs (representing faithful believers) issue in other examples of Early Christian art, such as the arch mosaic at Santa Maria Maggiore in Rome. When Emperor Honorius moved his capital to Ravenna, with its protective marshes, at the beginning of the fifth century, this area began to be an important Christian enclave. It was subsequently adopted by the Byzantine emperors as an Exarchate (a Byzantine province ruled by a governor known as an Exarch), providing a valuable link between Italy and Byzantium. Remains of many other early churches have been excavated (such as Castelseprio, a Byzantine work of the sixth century), while many others have been obliterated by the later edifices built on their sites. The remains of the early basilica can still be seen, however, beside its seventh-century counterpart with its splendid mosaics at Poreč, a Byzantine port on the other side of the Adriatic in Croatia.

Additional arts of Antiquity continued to be practised in Early Christian Italy, and metalwork and ivories (which continued to be produced until the mid-sixth century, the art form later being revived by the Carolingians) increasingly featured Christian as opposed to secular or pagan scenes. *Pyxides*, little ivory boxes, can carry iconographies; but when adorned with images such as miracles of healing, they are thought to have contained the Eucharistic wafers, holy oils or medication. Ivory panels of the form traditionally associated with consular diptychs (two carved ivory panels hinged together), celebrating the bestowal of high office, were joined by, or re-carved with, those depicting Christian subjects, such as the sixth-century depiction of an archangel, which formed part of a diptych. The large format and grandeur of this hellenizing piece, coupled with the accompanying inscription which reads 'Receive the suppliant before you, despite his sinfulness' and the victorious iconographic adjuncts (the cross, laurel wreath, orb and sceptre), have given rise to speculation that the other leaf depicted Emperor Justinian. It seems to have been used subsequently for writing prayers on the back, perhaps as a liturgical aid.

Ivory plaque depicting an archangel, second quarter of the sixth century, Constantinople. British Museum.

45

Origins of the Liturgical Veneration of the Cross

In addition to the cult of the Virgin, another Eastern introduction to the West that occurred via Rome was that of the veneration of the cross. Pope Symmachus (498–514 CE) provided a reliquary adorned with gems containing a fragment of the cross for a chapel of the Holy Cross at the Vatican, and Emperor Justin II presented another reliquary cross to the Vatican. During the first quarter of the seventh century the tradition of the veneration of the cross on Good Friday was introduced to Rome, under Eastern influence from Constantinople; a mass for the exaltation of the cross was composed in Rome and used in many of its churches. The earliest surviving liturgical text from Rome for the veneration of the cross in St Peter's, Rome, is the *Ad crucem salutandum in sancto petro*:

> 'Deus qui unigeniti tui domini nostri iesu christi praetioso sanguine humanum genus redemere dignatus es, concede propitius ut qui ad adorandam uiuificam crucem adueniunt a peccatorum suorum nexibus liberentur. Per dominum.'
>
> *('God, who has deigned to allow the human race to be redeemed by the precious blood of your only-begotten son our Lord Jesus Christ, grant we beseech you that those who come to adore the life-giving cross may be freed from the bonds of their sins. Through our Lord'.)*

This occurs in the Sacramentary of Padua – Paduense[1] – and was celebrated on 14 September, as the finding of the True Cross was celebrated at Jerusalem on that date. In 614 CE the Persians had captured Jerusalem and with it the relic of the True Cross. Emperor Heraclius recovered it and returned it to Jerusalem in 629 CE, but it was still at risk and so was transferred to Constantinople in 635 CE. Its triumphant entry – the imperial *aduentus* – was the focus of its exaltation there. This developed into the formal veneration of the cross on Good Friday. Roman liturgy emphasized the life-giving cross as an image of Christ, focusing on John 3:14 – the raising up of Christ on the cross, which also symbolizes resurrection: '…when you have raised up the Son of Man then you will realize that I am he' (John 8:28). The prayer mat (*oratorio*) was used to allow everyone to kneel and kiss the cross, as shown by a late eighth-century *ordo* (order of liturgical practice) adapted from Roman use for liturgy north of the Alps.[2] Carpet-pages in Early Coptic and Insular manuscripts may be meant to recall such prayer mats (standing as they do at the entrance to the holy ground of sacred text), which still feature in the observances of the churches of the Christian Orient and within Islam: their common origins lie within the shared worship rituals of the Middle East.

4

The Christian Orient

The Christian Art of Palestine, Armenia, Georgia and Syria

The Greek Church began to achieve ascendancy around the eastern Mediterranean from 381 CE, when an ecumenical (universal) council declared that Constantinople exerted an equal authority in the East to that of Rome in the West. At the Council of Chalcedon in 451 CE five supreme patriarchates were established: Constantinople, Rome, Alexandria, Antioch and Jerusalem. Constantinople was accorded jurisdiction over Asia Minor and the eastern Balkans and evangelized there. In 588 CE Patriarch John IV of Constantinople declared himself Ecumenical Patriarch – a title retained by the leader of the Greek Orthodox Church to this day, while the leader of Catholic Orthodoxy in the West retains the title of 'Pope'. The authority of the other early patriarchates was severely curtailed by the spread of Islam from the seventh century onwards, but the Coptic (Monophysite, named for its espousal of the doctrine of the 'single nature' of Christ) Church is still led by its own pope, the Patriarch of Alexandria.

Debate and Division

The theological debates that dominated the fourth and fifth century proved extremely divisive and led to a hard-line condemnation of heretical sects by the 'orthodox' church, which in the process increasingly defined itself. Almost as soon as the Edict of Milan sanctioned the existence of the church, disputes concerning its beliefs and practices arose. Eager to prevent division, Constantine convened the first international ecumenical council at Nicaea in 325 CE. This condemned Arianism – the heretical teaching of an Alexandrian priest, Arius, which claimed that Christ was one of God's created creatures and that his nature was similar to but not the same as God's – and promoted the concept advanced by another Alexandrian prelate, Athanasius, that they were of one substance. In 431 CE the Council of Ephesus condemned the thoughts of Nestorius, Patriarch of Constantinople, concerning the relationship between Christ and the Virgin, whom he viewed as mother of the human part of Christ, fearing that the implications of this would split Christ's nature into two; this caused the Eastern Syriac Church to splinter off. The crucial Council of Chalcedon (451 CE), however, pronounced that Christ did indeed possess two natures, human and divine, which coexisted but were not merged. The Egyptians objected, championing the Monophysite belief that Christ possessed only one nature, causing a breach between the Orthodox and Monophysite (Western Syriac or Jacobite, Coptic, and Ethiopic) Churches. The Armenians, busy fighting the Persians, did not attend Chalcedon and retained an ambiguous position regarding Monophysitism. Georgia broke with Byzantium following the Council, but resumed relations in 607 CE, becoming an autocephalous (self-governing) Orthodox Church – as did the Slavic Churches that were subsequently established. A number of independent churches therefore came into existence, each with its own languages, traditions and approaches to art.

Armenia (or Hay as its inhabitants called themselves) was the first nation officially to adopt Christianity as its state religion in the early fourth century. Its conversion is ascribed to St Gregory the Illuminator, who emerged from the pit in which he was imprisoned for fifteen years by King Trdat III to convert him, establish Christianity and become Catholicos of the Armenian Church in 314 CE. During the fifth century the church suffered persecution at the hands of the Persians (although there was also a Christian Persian Church which nonetheless survived), and in a Council at Dvin in 506 CE it was decided that Armenia would subscribe to the first three great ecumenical councils but would not subscribe to the rulings of Chalcedon – causing the Byzantines to regard it as heretical and aligned with the Monophysites.

The Development of Armenian Art

Armenia has produced a fine tradition of ecclesiastical art, knowledge of which has been constrained by its usual characterization, until recently, as an orientalized extension of mainstream Byzantine art. The Early Christian Eastern origins of its art are echoed by the stone funerary monuments known as *khatchk'ars*, which continued to be carved throughout the Middle Ages, and resembled the carpet-pages of Coptic and Insular manuscripts which all drew upon similar sources of inspiration in the Near East. Its development tends to be considered in three phases. During the first period (c. 300–750 CE), Syriac and Byzantine influences were experienced, the

RIGHT: Khatchk'ar of Aputayli, an Armenian funerary monument, Armenia, 1225. British Museum.

Armenian alphabet was invented (by St Mesrop, also responsible for devising written Georgian), and by 433 CE the Bible had been translated into the vernacular. Armenian architects, like their Byzantine counterparts, experimented with church buildings featuring a central dome and the Armenian and Byzantine traditions converged to influence the architecture and frescoes of the Cappadocian rock-cut churches. In the second period (c. 862–1021), the inspiration of the past was combined with continued inventiveness, producing monuments such as the tenth-century frescoes at Tatev and the carved exterior of Aght'amar. During the third period (c. 1150–1500), following the disruption from Seljuk invasion, Armenian Cilicia (Lesser Armenia) was formed, enduring from 1099–1375. Cilicia produced particularly vibrant art during the thirteenth century, stimulated in part by contact with the Crusader kingdoms and by Franciscan missionary activity that promoted an interest in Rome and Western traditions of faith and art – not always to beneficial effect: the novel *The Man In the Iron Mask* was based on the kidnapped Armenian Patriarch Avedick (1702–11), who was coerced to become a Latin priest.

The fall of Cilicia in the fourteenth century left Armenian colonies scattered throughout the empires of Safavid Iran, Ottoman Turkey and Tsarist Russia, all of which influenced them culturally to varying extents. These focused upon the four centres of the Armenian Church: the patriarchate of Jerusalem; the patriarchate of Constantinople; the catholicate of Cilicia; and the catholicate of Ējmiadsin. From at

49

least the sixth century the Armenian devotion to pilgrimage to the holy places resulted in the Armenian patriarchate of Jerusalem that helped to maintain the sites and offer hospitality to pilgrims through the offices of the Armenian Brotherhood of St James, which had a ministry akin to that of the Franciscans. The Armenian Lectionary preserves a translation of the Greek liturgy, which is the best surviving witness to worship in Jerusalem during the fifth century. Armenian royals and nobles made donations there and a number of mosaic pavements record their munificence in inscriptions, such as that in the funerary chapel of St Polyeuctos, Musrara, Jerusalem.

In the mid-fifth century another distinctive type of mosaic carpet became popular in the churches of the Near East: so-called 'animated landscapes' with scenes of everyday life, environs, flora and fauna (such as the Nilotic scenes in Cyrene Cathedral). Likewise, on Transjordanian church floors there was a vogue for depictions of cities and buildings picturing the 'Holy Land', for example, Gerasa, Sts Peter and Paul and St John the Baptist; Khirbet Samra, Large Church; and the Madaba mosaic pavement map, with Jerusalem at its centre.

The Armenian patriarchate later established good relations with the Crusaders, with the first three kings of the Latin kingdom of Jerusalem marrying Armenian princesses. One, Queen Melisende of Jerusalem (c. 1131–61), who was married to King Fulk, Count of Anjou (who fell from his horse whilst hunting a rabbit, leaving her as a successful regent), owned a resplendent psalter in which Armenian, Byzantine and Western styles were blended by collaborating artists (one named Basilius, a Greek name). The psalter is protected within intricately carved ivory covers of orientalizing fashion, depicting scenes from the life of King David and virtues and vices on the front cover, and the works of Charity/Mercy (Matthew 25:35–36) on the back cover.[1]

Armenia's greatest artistic contribution is deemed to be its manuscript illumination. One of the most prominent Armenian artists was T'oros Ŕoslin (his name suggests mixed Armenian and Western descent – might the surname even allude to the notorious Templar church of Rosslyn in Scotland?), who signed seven manuscripts dating from 1256–68 and was based at Hr'omklay in Cilicia. One fine example of his work, dated 1268–69, was commissioned by Catholicos Kostandin I as a gift for 'the handsome youth Het'um', who became King Het'um II.[2] Particularly detailed colophons are a feature of Armenian books, giving an unprecedented amount of information concerning those who commissioned and made such works. One of the oldest Armenian gospelbooks[3] contains a colophon which records that it was commissioned by an anonymous priest, 'with all his family, for the adornment and glory of the holy church'. His scribe and fellow priest, Sargis, added that he 'wrote these holy Gospels in the year 415 of the Armenian era' (966 CE). The text remains a significant witness to both the first Armenian translation of the Gospels

Virgin and Child, from an Armenian gospelbook,
Armenia, 966 CE. Baltimore, Walters Art Museum.

and the earliest revision following the Council of Ephesus in 431 CE. It contains a stylized miniature of the Virgin and Child (the Virgin is shown seated in the *orans* position of prayer and praise as an intercessor with the Child standing in front of her, rather than nursing him as the mother of God), and portraits of the evangelists Mark and Luke, clad in liturgical vestments, perhaps reflecting the priestly occupations of the book's patron and its scribe. Indeed, Sargis the scribe may also have been the painter. The pairing of evangelist portraits between the Gospel texts is rare; in Early Medieval gospelbooks a single portrait usually appears before each Gospel. This format, the preference for geometric stylization over figural modelling, and the largely earth-tone palette give a rare insight into Early Armenian illumination.

Georgian Manuscripts

Another important early kingdom of the Christian Orient was Georgia, strategically placed between the Black Sea, the Caucasus, Albania and Armenia. During Antiquity Georgia was contested between Rome and Persia and its kings trod a delicate path between the two until 522 CE, when King Tzathius received Christianity, along with his royal regalia, from the Emperor Justinian, as a result of which the kingdom of Lazica became bound to Byzantium. Christianity had been practised in the area perhaps as early as the 320s CE, however, and tradition links the conversion of King Mirian of the Iberian kingdom to the missionary work of a slave woman, St Nino, in 337 CE. How soon afterwards scripture was translated into the native language is uncertain, but at least the Gospels and other Christian writings were translated before the mid-fifth century. The oldest Georgian manuscripts, dating from the fifth to sixth centuries, are palimpsests (reused – erased and overwritten – manuscripts), and contain mostly biblical texts. The Georgian Church, which had a presence in Palestine from at least the fifth century, initially rejected the rulings of the Council of Chalcedon and favoured Monophysitism, but in the early seventh century it returned to Orthodoxy and communion with Byzantium.

The oldest known illuminated Georgian manuscripts date to the ninth century, the First Jrutchi Gospels[4] being one of the earliest examples. It includes colophons by Gabriel, 'the hasty scribe'; Grigol, son of Mirdat, the patron; and Tevdore, the illuminator, indicating that work on the manuscript took place at the Shatberdi Monastery in Georgia (now in Turkey), from 936–940 CE, with the miniatures added in the fourth year. It features canon tables, a portrait of Matthew opposite the Virgin and Child, and three scenes of healing opposite the other evangelist portraits: the Healing of the Blind, facing Mark; the Healing of a Man Possessed by the Devil, facing Luke; and the Healing of a Man Suffering from Palsy, facing John. Each scene has two inscriptions: one naming Jesus Christ, in three languages (Georgian, Armenian and Greek); and the other describing the miracle depicted (in Georgian).

From this point on, several stages in the development of Georgian manuscript decoration can be identified, each characterized by distinctive styles. Most are biblical volumes, such as psalters and gospelbooks; but secular illuminated works also survive, including astronomical treatises, vernacular literature, and Georgian versions of the fables known as *Kalila wa Dimna* and of Firdawsi's Persian epic *Shahnameh* (book of Kings). A significant number of tenth- to fourteenth-century Georgian manuscripts have survived. The Georgian kingdom was at its zenith: its monasteries were flourishing in Syria and Palestine and producing recruits for the community of St Catherine's, Sinai, who required servicebooks in their own language, or bilingually alongside Greek. One of the manuscripts in the Georgian

The Khakhuli Icon, with jewelled surround, Georgian, twelfth century. Tbilisi Museum, Georgia.

language found at St Catherine's (in the ceiling of the chapel of Sts Cosmas and Damian) is an eighth-century psalter from Palestine or Sinai[5] written on papyrus, as are several Georgian works of this period, rather than on the parchment generally used. Most Georgian manuscripts had a wooden binding covered with tooled leather, although lavish treasure bindings have also survived.

Georgia also produced some fine mosaics (such as those at Ghelat) and frescoes (including those at David-Garedja, Ghelat, Ateni and Ihari), using a sophisticated if occasionally somewhat severe version of mainstream tenth- to thirteenth-century Byzantine styles and featuring a preponderance of earth colours. From the ninth to the eighteenth centuries Georgian craftsmen also fashioned a marvellous array of metalwork, now mostly preserved in Tbilisi Museum, much of which is decorated with enamels imported from Byzantium or made in Georgia during the eleventh and twelfth centuries, such as the famous Khakhuli Icon.

Syriac Manuscripts

A further important tradition within the Christian Orient was that known as Syriac (divided into Orthodox and Monophysite 'Jacobite' Churches). Syriac is an Aramaic dialect that became the principal literary vehicle for Semitophone Near Eastern Christianity. This predominance stemmed from its connection with the important classical and Early Christian city of Edessa. The conversion of its populace is thought to date to the late second century, although tradition tells of one of its rulers, Abgar, who sent an embassy to Jesus. It allegedly returned with a letter of instruction and a portrait, which became the basis of a series of icons thought to be miraculous likenesses made 'not by human hand'. Missionary activity carried the Syriac tradition far into eastern Asia. Numerous manuscripts dating from the fifth century onwards have been preserved, including scriptures in the Old Syriac and the Peshitta ('simple') versions.

Perhaps the greatest monument of Syriac art in a Christian context, and to Early Christian manuscript art in general, is one of the earliest surviving illuminated gospelbooks containing illustrations of episodes from the New Testament: the imposing and intriguing Rabbula Gospels,[6] written by the scribe Rabbula in the Syriac language at the monastery of St John in Beth Zagba, a little-known site lying inland between Antioch and Damascus. Its scheme of illumination, although indebted to that of Byzantium, is highly original and inventive and is structured to emphasize the harmony of scripture in foretelling and relating the incarnation, death and resurrection of the Messiah. The Gospels are introduced by canon tables, a concordance system devised by Eusebius in the

RIGHT: The crucifixion from the Rabbula Gospels made in Syria at the monastery of St John in Beth Zagba, 586 CE. Florence, Biblioteca Medicea Laurenziana.

fourth century in which Gospel passages were numbered in the margins and the numbers correlated in tabular form, showing where the four Gospels agreed or diverged. These are adorned with the cross, birds and figures of the Prophets and evangelists, emphasizing their unity of purpose, and a series of marginal illustrations narrating events to which the numbers relate – from the Annunciation to Zacharias of the birth of John the Baptist, to the trial of Christ Before Pilate. The book also features several full-page miniatures, including the Crucifixion, the Women at the Tomb and the resurrected Christ Appearing to the Two Maries, scenes from Acts (the Choosing of Matthias, the Ascension of Christ, and Pentecost), the presentation of the manuscript to Christ, and an icon of Christ and the Virgin Mary (perhaps from a Palestinian model; for it corresponds to images on pilgrim flasks, or *ampulae*, and a pilgrim's box in the Vatican from that region). The manuscript of the Rabbula Gospels exhibits signs of extensive repainting, probably conducted in Renaissance Italy, and seems not simply to have been a restoration but a concerted attempt to normalize many unusual Syriac features. For example, in several of its depictions of Christ (including the Crucifixion – one of its earliest occurrences in art) he was originally portrayed with a pointed face and curling red hair – the so-called 'semitic' type of representation that was probably later considered inappropriate once such stereotypical characteristics had, regrettably, become associated with pejorative Christian depictions of Jews.

Out of Africa

The Art of the Churches of Coptic Egypt, Ethiopia and Nubia

During the post-Roman Period, in the Middle East and North Africa, the production of Christian art and scriptures increasingly centred on remote monasteries founded by Christian communities escaping persecution and tax hikes by following the lead of St Anthony, who had retreated to the Egyptian eastern desert in the late third century. In Caesarea, Armenia, Syria, Coptic Egypt, Nubia (an ancient region along the Nile in southern Egypt and northern Sudan) and Ethiopia monastic scriptoria developed distinctive styles of codicology (the ways in which books are put together), script and illumination. Some important monastic libraries survive, notably that at St. Catherine's, Mount Sinai, and Deir-el-Suriani ('the monastery of the Syrians') in the Egyptian Wadi Natroun, where additional caches of long-lost manuscripts have recently been found in forgotten corners. Their contents graphically portray the varied cultural influences that impacted upon these remote outposts, as do the carved architectural details, frescoes and icons that they contain.

From Pharaonic Temple to Coptic Church

When the Copts (Arabic *qibt*, from the Greek for 'Egyptian' – *aiguptios*, denoting the indigenous Christian population of Egypt) inherited the ancient pharaonic temples they did not always feel the need to redecorate, even though rough crosses were sometimes cut into images in order to deface them and thereby deprive them of power. Some traditional iconographies were retained, but imbued with a new Christian meaning. For example, carved or painted images depicting Anubis

Fresco of the Last Judgement, with the apostles and the Virgin and Child (derived from ancient Egyptian images of Isis and Horus), from the Monastery of Apollo, Bawit, Egypt. Cairo, Coptic Museum.

weighing the souls of the deceased before Osiris, god of the dead, were transformed into the measuring conducted by the archangels at the Last Judgement, which would later feature in the great Doom paintings and sculptural tympana above the entrances to Western Gothic churches. A particularly popular devotional image among the Copts was that of the Virgin holding the Christ-child upon her lap, and sometimes suckling him. This pose was quite evidently lifted from traditional depictions of the Egyptian goddess Isis nurturing Horus – a powerful talismanic image. This Marian iconography would soon travel to Byzantium and even to the farthest corners of the known world. In 698 CE just such an image of the Virgin and Child was carved onto the wooden coffin or relic box (*theca*) of the northern English St Cuthbert at Lindisfarne. It would go on to become one of the most popular Christian devotional images, painted time and again by Raphael and depicted by more recent artists, such as Josephina de Vasconcellos.

The Coptic development of this influential iconography probably had much to do with their Monophysitism, which emphasized the single nature of Christ, in which the divine and the human were at one, and focused upon the role of the Virgin as *Theotokos* – a doctrine devised by the Egyptian patriarch Cyril to address concerns regarding the definition of the nature of Christ discussed at the Council of Ephesus in 431 CE. The schism that resulted has endured to this day. Such images assumed an iconic character and are found painted on the walls of many Coptic churches, or on panels as independent icons, or as part of iconostasis screens – the partition that separated the Holy of Holies from the body of the church, which was covered with a series of icons. Written references to them escalate from the fifth century and by the sixth century icons of Christ and the apostles had been placed upon the *templon* barrier surrounding the sanctuary at Hagia Sophia in Constantinople; stone reliefs depicting them survive from the sixth-century church of St Polyeuktos in the same city.

The church in the Monastery of Deir-el-Suriani in the Wadi Natroun contains both early Coptic murals depicting the Virgin and Child, in iconic fashion, and a superb seventh-century apse-fresco of the annunciation in elegant Hellenistic Byzantine style. No longer in situ at the Monastery of Apollo at Bawit, but preserved in the Coptic Museum in Cairo, is an imposing sixth- to seventh-century fresco from a niche depicting Ezekiel's vision of the second coming. It features a bearded Christ enthroned in majesty within a mandorla (a 'burst of glory', usually almond-shaped), flanked by wheeled, many-eyed fireballs containing the heads of the evangelist symbols and by two reverent angels. Below sits the enthroned Virgin and Child, surrounded by the apostles and local saints, holding the Gospels to which they bore witness.

Encaustic Icons and Coptic Manuscripts

The figure-style of these apostles recalls a fine example of another form of early iconic painting: the painted covers of the Freer gospelbook (Codex Washingtonensis), one of the earliest witnesses to the Greek Bible, made in Egypt during the late fourth to early fifth century. During the seventh century its wooden binding boards were adorned with images of the four evangelists whose Gospels lie within.[1] They are depicted in bearded Byzantine fashion, each head framed by a nimbus, holding individual copies of their Gospels bound in jewelled treasure bindings. Their hands are draped in the attitude of veneration adopted by the deacon when carrying the Gospels in procession and reading from them during the liturgy. The vibrancy of the colours has been retained due to the use of the encaustic painting technique in which pigments were mixed with wax – a process particularly favoured in Coptic Egypt.

Wooden binding boards painted with images of the evangelists in wax (encaustic painting) from the Freer Gospels (Codex Washingtonensis), late fourth or fifth century, with original covers painted during the seventh century in Coptic Egypt. Washington, Freer Gallery of Art.

THE LION COMPANION TO CHRISTIAN ART

Encaustic paint consists of pigments mixed with beeswax, worked when molten, applied to a surface and reheated to fuse the paint, giving an enamel-like finish. The term comes from the Greek term 'to burn in', referring to the process of fusing the paint to its support. Encaustic painting was practised by the Greeks from the fifth century BCE, and Pliny, writing in the first century CE, tells of Roman encaustic painting on wooden panels, marble and ivory. Some of the finest examples of the art are the funerary portraits that adorned mummified burials in the Fayum during the first and second centuries, and the technique was perpetuated in Egypt during the Early Middle Ages. A difficult technique, it permitted a building up of paint in relief, with a jewel-like luminescence and a far better rate of preservation than tempera as it is moisture-proof and does not fade or discolour.

Metalwork fittings at the head of the binding prevent the volume from being opened very far, thereby protecting its structure but also preventing the text from being read. This amounted to its enshrinement as a relic, the images of the gospellers effectively serving as a substitute for the inaccessible Gospels contained within. The Copts seem to have pioneered this approach to the book as relic. Perhaps the earliest surviving example of a metalwork book-shrine, or plate from a treasure binding, is a silver and gilt panel depicting the cross from the Treasure of Bishop Abraham of Harmonthis, which dates to around 600 CE.[2]

The interiors of Coptic gospelbooks and lives of the saints were embellished with carpet-pages – ornamental pages introducing major texts, often featuring crosses composed of interlace. These would influence the gospelbooks of Early Christian Ireland and northern England and later Medieval Jewish and Islamic books. Headpieces framing the opening of texts, in Byzantine fashion, and images of the saints also occur, all in a distinctive palette of red, green and yellow.

Carving and Textiles

Richly carved architectural sculpture, in the tradition of Greece, Rome and Justinian's Byzantium, ennobled imposing basilican churches, such as the sixth-century ones at Bawit, Dendera (where the churches are inserted between the grandiose remains of the ancient temple and its pilgrim hospital). The church at Saqqara was also adorned by murals painted to resemble panels of geometric marble wall cladding, in the style of Late Roman interiors. Such embellishment was intended to summon up recollections of the grandeur of powers long entombed. Acanthus ornament, basket-weave ornament and bunches of grapes abound, and *erotes* (plump little figures of Eros which would later become fully fledged Christian cherubs) carry crosses framed in triumphal wreaths. All would have been brightly coloured.

Painted stone funerary *stellae* and moving diminutive headstones (or pillow-stones, to support the head of the deceased) often carried inscriptions in Coptic or Greek. They also bore motifs including: the *crux ansata* (its upper member in the form of a circle of life, descended from the ancient Egyptian ankh cross); the figure of the deceased with his or her arms raised in the Christian *orans* attitude of prayer, and perhaps flanked by the jackal form of the Egyptian god Anubis (guide of the dead in the afterlife) and the falcon of Horus (life-giving solar god); and an architectural arcade resembling depictions of the Torah Ark in Judaic art – and perhaps intended to represent the gateway to eternal life – from which the cross and the symbols 'alpha' and 'omega' are suspended.

Other distinctive features in Coptic art are stylized vine-scrolls inhabited by animated little grape-pickers, often carved into architectural friezes of wood or stone – a theme frequently found in the murals of ancient Egyptian tombs. Likewise, depictions of the hunting of water fowl in the marshes of the Nile are also typical. Scenes from classical pagan mythology continued to occur, either lacking religious symbolism or imbued with new Christian interpretations.

Among the more everyday items upon which the Copts would have seen Christian images – biblical scenes and secular celebrations, classical and Christian paradisiacal motifs – are the abundant textiles that have survived, such as gaily coloured woollen embroidery on linen garments (some worn by lay people and others as ecclesiastical vestments), bedspreads and curtains (some perhaps veiling the doorways into church chancels). Other everyday objects also carried biblical scenes, such as bone combs (some of which probably served a liturgical function), and items associated with the pilgrim industry that flourished in Egypt and Palestine from St Helena's visit onwards. Particularly numerous were clay pilgrim-flasks bearing depictions of St Menas (an Egyptian recruit to the Roman army who died for his faith), on which the saint is depicted as an *orans*, flanked by two camels who carried his body and indicated the place in the desert where it was to be buried. It gave rise to a healing spring that attracted splendid buildings constructed by the Byzantine emperors and became the Lourdes of its day.

The Spread of Coptic Christianity

Christianity spread from Egypt to Nubia, which extended from Aswan in Egypt to south of Khartoum, from the fifth century onwards. Its churches, such as that of Abdallah Nirqi (dismantled during the construction of the Aswan Dam – some of its art is now preserved in the Coptic Museum in Cairo), and the cathedral of Faras, feature frescoes exhibiting Coptic and continuing Hellenic Byzantine influences, for

Nubia retained a Byzantine identity for centuries after the Islamic conquests of lands to the north and became a refuge for fleeing Coptic monks. Its religious complexion was part Orthodox, part Monophysite, with the latter predominating. A comparatively unusual iconographic theme that was favoured in both Nubia and Egypt was that of the Three Hebrews in the Fiery Furnace, who were saved by the

Frescoes, tenth to eleventh century, Cathedral of Faras, Nubia.

cross, which is also sometimes encountered on the high crosses of Early Medieval Ireland – one of many signs of contact between these ascetic 'wildernesses'.

The arts of the Copts exerted an influence upon the Islamic peoples who became their rulers during the seventh century. This ensured the continuity both of much decorative vocabulary – such as traditional fretwork and interlace patterns, which continued to be carved and inlaid into the pierced wooden screens, doors and furniture of Medieval and Modern Egypt – and of individual forms, such as the stepped pulpit, a free-standing stone pulpit approached by a series of integral steps. (The Coptic Museum in Cairo contains a sixth-century example from the Monastery of St Jeremias at Saqqara, which is decorated with a cross in a shell and an inscription invoking the Trinity.) Their form may have been influenced by the steps leading to the shrines of pharaonic temples (as at Saqqara) and to Early Christian Episcopal thrones (as at Ravenna). The design of the *minbar*, or pulpit, in mosques derived from their Coptic forebears.

A particularly long-lived tradition of art survives to this day in Ethiopia (also known as Abyssinia or Axum, after its ancient capital), which received Christianity under Constantine via two shipwrecked Romans, Frumentius and Aedesius. Among the earliest monuments to survive from this period are the tall stone stelae, carved to depict multi-storey buildings – one such column at Axum being 110 feet (33.5 m) tall. The Nine Saints, who were among an influx of Syriac monks in the late fifth to sixth century, are said to have founded Ethiopian monasticism and contributed to Ethiopian Monophysitism. Until it was curtailed by the rise of Islam, the Axumite empire was regarded as one of the most powerful to have existed: its royalty claimed descent from Solomon, and the vast sixth-century Church of Maryam Seon in Axum (destroyed in the sixteenth century) claimed possession of the Ark of the Covenant. Islamic conquests of neighbouring territories served to render it an isolated Christian kingdom. It retained a strong ascetic tradition of monasticism and produced many beautifully written and illuminated copies of scripture and liturgical manuscripts from the Medieval Period onwards. Such books are still penned there by highly trained scribes in the South Gondar region, employing much the same methods and materials as when Christianity became Ethiopia's state religion during the fourth century. They can write an undecorated religious codex of some 400 leaves in around eight to twelve months, any decoration required being added elsewhere by specialist artists. They write for two or three hours per day amid agricultural and church duties, simply resting the leaves on their knees as they squat on the ground to write.

One of the earliest extant Ethiopic illuminated manuscripts is the Zir Ganela gospelbook,[3] written and illuminated in 1400–1401 according to the colophon,

which states that it was made for Princess Zir Ganela. The decoration comprises
twenty-six full-page miniatures, four illuminated incipit pages, and canon tables
that are thought to be earlier than the manuscript, dating from the tenth to eleventh
centuries. They may have been preserved because of their association with a valued
earlier manuscript and included within the princess's new commission to
emphasize the legitimacy of the rule of the dynasty from which she sprang, by
stressing links with the past. One miniature depicts the crucifixion. The angels and
the sun and moon watch on, the two thieves hang on their adjacent crosses, and the
spear and sponge bearers (Stephaton and Longinus, according to apocryphal
legend, here both shown holding spears) reach up to the body of Christ – which is
absent, the empty cross serving to demonstrate his victory over death in the
resurrection. There are many splendid Ethiopic books dating from this time
onwards, but survivals from earlier times are extremely rare. The destruction of the
Ethiopic kingdom by French and English forces during the nineteenth century
disrupted a long and venerable tradition, its treasures being despoiled and carried
off to Western museums. Nonetheless, this strong culture reasserted itself, and its
distinctive figures, with their benign rounded faces and large, gentle, kohl-rimmed
eyes, still frequent icons and cross-pendants by contemporary Ethiopic artists.

The New Rome

Emperor Justinian and Early Byzantine Art

Constantine's new capital of Constantinople was destined to become the focus of an empire that would inherit something of the role of the Roman empire in the East – Byzantium. The Virgin Mary came to be particularly closely associated with the city, where her girdle and veil were venerated as relics, and in 626 CE she was credited with protecting it from Persian and Avar attack, Patriarch Sergios carrying her icon around its besieged walls.

Women of Influence

The city enjoyed the patronage of other wealthy Christians, as well as the emperors. One of these was a redoubtable woman, Anicia Juliana (c. 461–528 CE). In a dedication inscription at her now lost foundation of St Polyeuktos in Constantinople, she ranked herself alongside Emperors Constantine and Theodosius as a benefactor of the city, stating that her temple surpassed that of Solomon. Related to the Theodosian imperial dynasty and claiming descent from emperors via both parents, she was a powerful figure who established herself as a champion of Chalcedonian orthodoxy. Her portrait survives as the frontispiece to a copy of the medical works of Dioscorides which she commissioned.

The alleged mausoleum of another powerful woman who held sway over the imperial court during the early fifth century, Galla Placidia, mother of Emperor Valentinian III, is one of the Early Christian masterpieces of Ravenna. Its interior is encrusted with exquisite mosaics, one of which depicts the martyrdom of St Lawrence, heading for the gridiron on which he was toasted, with an imposing

armarium (bookcase) in the background, symbolizing the cumulative wisdom of scripture and the patristics. The vault above has become an evocation of the heavens, its twinkling gold mosaic stars upon their rich blue ground illuminating the central golden cross and flanking evangelist symbols. The building may in fact have been an early fifth-century chapel dedicated to St Lawrence, to whom Galla Placidia also dedicated the martyrium of San Lorenzo in Milan; or the allusion to the saint in her burial place may be intended to recall her gifts to God. Nearby in the Orthodox Baptistery, elegant, slender mosaic figures of the apostles regard the baptism of Christ, and four gospelbooks and the *Crux Gemmata* sit enthroned (the *etimasia*); and in San Giovanni Evangelista mosaics celebrate the great saints of Asia Minor, Galla Placidia, and the imperial Theodosian family of the East. The Eastern orientation of the Ravennate court is also signalled by the importation of numerous Asiatic marble sarcophagi, often featuring single figures set in architectural niches decorated with scallop shells; others contain simple iconographic themes (including Marian imagery) or symbolism (such as the Mystical Lamb and peacocks).

Mosaic of St Lawrence going to his martyrdom on a gridiron, with a bookcase (*armarium*) containing copies of scripture and the patristics that served to inspire him; fifth century. Mausoleum of Galla Placidia, Ravenna.

The Churches of Ravenna

The seat of the Western emperor from 402 CE and site of the strategic nearby naval base of Classis, Ravenna was the working capital of Italy. It survived the demise of the imperial line in 476 CE, the rule of the romanophile Arian Ostrogoth, Theodoric (493–526 CE), and the Lombardic incursions of the 560s CE, to become a Byzantine Exarchate, finally falling to the Lombards in 751 CE. Henceforth, Byzantine power would be restricted to southern Italy. Several major churches in Ravenna were established in the early sixth century by the Ostrogoths, other monuments to their

Mosaics depicting Empress Thedora and her entourage, sixth century, San Vitale, Ravenna.

rule including the Mausoleum of Theodoric and a splendid copy of Ulfilas's translation of the Bible into the Gothic language, the Codex Argenteus.[1] These churches were completed under Emperor Justinian I (c. 482–565), who reconquered Italy from the Ostrogoths, North Africa from the Vandals and part of Spain from the Visigoths. His programme of building works included: Sts Sergius and Bacchus and the rebuilding of the cathedral of Hagia Sophia in Constantinople; and in Ravenna, the Arian Baptistery (one of several edifices begun under the Arian Ostrogoth Theodoric and completed under Justinian), the Archbishop's Chapel, San Vitale, Sant' Apollinare Nuovo and Sant' Apollinare in Classe. All are adorned with a splendiferous array of mosaics: those at Sant' Apollinare Nuovo incorporate Arian mosaics from Theodoric's time (including depictions of Classis and the Palace of Ravenna) into its solemn processions of prophets and panels of scenes from the life of Christ. One sort of image that is notably absent from Arian iconography is the depiction of the Virgin, for their belief in the indivisible nature of Christ denied her the title of 'Mother of God'. After the reconciliation with Orthodoxy in the sixth century, however, the Arian Baptistery of Ravenna was restyled Santa Maria in Cosmedin. The cult of the Virgin was now firmly established.

Among the mosaics in San Vitale are those depicting Justinian, his consort Theodora (died 548 CE) and their entourages. Theodora had a spectacular rise from circus performer, actress and possible prostitute to empress, ruling astutely alongside her husband from 527 CE onwards, discreetly but steadfastly championing the Monophysite cause and undertaking charitable works. This remarkable woman is commemorated by the distinctive iconography of the San Vitale mosaics (completed in the year of her death) in which she assumes parallel status with her imperial spouse as leader of court and state and as donor and protector of the church. In the apse of the circular building, Christ bestows his approval upon the bishop/donor, the local martyr, Vitalis, and Justinian and the forces that helped him to reconquer Italy and engage in his building programme. Opposite, on the sanctuary wall surrounding the place of Eucharistic offering, Justinian and Theodora present costly metalwork vessels to the church, their gifts to God's authority being prefigured by those of the Magi, depicted upon Theodora's cloak, and by Old Testament scenes of sacrificial offering below. The static monumentality of the figures, their frontal stance and exotic dress, are Byzantine in style, but their iconography and liturgical context speak of the art of Early Christian Rome, befitting the cultural fusion of the Exarchate of Ravenna.

Justinianic buildings also feature geometric *opus sectile* marble wall cladding, fine marble or porphyry columns and deeply drilled capitals, derived from those of classical architecture but featuring plant tendrils, basketwork or interlaced plaits

69

and Christian symbols such as the cross, the vine, doves, peacocks and lambs – all frozen in a stylized, rigid decorative concoction. Ravenna's other treasures include the outstanding ivory archiepiscopal throne of Maximian (Archbishop of Ravenna, 545–53 CE), thought to have been made in Constantinople during the sixth century, perhaps under Egyptian influence, which features scenes from the lives of Christ, the Virgin and Joseph. Another fine example of the ivory carver's art is the late fifth-century book cover, now in Milan Cathedral Treasury, upon which the busts of the evangelists and their symbols and scenes from Christ's infancy and ministry flank jewelled images of the Mystical Lamb (*Agnus Dei*) and the cross surmounting the four rivers of Paradise. Another gospelbook cover of sixth-century date, from St Lupicin (Jura) and now in the Louvre, features angels who are directly descended from the winged victories of Antiquity, bearing the cross within a laurel wreath. Beneath sit enthroned the Virgin and Child, flanked by scenes from the life of the *Theotokos*, the companion leaf featuring episodes from the life of her son.

The Golden Canon Tables, a system giving the concordance of the Gospels devised by Eusebius in the fourth century, painted around 600 CE in Constantinople. London, British Library.

70

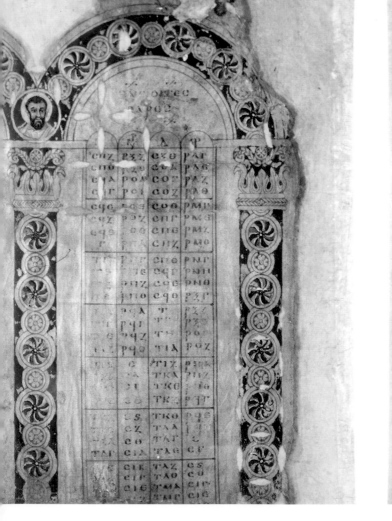
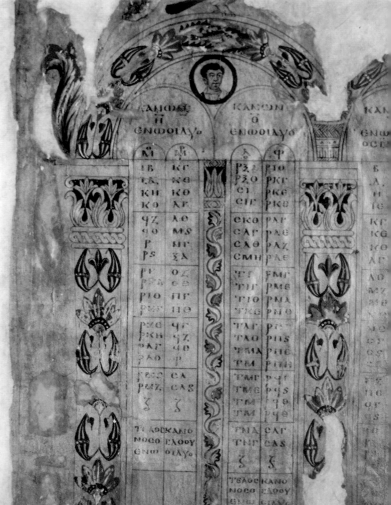

The Decoration of Christian Scripture

Early Christian copies of scripture were undecorated, but during the fifth and sixth centuries images began to be applied to biblical books – with great picture cycles illustrating books such as the Byzantine Cotton Genesis, the Vienna Genesis,[2] Codex Sinopensis and the Rossano Gospels, and the Syriac Rabbula Gospels.[3]

The Vienna Genesis, The Deluge, Eastern Mediterranean, early sixth century. Vienna, Österreichische Nationalbibliothek.

Pictures had not found favour with classical bibliophiles, but Italian publishers now even illustrated old literary favourites by Virgil, Terence and Homer. The use of opulent materials, with gold and silver scriptures on purple pages, also imparted imperial stature to the grandest Byzantine, Syriac and Italian tomes, such as the sixth-century Italian Codex Brixianus[4] and the Golden Canon Tables,[5] made in Constantinople around 600 CE. The passage numbers of the concordance to the Gospels are set upon pages impregnated with gold and contained within architectural arcades – like a chancel arch or *templon* (screen of columns) giving entry to the Holy of Holies, for the numbers formed a sacred computer encapsulating Christ's mission and message. Such opulent tomes were probably protected by treasure bindings, such as the Dumbarton Oaks Covers[6] – silver gilt covers adorned with cypress trees set beneath aedicule or the figures of Sts Peter and Paul – which probably once contained a Byzantine gospelbook of sixth to seventh-century date.

The Cotton Genesis[7] was once one of the most impressive and important of Early Christian illustrated biblical books, but sadly only shrunken fragments remain. It was made in the eastern Mediterranean (Alexandria, Egypt?) in the late fifth or sixth century and contained around 339 miniatures illustrating Genesis. It would have been an imposing volume of some 440 pages measuring around 10 x 13 inches (25 x 33 cm), the fragments having shrunk to about half their original size during a fire in 1731. Some impression nonetheless remains of the opulent picture cycle, with its late antique illusionistic paintings set in panels, resembling the series of frescoes and mosaics that adorned great metropolitan churches, such as Santa Maria Maggiore in Rome. It is not known whether other biblical books were also extensively illustrated during this period, but another Early Christian illustrated Genesis, the Vienna Genesis, survives and the Old English Genesis,[8] made around 1000 CE, contains an image cycle thought to be indebted to an Early Christian model. A near contemporary Anglo-Saxon English paraphrase of the Pentateuch by the homilist Aelfric[9] also contains a picture cycle which may be of Early Christian derivation, implying that the first five books of the Bible may also have circulated as one book (the Christian equivalent of the Judaic Torah).

The various peoples and kingdoms that emerged from the maelstrom of the Roman empire's demise also contributed their own distinctive forms of ornament to manuscript illumination. Copies of sacred text produced in the second half of the first millennium would be very different in appearance and character from the simple, disposable pamphlets used by Early Christian communities, and were not only the vehicles of Christian teaching but also potent symbols of local identity and of emerging powers. As such, they graphically portray the transition from Late Antiquity to the Early Middle Ages – and the role that religion played in this process.

7

The Art of Orthodoxy

Byzantium and the Iconic Tradition

Byzantium, ever concerned to contain the schisms that endangered its hegemony, led the way in the Early Medieval debate concerning the role of icons. Byzantine book production had flourished during the Early Christian Period, readily embracing imagery (although little now survives). The *Crux Gemmata* and the gospelbook already serve as the aniconic embodiment of Christ in the fifth-century mosaics of the Orthodox Baptistry in Ravenna, where they occupy the throne and the altar as symbols of orthodoxy. In 692 CE the Council *in Trullo*, held in Constantinople, passed a canon (no. 11) rejecting the established symbolic iconography of John the Baptist, the 'Precursor', pointing to the image of Christ as the Lamb in favour of a more literal representation of the crucifixion as an image of redemption. The Pope refused to subscribe to the Council, which perhaps accounts for the prominent retention of the John the Baptist imagery on the Ruthwell and Bewcastle crosses from northern Britain, but there nonetheless appears to have been an initial Western move towards depicting the crucifixion, in accordance with the canon. These were very much live issues and even though a greater tolerance towards images prevailed in the West, it did not go unquestioned, and the debate continued into the Carolingian age.

The Iconoclast Controversy

In 726 CE the iconoclast party in Constantinople, sponsored by Emperor Leo III the Isaurian, tore down the effigy of Christ on the palace gate and replaced it with a cross accompanied by a plaque, which read:

'*The Emperor Leo and his son Constantine*
Thought it dishonour to the Christ divine

That on the very palace gate he stood
A lifeless, speechless effigy of wood.
Thus what the Book forbids they did replace
With the believer's blessed sign of grace.'

This erupted into the Iconoclast Controversy (726–87 CE). Imagery was largely outlawed and many wonderful works of art were destroyed. Yet, even during the state-sponsored iconoclasm of eighth-century Byzantium, certain symbols could be used as an alternative to figural representation. Thus the cross and the book became acceptable symbols of orthodox Christianity. Such aniconic images were generally replaced by figural images following the demise of iconoclasm, although a simple mosaic of a cross survives in the apse of the Church of St Eirene in Constantinople, and as the later frescoes at Toqale Kilisse (a rock-cut church in Cappadocia) flake off, the underlying non-figural paintings from the iconoclast period are revealed. Only in Mesopotamia did such aniconic trends endure. The Council of Nicaea of 787 CE, however, supported attempts by the Empress Eirene to restore images and stated that:

'We therefore follow the pious customs of antiquity and pay these icons the honour of incense and lights just as we do the holy gospels and the venerable and life-giving cross.'

Some theologians, notably John of Damascus during the eighth century, championed the cause of iconography, writing:

'Of old, God the incorporeal and uncircumscribed was never depicted. Now, however, when God is seen clothed in flesh and conversing with mortals, I made an image of the God whom I can see. I do not worship the matter, I worship the God of matter who became matter for my sake.'[1]

As a result of the Council of Nicaea and the accession of Empress Eirene (797–802 CE) images were reinstated and, despite an iconoclastic resurgence in 814–43 CE, artistic production was stepped up again within the Byzantine empire. Its art tends to be categorized in three periods: the pre-iconoclast Early Byzantine Period (fourth to early eighth century); the post-iconoclast classicizing Middle Byzantine Period (ninth through twelfth centuries), sometimes also termed the Macedonian and Comnenan Period after the ruling dynasties; and the Late (or Palaeologan) Byzantine Period of the central Middle Ages, which followed the crusader occupation of Constantinople during the short-lived Latin empire (1204–61).

Orthodox Opulence in Art

The Byzantine and other Orthodox traditions are distinguished by opulent display and the use of precious materials. De luxe silver plate had begun to be used in the celebration of the Eucharist, as well as for purposes of state and in domestic dining rooms, by the fourth century. They were often bejewelled with carved gemstones and enamels. Pagan imagery continued to adorn pieces used as church plate (some reused items donated by Christian converts), just as Christian symbols graced pieces for use in homes. There was evidently a sense of continuity between the pagan past and the Christian present. Major hoards have been discovered as far afield as Syria (the Kaper Koraon Treasure), Asia Minor (the Lapsacus Treasure), North Africa (the Carthage Treasure), Rome (the Esquiline Treasure), and Britain (the Mildenhall, Water Newton and Hoxne Treasures, some of the Sutton Hoo burial goods and the Corbridge Lanx). Likewise, the technique of producing sumptuous woven silk textiles was introduced into Byzantium from Persia and the East by the fifth century and Justinian subsequently introduced silk cultivation to his territories. These were worn not only by the aristocracy but might also be incorporated into ecclesiastical vestments and used to wrap the relics of saints (such as the complex Nature Goddess silk from Byzantium, which was one of the covers of the incorrupt body of St Cuthbert in Anglo-Saxon Northumbria). Silk tapestries were also woven, joining the earlier wool and linen examples from Egypt. One, the Gunthertuch in Bamberg Cathedral, depicts the mounted emperor and was found in the tomb of Bishop Gunther who died on the journey back from Byzantium in 1065, perhaps bringing the tapestry as a diplomatic gift. Another famous Byzantine silk is the 'elephant silk', placed in the tomb of Charlemagne at Aachen by Emperor Otto III in 1000, to honour the anniversary of the re-establishment of the role of Christian emperor of the West with a treasure from that of its Eastern counterpart. The fall of Constantinople hit the silk industry hard and although it still produces textiles for use in the Orthodox Church it was largely replaced by Italian and Eastern competitors. From the early thirteenth century onwards Byzantine embroidery developed as an art, as an extension of the practice of enriching textiles by sewing on pearls, gems and enamels. Designs in gold wire (*chrysoklabarika / chrysokentita*, 'ornamenting / embroidering with gold'), often in raised designs over quilting, became popular for Greek and Russian Orthodox Church use and to convey secular pomp too.

As for the fine arts, three-dimensional sculpture – although not unknown on a small domestic scale – generally declined because of its associations with the pagan past and the worship of idols. The major exception to this trend was, as we have seen, funerary sculpture, notably Early Christian sarcophagi. Architectural embellishment and articulation also continued to offer scope for the sculptor, although demand was such that earlier columns and capitals were often recycled. The great age of basilican and domed church buildings in the Early Byzantine Period gave way to smaller churches, often monastic, based upon a cross inscribed by a square with a central dome, in the Middle Byzantine Period. The low chancel screen of the earlier period also developed into the heftier *templon*, which was adorned with stone slabs carved with motifs of increasingly Near Eastern inspiration, reflecting Byzantine military conquests in tenth-century Anatolia. During the thirteenth century areas under Byzantine influence, such as Venice and the Balkans, witnessed a revival of figural sculpture in high-relief on funerary monuments and architectural capitals and façades. A rare survival is the applied

The *Harbaville Triptych*, with the Deeisis (Christ flanked by the intercessory figures of the Virgin and John the Baptist), Constantinople, late tenth century. Paris, The Louvre.

THE LION COMPANION TO CHRISTIAN ART

sculpture adorning the exterior of the church on the island of Achthamar in Lake Van in Armenia, built for King Gagik by the architect Manuel in 915–21 CE. Such distinctive applied two-dimensional sculptural decoration, with its isolated figures, animals and plant motifs, would influence some Western Early Romanesque façades, such as Regensburg Cathedral and Cormac's Chapel on the royal/ecclesiastical citadel of Cashel in southern Ireland.

On a smaller scale, carved ivories continued in vogue. The consular diptychs of the Late Roman empire inspired (and were sometimes reused as) the covers of liturgical and biblical books and wax tablets upon which the church feasts of the day were inscribed, and the toiletry and work boxes of wealthy women metamorphosed into reliquaries and pyxes to contain the host and the holy oils of anointment. Such items were readily portable and served as stylistic, iconographic and technical conduits of influence from East to West, giving rise to vibrant Carolingian, Ottonian, Anglo-Saxon, Romanesque and Gothic traditions of ivory carving. A rare example of a free-standing statue is a 12-inch- (30 cm) high tenth-century ivory of the Virgin and Child; but perhaps the finest ivory from the Macedonian age of Constantinopolitan art is the late tenth-century *Harbaville Triptych* with the frozen stylized classicism of its hieratic figures of the Deesis (Christ flanked by the intercessory figures of the Virgin and St John the Baptist) and saints. This is in marked contrast to the emotive impact of the animated anticipation and humanity of the Forty Martyrs who await their fate on a twelfth-century panel in Comnene style.

Ivories were often combined on such items with enamelwork, in which Byzantine craftsmen excelled. Enamel is coloured glass that has been fused to metal by heating. Initially, the technique was a perpetuation of that inherited from ancient Greece and Rome, with gold filigree (droplets) soldered onto a gold ground to separate fields of different coloured enamels. From the mid-ninth century a refinement of the technique was introduced from the West, which had responded to the earlier form, replacing the filigree with strips of gold, sometimes as thin as wire, in what is known as the cloisonné technique (cells of colour) which Byzantium elevated to new heights of achievement. During the tenth century the champlevé technique, in which recesses are carved into the ground to receive the enamel, was introduced and rapidly spread to the West where it became the norm.

The reuse of earlier gold coinage, objets and mosaic tesserae meant that such costly materials were in relatively plentiful supply in Byzantium – unlike the West, which from the tenth century onwards relied increasingly upon a silver-based economy, rendering such eastern opulence even more exotic and desirable. Many such exotic items reached the West as a trickle of gifts and pilgrimage souvenirs

77

which became a flood with the sack of Constantinople by the Crusaders in 1204. En route to the Holy Land on the Fourth Crusade they had promised a share of their spoil to the Venetians in return for transportation and had diverted to plunder the wealthiest Christian city – an atrocity deemed excusable as the Latin and Greek Churches were in a state of schism. Such conflicts between members of the same religion, whichever that may be, serve to illustrate all too well that faith conflicts are often simply the result of the ambitions and fears of man, rather than the promptings of different religions. The Treasury of San Marco's in Venice preserves much of the Crusaders' booty: enamel and jewel-encrusted chalices and patens, their bodies of metalwork or semi-precious stones, such as onyx and jasper, recalling the apostle John's vision in the book of Revelation; reliquaries and treasure bindings. One of the finest such trophies was the mid-tenth-century cover of a reliquary containing a fragment of the True Cross, which was presented to the nuns of Stuben after 1204 and is now in Limburg an der Lahn. A striking and unusual instance of Persian influence on Byzantine cloisonné enamelwork can be seen on two panels depicting exuberant Eastern-style dancing girls on the crown of Emperor Constantine Monomachos (1042–55), now in Budapest.

Byzantine and Other Orthodox Mosaics

Among the most scintillating of Byzantine artworks are the mosaics that occur throughout its territories, a technique inherited from the world of Classical Antiquity and given renewed impetus during the reign of Justinian, under the stimulus of Italian Early Christian wall and apse mosaics. Centres such as Thessaloniki perpetuated these traditions, producing works such as the touching seventh-century image of a youthful St Demetrius with two suppliant children, one a mere toddler. The mosaics of Thessaloniki are a rare survival in Greece of pre-iconoclast monumental images.

The decorative scheme first established after the iconoclast period by the mosaics (now lost) in the Nea, in Constantinople, founded by Emperor Basil I (867–86 CE), was formalized by the Orthodox Church and passed from generation to generation, finally being preserved in written form in a handbook known as the Painter's Guide, of which a sixteenth-century copy survives. The handbook details the way in which churches should be decorated and how the scenes should be painted, and artists were not permitted to deviate from it. Christ presided over the New Jerusalem (the church) in its dome, accompanied in proximity by scenes from his life; the Virgin occupied the apse; at a lower level, or in a side chapel, were Old Testament scenes or the life of the Virgin; beneath were the intercessory saints, and

RIGHT: Mosaic of St Demetrius protecting two children, perhaps acolytes; seventh century. Church of St Demetrius, Thessaloniki.

79

THE ART OF ORTHODOXY

Christ Pantocrator,
c. 1100, in the dome at
Daphni, Greece.

in the lower part of the apse the Fathers of the Church who formulated liturgy. The mosaic of *Christ Pantocrator* (Christ the Almighty) in the dome at Daphni near Athens, made around 1100, depicts him as a grim and forbidding judge, his brows furrowed and his fingers gripping the Book – an expressionistic Old Testament Jehovah, rather than the empathetic embodiment of vulnerable humanity favoured in other phases of Byzantine art and in the West. Other subject matter might include depictions of the imperial family, such as that in the South Gallery of the Church of Sancta Sophia in Constantinople in which Christ is flanked by the Empress Zoë and her third husband, Constantine Monomachos (whom Zoë married in her sixties and whose head and inscription replace that of her first spouse), a notable patron of the arts whose reign brought the Macedonian dynasty to a close in 1055.

Monumental figural compositions also survive in frescoes from the Macedonian age onwards, such as those from the rock churches of Cappadocia – including those dating from the tenth and eleventh centuries at Kiliclar, Toqale Kilisse and the nearby chapel of Elmale Kilisse. Figures are slender, if sometimes somewhat static, with elegant draperies. Impressive as they are, they lack the animatic spirit, emotional content and approachability of their Comnene successors seen, for example, in the Deposition at Nerezi, Macedonia, painted by a Constantinopolitan artist in 1164. The elongated figures, with their exaggerated and well-choreographed postures, tend towards the expressionistic and invite the viewer to participate in the events depicted through a shared humanity. This humanism, particularly favoured under the Comnene dynasty (1081–1185), also expressed itself well in the arts of the mosaicist and the illuminator. The mosaics at Daphni exhibit an intimacy unknown before they were executed, around 1100, as do miniatures such as the portrait of Emperor Nicephorus Botiniates (1078–81) between St John Chrysostom and the Archangel Michael, in which the formality of the subject does not conceal the humanity of the figures.

The Western occupation of Constantinople from 1204–61 did not prevent the further development of Byzantine art, even if it disrupted it. The Palaeologan emperors established themselves in exile, with three branches of the imperial family settling themselves at Trebizond (near the Caucasus), Epirus (northern Greece) and Nicaea (some 60 miles or 100 kilometres from Constantinople in Asia Minor). The re-installation of Emperor Michael III Palaeologus in Constantinople in 1261 brought with it the Palaeologan Revival Style, which had been developing from as early as c. 1200 (the graceful and tender Deesis mosaic in the southern gallery of Sancta Sophia, Constantinople, should perhaps be dated this early), and had evolved during the period of exile in works such as the frescoes of Sancta Sophia, Trebizond. Its lively compositions and intimate figures, its tendency towards mannerism, and its use of white highlights to increase dramatic effect can be seen in masterworks such as the mosaics and frescoes of Mistra and the church of Kariye Camii (Christ the Saviour) in Constantinople, commissioned by a court official, Theodore Metochites, who retired from public office in disgrace to become a monk there. The manner in which the compositions fill the architectural space, such as the receding perspective of the bulbous wine jars in the miracle at Cana scene, are a tribute to the inventiveness of the artists when conveying a traditional iconography. Another more unusual iconography explored in this remarkable scheme is that of the first steps of the Virgin, in which Mary is shown as a toddler, taking her first hesitant steps between a nurse depicted as a classical muse, with her diaphanous shawl framing her head, and the outstretched arms of a tender St Anne, in a walled garden symbolic of virginity. It is fascinating to recall that these tesserae were being set at around the time that Giotto was painting the plaster of the Arena Chapel in Padua.

Mosaic depicting a scene from the childhood of the Virgin; Kariye Camii, Constantinople, c. 1310.

Also of Palaeologan date are a series of exquisite miniature mosaics, their tiny tesserae set into wax. Another earlier minor, but interesting, form of Byzantine painting is also worthy of mention; it survives on a few remaining ceramic tiles bearing images of saints (such as that of St Theodore from Patleina in Bulgaria), dating from the ninth to twelfth centuries.

Manuscript Illumination

Few illuminated manuscripts survive from the pre-iconoclast period, but those that do are, as we have seen, extremely ambitious and innovative in their use of costly materials, such as purple-dyed pages, gold and silver inks and multi-coloured painterly sequences of images, seen in fragmentary survivors such as the Golden Canon Tables and the Cotton Genesis, and in more complete works such as the Vienna Genesis, the Rossano Gospels and the Codex Sinopensis. A multitude of

illuminated books survive from the post-iconoclast periods, although the comparative infrequency of colophons and an innate conservatism of style in decoration and script make localization and dating challenging. The tenth-century Paris Psalter gives an insight into the classical and Early Christian inspiration underlying the Macedonian renaissance, with its depictions of Isaiah at prayer, accompanied by a glamorous female personification of night, with classical garb and her shawl held above her head, and its David composing the Psalms, in which the future king is shown as a young shepherd, playing his harp like Orpheus in a pastoral landscape. The continued classicism of figure-style can be seen combined with a mannerist dynamism of composition and colour and a feel for human

David (depicted resembling Orpheus) composing the Psalms, The Paris Psalter, Constantinople, tenth century. Paris, Bibliothèque nationale.

emotion in later Palaeologan works, such as the startling transfiguration in the Manuscript of John VI Catacuzenus, painted around 1370–75. Works might be produced in monastic scriptoria, sometimes by single artist-scribes working in solitude at their spiritual labours, or in urban workshops by laymen. The vast majority were biblical or liturgical tomes, with some illuminated saints' lives and homilies. Gospelbooks, with ornamented canon tables, headpieces and evangelist portraits depicting them as bearded scribes, were particularly popular, as were books containing these and/or the remainder of the New Testament, Gospel lectionaries, and Psalters containing prefatory cycles of images or sequences of marginal illustrations – as in the Theodore Psalter, written in Constantinople in 1066. The codicological practice of preparing the membrane leaves with a smooth, glassy finish has led to poor adherence of inks and pigments, resulting in flaking which often necessitated repainting across the ages. Nineteenth-century collectors in particular often had their prized acquisitions retouched and even added new images to restore them to connoisseur status.

The Sacred Role of the Icon

The most potent and characteristic form of Byzantine Christian artistic expression, however, is the icon. Images in books or other media are sometimes given this epithet, indicating their function as devotional images, but the term refers primarily to panel paintings, whether small, portable or domestic, or large patronal icons (depicting the saints to whom they were dedicated) in major churches. The role of the icon is a distinctly religious one. The act of 'writing' (rather than painting) an icon is in itself an act of prayer in which a direct channel of communication is opened between the sacred or saintly persons depicted and those who contemplate their images. This enables the subject to act as intermediary and intercessor between God and supplicant, heaven and earth, whether in the form of a compassionate Virgin and Child, a stern prophet, an ascetic saint or an archangel charged with the weighing of souls and the contesting of spindly Eastern-style devils.

The transmission of such sacred iconic images, like that of sacred texts, was considered to be achieved through the interaction of divine inspiration, the agency of the Spirit and the contemplative work of the transmitter. Certain famous icons depicting Christ (bearded, in Byzantine fashion, rather than in youthful unbearded Early Christian Hellenistic guise) were thought to have appeared miraculously (*acheiropoietos*) rather than being created by human hands, while some were attributed to St Luke, who was said to have painted the likeness of the Mother of God (*Theotokos*) from life. It therefore became extremely important that subsequent copies should preserve these images as faithfully as possible, instilling a powerful conservatism into the iconic tradition. Techniques were developed to assist in this, such as the use of cartoons onto which images were traced and transferred by pricking to enable mass-produced copies. Nonetheless, it is not unusual for an icon to carry numerous painting layers, as they were often reused and over-painted.

Strips of wood were mounted on a wooden support and often carved to form a recess and surrounding frame. The recess was sometimes lined with linen and then coated with layers of plaster gesso. Next the image was drawn in charcoal and the outlines frequently incised with a point. Those areas to be gilded were then often covered with red or yellow bole (clay) upon which gold leaf was laid and burnished with a dog's or wolf's tooth or the semi-precious agate stone. The images were painted in tempera (the yolk of an egg mixed with a drop of vinegar and a limited range of pigments: earth colours, malachite, azurite, verdigris, cinnabar, white lead and black), with encaustic wax sometimes being used as an alternative, especially in the pre-iconoclast period. Finally, a protective glaze was added.

Icons were usually designed so that they could be displayed on liturgical screens, on stands, as diptychs or triptychs, or carried in liturgical processions. The initial low chancel screen gave way to the Middle Period *templon* barrier and then to the Late Byzantine iconostasis – a full sanctuary screen separating the Holy of Holies from the congregation and carrying an established scheme of icons forming a symbolic cosmos. The lowest register of the iconostasis was the 'worship' row, comprising the royal doors and icons of local saints. Then came the Deesis row; the row of liturgical feasts of the Church; the row of Holy Days; the row of Old Testament kings and prophets; the row of Old Testament patriarchs; and the whole surmounted by the cross.

Icons were often paid heightened honour by encasing them in silver repoussé mounts which also served to raise parts of the design, such as haloes, giving a three-dimensional effect. An early example of this can be seen on a fourteenth-century double-sided processional icon, carried on a pole, from Ochrid, in which the Virgin is depicted as *Hodegetria*, the Indicator of the Way, gesturing to the infant. She has been given the title Saviour of Souls. By the Renaissance icons were being seen as works of art, as well as devotional and liturgical objects, in areas of Italian influence and they were often set within imposing frames and displayed on the walls of the wealthy in their homes and offices.

There is evidence that icons were in use since at least the fourth century, when Eusebius criticized their ill-informed veneration as potential idols while apparently appreciating their beauty and proper contemplative use himself, as discussed in Chapter 1. Some of the earliest and most powerful icons to have survived from the

Icon of St Peter, encaustic wax painting, sixth century. St Catherine's Monastery, Mount Sinai.

Early Period are preserved at the monastery of St Catherine, Mount Sinai, including a striking sixth-century encaustic icon of St Peter and a sixth- to seventh-century Ascension resembling that in the Syriac Rabbula Gospels. Another particularly fine collection of icons and manuscripts preserved in situ is that on Mount Athos, Greece. Some of the finest icons from the Middle Period were made in Constantinople itself. Following the Latin conquest of that city in 1204 and the consequent dismembering of the Byzantine empire, the impetus passed to other production centres. One of the most important of these was Crete, which became the Venetian colony of the Regno di Candia from 1210 to 1669. This became one of a number of areas of fruitful Italo-Byzantine economic and cultural interaction, where Constantinopolitan and Italian stylistic influences merged. Icons might be commissioned 'alla maniera greca' or 'alla maniera italiana/latina', according to style and iconography, by members of the Orthodox or Catholic Churches, often interchangeably. Cretan icon writers had an unusual tendency to sign their work, as a result of which it is possible to chart the existence of some 150 of them in the capital, Candia (modern Heraklion) by the sixteenth century. The anonymity of the icon writer gave way to the identity of the artist, in accordance with Italian trends, identifying for us painters such as the Ritzos family, Angelos, and Andreas Pavias during the fifteenth century and, in the sixteenth, Domenikos Theotokopoulos – better known as 'El Greco' – who once more transmitted the mystical and spiritual essence of the iconic tradition to Western art.

Angelos of Crete may have been responsible for giving the imagery of St George and the dragon its conventional form, with the serpent of evil becoming a winged dragon, vanquished by a crowned knight, representing the triumph of good, while

the imperilled princess and her people watch on and Christ and the angels bless his endeavours. St George, a military martyr in the eastern Roman empire, was adopted as a patron by Westerners occupying the Holy Land and the islands of the eastern Mediterranean and subsequently became the patron saint of England. An early example of Western interest in this imagery is a thirteenth-century icon of St George and the youth of Mytilene, a boy captive forced to serve the Saracens on Crete who was rescued by George. It was possibly painted at Lydda, the cult centre of St George in the Holy Land, or on Cyprus, and fuses Byzantine and Western styles in a manner typical of the Crusader kingdoms.

Icon of St George defeating the dragon, sixteenth century, Crete. Windsor Castle, the Dean and Canons of Windsor.

THE ART OF ORTHODOXY

Orthodox Art Beyond Byzantium

The decline of the Byzantine empire, from its sack at the hands of Westerners in 1204 to its fall to the Turks in 1453, led to the development of ever more distinctive regional traditions and styles of art in the kingdoms that had formed part of it and which now achieved increasing independence – much as their Western counterparts had following the demise of the western Roman empire a millennium earlier. Some of these have been discussed already: the considerable Byzantine influence on Sicily and Venice will be discussed below; of the remainder, the most significant were the Russian Orthodox Church and the Balkans.

The Balkans had long formed a distinct part of the Byzantine world and, with the weakening of centralized control, it produced a number of independent kingdoms: the Bulgars, who came from east of the Black Sea and brought with them Persian Sassanian influence, developing their own culture from the seventh century onwards; the Slavic Serbians, who emerged culturally in the twelfth century; and the Greek and Slavic Macedonians, who traced their descent from the empire of Alexander the Great. The small church at Boian near Sofia contains some of the finest Bulgarian painting, of mid-thirteenth-century date, which fully embraces the humanism of contemporary Byzantine art. Further outstanding examples occur at Tirnovo, Mesembria and St George in Sofia, but much other work is of provincial character and exhibits enduring Eastern influence, producing a distinctive regional style that is reflected in the few surviving manuscripts. The greatest of these is the Gospels of Tsar Ivan Alexander of Bulgaria, made in Tirnovo in 1355–56, which features an imposing image of the royal family.[2]

Macedonia and Serbia were producing fine examples of mainstream Byzantine art during the twelfth century, at sites such as Ochrid, Nerezi, Kastoria and Kurbinovo, the latter two already exhibiting an angularity and exaggerated articulation of the human form that would go on to form a local style. Some Serbian works, such as those at Studenica, favoured greater naturalism and modelling, however, under Italian influence, with Sienese painting providing a particular context for the beautiful, gentle head of the Virgin in the *Annunciation* at Mileševo – part of a scheme painted in 1230–37 by the artists Demetrius, George and Theodore. The finest Balkan

St Peter, from a fresco of the Agony in the Garden, by the artists Eutychios and Michael, c. 1295. St Clement's, Ochrid, Macedonia.

works of the age, however, are the frescoes at the Church of the Trinity, Sopoćani, commissioned by Uroš I around 1265, with their naturalistic, modelled figures which convey a profound spiritual involvement in the scenes they inhabit, whether saint or humble shepherd.

At the Church of St Mary Peribleptos, later known as St Clement's, Ochrid, Balkan artists signed their work for the first time (a practice that henceforward became normal) – the *Agony in the Garden* fresco being signed in 1295 by Eutychios and his colleague Michael.

Another, more regional, trend favoured heightened emotion and expression which resulted in works as innovative and moving as *Rachel Lamenting the Loss of Her Children*, and in the almost comic caricature of St Blaise, both at Markov Manastir from the mid-fourteenth century. An almost naïve quality is also apparent that endures in the recent revival of Balkan icon painting. Despite the traumas that beset Serbia, as Turkish incursions forced its people northwards to the Morava Valley during the fourteenth century, its art witnessed a final flourishing of almost effete beauty that was in stark contrast to the horrors of the age. The Christian virtues of gentleness and beauty were expressed here – as in the rest of Byzantium – through art at a time when the empire and its offspring were fighting for their very existence.

In Russia, the adoption of Orthodoxy led to the formation of a tradition of Christian art that has endured for a millennium. The Vikings had penetrated what became Russia in the late ninth century, basing themselves at Kiev. By 850 CE they had become known as the Varangians, raiding Constantinople and going on to trade and to form the Byzantine Varangian Guard. In 957 CE Princess Olga visited Constantinople and converted, and in 987/8 CE her grandson, Vladimir, christianized his state, importing Byzantine priests and craftsmen. The mid-eleventh-century mosaics and frescoes in one of the new churches, the Hagia Sophia in Kiev, are accordingly in Russo-Byzantine style, probably executed by Russian craftsmen supervised by a Greek master. Some iconographic innovations were introduced, such as Christ depicted as a priest and the inclusion of local Slav saints, and in Russian churches the frescoes extend to ground level, dispensing with the marble cladding of their Byzantine counterparts. In the early fifteenth century the iconostasis was enlarged to accommodate more icons, sometimes filling the entire height of the church. For the iconic tradition was embraced and adopted by the Russian Orthodox Church, which, along with Crete, became the focus of icon production after the fall of Constantinople, producing its own distinctive schools, such as those of Moscow and Novgorod. These were influenced by imports from Constantinople such as the outstandingly intimate and compassionate icon of the Virgin, clasped in tender embrace with the Christ Child, painted in Comnene style around 1125, which is

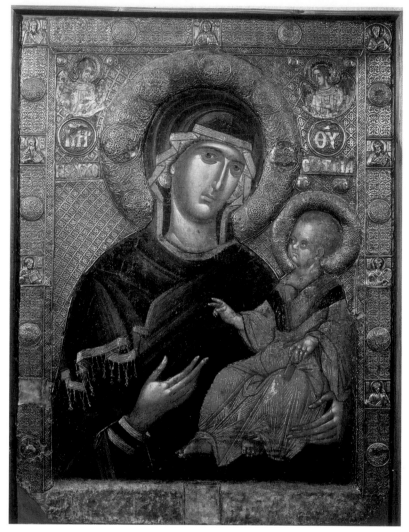

Our Lady of Vladimir,
Constantinople, c. 1125;
Tretyakov Gallery, Moscow.

FAR RIGHT: Icon of the Trinity,
depicted as the angels who
visited Abraham, painted by
Andrei Rublev, Russia, c.1400.
Tretyakov Gallery, Moscow.

known as *Our Lady of Vladimir*. Another such influential model was *Our Lady of Pimen*, probably painted at Constantinople in the late fourteenth century, but in what is known as the Graeco-Italian style, which held sway in the Adriatic and which exerted such a powerful and formative influence upon Italian Early Renaissance art. Such potent images served to inspire Russian artists such as Theophanes the Greek and Andrei Rublev (both active around 1400) to create works such as Rublev's famous *Trinity*, in the form of the three angelic visitors who announced to Abraham and Sarah the birth of a son, which has become both an icon of faith and a cultural icon. The enduring power of the tradition can be seen in late works such as the *Virgin Kazanskaya*, painted around 1915 by Dmitri Smirnov, a truly Russian icon which clearly proclaims its Byzantine ancestry. This is representative of the 'traditional' school of icon painting that endures to this day, along with the 'naïve' style, seen in many contemporary Balkan icons, for example, and the 'modern' style, practised by current icon writers in East and West.

THE ART OF ORTHODOXY

Icons: An Icon Writer's Perspective

Revd Regan O'Callaghan

Icons as religious artefacts are becoming more popular in the West. Today people from many different Christian traditions are learning about icons, have icons in their homes and are studying how to write icons. As an artist and an Anglican priest an icon is, for me, a wonderful way to make a connection between my priestly ministry, my Christian faith and my creative gifts.

When I was growing up it was always religious imagery that caught my imagination, deeply influencing my faith. In the church I attended as a child I would often peer up at the gold stars on the midnight blue ceiling, representing God's promise to Abraham that he would have many descendants. The church's stained glass windows cast beautiful colours on the congregation, with the highest window showing Jesus sitting on his throne gazing down on us all.

As an adult I continue to see and understand a lot of artistic works as portals of spiritual communication, by which I mean a window into the divine or spiritual realm. I also respect that what I might consider to be an icon others may not. However, the act of being creative, for me, is definitely connected to the creative spirit of God. If we believe in a creative God, then we, who are ourselves formed by divine hands and given breath by the Holy Spirit and who are made in God's likeness, must contain within ourselves the gift of creativity.

As well as being creative, writing an icon is an encouraging and prayerful act. I begin with prayer, asking for guidance and inspiration. The act of writing the icon itself is meditative, keeping the saint I am painting before me in my thoughts and prayers. It is a very slow process, and mistakes are easily made if the work is rushed, so I must be patient. In the Bible patience is one of the gifts of the Holy Spirit. In this sense, as an artist I am 'gifted' by the process of iconography, by having to learn to be patient.

The use of materials such as wood, egg yolk and coloured pigments gives an 'earthy' feel to the writing of an icon – I am reminded of the elements. When working with egg tempera I have to begin with the dark shades, slowly bringing in the medium tones then the lighter tints and finishing with the highlights. Applying layers of egg in between the layers of colour can give a distinctive luminous, transparent effect bringing an aura of spirituality to the image. This method of working from dark tones and gradually bringing in light ones reminds me of the story of Creation from Genesis, when in the midst of darkness 'God said, "Let there be light," and there was light' (Genesis 1: 3). The use of gold is another reminder of the precious inner light of divinity within us all.

I use the term 'writing' instead of 'painting' because I understand icons as visual sermons and as prayers of colour. As an Anglican priest I am called to proclaim the good news, holding tight to St Francis of Assisi's proclamation, 'go out and share the gospel and use words if you have to'. I often feel there is more to be gained from silently contemplating or touching an icon than from listening to too many words or a mediocre sermon. Icons have a form that can inspire serenity and a content that invites meditation. The saint in an icon will often be portrayed looking directly at you, waiting for you to communicate through prayer and meditation. Their hand gestures will be blessing or pointing to Jesus or to heaven. An icon

Icon of St Paul, Regan O'Callaghan London, 2006.

invites contemplation and interaction rather than just aesthetic judgement. The great theologian St John of Damascus pointed out that 'just as words encourage hearing, so do images stimulate the eyes'. The icon I have written of St Paul and the Huia takes this theme even further. St Paul is seen holding his letters upon which St Paul's Cathedral in London is carried. Above him is his tent and on his shoulder an exotic bird. The Huia, an indigenous bird of Aotearoa in my native New Zealand, is clearly not a typical orthodox image but I have included it for an important reason. The

Huia, above all other species in the forest, was sacred to Maori. It was closely associated with the great chiefs of the land and only chiefs of distinction could properly wear its tail. When it became rare Maori declared it tapu (sacred) but sadly this was not enough to save it as its tail feathers became sought after in Europe as well. The Huia became extinct in the early part of the twentieth century. As well as its plumage the Huia's call was very beautiful. The Huia that sits on St Paul's shoulder reminds us that even though its song has been silenced, we are all still called to listen for the inspired beauty of God's song found in creation and holy scripture.

Writing an icon can be a powerful act of encouragement for the iconographer. More specifically, the act of writing and praying with an icon involves what I call 'a mission of encouragement and enlightenment'. I once led an icon writing workshop for beginners. A woman in her eighties attended and was feeling slightly nervous as she had not done any art since she left school at the age of fourteen. She eventually decided to produce an icon of the fourth-century ascetic St Simeon the Stylite, who lived on top of a pole for thirty years. His desire was to be closer to God and yet God wasn't found up his little tower, but rather in the crowds of people who came to see this holy man. The story of St Simeon spoke to this woman in a profound way, and the process of writing the icon enabled her to express her faith, in the midst of what is an eternal mystery – the unknowability of God. Although she had not found it easy, she eventually finished with a great sense of achievement, much to her amazement, and had the icon blessed in her church. More importantly, her faith had been enriched by the creative process of icon writing.

The mission of encouragement is also an important element of the community art projects I am involved with. One recent large banner project I worked on with artist Lucy Brennan-Shiel drew inspiration from the famous Rublev *Trinity* icon, now housed in the Tretyakov Museum in Moscow. It depicts the three visitors to whom Abraham offered hospitality when they came to tell his wife Sarah that, old though she was, she would bear a child.

The image of the visitors at table offered an opportunity for all the participants in the project to consider the question of hospitality and of living next to people you do not know and whose customs may be different from your own. The Grade 1 listed St John's Church on Bethnal Green in East London, where I am based, exists in a very busy diverse community. The banners were for the front of the church and it was important they reflected this diversity. We worked with six different local community groups, focusing on the theme of hospitality. Some groups worked on the figures while others concentrated on what would be brought to the table. The end result was three vibrant and beautiful 10 x 40 foot (3 x 12 m) banners, which caused people who were passing to not only look up but to look within as well!

The resurgence of interest in icons throughout the church is perhaps a reaction against a world full of modern communication, which requires little fruitful dialogue or ability to listen. However, an icon is more than just an object of meditation. In the Orthodox Church its function – or functions – stem from its liturgical significance, in the course of which people will kiss and handle it. Icons are carried in processions, reminding people of the communion of Saints and of the Angels who pray for them and with them. The veneration of an icon is seen not as one-sided communication, but rather as a dialogue between heaven and earth, saints and pilgrims, divinity and humanity.

Icons have many functions across different traditions. They enhance the beauty of a church and instruct the faithful. They illustrate the sacred scriptures. They serve as reminders of Christ's crucifixion, his death and suffering. The icon as an aid for prayer can be part of the whole experience of the Eucharist and liturgy.

Icons are a means of worshipping God, though ultimately neither icons nor words can ever fully explain the substance of Christian faith. As blessed by the Orthodox Church, icons become sacramentals – channels of divine grace for the community. They are one of several ways in which the church communicates the gospel, and I believe they can provide the most direct and immediate way with the most permanent effect. I believe too that icons come very close to symbolizing the mysteries of God. They challenge the belief that 'God is up there' by confronting us face to face and reminding us of the divine presence all about us here and now and, in so doing, they have value for twenty-first-century Christians of which we, in the West, are only just becoming aware.

8

The Rise of Islam

Islam and Christian Art

95

In the seventh century another important power emerged on the international scene. The Prophet Muhammad began preaching in Mecca around 610 CE and died in 632 CE (11 *anno Hegirae*). By 641 CE his followers had come to dominate much of the Middle East and were rapidly expanding around the eastern and southern Mediterranean, their tribal origins being transformed by emergent bureaucracies modelled upon those of the Byzantine and Sassanian empires. The empire was led by a caliph and divided into provinces, such as that ruled by the Ummayad caliphate (Syria, centred upon Damascus), the Abassid caliphate (Iraq, focused upon Baghdad) and the Fatamid caliphate (based at Fustat, which would become Cairo, in Egypt). Not until around 900 CE did Muslims become the majority within the populations of core regions such as Arabia, Syria, Iraq, Iran and Egypt, with converts initially becoming attached as clients (*mawálī*) to the original Arabic tribes. Many, however, did not convert and continued to practise their faiths under Islamic rule. Some important early examples of Judaic and Christian scripture were transcribed in Arabic, which had become their language of everyday currency, or as Greek and Arabic bilingual manuscripts, some of which form a substantial part of important Christian libraries, such as that at the monastery of St Catherine's, Mount Sinai. The toleration of religious and ethnic minorities by the caliphate (the leading political power among Muslims) and its recognition of local religious leaders as simultaneously community representatives further promoted the development of self-contained regional churches with inextricably interwoven ethnic cultures and traditions of faith, many of which survive still and can periodically explode into conflict amid the pressures and competition of our sometimes less tolerant age.

Positions became more entrenched during the Crusades of the late eleventh to late thirteenth centuries as Western forces sought to gain control of the holy places. Closer contact with the churches of the East served only to deepen their estrangement, northern armies despoiling the heart of Byzantium in 1204. Finally in 1453 Constantinople, the Christian city founded by Constantine in 330 CE as a bridgehead between Occident and Orient, fell to the Turks: the unfortunate, artificial rupture of the world into East and West was complete.

Parallels between Early Christian and Early Islamic Art

The Ummayad architectural splendour of mosques such as Qubbat-a-Sakhara in Jerusalem derived ultimately from classical and Byzantine models, notably those constructed under Emperor Justinian. Echoes of parallel influence can therefore sometimes be detected between Early Islamic buildings and their sculptural and mosaic decoration, and those of contemporary and earlier Christian churches. The early caliphs sought the assistance of Byzantine craftsmen when erecting their palaces and mosques, such as the Great Mosque of Damascus, established under the patronage of Caliph al Walid in 715 CE. Its Byzantine courtyard mosaics depict paradisiacal landscapes, and are indebted to the mosaic views of Justinian's reign that adorned the floors of the imperial palace in Constantinople. The Islamic schemes, however, favour the ornamental repertoires of Late Antiquity and of Early Christian Byzantium rather than their figural iconographies, in religious contexts, although the figures of humans and animals were to be found enlivening Islamic secular buildings and adorning the trappings of everyday life.

Christian bibliographic traditions in Islamic territories, like those of Hebrew scribes, weathered the Islamic conquest of the eastern and southern Mediterranean from the seventh century onwards. Although it began earlier, Islamic book production did not get fully underway until the ninth century and Muslim artists, like their Jewish counterparts, did not use figural imagery in scripture for fear of idolatry, but evolved their own sacred calligraphy and decoration for the glorification of the Word. One of the most splendid examples is Sultan Baybars' Koran,[1] a sumptuous seven-volume copy of Islamic scripture made in Cairo in the fourteenth century CE. Its interlace, fretwork patterns and foliate rinceaux, known through their popularization in Islamic art as 'arabesques', sprang from the root-stock of the Antique vine-scroll, so beloved by Christian artists as well as their Islamic contemporaries.

The art produced by Christians living under Muslim rule often absorbed Islamic stylistic influences, as can be observed in a Christian Syriac depiction of the

RIGHT: Byzantine courtyard mosaics depicting paradisiacal landscapes, the Great Mosque of Damascus, established under the patronage of Caliph al Walid in 715 CE.

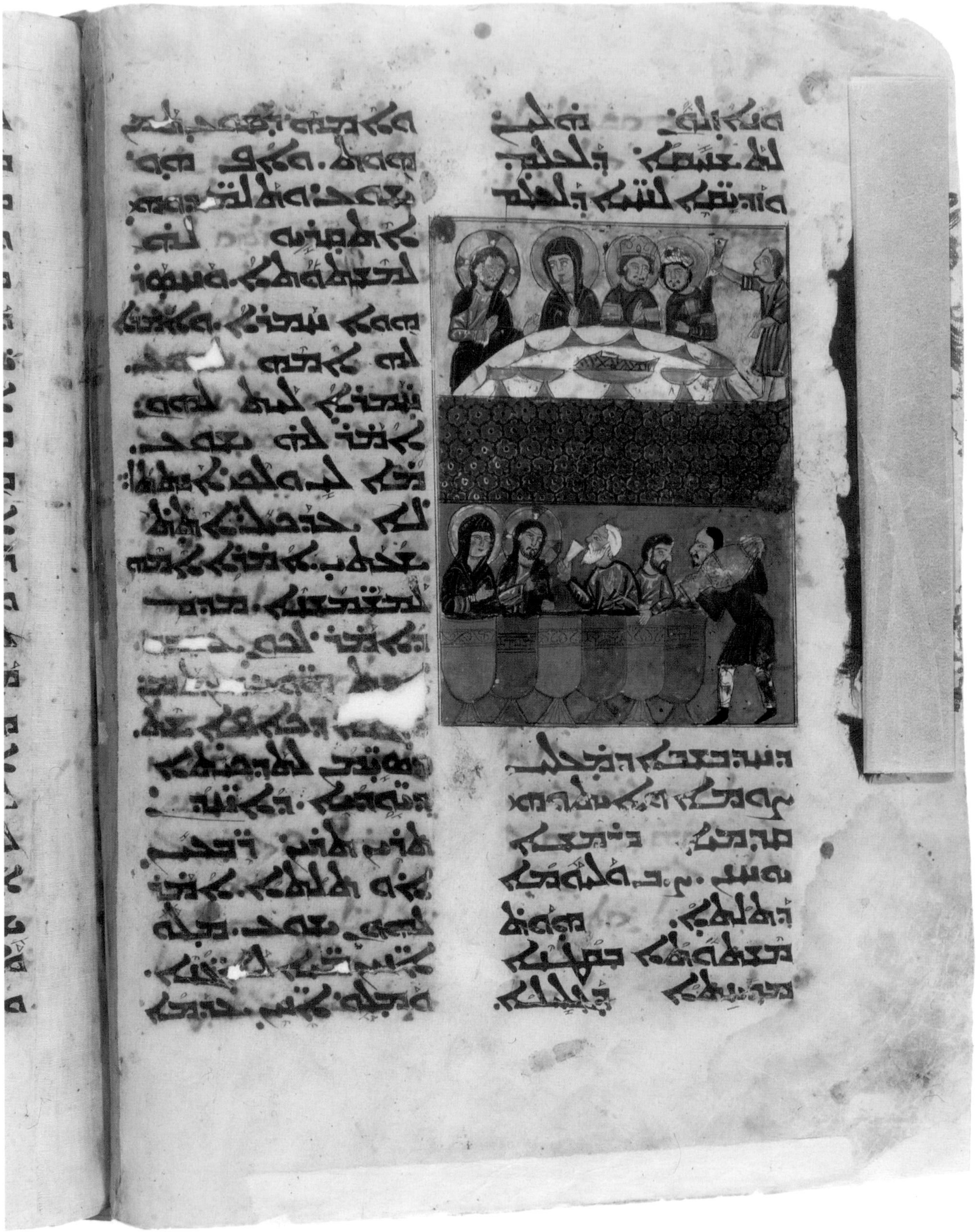

Marriage at Cana in a manuscript – made in the region of Mosul (in modern Iraq) around 1220 and now in the Vatican – in which the figure style is close to that of contemporary Islamic secular painting. Such circumstances gave rise to distinctive regional cultures such as that of the Mozarabs in Spain. Post-Roman Spain was occupied by Vandals and Visigoths. The latter converted and promoted Christian scholarship through the writings of figures such as Isidore of Seville. Potent symbols of Christian kingship survive, notably the bejewelled Votive Crown of Recceswinth, King of the Visigoths (649–72 CE), which was designed to hang above an altar or shrine. Visigothic scribes developed their own distinctive minuscule script, which they continued to use in many regions until the twelfth century as a sign of their independence from Carolingian dominance and their Christian identity under Islamic rule. In the 780s CE Beatus of Liebana composed his influential commentary upon the *Apocalypse of Saint John* (the book of Revelation), and the raw energy and Picasso-esque stylization of the images in the resulting copies of the *Apocalypse*, produced in Spanish scriptoria such as San Salvador de Tavara and Silos during the late tenth to early twelfth centuries, speak of the degree of cultural identity retained by the Mozarabic Christians under tolerant Muslim rule.

Intermittent Western contact with Islam brought many benefits. During the eighth century Muslims learned from Chinese captives how to make paper (*carta*) , a technology which they transmitted to Byzantium in the ninth century and to the West from the eleventh – via cultural melting pots such as Iberia and Sicily, which served as conduits for the exchange of techniques and ideas. The architecture and surface decoration of the churches of Norman Sicily, such as Palermo and Monreale, and of southern French pilgrimage churches, such as Le Puy and Conques, are very clearly influenced by the work of Islamic architects; while the Cosmati-work (patterns formed from pieces of coloured marble devised by the Italian Cosmati family) that adorns the pavements and pulpits of such southern Italian edifices speaks eloquently of Muslim contacts. Most significantly, important elements of classical learning were fostered by Islamic scholars, such as Avicenna (died 1037), who continued to build upon the scientific and medical learning of Antiquity, and who preserved Aristotle's works which had been lost to the West until reintroduced, via Crusader contact with Muslims, into the Medieval universities.

LEFT: The Marriage at Cana, c. 1220, Syriac (Mosul, in modern Iraq), a Christian manuscript influenced by secular Islamic art. Vatican, Biblioteca Apostolica.

Christian Art in Muslim Contexts

Professor Sheila S. Blair and Professor Jonathan M. Bloom

Christian art is generally understood to be the art of and for a specific faith; by contrast the term 'Islamic art' is reckoned more broadly to encompass not only the art made for the religion of Islam but also all the arts made in settings where Islam was the dominant, although not the only, religion. It includes everything from magnificently calligraphed and illuminated manuscripts of the Koran commissioned by rulers to humble crockery used in everyday settings. Large areas of the world that came under Muslim sway beginning in the seventh century CE – notably the Iberian peninsula, North Africa, Egypt, the Levant, Mesopotamia and Central Asia – had sizeable Christian communities, and it took several centuries for Muslims to become the majority population in these regions. Even today, Christian minority communities continue to survive – and some even to flourish – in such regions as Egypt, Syria, Lebanon, Turkey and Iraq. Christians, as well as Jews, Zoroastrians and others, shared the visual vocabularies of their Muslim neighbours, if not their faith, and it is often difficult if not impossible to distinguish a work of 'Islamic art' made for a Muslim from one made for a non-Muslim; many of the craftsmen making 'Islamic art' may have been Christians or Jews.

In some times and places, Muslims and Christians violently contested the same spaces, whether during the Reconquista of the Iberian peninsula or the Crusades in the Levant. Despite the bellicosity, in both cases artistic interchange occurred, creating distinctive traditions known as Mozarabic art (art made in the Iberian peninsula by Christians living under Muslim rule) or Crusader art (Levantine art made from the twelfth to fourteenth centuries when some areas of the

region were under Crusader rule). Three examples will serve to illustrate the range and variety of Christian Islamic art.

The first is a carved alabaster capital (height 10.2 inches or 26 cm) attributed on stylistic grounds to the city of Raqqa, the ancient Nikephorion, located at a strategic site 150 miles (250 km) east of Aleppo on the east bank of the Euphrates River. The city, which had been the seat of a bishopric, became the favoured residence of the Abbasid caliph Harun al-Rashid from 796 to 808 CE, but subsequent rulers returned to Baghdad in Iraq. The capital, of a type similar to those excavated at the site in the early twentieth century, is decorated with rhythmic and symmetrical repetitions of curved lines ending in dots that form abstract vegetal patterns in which the traditional distinction between subject and ground has been dissolved. This so-called Bevelled Style, which was first developed for

moulded and carved plaster, became typical of many arts produced under the Abbasid dynasty in regions ranging from Central Asia to Egypt. What makes this capital distinctive is the cross carved on one side in the central palmette. It shows that the capital must have come from a Christian building and that the 'Islamic' Bevelled Style did not carry specifically confessional associations.

A second example in a different medium comes from the period of the Crusades: a large (diameter 14.5 inches or 37 cm) brass canteen, chased and inlaid with silver and a black organic material. It has a flat back with a conical socket on which it could be fitted on a post, a convex front, and a short cylindrical neck. The shape derives from pilgrim flasks known since pre-Islamic times, but the style and technique of its decoration show that it was made in thirteenth-century Syria. The organization of the decoration, with linked medallions, follows the style of inlaid metalwork established in the city of Mosul, as do the Arabic inscriptions around the centre and along the shoulder, which offer the standard range of good wishes to the unspecified owner. The edge is decorated with thirty medallions presenting typical Islamic scenes of musicians, drinkers and a hawk attacking a bird. A second band contains an animated inscription, in which the Arabic letters have been transformed so completely into revellers that the specific text is illegible. The face is decorated with large figural scenes in which Christian themes predominate. The central medallion shows the enthroned Virgin and Christ Child and is surrounded by three scenes from the life of Christ: the Nativity, the Presentation in the Temple, and the Entry into

Jerusalem, separated by typical medallions of birds against an arabesque scroll. The back is decorated with an arcade of twenty-five pointed arches, each enclosing a haloed figure, including an angel, a warrior–saint and a person at prayer. The central ring shows a band of nine armed horsemen galloping anticlockwise.

This canteen is the most famous of a diverse group of eighteen pieces of inlaid metalwork with Christian scenes made around the thirteenth century. Some, of rather poor quality, were made for local Christians in Syria or Iraq, while others have Arabic texts dedicating them to specific Muslim patrons, such as the Ayyubid sultan of Syria and Egypt, al-Malik al-Salih (reigned 1240–58). Others were probably made for Crusader nobility, who developed a nouveau-riche taste for exotic objects with delicate chasing and glittering silver inlay of Arabic inscriptions, Christian scenes, and secular pleasures. Objects like this canteen were taken as souvenirs of the Holy Land back to Europe, where they became reliquaries or treasured objects in princely collections. This canteen, for example, was discovered in 1845 in the collection of the Italian prince Filippo Andrea Doria, and its pristine condition indicates how revered it had been since its manufacture six centuries earlier.

Our third example is All Saviours (or Vank) Cathedral in New Julfa, a district across the Ziyanda River from the city of Isfahan in central Iran. Around 1603 the Safavid Shah Abbas I ordered the resettlement of some ten thousand Armenian families from the Caucasus into this quarter to ensure that their skills in silk trading remained in Safavid hands. A royal decree of 1614

LEFT: Eighth-century alabaster capital showing influence from Byzantine art. A cross on the other side indicates that it came from a Christian basilica in the Islamic city of Raqqa on the Euphrates, then under Abbassid rule. Such art influenced the subsequent Islamic 'bevelled' style of sculptural decoration. Copenhagen, David Collection.

ABOVE: The Freer Canteen, an Islamic canteen made in Syria during the thirteenth century, modelled upon earlier pilgrim flasks and incorporating Arabic inscriptions, Christian iconographies and scenes of secular pleasure – the sort of object brought back from the Crusades as exotic mementos. Washington, D.C., Freer Gallery of Art.

states that the Shah, in order to show royal favour to his Armenian and Christian subjects, ordered a lofty church built on a plot of land granted by the Shah himself. The cathedral was intended to house some sacred stones that had been brought to Isfahan from a ruined church near Erevan on the Shah's orders. The Shah appointed two courtiers to supervise the plans and the project, and one of them was also the contractor for the royal mosque, built by the Shah at the same time. Indeed, although the spatial organization of the cathedral could not be more different from that of the mosque, the kite-shaped shields supporting the domes on both buildings are structurally identical.

The interior decoration of the cathedral, however, is decidedly Christian in content, although many ornamental details would not have been out of place in a Muslim context. Instead of the vegetal and geometric tilework that would have graced contemporary mosques, the church was covered with representational murals executed in vibrant colours, now darkened by centuries of candle soot and incense. The images, derived from

European engravings, were donated by a prosperous Armenian merchant in the 1660s and show the Creation, the Expulsion, and the Killing of Abel in the dome. Episodes from the Old Testament are paired with New Testament themes on the upper walls, with lurid scenes of martyrdom below. The painters may have been either Armenians living in Isfahan or Europeans attached to the various East India companies resident in this quarter.

To conclude, then, Christian art of the period flourished in Muslim contexts and partook of local materials, techniques and styles. While Christians living under Islamic rule may well have shared with their Muslim brethren a taste for Islamic secular arts, their sacred art retained a distinctively Christian – and often representational – iconography.

Interior of All Saviours (Vank) Cathedral, Isfahan, Iran, built in the early seventeenth century at the command of Safavid Shah Abbas I to show favour to resettled Christian Armenian silk traders. The interior combines Islamic decoration and Christian iconographies influenced by European engravings.

9

Barbarians!

Art and the Re-conversion of the West

With the fragmentation of the Roman empire in the early fifth century CE, the urban nature of classical civilization was transformed into a new network of power-bases and intellectual centres. Some towns continued to trade, becoming bishoprics or royal centres, and were joined by rural manors, princely citadels, and monasteries, which proliferated throughout the Middle East and Europe. Literacy contracted among the general populace, but book production – no longer undertaken by secular scribes and publishers – was perpetuated and carried beyond the old empire's frontiers by the church.

The Development of Book Production in Western Europe

In Europe, book production became firmly established in the centuries between the retraction of the Roman empire's frontiers in the early fifth century and the Viking raids, which commenced in 793 CE with the sack of Lindisfarne – a period often inappropriately termed 'the Dark Ages', but one that was illuminated by its manuscript culture. One of the major achievements of the age was the construction of northern European successor states, underpinned by the Christian zeal of the newly converted and a re-emerging stability of administration and social structure based upon effective collaboration between church and state. Crucial in this was the dissemination and reception of Christian scripture, with its emphasis upon law, social reform, and teaching by example. The great bibles, psalters and gospelbooks of this age stand as its enduring monument.

The pagan Celts and the Germans of northern Europe had developed proto-writing systems of their own – ogam and runes – in response to Roman script but used them only for short commemorative or talismanic purposes, preferring to

Opening of the Office for the vigil of the Nativity, with initial I in the form of Mary in eastern garb, holding the cross and a container of spices to anoint Christ's body, and with birds eating from the tree of life. The Sacramentary of Gellone, late Merovingian / early Carolingian, second half of the eighth century; Gellone, or Rebais in the diocese of Meaux. Paris, Bibliothèque nationale.

cultivate the memory and oral literacy. They embraced written literacy along with Christianity and, faced with the challenges of learning to speak and write Latin as a foreign language, made major contributions to book production. They evolved their own distinctive scripts and written languages, introduced word-separation and systematic punctuation, promoted decoration to help navigate the text, and integrated their indigenous styles of art and poetry. Due largely to their enthusiastic espousal of its potential, the codex assumed much of its distinctive appearance and apparatus.

One of the most enduring successor states was that of the Franks in what had been Roman Gaul. The durability of the Merovingian dynasty (480–751 CE), which paved the way for that of their Carolingian heirs (751–962 CE), owed a lot to the continuity of much of the urban structure under the aegis of their bishops, whose dioceses perpetuated the Roman administrative divisions. The incoming Germanic settlers integrated, assisted by the rapid conversion of their leaders to Catholic orthodoxy, rather than to the Arian heresy favoured by many other Germanic converts, thereby ensuring them the support of the post-Roman Church in Gaul.

The Merovingians' chancery script evolved from Late Roman bureaucratic cursive – a rapidly written script with many loops and ligatures causing it to resemble the wanderings of a demented spider – while their books feature uncial script (a formal, rounded hand inherited from Rome) and a plethora of local scriptorium-specific minuscule scripts (less formal, lower-case hands, such as Luxeuil minuscule and Corbie 'ab' minuscule). These were enlivened with initials and display lettering constructed from colourful birds, fish, beasts and human forms that were derived from their own art and that of Byzantium and Italy. Among the finest examples of this style of illumination are the eighth-century Sacramentary of Gellone and the Gelasian Sacramentary. This stylized form of decoration is also to be found on Merovingian sculpture, of which little survives, such as the tomb of Bishop Agilbert from the crypt of Jouarre and the underground mausoleum of Abbot Melebaudus known as the Hypogêe de Dunes in Poitiers, with its Atlas-like supporting figures and its frieze of angels. These date from the seventh century and represent a Frankish response to the art of Roman Gaul. A remarkable symbol of continuity from Early Christian to Medieval Gaul is the bejewelled golden statuette of the child-saint, Sainte Foy, at Conques in southern France, which was created in the fifth century and continued to be studded with additional gemstones until the tenth century, becoming an important focus of pilgrimage.

As we have seen, post-Roman Spain was occupied by Vandals and Visigoths. The latter converted, initially to Arianism and then, perceiving the diplomatic advantages, to Catholic orthodoxy. Christian scholarship flourished through the writings of influential figures such as Isidore of Seville. Visigothic minuscule script continued to be used in some areas until the twelfth century, signalling Christian identity under Islamic rule and independence from Carolingian domination. Book decoration consisted of stylized initials formed of animals and birds, as in Frankia, but under Islamic rule the Mozarabs would develop a semi-abstract figural art used in works such as the great copies of the *Apocalypse* (see Chapter 8). Visigothic architecture and its sculptural decoration, preserved in centres such as Merida in Estremadura and San Julian de los Prados in Oviedo, were indebted to that of Early Christian Byzantium and Italy, through which the Visigoths had passed as migrants in their search for a home, before finally being allowed to settle in Iberia.

Bejewelled golden statuette of Sainte Foy, Conques, a focus of pilgrimage which continued to be adorned with votive gifts of jewels from the fifth to tenth centuries. Cathedral Treasury, Conques.

The Art of Post-Roman Italy

In fifth- to sixth-century Italy power passed to the Byzantine Exarchate of Ravenna (see Chapter 6), the papacy in Rome, the Ostrogoths and the Lombards of northern Italy and Benevento and, from around 800 CE, the Carolingian empire. The romanophile Ostrogothic kingdom did not survive, owing to its Arianism which alienated the indigenous population and its neighbours; but within it were written several influential works including those by Cassiodorus, who founded the monastery of Vivarium in Calabria and whose teachings exerted great influence upon Early Medieval scribes and authors, encouraging them to view their labours as an act of prayer and evangelism.

The Lombards, a barbarian people who invaded Italy, resisted these other powers and fused influences from Mediterranean art with traditional Germanic animal ornament. They favoured their own Beneventan minuscule, which endured in the Duchy of Benevento in southern Italy, notably in Saint Benedict's monastery of Montecassino, until 1300. In north-east Italy stands Cividale, which the Lombards adopted as their focus for control of the Veneto and which became the patriarchate of Aquileia in 730 CE. Its importance during the eighth century is evinced by the Tempietto, still almost intact and preserving its marble, mosaics, frescoes, stuccowork and architectural sculptures. These include elegant attenuated human figures, some dressed in Byzantine fashion, depicting Christ, the Virgin, saints and rulers, and cityscapes – the heavenly Jerusalem (with trompe l'oeil architecture encrusted with precious stones), stuccowork friezes of vines, acanthus and rosettes embedded with jewel-like coloured glass. The appearance in the essentially Italo-Byzantine ornamental repertoire of Insular-style interlace and the two-dimensional stylized carving of figures on other pieces at Cividale, such as the altar of Duke Ratchis with its Christ in Majesty, speak of other influences that had travelled over the Alps with Irish missionaries such as Columbanus. Similar resonances of Insular manuscript illumination can be observed in what may be a survival of Lombardic fresco painting from around 800 CE at St Procul, Naturns (South Tirol), where the apostle Paul is shown escaping Damascus by being lowered from its walls on a swing-like rope. The range of cultural resonances and abilities demonstrated by the Lombards can be seen by comparing such works with the splendid eighth-century Codex Beneventanus,[1] in which the canon tables are set beneath imposing architectural arcades of Antique and Byzantine inspiration. Recent excavations at the monastery of San Vincenzo al Volturno have also revealed a major decorative scheme of frescoes which date to the eighth century, when Carolingian rule extended into parts of Italy.

In the late eighth century the Lombardic kingdom, then ruled by Desiderius, fell to the Carolingian expansion into Italy. Yet the southern Lombardic duchy of Benevento survived under Duke Arichis who, despite being forced to submit to Charlemagne in 786 CE, managed to secure it an independence that endured until the thirteenth century by becoming the Byzantine representative in Italy. He boasted of receiving silks and purple textiles, precious metalwork and trade goods from Arabia, India and Ethiopia, and although the dedication of his great church of Sancta Sofia, Benevento, may have been intended to recall its namesake in Constantinople, its plan has more in common with the Islamic Ummayad splendour of Qubbat-a-Sakhara in Jerusalem, since both ultimately derive from Byzantine models. Such areas continued to form a valuable conduit between East and West.

In Rome itself the church, the arts, and learning were given a tremendous boost under Pope Gregory the Great (died 604 CE). This great missionary, intent upon reviving Rome's western empire in Christian guise, was a gifted theologian

107

The Tempietto, interior view with sculpted figures of female saints, Lombardic, eighth century, Cividale.

whose writings helped mould the Western Church. Books from Gregory's Rome (see Chapter 3) feature elegant uncial script and initials decorated with crosses and fish. The Saint Augustine Gospels (on which the Anglican archbishops of Canterbury still take their oaths) feature a classical author portrait and 'cartoon-strip' scenes from the life of Christ. The Gospels are said to have accompanied Augustine when he was sent by Gregory to convert the pagan Anglo-Saxon settlers of England in 597 CE. These books – along with other portable artworks such as painted panels, ivories, metalwork and textiles – provided valuable models which inspired English artists to create works such as the Codex Amiatinus[2] and the Ruthwell Cross; while Frankish masons and glaziers, imported to Northumbria by Benedict Biscop in the late seventh century, taught them the arts of building in stone and of stained glass, the earliest extant examples of which occur at the monastery of Jarrow.

Celtic and Anglo-Saxon Illumination

The Codex Amiatinus was one of three great single volume Bibles (pandects) made at the twin monasteries of Wearmouth and Jarrow in the kingdom of Northumbria (north-east England) before 716 CE, when their commissioner Abbot Ceolfrith set off for Rome to retire, taking with him the Codex Amiatinus as a gift for the Pope. The dedication inscription naming him was later erased and replaced with that of a local saint, and it was not until the 1880s that the book was recognized as English, rather than Italo-Byzantine, work as its style of illumination and script and its text (a particularly good version of St Jerome's Vulgate) are so Mediterranean in their affiliations. However, this was no slavish copy of its models but a dynamic fusion of influences, brought together in one of the best scholarly editions of the day, no doubt overseen by Wearmouth-Jarrow's most famous son, Bede (who also served as one of the scribes). The apostolic mission had come of age and the farthest outposts of the known world were signalling to its old cultural centre that they were now making outstanding contributions of their own to the Christian tradition.

The Ruthwell Cross was also carved during the eighth century by Northumbrian sculptors, although it was located within the ancient British kingdom of Rheged (south-west Scotland) into which Northumbria was extending its rule. This may account for the prominent display of Germanic runes on the monument, quoting passages from a poem that was later worked up to form 'The Dream of the Rood', in which the wooden cross laments the role it was forced to play in the crucifixion and is duly elevated to a position of honour as the precious *Crux Gemmata* ('jewelled cross'). The imposing shaft of this tall monument, one of the finest examples of sculpture in the post-Roman world, is also adorned with scenes depicting Christ's miracles (such as the healing of the blind man) and crucifixion, the anointing of his feet by Mary Magdalene, and the Visitation, providing a contemplation in stone on the active and contemplative lives.

Another force in the conversion of the English was Ireland, operating through monasteries such as Iona and Lindisfarne, founded by the Irish St Columba and his followers. Ireland had received Christianity during the fifth century, when Palladius was sent from Rome in 431 CE as bishop to those who already believed and St Patrick launched his mission from the Romano-British Church. Irish scribes developed decorated initials, formal half-uncial hands for scripture, and calligraphic minuscule scripts for less formal works. They also introduced spaces between words and systematic punctuation to clarify legibility and meaning, stimulated by Augustine, Gregory, Isidore of Seville, and Bede, who advocated silent reading to facilitate meditation and comprehension, rather than the classical emphasis upon reading out loud to foster oratory and rhetoric.

The Anglo-Saxons further developed the range of scripts used, under renewed Roman influence via Canterbury and Wearmouth-Jarrow, adding Roman capitals and uncials, perfecting half-uncials and evolving minuscules of varying levels of formality. Within this sophisticated system of scripts, termed 'Insular' (meaning 'of the islands of Britain and Ireland, c. 550–850'), form was suited to function, recognizing that it was

Ezra the Scribe, the Codex Amiatinus, before 716 CE, Wearmouth-Jarrow, north-east England. Florence, Biblioteca Medicea Laurenziana.

King David composing the Psalms (left) and historiated initial showing him shaking hands with Jonathan (right), Anglo-Saxon, Kent, 720s to 730s CE, with gloss (the oldest extant translation of Christian scripture into English) added in the mid-ninth century. London, British Library.

inappropriate to use the same script for sacred texts as that used for informal correspondence or books intended for study in the library. The power of writing was reinforced by the iconic nature of the book in a religious context. Secular rulers were quick to perceive the value of this new medium and enlisted the support of the church in penning law-codes, charters, and genealogies to help establish secure states. Augustine committed King Æthelberht of Kent's Germanic law-code to the 'safe-keeping' of writing, thereby inventing written Old English and integrating the church into the social structure. Unlike their continental counterparts, seventh-century English documents are written not in the excessively cursive scripts inherited from the late Roman bureaucracy but in the high-grade uncials used for scripture – perceptions of the importance of writing in the context of sacred text and liturgical ritual serving to imbue such instruments of government with enhanced authority.

The Vespasian Psalter was made in Kent around the 720s to 730s CE, either at Canterbury or perhaps by the nuns of Minster-in-Thanet who are known to have made de luxe copies of scripture around this time for St Boniface's mission to Germany. It is written in impressive Roman uncial script modelled upon that used in the Rome of Gregory the Great, and contains a miniature depicting King David with his scribes and musicians, composing the Psalms. He is shown in the guise of a contemporary ruler, playing a lyre which parallels one excavated in the great early seventh-century ship burial at Sutton Hoo. The text opposite opens with an initial depicting David and Jonathan shaking hands in which word and image provide mutual validation through the very letters of the text. This is the earliest occurrence in art of the historiated (storytelling) initial that would prove so popular and effective in Medieval illumination. The tiny, lower grade minuscule script between the lines was added in the mid-ninth century, during the Viking invasions, and represents the earliest surviving translation of any part of the Bible into English. For the Anglo-Saxons and the Irish, like their counterparts in the Christian Orient, saw no obstacle to using whatever tools were at their disposal – including their own languages – to share the Good News (Gospel, for the Old English 'Godspell'), giving them the oldest written European vernaculars. On his deathbed in 735 CE Bede was translating John's Gospel for all. This was a very different cultural climate to the Late Middle Ages when Wycliffe and Tyndale would be persecuted as heretics for daring to do the same.

Insular Gospelbooks

Insular missionaries evangelized the courts and countryside of their islands and continental Europe through extensive monastic federations – monasticism having achieved tremendous popularity among them from around 500 CE via the influence of the Eastern desert fathers (the early founders of the monastic tradition in the Near East, such as Sts Anthony, Pachomius and Basil), Italy and Gaul. Their inspirational preaching of the Christian message could lead seasoned warriors to embrace pacifism and kings to free slaves, radically transforming society. The role models provided by such energized, charismatic, ascetic individuals – publicly acclaimed as saints during their lifetimes – set new levels of social and spiritual aspiration. Some of the most beautiful Medieval gospelbooks were made as the focal points of their shrines and symbolized the processes of integration and transmission that characterized the transition from Late Antiquity to the Early Middle Ages.

Among the most magnificent and influential of these Insular gospelbooks were the Lindisfarne Gospels and the Book of Kells. The former was probably made on the tidal island of Holy Island (Lindisfarne) in Northumbria around 710–20 CE and is the work of a single artist-scribe (perhaps Bishop Eadfrith who died in 721 CE). That one of the most elaborate books ever to be made by hand was the work of one person says something important concerning the underlying spirituality and motivation, for Lindisfarne had been founded in 635 CE by Irish monks from Iona (itself founded by St Columba in 563 CE) and inclined towards an eremitic style of monasticism. Like St Cuthbert of Lindisfarne, for whose shrine the Lindisfarne Gospels were probably made as a focal point and who spent part of his time in prayer as a hermit on the harsh rock of the nearby island of Inner Farne, the scribe entered the desert of the book to undertake his gruelling act of physical labour and focused meditation. Its decorated pages include: architectural canon tables; carpet-pages in which are embedded crosses from the different ecumenical traditions, designed to recall jewelled processional crosses and prayer mats; incipit pages in which the opening words of each Gospel explode across the page, becoming icons in their own right and glorifying the Word; and evangelist portraits, set like framed icons on the page, symbolizing the various aspects of Christ (according to the exegetical interpretations of Gregory the Great and Bede, Matthew represents incarnation and humanity; Mark, kingship and resurrection; Luke, sacrifice; and John, ascent and second coming). The book's style of decoration carefully blends ingredients from the Celtic, Germanic, Roman and Middle Eastern cultures to form a new vision of collaboration and harmony. Eadfrith's stately half-uncial Latin script was glossed between the lines around 950–60 CE by a later member of the community, Aldred, and is the oldest surviving translation of the Gospels into the English language.

These themes, and many individual artistic elements, are perpetuated in the Book of Kells, probably made on Iona around 800 CE as one of the great cult books celebrating St Columba. Its team of artists and scribes extended the minor decoration, ornamenting as much of the text as possible with decorated initials and lively little human and animal figures which act as a visual gloss upon its meaning. For example, in the genealogy of Christ a merman grasps the name Iona, which is Hebrew for dove and in Latin is 'columba', thereby both drawing attention to the founder saint and referring to Jonah's sojourn in the belly of the whale. They also designed a number of striking full-page miniatures with stylized figures that expound the underlying meaning, or meanings, of the text; for the Insular mind (following the teachings of Augustine and Jerome) considered it naïve to settle for just the literal meaning when a number of symbolic and metaphorical meanings might also be understood. Thus the image of the Temptation of Christ, in which he is shown atop the Temple (depicted in the form of Irish chapels of the period and

the metalwork house-shaped reliquaries that echoed their forms) resisting the blandishments of a spindly black devil of Eastern fashion, is also a schematic *figura* (plan or diagram) of the Communion of Saints. In accordance with this theological doctrine, Christ is literally the head of the body of the church (from which his bust

Cross carpet-page introducing St Matthew's Gospel, the Lindisfarne Gospels, Holy Island, north-east England, c. 710–20 CE. London, British Library.

BARBARIANS!

114

The Temptation / Communion of Saints, the Book of Kells, Iona, c. 800 CE. Dublin, Trinity College Library.

appears to grow) and is joined by the Church Triumphant (the angels who hover above his head), the Church Militant (the apostles and believers who stand alongside watching) and the Church Expectant (those who have died and are awaiting resurrection, symbolized by the figures beneath the church, presided over by a figure resembling Osiris, Egyptian god of the dead).

Another of the Book's images depicts the Virgin and Child accompanied by angels bearing Eastern liturgical fans (the *flabellum*) and enthroned, recalling the ancient Egyptian imagery of Isis and Horus, which was Christianized by the Copts and had appeared in these western islands earlier, carved on the wooden coffin made to contain the miraculously incorrupt body of St Cuthbert in 698 CE. Inside that coffin, redolent of the Egyptian practice of interring the Book of the Dead with the deceased to help them on their way to the afterlife, was placed a little copy of John's Gospel which preserves it original binding – the earliest in the West, made at Wearmouth-Jarrow but bound in a complex manner known as 'Coptic sewing'. It is one of many tangible indications of the influences that flowed from the deserts of the Middle East to the watery wildernesses of northern Europe. Insular missionaries and ecclesiastical pilgrims carried those influences into continental Europe, their foundations producing scriptoria in which Insular traditions fused with more local ones to produce distinctive works such as: the Milan Orosius from St Columbanus's monastery at Bobbio in northern Italy or the St Gallen Gospels from another of his houses at St Gall in Switzerland; the Trier Gospels from St Willibrord's Echternach (Luxembourg); and the Cutbercht Gospels from eighth-century Salzburg (founded by the Irish monk, Virgil).

In the late eighth and ninth centuries continental styles were once more introduced into Britain and Ireland, producing elegant classicizing works that combined Insular, Eastern and Carolingian influences. This produced works such as the architectural friezes of Breedon-on-the-Hill with its centaurs and Syrian hunting scenes, the carved Lichfield Angel, the Barberini Gospels, and the Stockholm Codex Aureus and the Royal Bible with their purple pages and chrysography – all of which came from the Anglo-Saxon kingdom of Mercia (and its annexe, Kent) where, in the late eighth century, King Offa had proclaimed his kinship with Charlemagne and had minted gold coins modelled on Arabic dinars, his own name alongside that of Allah.

The Lichfield Angel, sculptured panel retaining purple and white pigments, probably from the shrine of St Chad, Mercia, late eighth century. Lichfield Cathedral.

Carved Crosses

The Eastern cults of the Virgin and of the cross won particular popularity in the Insular world. The Stations of the Cross were followed by pilgrims on Holy Island and in Irish holy places from at least the eighth century onwards, and monumental stone crosses were often erected as part of this practice or to demarcate different parts of the monastic precinct, and to commemorate burials or events. They were probably brightly painted, resembling the cross carpet-pages in contemporary manuscripts, and some carried metalwork bosses covering relics. Particularly

RIGHT: A sermon in stone: Muiredach's Cross, an Irish high cross with biblical scenes, tenth century. Monasterboice, Ireland.

BELOW: A cross carpet-page in stone: the front of the Pictish Aberlemno Churchyard Cross, eighth century. Aberlemno Church, Angus, Scotland.

impressive examples were erected in Ireland during the ninth and tenth centuries and are known as 'scripture' or 'preaching' crosses as they carry a wealth of visual imagery in stone, narrating biblical scenes which are arranged in schemes designed to draw analogies between the Old and New Testaments. This was a theological device known as typology, which was advocated by St Jerome; images featuring such typology had formed part of the series of panel paintings brought back from Rome in the late seventh century to grace the churches at Wearmouth-Jarrow. Thus Abraham's sacrifice prefigured that of Christ; King David was an Old Testament type, or precursor, of Christ; and the Temptation of the first Adam is redeemed by the crucifixion of the second – Christ. Fine examples occur at important monasteries such as Kells, Clonmacnoise and Monasterboice.

In other Celtic regions, such as Wales, Cornwall and Brittany, simpler stone crosses are to be found, many erected as wayside places of devotion, and from the earliest Christian times standing stones were carved with inscriptions and symbols as memorials to the dead. The Picts of Scotland (named by Julius Caesar for their practice of tattooing and painting their bodies) also developed their own distinctive form of decoration that survives on metalwork and on an extensive corpus of incised stones, which may date from as early as the Roman occupation onwards. In the early eighth century the Pictish Church, established earlier by St Columba, was reformed under Northumbrian influence, producing a beautiful series of carved crosses, like carpet-pages in stone, which still retain some of the enigmatic Pictish symbols that adorned the earlier carvings: animal symbols (perhaps clan badges); crescents and notched rectangles (buildings resembling the Pictish towers known as brochs?) overlaid with 'V'- or 'Z'-shaped rods (like broken sceptres or spears); double-handled cauldrons viewed from above; and mirrors, combs, shears and the like. These were now combined with crosses and with scenes from scripture and from Pictish life.

The Creation of 'Insular' Culture in Early Christian Britain and Ireland

The decorative arts also flourished in Early Christian Britain and Ireland, producing impressive suites of church plate modelled upon that of Byzantium, such as the Ardagh Chalice and the Derrynaflan Hoard from eighth- to ninth-century Ireland, and jewellery such as the Irish Tara Brooch and the Anglo-Saxon Fuller Brooch, with its iconography of the five senses of the sort worn by clerics as well as nobles. Book covers and shrines were also adorned with metalwork, such as the eighth-century Irish Athlone Crucifixion Plaque. On this Christ is depicted as a young

The Athlone Crucifixion Plaque, with Christ flanked by angels and by the spear and sponge bearers, Stephaton and Longinus, a metalwork plaque perhaps from a book cover or shrine; Irish, eighth century. Dublin, National Museum of Ireland.

victor upon the cross, protected by his breastplate (certain protective Irish prayers were known as breastplates, or *loricas*) and captivating the viewer with his iconic eyes which stare spiritually into eternity (recalling the sculptures of Constantine's era and those of the Celtic Iron Age). He is accompanied by angels, and the spear and sponge bearers, Stephaton and Longinus (popular in Irish apocryphal legend).

Insular culture undoubtedly preserved its own distinctive character, or characters, derived from the many peoples who inhabited these islands, some styles and iconographies stretching back into their prehistoric pagan past. And yet, such long-lived traditions were effectively Christianized and fused with incoming influences from the Continent and the Middle East to produce a vibrant Christian culture in which past, present and future were reconciled. Nowhere is this better expressed than on the Franks Casket, a whalebone box perhaps made in eighth-century Northumbria to contain a book, perhaps one of the royal genealogies which traced the descent of Anglo-Saxon rulers back through the historical line to pagan deities such as Woden (whose lineage was traced, in turn, back to Adam). It is modelled on a late Roman continental form and its faces carry scenes from classical literature (Achilles?), the suckling of Romulus and Remus (founders of Rome) by the she-wolf, the sack of the Temple in Jerusalem by General Titus, the Germanic saga of Wayland the Smith, and the Adoration of the Magi – all captioned in a mixture of Roman capital lettering and runes. This visual encyclopedia effectively integrates the Anglo-Saxons into a view of world history in which pagan past and ancestry is not expunged, but gives way to Christian present.

10

The Art of Imperialism

Art in the Carolingian and Ottonian Empires

The memory of the Roman concept of empire and of classical art and learning continued to haunt the peoples who carved new nations out of its previous territory. In the West an attempt to re-establish a Christian empire, along Late Antique lines, was fulfilled by Charlemagne (742/747–814 CE), a scion of the Carolingian dynasty, members of which began their rise to prominence as eminent household officials at the Merovingian court during the seventh and eighth centuries. Charlemagne successfully conquered a number of territories, forcing some, such as the Saxons, to convert to Christianity at sword-point. In recognition of this de facto power, which brought together Roman Gaul, Germany, parts of northern Spain and much of Italy, he was symbolically crowned as emperor by the Pope in Rome on Christmas Day in the year 800 CE. At his court, which focused upon a newly constructed palace with dynastic chapel (*capella palatina*) at Aachen/Aix-la-Chapelle, built to resemble foundations by Constantine and Justinian, Charlemagne assembled an array of intellectual and artistic talent, drawn from as far afield as Byzantium, Italy, Spain, Anglo-Saxon England and Ireland, as well as from the heartlands of his empire. The conscious classicizing revival that ensued is known as the 'Carolingian renaissance' – one of many 'rebirths' of classical influence in art.

The Carolingian Renaissance

One of the earliest works produced by this movement is the Godescalc Evangelistary of c. 781–83.[1] Its miniature depicts the fountain of life, and its elegant and tranquil image of the youthful Christ enthroned is perhaps indebted not only

Christir in Majesty, Godescalc Evangelistary, commissioned by Charlemagne and his wife, Hildegard, from the Court School, Aachen, Germany, 781–83 CE.

to Early Christian art but also to works by Insular artists who formed part of the missions to the Continent. Other examples of such influence can be seen in so-called 'Anglo-Carolingian' works such as the chalice made for Duke Tassilo of Bavaria, the jewelled processional Rupertus Cross, and the Valenciennes Apocalypse from Liège, c. 800 CE, with its extensive cycle of images illustrating the book of Revelation. Manuscripts made at the Palace School around the year 800 CE feature illumination in the lively illusionistic style of painting favoured by Byzantine artists (who may have been imported for the work) and inherited from ancient Rome. The evangelists depicted in the Ebbo Gospels[2] can hardly keep still, so great is their emotional and spiritual stimulation. This distinctive style would go on to influence a series of exquisite works made in the diocese of Reims during the first half of the ninth century, including engraved crystals, ivories, and manuscripts, the most famous of which is the Utrecht Psalter,[3] with its extensive series of images thought to have derived from an Early Christian exemplar and which itself served as the model for several eleventh- and twelfth-century English versions. The great gospelbooks produced by the Court School for Charlemagne around 800 CE – such as the Harley Golden Gospels and the Lorsch Gospels[4] with its ivory cover, which rendered it equally powerful and impressive when closed – are stately images of imperial power and Christian faith. Their trompe l'oeil architectural canon tables, their enthroned naturalistic evangelist portraits, and their incipit pages of gold and silver on purple pages are designed to conjour up thoughts of the imperial Roman past and the Byzantine and Carolingian imperial present.

Faith, scholarship and books were intended to play an important part in holding the disparate territories of the Carolingian empire together, bestowing some semblance of unity by promoting the use of the same biblical edition and of

120

an homogenous script – Caroline minuscule. This was developed at Corbie and the imperial court from around the 780s CE onwards, replacing the plethora of local hands that were favoured in the many monastic scriptoria throughout Carolingian territory. It looks familiar to us today because it was revived by the humanists during the Renaissance and came to form the basis of our modern typfaces. A crucial factor in its dissemination was the circulation of a single-volume revision of the Vulgate Bible produced in 800 CE by the English scholar Alcuin of York, who was appointed by Charlemagne as Abbot of Tours (796–804 CE). Alcuin's was not the only Carolingian biblical edition – Theodulf of Orléans relied upon the mixed Spanish tradition of his homeland when preparing his revised text – but it became the most influential and formed

Picturing the Psalms: Psalm 26, the Utrecht Psalter, Hautvilliers (diocese of Reims), 830s CE.

the basis of the 'Paris Study Bibles' used during the Middle Ages in Paris University. The scriptorium that Alcuin established at Tours was able, under his successors during the first half of the ninth century, to turn out as many as three of these massive pandects per annum, for distribution to other scriptoria where they served as models for further copies, ensuring unity of observance and style. These Alcuin or Tours Bibles contain elegant, restrained initials and full-page illustrations, some arranged in comic-strip-like registers resembling Early Christian cycles such as the mosaics of Santa Maria Maggiore in Rome.

The Carolingian debate on imagery, in which scholars such as Alcuin of York participated, was a conflicted one. They perceived its usefulness in emphasizing the interdependence of church and state, and employed it to demonstrate that in the person of the emperor the symbolic roles of king and priest were reconciled and unified; but they remained troubled by the issue of idolatry. The Carolingian response to the Council of Nicaea (787 CE) took the form of the *Libri Carolini* composed by Theodulf of Orléans, in which the primacy of the word was asserted over images, which were permitted but deemed to possess no inherent holiness or

121

THE ART OF IMPERIALISM

iconic value. Nonetheless, Theodulf's own chapel in his villa at St Germigny des Prés was adorned around 800 CE with stuccowork and mosaics in Byzantine fashion depicting the Ark of the Covenant, cherubim and the Hand of God. Other large-scale Carolingian images include the mid-ninth-century frescoes in the crypt of the abbey church of St Germain, Auxerre. Copies of scripture produced from this time until c. 810 CE (when the Lorsch Gospels once more dared depict Christ in Majesty) are noticeably devoid of pictures of the divine, preferring illustrations of biblical narratives or evangelist portraits. This of course made way, conveniently, for the development of royal iconography.

Carolingian annexation of parts of Italy, the Alpine regions, southern France and Germany brought access to the contents of many fine monastic libraries and archives. These contained much classical learning, much of which had lain undiscovered or had fallen out of vogue at a time when the focus of book production had been the supply of biblical texts and patristic commentaries for preaching and studying the Word, and for liturgical use. Many classical pagan texts

Mosaic depicting the Ark of the Covenant, cherubim and the Hand of God, from Carolingian scholar / iconoclast Theodulf of Orléans' chapel in his villa at St Germigny des Prés.

would not have survived had they not been copied at this time. For Early Medieval Christians did not reject potentially useful scholarship simply because of pre-Christian authorship. Insular and Merovingian scribes had preserved such works, when available, but many more now came back into scholarly circulation. During the ninth century, Carolingian authors such as the Irishmen Duns Scottus and John Eriugena, Walafrid Strabo, the Visigoth Theodulf, the Italian Paul the Deacon and Einhard (Charlemagne's biographer) composed new works of scholarship, poetry, history and theology, adding to works from Antiquity that were already known, such as Cicero's *Aratea* (his Latin translation of the Greek *Phenomena* of Aratus, dealing with the constellations and their mythology), Vitruvius's works on architecture, and medical texts by Dioscorides and Pseudo-Apuleius. Hrabanus Maurus's œuvre included *carmina figurata* – word poems featuring a series of meditations on the cross (*De Laudibus Sanctae Crucis*), in which figural images such as a portrait of Emperor Louis the Pious as *miles Christi* ('soldier of Christ') were superimposed upon a grid of letters, isolating some to form a poem with a poem, in the manner popularized by Emperor Constantine's court poet, Porphyrius. What better way of asserting the primacy of the word over the image?

The impetus towards cultural renovation begun during the heyday of the Carolingian empire was to outlive its territorial reality. Frankish inheritance laws necessitated its partition between Charlemagne's grandsons: Charles the Bald, Louis II and Lothar. (The survival of just one of his sons, Louis the Pious, only temporarily delayed this.) The contest for supremacy between these rulers split the empire and laid the foundations of the development of France and Germany. All three were patrons of the arts. Among the most opulent books of the ninth century were the First Bible of Charles the Bald, or the Vivian Bible (made at Tours in 845 CE as a gift to Charles from Abbot Vivian),[5] and the Lothar Gospels,[6] also made at Tours around 850 CE as a gift for its monastic community at the behest of Charles's rival sibling, Lothar, to help extend his influence. Such books, designed for public display, carried forward the use of royal iconography as an adjunct of power. They depict the ruler enthroned, like Christ in Majesty, his power acknowledged by supporting figures representing church and state or personifications of the territories ruled.

The Ottonian Renaissance

The Ottonians succeeded the Carolingians in the Lotharingian (Lorraine/German) and Italian parts of their empire from the accession in 936 CE of Otto I (who was crowned emperor by the Pope in 962 CE), until the death of Otto III in 1002. Their influence was to endure into the 1050s. The Benedictine Reform that was sweeping

France and penetrating England also reached Ottonian territory during the 930s CE, adding an impetus to artistic production within the monasteries. In their art, as in their politics, the imperial imperative persisted, along with conscious allusions to the symbolism and scholarship of the Roman and Carolingian empires and to Early Christian art. Massive churches were built, such as St Pantaleon, which contains the tomb of the Byzantine Princess Theophanu, and Santa Maria im Capitol, with its eleventh-century carved wooden doors – both of which are in Cologne. Another fine example is St Cyriakos in Gernrode, inspired by earlier Carolingian edifices such as St Riquier, which features imposing westworks incorporating towers, a narthex or porch, an upper chamber, and perhaps an internal royal gallery from which services could be viewed. At St Michael's, Hildesheim, Abbot Bernward commissioned some major pieces of metalwork to adorn his church, including a set of great bronze doors made in 1015. Its panels contain scenes of New Testament types paralleling Old Testament antitypes, perhaps inspired by the wooden doors of Santa Sabina in Rome. He also ordered bronze columns, derived from Roman triumphal monuments such as Trajan's Column in Rome, with scenes from the life of Christ replacing the heroic feats of the emperors.

Smaller metalwork masterpieces were also produced: crucifixes, and walrus ivory carvings influenced by those of the Early Christian and Carolingian periods, such as one in Chantilly depicting Gregory the Great, writing while inspired by the dove of the Holy Spirit, and observed by his assistant who peeps through a hole he has made with his stylus in the shielding curtain. Such domestic products formed part of the treasure bindings and portable altars of the day, while on occasion de luxe pieces were commissioned elsewhere – for example, the ivory bookcover depicting Otto II and Theophanu holding the infant Otto III that was made in Milan c. 980–83 CE. More monumental sculpture was also produced, such as the imposing, sorrowfully serene Gero Crucifix, located in Cologne Cathedral and presented to it by Archbishop Gero (died 976 CE) – the oldest monumental crucifixion to have survived.

The emphasis of Ottonian scriptoria, such as Trier, Cologne, Echternach, Regensburg and Reichenau, however, fell on the production of imposing illuminated gospelbooks and liturgical volumes for use in public performance of the liturgy and in the private devotions of royalty, aristocracy and leading prelates. Among the most important to have survived include: the Gospels of Otto III, made at Reichenau around 996 CE;[7] the Sacramentary of Henry II, made in Regensburg, 1002–1014;[8] and the Gospels of Abbess Hitda of Cologne, c. 1000.[9] As in their Carolingian and later Anglo-Saxon counterparts, an adherence to classically inspired, yet stylized, figures and the lavish use of imperial purple, gold and silver, prevails. Evangelist portraits and images of Christ in Majesty were popular, along with donor portraits in which

diminutive royals, nobles or leading clerics are presented to Christ by their patron saints. Series of full-page illustrations of New Testament scenes also feature in some volumes, all in thick layers of pigments in pastel shades. Like the gospelbooks of Charlemagne's Court School, entire books might be written in gold ink (chrysography), and some pages are painted in illusionistic fashion to emulate woven Byzantine silks. Such trends received a stimulus from renewed Byzantine influence following the marriage of Emperor Otto II and Princess Theophanu in 972 CE. This political coup brought Eastern goods and craftsmen into the Ottonian court and its orbit, producing an opulent, exotic style that would also spread across the Channel to Anglo-Saxon England and would help to influence the formation of the more widespread European Romanesque.

The Gero Crucifix, Ottonian, donated to Cologne Cathedral by Archbishop Gero (died 976 CE).

'Words Passed Down': Carolingian Pictures of Translation and Transmission

Professor Herbert L. Kessler

A tenet of Christianity holds that sacred scripture, written in various languages over centuries by more than forty holy men, records words spoken by a single voice, that of the Holy Spirit. For instance, when discussing the book of Job, Pope Gregory the Great, in his influential *Moralia*, considered its Gentile author to be merely instrumental when he stated: 'In raising a question about the writer we do nothing more than ask about the pen.' Unlike the Jews, who safeguarded unchanged the writ they believed had been written by God himself and delivered directly to Moses, Christians therefore translated the Bible's original Hebrew and Greek into diverse tongues and, in art, developed schemes of images that revealed that all the texts were speaking for the one God. In the *Maiestas Domini* (Christ in Majesty), for example, they gathered the four evangelists around a single figure of the heavenly Lord, and in a striking move they actually mapped Christ's features onto individual authors; in the Book of Kells, for instance, St John resembles Christ because as a visionary he witnessed all of sacred history.

No manuscript makes visible the notion that each prophet and evangelist is but God's mouthpiece more inventively than the First Bible of Charles the Bald.[1] Produced in St Martin's at Tours in 845 CE and gathering all the books of the Bible into one enormous volume, it is adorned with eight great frontispieces that make scriptural unity a central theme. The miniature before the Gospels, for instance, elaborates the standard *Maiestas Domini* by inserting the four major Prophets; and the pictorial

St Jerome's work in researching, teaching and distributing his Latin Vulgate edition of the Bible, from the First Bible of Charles the Bald or Vivian Bible, Tours, 845 CE.

127

counterpart before the book of Psalms figures David as a prophet of Christ by portraying him within a mandorla accompanied by four co-psalmists. Moses is represented with the apostle Paul's distinctive facial features, bearded and with a bald head sporting a widow's peak, to show that the preaching of Christ's Gospels had superseded the written law given on Sinai. This pictorial argument culminates in the Apocalypse frontispiece, which depicts a codex displayed god-like on a throne – surrounded by the apocalyptic beasts and being unsealed by the Lamb of God – juxtaposed to a mysterious enthroned man bearing the features of Moses and Paul, which are unveiled by the four evangelist symbols. Matthew's symbol lifts a long trumpet to the man's lips to make explicit the claim that all the texts convey a single message: Old Testament and New, book and person.

The first frontispiece depicts St Jerome preparing the Latin Vulgate and introduces the volume. Jerome's Latin translation had been a special focus of manuscript production at Tours

'WORDS PASSED DOWN'

since the 790s CE when Charlemagne dispatched Alcuin to St Martin's monastery to oversee the production of a correct version; and this frontispiece was created as a response to the monastery's special interest in the Vulgate. The pictures were based on illustrations in an early fifth-century copy of Vergil's *Aeneid*,[2] which was at Tours during the ninth century, and are elucidated by captions composed by one of its monks, Audradus Modicus.

The story begins with Jerome departing from Rome and boarding a trireme for the Holy Land; once arrived in Lydda, Jerome counts coins into the hand of Baranius, to whom he says he 'paid not a little money' for Hebrew lessons. The caption below reads:

'Jerome leaves Rome for Jerusalem to learn well The words of the honorable Hebrew law.'

The second register shows Jerome teaching his flock, including the matron Paula and her daughter, in Bethlehem near the *turris gregis* where earlier Christ's birth had been announced to actual shepherds; its caption characterizes the saint as an inspired author:

'Strengthened everywhere by God, [who is] enthroned on high, he gives The divine laws of salvation to Eustochium and also to Paula.'

The first two registers encapsulate the prologue to the work, which precedes the frontispiece and concludes by praising various acts of translation – Ptolemy's, Origen's, and most of all Jerome's which, it points out, was based on the teachings of a Jew and tested in the work of writing and dictating so that its language is clear and its meaning carefully conveyed.

In the final register Jerome hands volumes from open chests to some monks while others transport the heavy codices into a church and a monastery. The caption underscores the point that the saint is not only a translator but is also an author:

'Here bountiful Jerome himself bestows on these men the words passed down. Which he translated, [and] with them those he composed.'

Jerome wrote many interpretive prefaces for the Bible, of which a number are included in this very volume, including the *Frater Ambrosius* facing the frontispiece which sets out the unity of all scripture with the very claim that is realized in the manuscript's final frontispiece:

'The Law is spiritual; one must raise the veil in order to understand it and so that we can contemplate God's glory with face uncovered.'

Provided with a status nearly equal to that of the prophets and evangelists, Jerome is pictured sitting on a *sella curulis*, a symbol of earthly authority. This also positioned the sainted monk in the struggle over monastic governance – the quarrel over lay abbots – that was occupying his successors at St Martin's at the moment the manuscript was being produced.

A nearly identical frontispiece adorns another Bible produced for Charles the Bald,[3] illuminated a quarter of a century later at Reims. Based certainly on an exemplar from Tours, its captions are different, however, hence also the understanding of Jerome's work of translation and transmission.

Accompanying paired episodes quite like those in the First Bible, the initial verses characterize Jerome's journey and praise his philology:

'Jerome departs from Roman soil and, under full sail he crosses the briny sea to seek out the holy places. Instructed by the master in Hebrew and strong in faith and in work, he redeems the language's elements.'[4]

In contrast to that of the earlier frontispiece, the second register maintains the narrative aspect. Divided into two distinct episodes, it first shows Jerome pointing to passages in his book to dispute the interpretation of the Bible being advanced by opponents who also cite scripture; as the caption makes clear, the animated debate is about predestination (on which Jerome had written a tract, *Dialogus adversus Pelagianos*):

'Pelagius's error he crushes and forces confession that heavenly gifts are not bestowed for the merits of man.'

The scene's counterpart at the right shows Jerome at work in his monastery with two women, of whom one holds an open codex and Jerome's inkwell and the other a scroll, while a scribe records his dictation on a wax tablet:

> 'He teaches you Paula and your offspring
> (Eustochium) in whom the gift of faith,
> that is poured upon you, was doubled by the
> intimate grace of Christ.'

Most curious is the woman at the far right who is apparently eavesdropping on the cloistered group and who also writes Jerome's words down on a tablet – a spy perhaps for the Pelagians, who had criticized Jerome's Vulgate and had in fact persecuted him and his followers for their work.

The third register begins by showing Jerome, depicted like King David composing the Psalms, dictating to four scribes who transcribe his words – most likely as the caption implies his interpretive prefaces – in four great volumes:

> 'Penetrating into the Hebrews' archives by the
> light of his heart
> Jerome reopens the holiest of holies and the
> ivory temples.'

As in the First Bible, this sequence of scenes ends with a picture of the saint distributing his work, completing the circuit when he left Rome for the Holy Land:

> '...to his disciples and to Latium he sends what
> one must have,
> and entering the Judaic grove hitherto closed,
> impassable to our own.'

Here, however, a quatrain at the bottom completes the miniature, praising Jerome's learned and eloquent translation as divinely inspired:

> 'He illuminates it with the light of his mind.
> And he expounds, captivating the ear by the
> genius of his mind.
> And forthwith he reveals the vast double and
> triple constellation,
> and beginning from here his attic pen surges
> forward with sturdy vigour.'

If the frontispiece in the First Bible of Charles the Bald was constructed to support claims being advanced by the brethren of St Martin's, the miniature in the San Paolo Bible too engages specific interests of the monastery that produced it – in this case, doctrinal not political issues. During the decades before the Bible was being made,

Hautvilliers at Reims was occupied with the very controversy about predestination that is introduced in the third episode. Indeed, Gottschalk of Orbais, who had championed what is called 'double predestination', had been exiled to Reims and died there only a year or so before the manuscript was completed. Hincmar, one of Gottschalk's leading opponents, was the monastery's abbot who, in his own arguments against the heresy, cited Jerome's refutations alongside Augustine's *Retractions*. While Hincmar would surely have been involved in the planning of the illuminations, it is Florus of Lyon who seems best to explain the miniature's special emphasis on translation. He had pointed out that many disagreed with Augustine's great work against the Pelagians because the church father had not deployed Jerome's '*testimoniis ex Hebraica translatione.*' Therefore, Florus cited only the Vulgate in his confutation of Gottschalk's renewed Pelagian claims (as did Hincmar). That is an underlying message of the miniature too: only a reliable rendering of scripture can truly serve orthodoxy, specifically the translation prepared by Jerome and transmitted in the pages that follow.

Through the story of Jerome, the Carolingian frontispieces set forth the claim that such a translation is the product of a single person 'strong in faith and in work' who mastered the original scriptural languages, studied the diverse texts and debated their meaning, and reiterated them in his own tongue. By deploying borrowings from the Vatican Vergil, they added credibility to that assertion by returning the saint's biography to early fifth-century Rome and by providing a pictorial counterpart to the saint's own use of Vergil, explicitly alluded to in the San Paolo Bible's reference to Jerome's 'attic pen [that] surges forward with sturdy vigour'. In this way, the frontispieces also reinforce the Vulgate's position as the Aeneid's replacement, a notion of particular value in a culture that aspired simultaneously to transmit the pagan past to its people and to supersede it. Most important, by assimilating contemporary issues of governance and doctrine into the authentic account they created of the saint's story, the Carolingian narratives bring ancient scripture back home, transmitting not only the '*words* passed down' in Jerome's version but also the *meaning* they had for a new people of God. Picturing translation, the frontispieces are thus, in every sense of the word, themselves translations.

129

11

Roods, Rituals and Christian Rule

Later Anglo-Saxon Art and the Benedictine Reform

The Viking raids and settlements of the ninth century had a significant impact on Britain and Ireland. It was not all rapine and pillage, for the islands became part of their growing northern trading empire. They introduced towns (including Dublin, Waterford, Wexford and Cork) to the Irish rural environment and served as a catalyst to the formation of a united England under a single monarch. During the third quarter of the century most of England was occupied and its various kingdoms and their rulers fell before their onslaught. Only Wessex and parts of western Mercia (south-west England and the Welsh Marches) were able to resist, although at one point the West Saxon king, Alfred the Great, was reduced to hiding out as a guerrilla in the Athelney Marshes. His pushback was successful and he retook London and most of the southern counties, negotiating a partition of the country into England and the Danelaw. His conviction that the flood of paganism unleashed on his people was the result of their neglect of their Christian faith and of learning led Alfred to look to the spiritual health of the nation as well as its military defence. To assist him in this revival he assembled a circle of learned clerics drawn from England (Bishop Werferth of Worcester), the Celtic lands (the Welshman Asser), and the Carolingian empire (Grimbald of St Bertin). His stepmother, Judith, was a Carolingian princess, and Alfred was familiar with the ways of her court and of Rome, which he had visited as a boy. His reign was not marked by an artistic revival, given his other priorities, but the founding of schools and the writing of books were high on his agenda. The use of the vernacular language, Old English, was promoted to facilitate learning, giving rise to a growth in a thriving indigenous tradition of literature and poetry and of English and Latin Christian scholarship.

The reconquest of the Danelaw continued apace under subsequent West Saxon rulers Edward the Elder and Athelstan until the latter became king of England, governing both English and Anglo-Scandinavian subjects. Most Vikings in England assimilated into local society and converted to Christianity, but they also brought with them an injection of renewed Germanic culture and mythology. Christian iconography is juxtaposed with scenes from pagan Germanic legend on many of the sculptured monuments of tenth- and eleventh-century England. Examples include: the Gosforth Cross on which the crucified hero Christ is joined by Nordic figures, such as the Valkyrie who extends a chalice to a fallen hero; or the ninth- to tenth-century Nunburnholme Cross on which a scene depicting the celebration of the Eucharist is paralleled with that of Sigurd, the dragon-slayer, who had also come to symbolize the triumph over evil – a Germanic 'type' of Christ, just as David was his Old Testament precursor.

Anglo-Saxon Scriptoria

Athelstan was a noted collector of books and relics. The Coronation Gospels,[1] a little Carolingian illuminated volume from Lobbes, c. 900 CE, upon which the kings of later Anglo-Saxon England are thought to have sworn their oaths of accession, was sent to him as a gift from his brother-in-law Emperor Otto the Great, founder of the Ottonian dynasty. Such continental influences were accelerated from the mid-tenth century by the Benedictine Reform movement implemented within the English Church by Sts Dunstan, Æthelwold and Oswald. St Dunstan, himself a distinguished metalworker and artist, may have left us a self-portrait in a masterly line drawing depicting him kneeling at the feet of Christ in his own Classbook[2] (a collection of texts for his own study). Canons were expelled from the cathedrals and the individual rules of life favoured by monasteries and nunneries were replaced by the Benedictine Rule. The beauty of worship figured large in this programme of renewal, and art flourished alongside rich traditions of music and liturgy enacted within grand stone buildings such as the New Minster in Winchester. There Bishop Æthelwold would have been seen presiding on major feast-days, pronouncing episcopal blessings from his magnificent Benedictional,[3] written in the Winchester scriptorium between 971–84 CE by the scribe Godeman, who recorded in a poem of golden letters that the 'Son of Thunder' commanded that the book be made, using gold and many colours. Use them he did, on figures that combine the calligraphic penmanship of the Insular tradition with lively flying draperies and figure-style ultimately indebted to the Carolingian tradition. These are contained within heavy decorative borders composed of exuberant acanthus

Picua et scriptura huius pagine subtus uisa : est de propria manu sci dunstani.

NE·D·2·19·
(2176)
Bod·578·

St Dunstan's Classbook, drawing of St Dunstan kneeling before Christ, with an accompanying prayer, both in his own hand. Glastonbury, mid-tenth century.

ornament. This has become characterized as the Winchester style or 'First' style of later Anglo-Saxon art, although its popularity led to it also being used in other Anglo-Saxon scriptoria. The full-page miniatures in the Benedictional of St Æthelwold depict the saints or events celebrated on specific feast days, such as that for Easter Sunday, which depicts the women greeted by the angel at the empty tomb from which Christ had risen. The somewhat masculine physiognomies of the women and the cupboard-like appearance of the tomb have been interpreted as relating to the performance of liturgical drama in Anglo-Saxon England, a tradition first evidenced in the eighth century, with monks playing the part of the women and the tomb a moveable stage prop.

The Winchester style could also be produced as elegant tinted drawings, as well as fully painted and gilded, harking back once more to both Insular draughtsmanship and increasingly to the Carolingian drawing style of Reims, as epitomized by the Utrecht Psalter. This phase has therefore been termed by scholars the 'Utrecht' or 'Second' style of later Anglo-Saxon art. In the early eleventh century this influential work was acquired as a model for his scriptorium by the Archbishop of Canterbury, who commissioned a version known as the Harley Psalter,[4] one of several 'copies' made in England. It is extremely rare for an exemplar and its responses to survive, enabling them to be compared and contrasted – hence the secret of the Utrecht Psalter's fame. The scriptorium learned a great deal about the challenges of integrating an extended picture cycle with the text and adapting the iconography to draw out varying theological nuances. Also from

Canterbury around this time were two more remarkable books that conflated the Anglo-Saxon world with that of the Early Christian past and with the Israelites' experiences of exile and migration in the fully illustrated Old English Genesis and the Old English Hexateuch.[5] Superb examples can be seen among the work of the so-called Ramsey Psalter artist, thought to have been a monk of Winchester (or perhaps Ramsey), who travelled in Frankia and painted or scribed for his supper en route, collaborating with members of Carolingian scriptoria such as Fleury and St Bertin. His masterwork, the Ramsey Psalter,[6] which he wrote and decorated in the late tenth century, features a moving depiction of the crucifixion in which Christ hangs heavily on the cross – his limp, tortured form proclaiming his humanity – lamented by the sorrowing Virgin and the apostle John, who is inspired to write his Gospel. Monumental crucifixions were also made in ivory and metalwork and in stone, such as the Langford and Romsey Roods.

The cult of the Cross and that of the Virgin continued to form important focal points in English devotion throughout this period. In the Ælfwine Prayerbook[7] – made around 1023–35 by the Winchester scribe Ælsinus for Ælfwine, Abbot of the New Minster, when he was still a deacon – the Virgin and Child even join the members of the Trinity in an extended Holy Family, enthroned upon the rainbow symbolizing God's covenant with humankind (an iconography derived from the Carolingian Utrecht Psalter), with Satan, Hades, Judas and the heretic Arius cowering below. Christ sits alone upon his rainbow as Christ the King, enthroned in majesty at Doomsday on a highly modelled ivory pectoral cross, worn by a bishop during the early eleventh century. Another fine image of Christ in Majesty occurs at Barnack, one of a series of impressive stone sculptures from later Anglo-Saxon England, which produced stone crosses, shrines and tympana, continuing an indigenous tradition of stone carving that extended back into Roman times and Celtic prehistory.

A series of opulent gospelbooks were also made around this time, including the Copenhagen Gospels (the Matthew miniature of which was partly based upon that in the earlier Lindisfarne Gospels), the Arenburg Gospels, the Trinity Gospels, the York Gospels, the Eadui Codex, the Grimbald Gospels and the Bury Gospels.[8] Many appear, stylistically, to have been Canterbury products. One leading artist-scribe in particular worked on a number of them. His name was Eadui Basan (Eadui 'the fat'), a monk at Christ Church Canterbury. He can be identified as he signed a colophon in the Eadui Codex and wrote a series of charters dating from 1012–23. He seems to have attracted the attention of King Cnut and Queen Emma, and to have been pulled out of the Christ Church scriptorium to follow the court and pen important royal charters and opulent books for the royal couple to bestow

FOLLOWING SPREAD LEFT: St Benedict, enthroned, presents his Rule to the community of Christ Church, while the artist–scribe, Eadui Basan, embraces his feet in the Eadui Psalter, Christ Church Canterbury.

RIGHT: The Gospels of Judith of Flanders, Crucifixion – either the owner, Countess Judith of Flanders (1032–94), is embracing the cross, or this is the earliest such depiction of Mary Magdalene. Made in Canterbury, Winchester or East Anglia c. 1051–64.

135

ROODS, RITUALS AND CHRISTIAN RULE

as gifts to regain the goodwill of their English subjects – for Cnut was a Dane and came to the throne as a result of Viking invasion. Eadui can be seen in one of his works, the Eadui Psalter,[9] kneeling at the feet of St Benedict, who bestows his Rule upon the Christ Church brethren. The juxtaposition of full painting and tinted drawing here may be intended to denote the distinction between eternal sacred space, occupied by Benedict, and contemporary time in which the monks dwell. Eadui, despite the proclamation inscribed upon his belt that he inhabits the 'zone of humility', is depicted fully painted like the saint.

The Convergence of Anglo-Saxon and Norman Art

Queen Emma, formerly wife of Anglo-Saxon king Ethelred the 'Unready', was one of a number of prominent Normans at the English court. Another incomer was Countess Judith of Flanders (1032–94), who came to England in 1051 as wife to Tostig Godwinson, Earl of Northumbria and protagonist in the scramble for the English throne which lead to the Norman Conquest in 1066. In one of three gospelbooks[10] associated with her patronage, Judith is shown embracing the foot of the cross. Anglo-Saxon artists contributed to a number of themes that were to become central to Medieval art, notably the iconography of the Trinity, the Virgin and the Crucifixion. If the woman clutching the Rood on which her Saviour hangs was not intended to be Judith, this would be the earliest such depiction of the Magdalene – or it may even have been meant to represent both women. Its heightened emotion and mannerism distinguished the 'Third' style of later Anglo-Saxon art, in which the Winchester and Utrecht styles fused and assumed an even greater monumentality, which is also seen on its resplendent jewelled cover.

There was a constant two-way stream of political and cultural influence running between England and Normandy throughout the eleventh century. Scribes and illuminators did not wake up after the Conquest in 1066 and re-tool for Norman-style book production. Norman scriptoria had for some time been influenced by those of Anglo-Saxon England, and by its advanced written bureaucracy and legislature. Late eleventh-century Norman manuscripts such as the Jumièges Gospels and the Préaux Gospels[11] are clearly indebted to the Winchester style, being heavily influenced by Winchester style illumination and English Caroline script. The 'Channel School' of the twelfth century can be seen to have its origins in a trans-manche cultural milieu of the tenth and eleventh centuries, linking England, Normandy, northern France and the southern Netherlands. In English post-Conquest scriptoria a protracted merger of styles and practices can be traced as Norman England emerged.

12

Romanesque

Pilgrims, Crusaders and European Style

During the eleventh and twelfth centuries the European political and cultural scene was largely dominated by a new factor – the Normans – and by an international style that has been called 'Romanesque'. This term was first coined in the nineteenth century because of the perception of an indebtedness to Roman architecture in the ambitious building programmes of the age, and in respect of its cultural relationship to the simultaneous rise of the Romance languages in Europe. This was an age when western Europeans were on the move, journeying on pilgrimage, conquest and crusade, and the impact of the peoples and places they encountered is reflected in their art, which blends the traditions of their own regions with those of Byzantium, the Christian Orient and Islam. The result is a monumental style of art that conflates decorative stylization and echoes of classical naturalism and which makes a direct appeal to the emotions. Opulent metalwork, frescoes and sculptures combine to evoke awe and wonder in the viewer, who is left quaking with excitement and anxiety at the prospect of an apocalyptic end to the human story and the fate of their own soul at the Doomsday to come.

The Normans and Romanesque Art

It should be apparent from preceding chapters that this style was less a reinvention of the classical past, however, than a natural evolution from the traditions of the Anglo-Saxon, Hispanic, Carolingian, Ottonian and Byzantine regions, which received renewed impetus from the energies of an ambitious new power. Normandy was founded in 911 CE when Emperor Charles the Bald granted a

Viking, Duke Rollo, land around the mouth of the Seine in fiefdom, to stave off raids. Rollo adopted the name Robert, along with Christianity, in 912 CE and established a dynasty that shot to prominence in 1066 when Duke William enforced his claims to the English throne. One of the greatest, and undoubtedly the most famous, of Medieval textiles records his version of events in the Bayeux Tapestry, a long banner of linen embroidered in coloured wools, probably by English needlewomen, for William's brother, Bishop Odo of Bayeux. It is thought that this was suspended from the columns of his church's nave. Its technique and the lively, loquacious images and inscriptions obscure the immediacy of its debt to centuries of Christian narrative cycles. Its subject matter may be political and secular, but it conveys matters of tremendous import for the history of Christianity.

The acquisition of the Anglo-Saxons' advanced administration gave an added impetus to the success and consolidation of Norman rule, in England, Normandy and elsewhere, enabling the construction of the Angevin Empire during the twelfth

Death of Edward the Confessor, from the Bayeux Tapestry, c. 1090s, England. Bayeux, Normandy.

century. An early manifestation of this new power was a book – the Domesday Book of 1086 (now in the National Archives in London), the first full census of property ownership and demographics to be undertaken in the post-Roman world, and a major source for English history. Out of such political and cultural fusion, and from the Norman espousal of reformed Cluniac monasticism and their political and military expansion into other parts of France, Italy, Sicily, Byzantium and the Crusader kingdoms, was born the 'Romanesque' culture that was to characterize the age.

The Normans were great builders – of kingdoms, of castles and of churches. Not only did they build or rebuild many cathedrals, such as Durham, Winchester and Peterborough, they also ploughed ahead with the provision of parish churches at a local level, all of which required books and liturgical furnishings. As reform of the English church and the introduction of more Norman personnel escalated in the latter part of the eleventh century, so the work of more Norman scribes, trained in scriptoria such as Mont St Michel, Jumièges and Bec (whose traditions had been formed with reference to English and French book arts), can be detected working alongside their English counterparts in leading scriptoria such as Canterbury and Durham. So close are the connections that books made during this transitional period are attributed to a 'Channel School', incorporating English, Norman and northern French scriptoria such as St Bertin (near St Omer) and St Vaast, Arras. The earlier use of zoomorphic and anthropomorphic initials (letters shaped from animal and human forms) and of historiated (storytelling) initials continued and flourished, with lively gymnastic initials, in which the postures of living creatures become ever more contorted, joining the repertoire (as seen, for example, in the Psalter of Robert de Bello). These were joined by their counterparts in stone on the voussoirs and jambs of doorways, on capitals and corbels and on the bowls of fonts (such as those of the Herefordshire school, as at Eardisley with its Harrowing of Hell and Viking-like warriors battling evil). Often they were imbued with symbolism, representing the virtues and vices, the labours of the months and the zodiac sign; or they stemmed from classical mythology and the marvels of the East, such as the centaur, the siren and the human-headed lion known as the manticore – harbinger of death. Some, like the hermaphrodite *sheelagh-na-gigs* (Gaelic for 'the witch on the wall') who expose themselves on the exteriors of some Irish and British churches, such as Kilpeck in Herefordshire with its humorous twelfth-century corbel table, served an apotropaic function, scaring off evil and providing a link back to the indigenous pagan past.

Norman architecture had drawn inspiration from important Benedictine foundations, such as Cluny and St Benoît sur Loire (from where the relics of St

Benedict of Nursia, founder of the order, had been brought from the ruined Monte Cassino). The reforming zeal of the order during the tenth and eleventh centuries had contributed to a burgeoning of art and ritual. At St Benoît the choir and massive porch still retains its late eleventh-century sculptures of Old and New Testament scenes and depictions of the life of St Martin of Tours, who inaugurated monasticism in France. The splendour that was Cluny may lie in ruins, but its awesome scale can still be appreciated, along with the quality of its capitals, probably carved during the late eleventh century, which depict not only biblical themes but some derived from Antiquity, such as personifications of the Liberal Arts, the tones of music and the Rivers of Paradise. Other fine examples of Cluniac architecture and sculpture are preserved at fellow Burgundian foundations such as Paray le Monial (c. 1100) and Autun (c. 1120–32), and in smaller parish churches, such as those of the Brionnais. The name of one of the master sculptors has survived from Autun, namely Gislebertus, who carved the superb tympanum above its west portal that depicts the Last Judgement in graphic detail, bringing all who entered to a sense of their own urgent need for redemption. This is poignantly conveyed by the sensuous yet vulnerable figure of the naked Eve. The themes of the carvings that enliven the fabric of such buildings combine the didactic and the admonitory, forming sermons in stone.

Capital depicting the personification of the Liberal Arts (or the tones of music), early twelfth century, from one of the most important Romanesque abbeys, Cluny. Burgundy, France.

Such aesthetic and intellectual trends did not find favour in all quarters, however, and their most vociferous critic was the prominent churchman Bernard of Clairvaux, a member of the Cistercian order, founded in 1098 as an attempt to reform Cluniac Benedictinism and adhere more strictly to St Benedict's Rule of common life. The abbot of Benedictine Molesmes, Robert, and two of his monks, Alberic and the Englishman Stephen Harding, left to found the monastery of Cîteaux, near Dijon in Burgundy, dedicated to monastic worship and agricultural labour. In 1112 they were joined by a band of new recruits, including Bernard of Clairvaux, whose writing and preaching promoted the popularity of the order and advocated Crusade to regain the Holy Land. Many Cistercian monasteries were founded across Europe, including sites later romanticized as ruins such as Fountains and Tintern Abbeys – notable for their austere plans, their comparatively restrained decoration, their accommodation for large numbers of lay workers, their 'desert' riverside sites, and their specialization in profitable sheep farming. One area in which the Cistercian ethos did find artistic expression, however, was in their books, which contain particularly inventive anthropomorphic and gymnastic initials – perhaps partly inspired by Harding's familiarity with English illumination, seen in the Cîteaux Bible.[1] The lively initials

Detail depicting Eve, from *The Last Judgement*, carved by Gislebertus, c. 1120–32, typanum of the West Portal, Autun Cathedral, Burgundy, France.

of Cistercian manuscripts reflect the emphasis placed upon monastic labour – 'to work, is to pray'. Bernard's influence was felt widely, extending to Benedictine houses such as Anchin in France, where his treatise on the Twelve Degrees of Humility is illustrated with an image of angels climbing a ladder to ascend to Christ, St Benedict and St Bernard while Satan lures them to their fall – the origins of the game of 'snakes and ladders'.

Initial 'Q' depicting Cistercian monks chopping wood, Cîteaux Bible, c. 1125–50. Cîteaux Abbey, France.

Pilgrim's Progress: The Popularity of Pilgrimage

During the eleventh century the vogue for pilgrimage, first manifested in the third century, took a firm grip upon the European imagination, perhaps encouraged by millenarianism and the upheavals of the Viking age. Visits to local shrines were augmented by more arduous and spiritually challenging (and exciting) journeys to sites that claimed the relics of biblical figures or prominent saints, such as Vézelay in Burgundy (close to the home of the modern Taizé community), an early pilgrimage church that fell into decline during the Viking age and which reversed its fortunes in the early eleventh century by asserting that it possessed the relics of Mary Magdalene. The splendid Romanesque church that was built there is enlivened with loquacious capitals relating biblical and symbolic scenes, such as the Mystic Mill in which the wholesome grain of the Old Testament is poured into a cross-shaped hand-quern that transforms it into the purified, life-sustaining flour of the New Testament.

Vézelay was not only a destination but also a staging post on the greatest of all European pilgrimage routes – that leading to Santiago de Compostela in Galicia, which housed the shrine of the apostle James, whose symbol, the scallop shell, became a cipher for pilgrimage and gave rise to a gallery of subsequent pilgrim badges certifying a successful penitential trip. Many such shrines were noted for their miracles of healing – an ancient attribute of religious sites (and one that features in most religions) which is perpetuated today at shrines such as Lourdes and Knock. A growth in the papal practice of granting indulgences (time-off for good behaviour from the sojourn of the soul in Purgatory) to those who undertook such pilgrimages further stimulated the trend, drawing pilgrims from northern European territories, such as Germany and England, to southern France and Spain. The sites they saw en route inspired them to transmit the influence of Moorish and Mozarabic architecture and that of Romanesque France throughout Europe, along with the lively sculptural styles of Burgundian and southern French churches such as Moissac and Souillac, with their superbly stylized column-figures, and Nîmes and Arles, with the abiding figural classicism of their Roman past. Their influence can be seen in the twelfth-century sculptures in the porch at Malmesbury, for example, and in the panels depicting the Raising of Lazarus and Martha and Mary at Chichester Cathedral. The plans of churches changed to accommodate the problems of visitor flow stimulated by the lucrative pilgrimage trade, with stepped-up construction of campaniles and bell towers to summon the faithful, narthex holding areas, aisles, ambulatories and crypts – all requiring sculptures, frescoes and reliquaries to instruct and stimulate the eager religious tourist and to prepare them for their spiritual encounter.

Visits to these places – along with those to more local sites such as Croagh Patrick in Ireland, St David's in Wales, St Boniface's shrine at Fulda in Germany, that of the Magi in Cologne and, following his shocking assassination by Henry II's knights in 1170, that of Archbishop Thomas Becket at Canterbury – became acceptable alternatives to pilgrimage to the Holy Land.

The Crusaders

The Holy Land had become less accessible since Jerusalem was captured by the Seljuk Turks in 1071, prompting a plea from the Byzantine emperor for Western assistance in retaking it. This led to the fateful series of military and popular expeditions known as the Crusades, the first of which was preached in 1095 and the fourth of which culminated in 1204 in the despoiling of Constantinople itself. In the interim the Crusader kingdoms were forged and the Western imagination so fired that even a tragic children's crusade was launched, most of them expiring en route. Western knights based in the Latin kingdom and its neighbours developed a taste for exotic Eastern and Byzantine arts; the work of local and Greek artists was sometimes blended with that of Westerners to form distinctive cross-cultural works such as the Melisende Psalter of c. 1131–61, discussed in Chapter 4. They also commissioned icons such as those of the prominent military saint, George, discussed in Chapter 7. Such contacts stimulated another great phase of influence from the Christian Orient and Byzantium upon Western art.

The staging posts for Crusaders led them through Italy and to maritime bases such as Venice, southern Italy and Sicily. The external arcades of northern Italian architecture (such as that of the cathedrals at Parma and Modena) exert their influence as far afield as St Maria im Capitol in Cologne, and the distinctive watchful lions – symbols of resurrection and prophetic kingship, thought never to sleep – that support the column bases of Lombardic church portals, such as those at the influential church of San Zeno in Verona, recur throughout Romanesque art. Also at San Zeno can be seen another feature of Italian churches that inspired many northern European responses – bronze doors bearing biblical narrative cycles, with panels cast in the eleventh century being incorporated into their twelfth-century successors when a larger doorway was needed. Antique and Byzantine exemplars once again served as models, and at San Michele at Monte Sant'Angelo are doors commissioned by Pantaleone of Amalfi from Byzantium in 1076. Imposing European Romanesque examples survive at: St Maria im Capitol in Cologne; the Porta di San Ranieri at Pisa Cathedral, made around 1190 by Bonanno Pisano; Trioa Cathedral in Apulia, which has two sets of doors made in 1119 and 1127 by Odorisio da Benevento; and Master Buvina's doors carved in 1214 for Split Cathedral. Doors also sometimes carried massive sanctuary knockers, such as that guarding the main portal to Durham Cathedral, in the form of a roaring lion's head.

Artistic influences could flow from in both directions. The sculpted façade of Modena Cathedral, carved by the twelfth-century mason, Wiligelmo, exhibits southern French influence in its depictions of the prophets and of scenes from

144

Genesis. Likewise, the sculptures carved around 1200 by Benedetto Antelami *dictus* ('called Antelami') at Parma Baptistery are so Francophile in their style and iconography (which includes Ecclesia and Synongogue, Solomon and Sheba, the Nativity, the Deposition and the Last Judgement) that it has been suggested that he trained in Provence, perhaps at St Trophime in Arles.

Southern Italy had long been a multi-cultural area. It was nominally subject to Byzantine rule until the rebellions of 1009–1012, but was frequented by Greek, Muslim and Latin mariners and mercenaries, and by pilgrims to shrines such as that dedicated since at least the fifth century to St Michael in a cave on Monte Gargano. By the end of the eleventh century William of Hauteville, one of the many Norman mercenaries who roved around Europe and the Near East intent upon carving out a fortune and a territory, had taken control as Count of Apulia and in 1059 the Pope promised another Norman, Robert Guiscard, not only the fiefdom of Apulia and Calabria but also Sicily, if he expelled the Saracens. By 1091 the resulting Norman conquest of Sicily was complete. During the early thirteenth century this enlarged kingdom passed to the Hohenstaufen Emperor Frederick II (1220–50) and then to Charles of Anjou, who relocated his capital – giving birth to the kingdom of Naples.

The Italo-Byzantine Tradition

Byzantine artistic influence continued to be exerted in the region. The Monte Gargano shrine was given bronze doors made in Constantinople in 1076, inspiring those made by Barisano in 1175–79 for one in the upper church at Trani. He also worked at Ravello and at Monreale. In establishing new centres of worship the Normans of southern Italy engaged in the popular pastime of relic stealing – seizing the relics of St Nicholas from Myra in Greece and making them the focus of his cult at the basilica of San Nicola in Bari, completed in 1197. Another new-build was Otranto Cathedral, commissioned by Bohemund in 1080–88, with one of the largest pictorial mosaic floors of the age; while Salerno Cathedral, begun for Robert Guiscard in 1076, contains the finest examples of the style of coloured marble intarsia pavements, altars and pulpits known as Cosmati work – another manifestation of combined Latin, Greek and Muslim tradition.

In southern Italy and Sicily, as in Venice, lingering Byzantine influence continued to find majestic expression in mosaics and in painted crucifixes and retables that hung behind altars. This Italo-Byzantine tradition would serve both to inform and to prompt the counter-reaction that was the early Renaissance. The mosaics that adorn the palace, the Capella Palatina, other churches in Palermo (which became the capital in 1130), Cefalù Cathedral, and Monreale Cathedral and churches

Mosaic of Christ
Pantocrator, in the apse
of Cefalù Cathedral, mid-
twelfth century, Sicily.

– like their Moorish and Greek inspired architecture – are both a fine epitome of the cultural synthesis of the area and a splendid regional expression of Byzantine art. The gracious Christ in the apse at Cefalù, completed before King Roger's death in 1154, is the work of mainstream Byzantine artists, but the book he holds open at the words 'I am the Light of the World' bears the text in both Greek and Latin. The mosaics in the dome area of the Capella Palatina in Palermo were also by Byzantine craftsmen, while those in the nave, undertaken in the late 1150s, are by Sicilians working in a more robust Western narrative style and are captioned solely in Latin.

In the late eleventh century, an ambitious cycle of frescoes was painted at Sant'Angelo in Formis, near Capua, by a Byzantine artist and a team of indigenous artists influenced by Monte Cassino. Other wall paintings in southern Italy are of humbler, provincial Greek style. The distinctive blue backgrounds of the Sant'Angelo in Formis paintings is echoed in Burgundy, which also produced a vibrant school of fresco painters (known in France as 'l'école au fonds bleus'). The imposing Christ in Majesty handing St Peter the scroll of the new Law in the apse of Berzé-la-Ville is the work of artists from Cluny, c. 1103–09, which had adopted the Italo-Byzantine style a little earlier. Little such work survives, but echoes can be found along the pilgrimage route, at churches such as Paray-le-Monial, on the way to Catalonia.

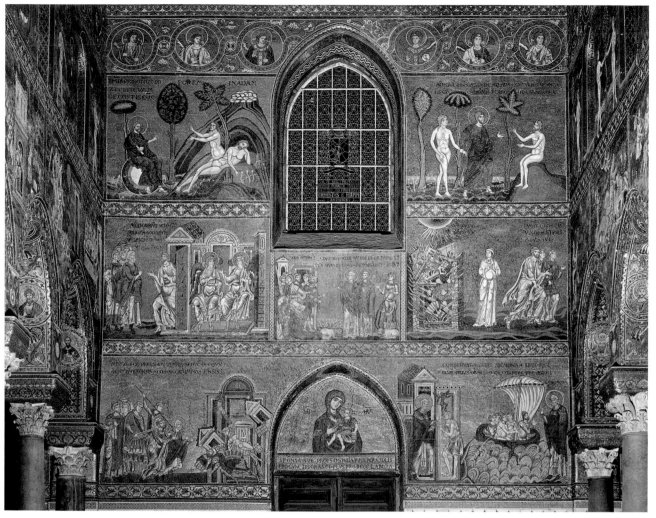

Spanish Romanesque Art

French and Italian influence can be clearly seen in the architecture and sculptures of Iberian churches such as: the impressive two-storey cloister of Santo Domingo de Silos with its late eleventh-century carved capitals and piers, some of the recorded names of the sculptors indicating their Moorish origins; and Ripoll, built in 1020–32 on the plan of Old St Peter's by the abbot of Vich in France, with a fine sculpted west front which later incorporated the earliest Romanesque portal in Spain, dating from the 1160s. The Ripoll Bible[2] of c. 1040, which contains the most extensive illustrative cycle of the period, relates to the sculptures of its west façade. Seo de Urgel and Tarragona display similar influences. The crusade to regain northern Spain from the Moors, energetically pursued under King Alphonso VI (reigned 1065–1109) after Portugal had been reconquered in 1055–64, led to an influx of French and the transmission back home of Moorish architectural features. These

Creation of Adam and Eve, c. 1158, part of the mosaics adorning the nave of the Capella Palatina, Palermo, Sicily.

include the horseshoe arch and the alternation of black and white stone for decorative articulation of arches, seen in French churches such as the cathedral and the little chapel of St Michel d'Aiguilhe atop its rocky pinnacle at Le Puy. Shrines to St Michael were usually located in the high places (for example, Mont St Michel in Normandy, St Michael's Mount in Cornwall) where he did battle with evil, at the meeting place between heaven and earth. Iberian buildings such as the Old Cathedral of Sé Velha in Coimbra, Portugal, and the cathedrals of Zamora and Salamanca likewise combine aspects of Moorish and Romanesque art.

The strength of indigenous Mozarabic culture is evident in the illuminated manuscripts of Romanesque Spain, notably the many copies of the *Commentary on the Apocalypse* by Beatus of Liebana that were produced at scriptoria such as Las Huelgas and Silos. The Silos Apocalypse[3] contains a colophon declaring that it was written in 1091 by the monks Domingo and Muño but that it was not completed by the illuminators to whom they passed on their work until 1109. The strange mystical symbolism of the apostle John's vision lends itself perfectly to their bold colours, simplified fields of composition and stylized figures, which verge on abstraction in Picasso-esque fashion, portraying the awe and attendant horrors of the apocalypse as effectively as Picasso's *Guernica* would later do in the face of the Spanish Civil War. The artistic language of both is the Spanish vernacular.

The comparative lack of wealth in Spain meant that frescoes and painted altar frontals and retables were the most popular forms of decoration for church interiors, rather than mosaics, marble and metalwork, as they could be cheaply produced. Where war has spared them they have survived, as they did not invite despoiliation for gain and Catholic Spain was not subject to iconoclasm. An unusual antependium (altar frontal) remains from Silos which is partly painted,

Christr in Majesty, apsidal fresco, c. 1120–50. San Clemente de Tahull, Spain.

partly enamelled, with raised copper gilt heads to its figures. Byzantine influence can also be seen in the frescoes of north-east Spain, which are thought to have accompanied Lombardic masons. Among the finest are those of San Clemente de Tahull (c. 1120–50) and the apocalyptic cycle at the Panteón de los Reyes at León (1167–88). Those at Sigena, with their beautiful naturalistic and modelled figures, stand on the threshold of Gothic art and show just how effective the pilgrimage routes were in promoting cultural interaction across Europe, for they were probably painted by English artists.

Jesse Tree, depicting the genealogy of Christ as a family tree springing from the loins of Jesse, from the Psalter of Henry of Blois (or Winchester Psalter), Winchester, c. 1150.

English Romanesque Painting

Few earlier examples of fresco painting have survived from England itself, owing to a trend for successive modernizations of parish churches, to puritanical iconoclasm, and to the whitewashing or stripping away of plaster according to liturgical and aesthetic fashion. A few precious survivors include: the twelfth-century procession of knights at Claverley, Shropshire; the realization of St John's vision of Revelation at Kempley (Gloucestershire); and a fine panel depicting St Paul in St Anselm's Chapel, Canterbury Cathedral.

The superlative quality of English Romanesque painting can best be appreciated, however, through its illumination. Under the governance of leading churchmen such as Lanfranc, Anselm, William of St Carilef and Henry of Blois the scriptoria that had characterized the Anglo-Saxon sacred arts continued to flourish, combining indigenous, continental and Byzantine influences. Among their many outstanding products are the Bury Bible, the Dover Bible, the Lambeth Bible, the St Alban's Psalter and the Eadwine Psalter,[4] a mid-twelfth-century version of the Utrecht Psalter, perpetuating Canterbury's obsession with that iconic Carolingian work. The artist-scribe Eadwine, the monk who led the work, has depicted himself at his labours and modestly describes himself in the surrounding dedicatory inscription as the 'prince of scribes' – was he emulating his forebear, Eadui the fat, in so doing, or is this perhaps a tribute to that Anglo-Saxon master? The Bury Bible was made at the abbey of Bury St Edumund's in 1121–48 by a team led by a lay artist, Master Hugo, who also worked in metals and who has left an image of himself and an assistant painting a border. That Bible was probably for the use of the monastic community, whereas the St Alban's Psalter was commissioned as a gift for Christina of Markyate, a well-regarded anchoress (spiritual recluse). Other outstanding books were commissioned for personal or institutional use, such as the Henry of Blois Psalter and the Winchester Bible[5] made at Winchester around 1160–70 for Bishop Henry of Blois, brother of King Henry I. The style of painting in the Winchester Bible features a new naturalism and humanism in its figure style, which may in part be a response to contemporary Byzantine art, and which can also be found in the Westminster Psalter,[6] made at Westminster Abbey around 1200, and the frescoes of Sigena in Spain painted by English artists. This is known as the 'Transitional Style' and, with such works, Europe stood on the threshold of Gothic art.

Roman porphyry vase, converted to form an eagle, symbol of St John and of the Risen Christ, for art lover Abbot Suger of St Denis, 1122–51. Paris, Louvre.

Storing up Treasures in Heaven: Medieval Metalwork

The ravages of the Reformation led to the seizure and melting down of most of the Medieval metalwork of Britain, but a few stunning objects have survived to attest to their splendour. These include the Gloucester Candlestick and other items less prized for their bullion value, such as the exquisite and highly decorative ivory depicting the Adoration of the Magi, made around 1140, in which the composition is skillfully tailored to the natural shape of the material. But it is to France, Germany and the Netherlands that one must look to truly recapture the opulence and imagination of the rich trappings of faith during the Romanesque age. Their greatest intellectual and theological advocate, in the face of criticism from Cistercian circles, was Abbot Suger of Saint-Denis, near Paris, whose refined aesthetic tastes extended to collecting antiquities – including a fine Roman porphyry vase which was converted (sometime during his abbacy in 1123–51) to form the body of an eagle, the symbol of the apostle John and of revelation.

The imperial art of Rome, Byzantium and Carolingia provided a wealth of such inspiration. Resplendent golden altars were made for a number of liturgical focal points across the Early Middle Ages: Sant' Ambrogio in Milan, c. 850; the Capella Palatina, Aachen, c. 1020; Basle Cathedral, Switzerland,[7] c. 1022–24; and Santo Domingo de Silos, c. 1140–50. Some of these perhaps drew inspiration from the Byzantine reredos, such as the Pala d'Oro in San Marco, Venice, commissioned from Constantinople in 976 CE and remade several times between then and 1345. Enormous candelabra peopled with allegorical and biblical figures were commissioned for Hildesheim Cathedral (1054–70), Gross-Komburg (c. 1130) and, by Frederick Barbarossa, for Aachen Cathedral (1166). Ciboria (altar canopies), chalices, patens, censers (such as that in the form of the Temple of Solomon from Trèves, c. 1000), aquamaniles (water carriers for use during the Eucharist), liturgical buckets for aspersion, book covers, croisiers, processional crosses, suspended crucifixes, ivory liturgical horns (oliphants) and reliquaries also abound. The latter often assumed the form in metalwork of the relics they contained, such as the foot reliquary of St Andrew at Trèves or the head reliquary of Pope Alexander made for Stavelot Abbey, c. 1146, which makes obvious allusions to ancient Roman portrait busts.

Notable among the many gifted metalworkers of the age was the monk Roger of Helmershausen who, in 1100, was paid by the Bishop of

Head reliquary of Pope Alexander made for Stavelot Abbey, Belgium, c. 1146.

Christ in Majesty, from the
Stavelot Bible, 1093–97.
Stavelot Abbey, Mosan
region, Belgium.

Paderborn for a portable altar. He is thought to be Theophilus ('lover of God'), who wrote the earliest and most influential Medieval treatise on artistic techniques, the *de diversis artibus*, indicating his expertise across a wide range of media. Such versatility was probably also granted to Rainier (or Reiner) of Huy who around 1107–18 made an extraordinarily graceful bronze font for St Bartèlemy in Liège and is also thought to have carved two ivory book covers (one depicting the crucifixion, in Tongres) stylistically indebted to Early Christian or Byzantine models. His figures are characterized by their slender forms and the expression and life with which they are imbued. The innovative design of the font depicts scenes of baptism in the ministry of John the Baptist and is supported upon the twelve oxen bearing the molten sea – symbolizing the apostles bearing the Word.

The Rhine and Meuse Valleys proved fertile artistic soil during this period, producing many fine pieces of metalwork and illuminated manuscripts. The latter included a number of imposing complete Bibles (pandects), such as the Floreffe Bible (c. 1160) and the Stavelot Bible[8] (1093–97), with its imposing Christ in Majesty, seated in a mandorla, which conflates Ottonian and Byzantine influences. The initials of such volumes are historiated with multiple biblical scenes, with an emphasis upon typology in which Old and New Testament analogies are drawn and prophecies are seen to be fulfilled. The graphic linear drawings of the quill are eloquently transcribed by the engraver's tool into metalwork form, and the cloisonné enamels produced earlier under Byzantine influence give way increasingly to bold champlevé Western counterparts. One of the finest late Romanesque practitioners of these arts was Nicholas of Verdun, whose works included a fine champlevé pulpit for the abbey of Klosterneuburg, near Vienna – completed in 1181 and still preserved there but converted into a retable – and much of the work on the Shrine of the Three Kings in Cologne Cathedral which had been commenced in the late eleventh century. Another metalworking centre that combined Ottonian and Italo-Byzantine traditions was Salzburg, where manuscripts were also made. The contemporary political climate fostered such cultural fusion, especially when, in resolution of the contest for imperial power between the Guelph and Ghibelline parties in the aftermath of Ottonian and Saxon rule, Frederick I of Hohenstaufen (Frederick Barbarossa) was elected Holy Roman emperor in 1152. He and his heirs, Henry VI and Frederick II, pursued ambitions in Italy, annexing southern Italy and Sicily. Meanwhile, in England, the aftermath of civil war in which the crown was contested by Stephen and Matilda resulted in the accession in 1154 of Henry II Plantagenet, a powerful ruler who also traced his ancestry from Anjou and who extended his territories to form the Angevin empire, which embraced England, Normandy, Anjou and Aquitaine.

Art on the Fringes of Faith

The Scandinavian countries that had launched the Viking impetus upon Europe were now drawn increasingly into the mainstream themselves as the church established itself under German, English and, to a lesser extent, French influence. Scandinavian wooden churches, known as stave churches, became ever more elaborate and contained painted wooden retables and wooden or metalwork effigies of the Virgin and crucifixes, such as that of c. 1140 at Tirstrup, Jutland. Such regional works are often imbued with a vigour and character all their own. One such area that gave rise to its own distinctive form of Romanesque – enriched by the retention of strong indigenous tradition – was Ireland, which fused Celtic, Viking and Norman stylistic elements to produce marvellously intricate and robust works such as the Cross of Cong.[9] What might almost be thought of as folk piety could also give rise to simple but supremely moving expressions of the grand international style, seen in works such as the large wooden crucifixes of Spain and Germany, which compel the viewer to identify with Christ's humanity and suffering on their account.

Such political webs wove into their very fabric the warp and weft of complex international relations and of cultural exchange, which unfolded into the Central Middle Ages and what is now known as the Gothic age.

154

Gilt bronze crucifix, c. 1140, a regional Scandinavian expression of Romanesque style. Tirstrup, Jutland, Denmark.

Monastic Aesthetics and the Rise of Gothic Art

Professor Conrad Rudolph

Shortly before the end of his life, Suger (c. 1085–1151), abbot of the great monastery of Saint-Denis, then a good half-day's walk north of Paris, wrote a strikingly detailed account of the lavish works of art of his ancient abbey. More unusual still, he then went on to describe the reaction he sometimes had to gazing upon them:

> When, at times – from love of the beauty of the house of God – the splendour of the many-colored gems has called me away from my cares, and fitting meditation has induced me to reflect upon the diversity of the sacred virtues, being transported from the material to the immaterial, I seem to see myself lingering, as it were, in some strange region of the planet that is neither completely in the impurity of this world nor entirely in the purity of heaven, and I seem to be able to be transported, by the gift of God, from this lower world to that higher one in an anagogical manner.

A fair idea of what Suger had been gazing upon is given from a fifteenth-century painting of the main altar of Saint-Denis, the closest we can ever come to a colour photograph of the interior of that famous church in the abbot's time.

Suger was perhaps the second most influential figure in the very influential world of monastic politics of mid-twelfth-century France, and the statement he quite consciously recorded for posterity was certainly expected to resonate with the majority of the monastic public. A considerably different attitude, however, was expressed by one of Suger's close contemporaries and occasional political ally, Bernard of Clairvaux (1090–1154), a Cistercian abbot who was unquestionably the most influential monastic figure of the day. After a description of liturgical art every bit as observant as Suger's, the great writer and preacher then went on to share his own very different reaction with his fellow monks:

> But we who have withdrawn from the people, we who have left behind all that is precious and beautiful in this world for the sake of Christ, we who regard as dung all things shining in beauty... whose devotion, I ask, do we strive to excite in all this?... The compunction of penitents, or the astonishment of those who gaze at it? O vanity of vanities, but no more vain than insane!... What are these things to poor men, to monks, to spiritual men?

We can still get a very good sense of the sort of monastic church environment Bernard held up as ideal from a glance at the interior of the Cistercian church of Fontenay, a place founded by Bernard himself and one whose interior decoration has probably changed relatively little since the mid-twelfth century, unlike the vast majority of other surviving Medieval churches.

The texts from which these two passages come are perhaps the most important written sources we have from the entire Middle Ages on the Medieval attitude towards art. They are both monastic, they were both written around the same time, they both come from the same general intellectual environment, and they are both by men who knew each other well. Originating in a profession that is famous for the uniformity of its conceptual basis,

Abbot Suger celebrating the Eucharist in his Cathedral of St Denis, reconstructed in a fifteenth-century Flemish painting by the Master of St Gilles, *The Mass of St Gilles*, c. 1500. National Gallery, London.

education, and thought over the millennia, the question arises as to what motivated these two very different monastic aesthetics, and what effect they had on the wider world of medieval artistic culture.

Already, before its widespread establishment in the early fourth century, Christianity had become so integrated into mainstream culture that it was believed by some to be in danger of losing its original values. Those who felt that a communal life of self-denial constituted the most effective

expression of Christian principles began to 'flee the world' to 'flee to the desert' (since this first took place on a large scale in Egypt), where they formed themselves into communities practising constant prayer. This was the beginning of monasticism, a communal life of celibate self-denial in which the material was to be rejected in favour of the immaterial. In regard to art, this encouraged an attitude that saw the material work of art as inhibiting progress towards the immaterial divine

on the part of the spiritual person. But since no doctrinal or theological position on the use of art had been articulated by the church in the West in the Middle Ages – there was only a vague formulation of long-standing tradition by Gregory the Great in 600 CE that permitted the use of art to educate the illiterate, including the spiritually illiterate, and the more cautious approach to the use of images expressed in the Carolingian *Libri Carolini* – actual practice remained local and individual.

The period of the Early Middle Ages was an enormously turbulent one. As the old structure of the Roman empire fell apart, the integrity of the secular church often crumbled with it. The monastic wing of the church, however, was frequently able to maintain its standards. This caused it to become increasingly integrated into secular society, despite the fact that it had fled 'the world'. In fact, it was precisely because it had fled the world that it soon became the most prestigious practitioner of the Cult of the Dead, the complex system of prayers and liturgies performed for the souls of the dead. The most prominent benefactors of the Cult of the Dead were kings, their families and nobles, who often gave great gifts of land to be commemorated in it. In regard to art, much of the wealth that came into the monasteries this way was 'reinvested' in those works of art that aggrandized the Cult – typically liturgical art, sometimes more broadly called the minor or precious arts.

As society slowly began to stabilize itself, the economy improved, a money economy became re-established, and the common people became increasingly free. As one manifestation of their new freedoms, those of common birth sought to improve their own chances of spiritual salvation, just as the aristocracy had. And one way they did this was by participating in the Cult of Relics, the veneration of some aspect of the physical presence of the holy on earth, usually in the form of pilgrimage to the remains of a miracle-working saint. Unable to give large tracts of land like the nobles, these commoners gave small amounts of money that, because of the greater number of givers, added up significantly. Just as a portion of the income from the Cult of the Dead had been

reinvested into that form of art that most enhanced it in the eyes of its lay public, so a part of the income from the Cult of Relics was now reinvested in those forms of art that enhanced this Cult: monumental architecture, painting and sculpture. The pilgrims who had travelled so hard and so far expected to see something. And while the church denied, theologically, that the holy could be localized, practically speaking, the creation of massive programmes of lavish art greatly contributed to the sense of the physical presence of the holy at the great pilgrimage churches in the popular conception. Indeed, the sources show that there was a very strong awareness on the part of many churches of the role – even the necessity – of art in the pilgrimage, one of the greatest manifestations of popular spirituality of the Middle Ages.

Eventually, the great successes of the Cult of the

Dead and the Cult of Relics, the twin foundations of the monastic economy, brought such wealth into many of the monasteries that a 'crisis of prosperity' ensued. Monasticism had been so successful that it was in danger of losing its integrity in the eyes of some. Soon, a new reform movement sprang up that challenged traditional monasticism on a number of issues. The most articulate of the new monastic reformers was the charismatic Bernard of Clairvaux. And those issues to which he gave the greatest weight – the 'things of greater importance', as he called them – were not the usual points of contention related to daily monastic life but a series of criticisms of the use of art by monasticism arising from its relatively newly exploited source of income, the Cult of Relics. With wonderful style and penetrating insight, Bernard incisively attacked the monastic investment in art, the sensory saturation of the holy place (particularly through excess in material and craftsmanship), the manipulation through art of the equation between excessive art and holiness in the popular conception, expenditure on art rather than on the care of the poor, and art as a spiritual distraction to the monk.

Under the general influence of Bernard, his own order, the Cistercians, confronted the question of the use of art by monks in a systematic way. In theory, they refused to participate in the Cult of the Dead, either by accepting burials of wealthy nobles or through the use of excessive liturgical art. Similarly, at least in theory and at least in the beginning, they refused to allow the development of the Cult of Relics at their monasteries, and legislated against the use of the monumental figural art that had become such an integral part of the pilgrimage. And they tried, by law, to radically limit the use of art because of its potential for spiritual distraction. The result was Fontenay and hundreds of churches like it; in essence perhaps not so different from many other monasteries that had come before, but now institutionalized through 'unchanging' legislation. In a sense, this was the artistic equivalent of fleeing to the desert, as their predecessors had done so many centuries before in Early Christian Egypt.

While traditional monasticism did not have to accept the strident artistic asceticism of the Cistercians and others like them, it did have to address the issues so publicly raised if it wished to appear contemporary. The definitive response, according to the working out of history, was the art programme of Suger at Saint-Denis. Suger's natural instinct was an aesthetic of excess, something suggested by the painting mentioned earlier. But in addressing the challenges of artistic asceticism, he found it useful to respond with an art that claimed to be 'accessible only to the *litterati*' – that is, intellectually accessible only to the literate choir monk (or *litteratus*, in twelfth-century monastic terminology, which equates to 'fully Latinate and culturally aware') – and not to the visiting pilgrim, whose pilgrimage art Bernard felt upset the spiritual ecology of the monastery. In striking this balance between excess and justification, Suger did three things that were to have important consequences for the history of art. First, he put a new emphasis on visual exegesis (the use of visual art to expound the typologies of the Old and New Testaments) – something that could claim to be the equivalent of scriptural study. Second, he greatly developed the medium of the stained glass window, an art form that had been around for centuries but that had never been fully exploited. Third, he multiplied and systematized the sculpture of the church portal, the primary point of interaction between the church's programme of imagery and the lay public. The result was the artistic movement known as Gothic.

It certainly meant little to Suger that there was a contradiction here: that the complex works of art that claimed to be intellectually accessible to monks alone were also quite visually accessible to the hordes of pilgrims who flocked to Saint-Denis. Bernard, however, must have been more than a little alarmed that the appeal of the newly exploited stained glass window was so powerful that the Cistercians themselves were forced to legislate against its use within their Order even in his own life time. With these developments by Suger, the leading edge of artistic development shifted from the elite, rural monasteries to the secular, urban cathedrals. The age of the dominance of the monastic aesthetic – of whatever kind – was over. But it had only been as a direct result of the controversy over art within monasticism, with its multiple spiritualities and multiple aesthetics, that this new form of artistic expression, Gothic, had come about.

13

Gothic

Cathedrals, Universities and Urbanization

The Gothic age extends broadly from the mid- or late-twelfth century (depending on area) until the permeation throughout Europe of humanist scholarship and the artistic movement known as the Renaissance, which occurred at varying times in different regions but had generally taken root by the early sixteenth century. The term was first coined by the art critic Vasari (1511–74) to describe what he viewed as barbaric art produced under Germanic rule between the fall of the Roman empire and the Renaissance. Whereas the monasteries were the main foci of artistic production and commission during the preceding age, Gothic art was generated primarily in the urban environment of cathedrals, universities, guilds, communes and mercantile middle classes, and in the court milieux and manors of the aristocracy and rural gentry. The creativity of monks and nuns was increasingly augmented by that of specialist lay craftspeople, clerks in minor orders and the friars.

The Rise of the Gothic Style

Suger's building programme and beautification of Saint-Denis is now seen as a major stimulus to the movement that commenced in the Île-de-France in the mid-twelfth century, producing works such as the Royal Portal at Notre Dame de Chartres (1145–55) with its elegant elongated biblical figures in the form of supporting columns, derived ultimately from classical caryatids. This period also witnessed the rise of scholasticism, in which methods of examining philosophical and theoretical questions were developed and reason was exercised in an attempt to reconcile differing theological viewpoints. Schools grew up around influential teachers such as Abelard and Hugh of Saint-Victor, and those of the abbey of Saint-Victor and the cathedral of Notre Dame de Paris gave rise to the foundation of its university. The reintroduction of Aristotelian logic around 1200, as a result of contact with the scholarship of Islam, provided a basis for its syllabus, although it was treated with caution by the friars. Other major universities included Bologna (with its emphasis upon law), Salerno (which specialized in medicine), Oxford, Cambridge, Heidelberg and Prague. Such intellectual centres fostered the book trade and, as towns burgeoned, trade guilds were formed which guarded their prerogatives and promoted specialization in the arts and crafts. A drift from the land, which increased throughout the age, brought more people to towns seeking to earn money, and to spend it. Their spiritual needs had to be catered for, as well as their material ones.

While pastoral care was undertaken at the parish level, there had been a growing disillusionment with the church and its personnel, who were often criticized for abuses and avarice. Heresy and dissent became a major problem for the papacy during the twelfth century. Most dissenters were condemned by church authorities, but two were recognized during the early thirteenth century by Pope Innocent III as potentially valuable tools and became saints rather than sinners. These were two young noblemen, one from Italy, the other from Spain – namely Francis of Assisi and Dominic Guzman. Their popular preaching skills and their commitment to embracing poverty and chastity within the world, rather than the cloister, made them an invaluable conduit into people's lives, especially within the towns, and formidable allies in combatting heretics such as the Cathars of south-west France. Scholarship and the arts were considered valuable components in their roles as spiritual confessors and counsellors, and the friars who belonged to these mendicant orders – the Franciscans (Grey Friars), the Dominicans (Black Friars), the Austin (Augustinian) friars and the Carmelites (White Friars) – often acted as authors, scribes and artists, especially the Dominicans who prized learning as a defence against heresy.

The rationalism and nascent humanism prevalent around 1200 combined, in artistic terms, with an interest in the naturalism and classicism of contemporary Byzantine Comnene art, especially following the sack of Constantinople by Crusaders in 1204 and the consequent influx of Byzantine art into Europe. Late twelfth-century Western artworks such as the Winchester Bible, the Westminster Psalter and the Trivulzio Candlestick (Milan Cathedral) from England (the latter so classicizing that manufacture in Milan or Lorraine has also been credibly postulated), the frescoes of Sigena in Spain, and the sculptures of the Île-de-France

(such as the portals of Senlis and Chartres) assume a calm, monumental tranquillity in their figures, which are well-proportioned and modelled in accordance with classical artistic principles. By the 1230s, when the west façade of Reims Cathedral began to be carved, figures such as those of the Virgin and St Elizabeth, who greet one another at the Visitation, resemble Graeco-Roman matrons with their serene classicizing visages and draperies sculpted to suggest the underlying human forms. The famous smiling angel that graces another part of the building, however, is

West portal, c. 1170, Senlis Cathedral, France. Christ in Majesty, with evangelist symbols, apostles, prophets and Old Testament figures.

The Smiling Angel, c. 1230,
Reims Cathedral.

imbued with a sweetness and whimsy that is pure Gothic. The influence of French
portal sculpture pervaded Europe, inspiring that of German cathedrals such as
Strasbourg (now in Alsace, France), with its elegant figures such as those of Ecclesia
and blindfolded Synagogue, Bamberg, Regensburg, Cologne and Naumburg;
English cathedrals such as Salisbury, Lincoln and Exeter; the Bohemian cathedral of
Prague; and Spanish cathedrals such as Seville, Burgos and Grenada. Italian
architecture and, to a lesser extent, its art also went through a Gothic phase, but
Italy was always a law unto itself and is considered separately (see Chapter 14).

The Gothic Cathedrals: Theology in Stone

The rise of the towns led to ambitious building programmes for their cathedrals,
the carved exteriors of Amiens, Chartres, Reims and Notre Dame de Paris
embodying a complete theological syllabus in stone. Saint-Denis had introduced a
new aesthetic of lighter structures with ribbed vaulting (developed from
Romanesque experiments with vault and dome construction) supported on
pointed, rather than round, arches which enabled greater height and window space
to be achieved. These ambitious buildings were the work of the master masons, the
architects of their day, who took a practical hands-on approach to their work. Some
even died on the job, such as William of Sens who plummeted from the scaffolding
of his masterpiece – the east end of Canterbury Cathedral. This airy structure is

RIGHT: South rose window, with
Christ in Majesty (centre)
surrounded by angels and elders
of the Apocalypse, with the Virgin
and Child and evangelists,
supported by the Old Testament
prophets Jeremiah, Isaiah, Ezekiel
and Daniel below, 1221–30,
Chartres Cathedral, France.

characterized, like that at Saint-Denis, by its lightness. Its many windows are filled with an extensive programme of stained glass, inserted during the late twelfth century, which narrates the Life of Christ, Old Testament episodes, and the lives of saints, notably that of Thomas Becket upon whom its pilgrim trade relied. The influence of illumination can be clearly traced in the lively compositions and glowing jewel-like colours of the glass, with its rich primary colours. The windows of Chartres Cathedral, glazed over three decades beginning around 1200, form a theological encyclopedia in glass, composed with reference to scholarly texts. A mystical realm of light was created that would have appealed to the sensuous approach of Suger and pained Bernard; indeed, the Cistercians legislated against its use in their churches. A rare example of the sort of working sketches used in designing glass may be the Guthlac Roll of around 1210–20, which carries a series of roundels containing outline drawings illustrating the Life of St Guthlac, an Anglo-Saxon warrior-prince turned hermit, whose visions of heaven and hell helped prepare the way for Gothic grotesques and the visionary genre that would later inspire Dante and Bosch. The drawing style harks back to Anglo-Saxon work and regained popularity largely due to its use in the second quarter of the thirteenth century by the chronicler-monk of St Alban's Abbey, Matthew Paris, who illustrated his own texts with lively marginal images.

A rare survival of an important sketchbook that gives a valuable insight into the thoughts and working practices of the Gothic artist is that compiled by Villard de Honnecourt in the 1220s. No buildings have been attributed to him, but he was obviously a gifted and well-educated mason, draughtsman and sculptor who worked in the Cambrai area. He tells us that he had spent time travelling, including a spell in Hungary, and that he designed the rose window of Lausanne Cathedral, and his sketches relate to the architecture and sculpture of northern French cathedrals such as Laon and Chartres, Vaucelles and Cambrai. He was familiar with Latin, the works of the Roman architect Vitruvius and the principles of geometry, and with mechanical devices for surveying, stone-cutting and proportions for the construction of figures; and his designs indicate reference to models such as ivories and illuminated bestiaries, as well as architecture and its ornament. The Gothic artist could evidently be a talented all-rounder as well as a commercial specialist.

The various arts came together to stunning effect in the Sainte Chapelle in Paris, constructed to contain the prized relic of the Crown of Thorns by the Capetian King Louis IX (reigned 1226–70), later canonized for his piety and good governance. Its walls are almost completely transparent, with tall lancet windows of glowing glass, and its vaulting columns and walls are covered with rich paint effects and gilded symbols of the royal fleur-de-lys. The chapel would have

RIGHT: A reliquary in stone and glass: the interior of the upper chapel of the Sainte Chapelle, Paris, completed in 1248 for King Louis the Pious of France to contain the relic of the Crown of Thorns.

166

La Somme le Roy ('The Dream of the King'), dedicated by Frère Laurent in 1279 to King Louis IX, illuminated by Maître Honoré, late thirteenth century, Paris.

TOP LEFT: Sobriety, a crowned female figure standing on a bear (inscribed above '*sobriete*').

TOP RIGHT: Gluttony, a youth seated at a full table, vomits (inscribed above '*gloutonnie*').

LEFT: A seated man cuts a loaf, while a dog waits expectantly, typifying sobriety, and the sharing of the Word with the Gentiles – the crumbs from the table.

CENTRE: Dives and a female companion dine at table. He gestures to his steward who bars the way to Lazarus, dressed as a pilgrim, two dogs licking his sores.

BOTTOM: a depiction of Dives in Hell (inscribed '*le riche homme auer*').

contained similarly opulent metalwork, ivories, textiles and illuminated manuscripts. It resembles a precious metalwork reliquary in stone, recalling pieces such as the Becket Chasse, containing relics of Thomas Becket, a fine thirteenth-century example of the popular colourful champlevé enamelwork produced at Limoges. The Sainte Chapelle stimulated competition from Louis's English rival, King Henry III, with whom he contested control of English territories in France, who began rebuilding Edward the Confessor's royal abbey at Westminster as a symbol of his own Christian monarchy. His tomb effigy that resides there is in courtly French style. A rare survival at Westminster is a retable, painted in the thirteenth century and set within a wooden and gesso (plasterwork) frame emulating jewels and cameos, in Italianate fashion. Other major building campaigns were undertaken at several English cathedrals during the thirteenth century, among the most inspiring of which are Salisbury and St Hugh's Choir at Lincoln, which heralded the angel ceilings of Medieval English churches, their roofs borne upon celestial wings.

Illuminating the Bible in Gothic Art

Many scholarly works were dedicated to St Louis, such as the *Speculum Maius* of the Dominican scholar Vincent de Beauvais, completed around 1250 and arranging all possible knowledge in three branches – naturale, doctrinale and historiale – as a mirror (*speculum*) of reality up to the time that Louis set off to lead the Seventh Crusade. Another was *La Somme le Roy*,[1] written in the form of a king's dream concerning good and bad conduct, by the friar Frère Laurent. A copy – perhaps presented to the king himself – was illuminated by the leading Parisian painter of the day, Maître Honoré, in the supremely elegant, courtly style associated with the French court during the thirteenth century. It contrasts virtues with vices, such as temperance with gluttony, or charity with avarice, in a painted moralistic lecture. The connection that St Louis and his contemporaries made in their minds between beauty and good works is made explicit by the Medieval historian Jean de Joinville, who describes Louis's programme of building thus:

> '*Like the scribe who has finished his book and illuminates it in blue and gold, so the king illuminated his kingdom with a host of hospitals and monasteries for Dominicans, Franciscans and other orders…*'

Like others who witnessed the impact of warfare and disease on crusade, Louis was inspired to found charitable hospitals in Paris and the provinces.

The *Bible Moralisée*, in which Old and New Testament scenes are paralleled in a theological juxtaposition known as typology. Paris, mid-thirteenth century.

168

THE LION COMPANION TO CHRISTIAN ART

Maître Honoré ran a workshop on Rue Boutebrie, one of thirteen prominent Parisian ateliers of illumination known from tax records dating from the second half of the thirteenth century. Such masters, like the later artist Van Dyke, employed assistants trained in their style to enable more commissions to be fulfilled. In such towns commissions were generally channelled through stationers (the *librarius*, also known in Italy as *cartolai*), who sold materials for the making of books and who subcontracted the work to a number of specialists living in nearby streets: scribes, illuminators concentrating on borders and other minor decoration, and figural artists skilled in major decoration and miniatures, gilders and binders. The entrepreneurial stationer would discuss the project with the patron, unless they could be sold something from stock, and would carefully cost all the various components, down to the sort of script used and the size and colour of the minor initials. Some of their clients were students, buying books for study or professional reference, such as the *Livre de Chirurgerie* made in Paris around 1300, which illustrates treatments for ailments from dislocated shoulders to frontal lobotomies, paralleling the medical procedure with scenes from the life of Christ in an holistic approach to spiritual/psychological as well as physical well-being. Each friar who graduated was equipped with a Bible to inform their preaching, and they and other students of theology would wish to possess a copy of the Paris Study Bible, a small, portable volume (resembling modern printed Bibles in format) using tiny script and minute historiated initials to convey the entirety of scripture. Parisian theological studies also produced, around 1240–50, the *Bible Moralisée*[2] – a lavish work containing some five thousand biblical scenes arranged in eight roundels per page accompanied by captions. Their arrangement is derived from the typological comparison of Old and New Testament scenes based on commentaries going back to Hrabanus Maurus and the Carolingian Period and from there back to St Jerome. During the fourteenth and fifteenth centuries another heavily illustrated form of bible appeared – the *Biblia Pauperum*, or 'Poor Man's Bible' – ironically often lavishly illuminated for wealthy patrons – in which the Bible story is narrated solely by pictures captioned in the vernacular. Such didactic tools were probably used to teach both children and adults, the deeper meaning being explained to them by their confessors.

Layfolk also wished to participate in a growing popular piety. For centuries the Psalter had formed the basis of both liturgical and private prayer, and its recitation formed a mainstay of the monastic divine office, being intoned along with lections eight times every day and night at appointed hours (matins, lauds, prime, terce, sext, nones, compline and vespers). Around 1240 an Oxford artist, William de Brailes, who ran a workshop with his wife Selina in Catte Street near what is now

Mary of Burgundy reading from her book of hours before her namesake, the Virgin Mary, and Child, from the Hours of Mary of Burgundy, Ghent or Bruges, before 1482, probably late 1470s.

the Bodleian Library, produced an example of a new devotional manual that was to become the Medieval bestseller – the Book of Hours. This brought together abbreviated versions of the devotions of the hours, such as the Little Hours of the Virgin, the Hours of the Cross, and the Office of the Dead, accompanying them with calendars and litanies celebrating the saints – some of them universal and some local to the place of manufacture or specific to the devotional preferences of patrons or makers. The genre spread throughout Europe but enjoyed particular vogue in England, France and the Netherlands and was especially favoured by women. Outstanding examples include: the Hours of Mary of Burgundy,[3] who died in 1482 and is depicted therein before the Virgin, reading from her book which is held in a protective chemise binding; and the *Bedford Hours*,[4] commissioned from a leading Parisian artist, the Bedford Master, in 1423 by John, Duke of Bedford, brother of King Henry V of England and regent of France on behalf of the young Henry VI. It celebrated his marriage to Anne of Burgundy, cementing an alliance that would ensure the immediate future of English rule in France, and this is reflected in its inclusion of unusual iconographies such as the marriage of King David and Bathsheba. Perhaps the most famous and beautiful, however, are the *Très Riches Heures of Jean, Duc de Berri*,[5] illuminated in the Burgundian version of the 'International Gothic' style by the Limbourg brothers and interrupted by their death during an epidemic in 1416. Many artists won renown for their work on such high profile commissions during the fourteenth and fifteenth centuries, including: the French illuminators Jean Pucelle, the 'Boucicaut Master', Jean Fouquet, Simon Marmion and Jean Poyet; the Netherlandish painters Gherard Horenbout, Gerard David and Simon Bening; and the Rhenish artist Hermann Scheere who worked in London.

Another leading English illuminator was the Dominican John Siferwas, who led the work on the largest and most opulent servicebook of the Middle Ages, the Sherborne Missal,[6] made for the Benedictine Abbey of St Mary's, Sherborne, Dorset, around 1400–07. It contains all the texts necessary for the performance of the Mass throughout the church year, along with some of the music accompanied by lifelike

The Sherborne Missal,
Crucifixion illuminated in
the 'International Gothic'
style by the Dominican
John Siferwas, Benedictine
Abbey of St Mary's,
Sherborne, Dorset.

GOTHIC

The Wilton Diptych, depicting Richard II presented to the Virgin by his Patron Saint John the Baptist and Saints Edward and Edmund, English (or possibly French), 1395–99.

depictions of the British birds who form a choir of their own to sing along. The Sherborne Missal is a fine example of the Late Medieval style known as International Gothic, owing to its conflation of stylistic and iconographic elements from various regions, its crucifixion miniature combining the courtly French and English style, the lively crowd scenes of Burgundian and Netherlandish art, and a swooning Virgin whose substantial form is reminiscent of Giotto's work in Italy while her female companions recall that of Simone Martini. This influential Late Medieval style, which developed from around 1350 onwards, favoured naturalism and close observation of details of dress and the like. Simone Martini and the school of Avignon in southern France, where the papacy spent time in exile during a contest for power with the Holy Roman empire, played an important role in opening a two-way street of cultural influence between France and Italy. Pisanello and Gentile di Fabriano carried International Gothic to Italian city-states such as Rome and Florence. Bohemia had also played an important part in the evolution of the movement, but itself continued to favour a sentimental 'soft style' (*weiche stil*), featuring sweet, tender female figures in charming settings, such as the *Garden of*

172

THE LION COMPANION TO CHRISTIAN ART

Paradise of c. 1420 in Frankfurt. The style rapidly spread to towns such as Nuremburg and Cologne, serving in turn to soften German art. Northern expressions of International Gothic style, with their ultra-realism of landscape, interiors and figures, even spread to Spain and Portugal, and the Portuguese *Genealogy*,[7] emphasizing the links between the Portuguese and English monarchies, was commissioned from Simon Bening in the far off Spanish Netherlands.

John Siferwas left six portraits of himself in the Sherborne Missal, alongside the one hundred or so of his patron Abbot Robert Bruyning, and others of the Benedictine scribe, John Whas – a poor Sherborne cottar's son – and of Richard Mitford, Bishop of Salisbury. The portrait proper had appeared in the fourteenth century, with the heads by Peter Parler in the choir of Prague Cathedral. Claus Sluter's sculptures at the Abbey of Champmol, Dijon, around 1402 are similarly veristic. Bohemian art enjoyed particular influence during the later part of the century, after Emperor Charles IV (reigned 1316–29) established his court there. It even reached England, partly through the agency of Anne of Bohemia, wife of King Richard II (1367–1400), who is thought to be the young monarch depicted in the Wilton Diptych[8] being presented to the Virgin and Child by his patron saints, and accompanied by his emblem, the white hart.

Women as Patrons and Scribes

The desire of women to lead active spiritual and God-centred lives made them enthusiastic patrons of Christian art, and of books of hours, vernacular prayer books and homiletic literature in particular. They became anchoresses or joined religious orders, including mendicants such as the Poor Clares and the Beguines (their male equivalents were Beghards), communities of relatively wealthy urban women who lived together in beguinages (mini villages within towns) following an ascetic lifestyle and ministering to the care of the sick, including lepers, and the poor. They flourished particularly in Belgium, Holland and Cologne. They and their secular counterparts would have owned many of the numerous books of hours made in these areas. Women also continued to make books, either in the scriptoria of convents or as laywomen within the towns, for despite the restrictive guild regulations which jealously guarded the rights and areas of activity of the various crafts, the limners' and stationers' guilds were uniquely liberal in permitting women to inherit workshops from their fathers and husbands and to continue to run them. One such was Christine de Pisan who, following the loss of her menfolk to an epidemic, set about earning her living as an author, scribe and publisher in early fifteenth-century Paris. The traditional female preserves of embroidery and tapestry also moved into a wider commercial milieu during the Gothic period, with French and Flemish weavers producing imposing wall tapestries (essential insulation) on religious, mythological and allegorical themes – such as the Lady and the Unicorn sequence in the Musée de Cluny, Paris, made in the late fifteenth century for Jean le Viste of Lyon and based upon the bestiary theme of the unicorn, which could only be captured when it rested its horn in the lap of a virgin!

Life on the Edge: Reading Images on the Margins of Gothic Art

Gothic psalters are more often associated with liturgical use and with male patronage. One whose production was also probably halted by the patron's death and by the outbreak of the bubonic plague that swept across Europe in 1348 was the Luttrell Psalter.[9] This was commissioned by Sir Geoffrey Luttrell (1276–1345), lord of the manor of Irnham in Lincolnshire, a member of the English nobility on the borderline between the baron and the rural squire, and was intended to serve as his memorial. It has certainly kept his name alive. The book is remarkable in incorporating scenes depicting the entirety of life on the Medieval estate and including the ordinary workers as well as their lord and his family. The two Dominican or Austin friars depicted feasting with the Luttrell family may have been involved in planning and making the book for other fourteenth-century bibliophiles, the Bohuns, who kept Austin artists on a retainer at their castle of Pleshey in Essex. The composition of the scene is intended to recall that of the Last Supper on a preceding page, with Sir Geoffrey presiding in priestly fashion as he holds the chalice to his lips in an eternal celestial feast. The style of the painting is robust and the margins are inhabited by fantastic hybrid creatures (grotesques or *babewyns* – the Middle English origin of 'baboon') which represent the forces of chaos that prowl the borders of consciousness, ever ready to pounce unless God (and in this case, his earthly representative at a local level – Sir Geoffrey) ensures stability and safety. The liminal space of the margins is also home to beggars, the disabled, and the troubadours and peddlers who travelled within and yet without of society, serving a variety of moralizing didactic functions and reflecting the mendicants' preaching of charity and social inclusion. On a far less positive note, however, images of Saracens and Jews also occur, coloured blue and with caricatured grotesque features – then prevalent Western Gothic conventions for depicting otherness – some of them defaced by rubbing by generations of readers' fingers, intent on eradicating evil. Such trends are amongst the low points of religious art and, acceptable in their day, are now lamented.

Tribulacionem + dolorem inueni:
nomen domini inuocaui.

Grotesques appear in all sorts of nooks and crannies in churches and cathedrals, including the underside of the bottom-rests for monks and clergy in their choir stalls – misericords. This somewhat undignified location lent itself to the scatological and unseemly, and many humorous and ribald subjects are to be found under these wooden ledges.

Images depicting aspects of religious belief surrounded the people of the Gothic age. Frescoes continued to be painted, an outstanding example being the painted ceiling of St Sevin, Poitiers. Rood screens were erected and chantry chapels and side altars constructed and equipped for the commemoration of the dead and in honour of the saints. These images took many forms: there is evidence of illuminated altarpieces on vellum, such as an early fourteenth-century example from Croatia now in the British Library;[10] many altarpieces were made, of which the most elaborate was the German *Schnitzaltar*, the most striking and influential of which is the Isenheim Altar painted by Grünewald with sculpture by Nikolaus von Hagenau; and free-standing statues of saints and of the Virgin and Child were carved in stone, wood, ivory and alabaster, in which latter craft Nottingham specialized. Gothic styles of sculpted and painted wooden artworks also spread to Scandinavia, where some remarkable examples have survived; those of England were largely destroyed by seventeenth-century puritans. Metalwork reliquaries and liturgical book covers abounded. Jewellery and rosary beads carried tiny iconographic scenes. Encaustic tiles carried images and symbols. The skill of the embroiderers can be seen on altar frontals, clerical vestments and book bindings,

The Luttrell family, their Dominican friar confessors / artists, and their servants at the New Year feast, which is intended to resemble the Last Supper and signal their participation in the eternal feast, from the Luttrell Psalter, 1330s–40s, Irnham and Norwich or Lincoln.

German *Schnitzaltar* altarpiece, by M. and G. Erhart, 1483–84, Blaubeuren Abbey, Germany.

with English women excelling in the production of *opus anglicanum*, and textiles such as silk were also painted. One textile that has proved particularly intriguing is the Turin Shroud (or *Sacro Sindone*, now in Turin Cathedral), which was first documented in the diocese of Troyes in 1360 and has been radio-carbon dated to around the fourteenth century, despite claims that it carries the imprint of Christ's body and was his winding sheet. Ivory carving also flourished, and was especially favoured for small devotional objects, such as tiny polyptychs, the covers of wax writing tablets, caskets and mirror cases. Scenes from the lives of Christ, the Virgin and saints were popular narrative themes for the adornment of such items, as were subjects imbued with a moralistic interpretation, such as the virtues and vices and the bestiary.

177

The lover seeks entry to the garden, symbolizing virginity and virtue, from the *Roman de la Rose* by Guillaume de Lorris and Jean de Meun, southern Netherlands (Bruges), c. 1490–1500.

These were also popular subjects of manuscript illumination, as were the more secular tales that appealed to an increasingly literate urban lay audience. Among the most popular of these was Arthurian literature, especially the *Roman du Saint Graal* by Chrétien de Troyes (although the genre has earlier British roots), and the *Roman de la Rose*[11] by Jean de Meun. Although part of the secular romance genre, their illustrations might properly be considered as 'Christian' in allusion, for the Arthuriana dealt with themes such as temptation, trials of virtue and the quest for the goal of redemption, symbolized by the Holy Grail – the cup used by Christ at the Last Supper and in which his blood was collected at the crucifixion and allegedly brought to Britain by Joseph of Arimathea. The *Roman de la Rose* is framed around the concept of the *hortus conclusus*, the enclosed garden that symbolized virginity, to which the lover seeks entry in order to pluck the rose – the beloved/virtue. An outstandingly fine copy was made in the late fifteenth century for Prince Engelbert of Nassau and depicts the tale in contemporary courtly setting.

For the Medieval mind made no distinction between the religious and the secular; faith pervaded every aspect of life, and of death. These can be seen in stark complementarity in one of the most beautiful and poignant of Late Medieval works, the *Hours of Joanna the Mad*,[12] daughter of Ferdinand and Isabella of Spain, who married the most eligible prince of the age, Philip the Fair of Burgundy, who was killed at the joust, causing her to lose her mind with grief. This exquisite little book was her solace during the long years of effective confinement in the family palaces. It was painted in Ghent or Bruges in the early sixteenth century by Simon Bening, the leading illuminator of the Spanish Netherlands. His depictions of urban and rural scenes in the labours of the months accompanying the calendar offer the most vivid evocation of Late Medieval life, from harvesters taking their lunch breaks in the field to butchers' stalls in the marketplace. The main text that follows opens with a grim reminder of the ever-present spectre of death and the need to repent of one's failings, with Adam and Eve being expelled from Eden by an angel glowing with anger and disappointment facing a convex mirror (*speculum*) in which the reader beholds their image – a skull; as effective a *memento mori* (reminder of death) as one might encounter in art.

Bening's work is closely akin to that of contemporary Netherlandish panel painters and marks the transition from Late Gothic art to that of the northern Renaissance. It was fitting that it was to the Netherlands and to Italy that the English monarch Henry VII (1457–1509), founder of the Tudor dynasty, turned for the sculptures of saints that peopled the walls of his funerary chapel at the east end of Westminster Abbey: his own unnervingly lifelike tomb effigy, and that of his queen, were cast in bronze in 1517 by the Italian Renaissance artist Pietro Torrigiano. It lies staring in perpetuity at the elegant fan vaulting above – the final flourish of the Middle Ages.

Medieval Stained Glass: Patron and Purpose

Professor Virginia Raguin

Stained glass windows expressed the ideas of their makers – aesthetic, philosophical, and also personal in pre-modern Europe. Primary importance is attached to glass's association with religious and philosophical concepts concerning light. Contemporary thinkers were familiar with Old Testament references associating light with good, and darkness with God's displeasure. The very first verses of Genesis announce to the reader that 'the earth was void and empty, and darkness was upon the face of the deep', until God created light and 'saw… that it was good' (Genesis 1:4). Light was associated with knowledge and power, 'the brightness of eternal light, and the unspotted mirror of God's majesty' (Wisdom 7:26). Light also functioned as a symbol of God's protection. The apocryphal book of Wisdom proclaimed God's shepherding for the Israelites as they fled from Egypt, when 'the whole world was enlightened with a clear light'. For the impious Egyptians the opposite was true: 'over them only was spread a heavy night, an image of that darkness which was to come upon them' (Wisdom 17:19–20). New Testament references are even more explicit and allude to the nature of God… 'God is light, and in him there is no darkness at all' (1 John 1:5). The Gospel of John further associated light with the nature of Christ and the means of spiritual awakening; 'In him was life, and the life was the light of all people. The light shines in the darkness, and the darkness did not overcome it… The true light, which enlightens everyone, was coming into the world' (John 1:4–5, 9).

Neoplatonic and Augustinian philosophy during the Middle Ages conceived of creation as a process of emanations of Divine light, from the 'first radiance', Christ, down to the lowliest speck of matter. In order to ascend from the lowest to the highest, one searches for the trace of Divine light in all creatures. God is not only light, but also harmony and beauty; thus the radiant beauty of sparkling stones and stained glass became for many of this period an intimation of God's very nature and therefore important as a contemplative aid. As a transparent as well as a coloured material, glass resonated profoundly with the concepts of clarity and opacity that functioned as primary dichotomies for both moral and ontological systems. Light was transparent as it left the Creator, acquiring colour, and thus its ability to be visible, as it penetrated the material world. Thus colours can be seen as imperfections, but betray the radiance of their origin.

Suger, abbot of Saint-Denis in the mid-twelfth century (see page 157), wrote explicitly of colour, light and brilliance – all qualities of stained glass – as essential aspects of the purpose of religious architecture. He maintained that his 'delight in the beauty of the house of God – the loveliness of the many-coloured gems' allowed him to redirect his thoughts from his temporal obligations to the immaterial world of divine virtues. Such commentary on the importance of colour and light reinforces the assumption that to Medieval spectators the church was a premonition of the heavenly Jerusalem. The colours of stained glass windows corresponded to the foundations of the heavenly city (Revelation 21:19). Authors such as Marbode of Rennes (1035–1123) attributed magical powers to the colour and clarity of precious stones in works such as his *De Lapidibus*. Like other writers, he also developed symbolic commentaries linking human virtues to different stones, the 'lapidarium' in some ways complementing animal lore preserved in the Medieval bestiary. One of the most frequently quoted commentaries, and one particularly cited during the Ecclesiological revival of the nineteenth century, was by Durandus of Mende (c. 1220–96), who wrote: 'For the material church, wherein the people assemble to set forth God's holy praise, symbolizes that Holy Church which is built in Jerusalem of living stones.' References to gems as part of the building materials formed part of the texts read during the dedication rite of churches, and Suger even suggested that precious stones were placed in the foundation of the walls during the dedication of Saint-Denis.

The symbolism of stained glass windows was pervasive and even their physical properties, such as protection against the elements, gave rise to analogies. Honorius of Autun (1080–1156) explained that windows, which let in light but separate us from storms, are the doctors of the church. Durandus compared the windows' iron lattice-work to prophets and teachers. More specifically, the miracle of the Virgin Birth was likened to light passing through glass without breaking it – in the same way as the Word of God, light of the Father, penetrated the womb of the Virgin. The concept appeared in popular contexts, such as the verse play the *Miracle of Theophilus* by Rutebeuf (c. 1230–85). Mingling the tragic and the comic, the play likened Mary's virginity to seeing the sun each day, entering and leaving a window without breaking it.

Medieval literature also abounds with allusions to sensual delight similar to Suger's extolling of 'the loveliness of the many coloured gems'. The *Pearl* poet, writing in the 1380s in western England, easily displays a craft of language and precision of form similar to Saint-Denis's windows and Suger's text. *Sir Gawain and the Green Knight* is visually tactile and replete with exuberant descriptions of textiles, forms and colours, in which the challenging apparition 'glemered and glent al of grene stones'. The text of the *Pearl* bristles with vivid detail such as the gleam of gems or the glitter of light on water. In the heavenly city Christ's presence transfigures light and 'Thurgh Hym blysned the borgh al bryght' ('Through Him shone the city, all bright'). The *Pearl*'s structure, however, is the true gem. In alliterative verse, the poem

comprises 1212 lines grouped in 101 stanzas to suggest beginning and return, using skillful repetition of first and last words within each division. For the true meaning of the story, already compelling in its superficial narration, word structure and richness of the description must be seen as reciprocal.

Since the costly nature of stained glass was so linked in the twelfth and thirteenth centuries to the aesthetics of precious stones, its placement was carefully planned. In Canterbury Cathedral, the windows of the monks' choir (1179–80) were embellished with particularly complex, theological statements. These were the windows that the monks saw routinely as they gathered at fixed hours during each day to sing the Divine Office. They set an erudite programme, showing the contrast of the Old and the New Testaments, in a system called 'typology': in one window scenes from the life of Christ were aligned in the centre, while the Old Testament prototypes were set at the sides. The scene of the Adoration of the Magi is flanked on the left by an image of Solomon receiving the Queen of Sheba. She entered Jerusalem with 'a great train, and riches, and camels that carried spices' and she declared Israel blessed for its king who dispensed justice and wisdom (1 Kings 10:1–13). On the right is the scene of Joseph and his brothers. Joseph had interpreted Pharaoh's dreams of years of plenty and years of want, as a result of which he was made Egypt's governor. During the time of famine, Joseph's brothers travel from Canaan seeking the resources of grain stored up in Egypt (Genesis 42). In the centre, Christ is depicted surrounded by those who pay him homage. In strict frontality, the Virgin holds the Child in a pose reminiscent of the twelfth-century *Sedes Sapientiae* or 'throne of wisdom'. Rather than a humble stable, the Virgin is enthroned under a building topped by a pediment and with rounded arches on either side. To the left are three kings, to the right three shepherds; the central Christ Child holds the orb of the world in his left hand and blesses with his right. The image thus speaks to the monks' meditation on the power of the incarnation; Christ is both God and Human, infant in the flesh but ruler of the world he created. Revelation is brought equally to the Jews – even the lowliest of their social outcasts – represented by the shepherds, and to the Gentiles, represented by the Magi.

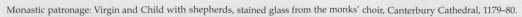

Different patrons and users set different programmes. In the late Middle Ages, society had so transformed that the laity exerted far more influence on the life of the church. An increase in population and commerce made the fifteenth century in England the era of the parish church. The church of Sts Peter and Paul that served the community of East Harling (Norfolk) was largely reconstructed and provided with stained glass between 1463 and 1480 by Anne Harling, heiress of the Gonville and Harling families. Although childless, she had previously married twice, first to Sir William Chamberlain, who was buried with her in the church. Her second husband was Sir Robert Wingfield (1432–81), Controller to the Household of Edward IV and Knight of the Shire for the county of Hertford, who was buried, according to the provisions of his will, in the church of the Black Friars in Thetford. Both husbands are depicted in the windows. Anne subsequently married John Scrope, fifth Baron Scrope of Bolton (1435–98), not imaged or buried in East Harling. Anne's tomb with that of her first husband was placed close to the altar, in a privileged position to the north side of the chancel, where Easter ceremonies involved placing the consecrated host on the tomb in a ceremony named the 'Easter Sepulchre'. The great east window contains fifteen scenes of the *Joys and Sorrows of the Virgin*, executed by the same workshop responsible for a similar window in the church of St Peter Mancroft in Norwich (Norfolk). The sequential placement of scenes focuses attention on a vivid, chronological narrative rather than theological meditation. In intimate detail, each panel appeals to the experience of the lay viewer. Most memorable may be the Visitation scene, where, after learning that she will give birth to the Saviour, the Virgin Mary journeys to help her cousin Elizabeth await the

birth of a son who will be John the Baptist. In the advanced stages of pregnancy, Elizabeth greets Mary wearing a split gown over her abdomen held together by laces. Such homely details would have importance for a society where female social bonds were vital in the birthing of children and the care of the mother and infant.

The spiritual emphases and chosen iconographic routes for contemplation and comprehension may have been different for the monks of late twelfth-century Christ Church Canterbury and for a wealthy fifteenth-century laywoman, but images illumined by celestial light spoke eloquently to them all, as they still can today.

14

Italian Gothic

Art and the Seeds of Rebirth

Italy has tended to be something of a law unto itself where the development of art is concerned. In architectural terms Milan is the only cathedral that can be considered fully 'Gothic' in style. Elsewhere the Romanesque, with its classical allusions, lingered on until the Renaissance, although there are a few smaller Gothic churches and some Franciscan and Dominican edifices, such as Sta Croce and Sta Maria Novella in Florence, which introduce northern features such as the pointed arch. Simplicity and space were valued and walls often remained solid rather than pierced by large stained glass windows, leaving more scope for frescoes in structures such as the three-tier church at Assisi, commenced in 1228. Some of the greatest painters to adorn church walls are also thought to have been architects – such as Giotto. The fashion for lavishly adorned west façades and portals certainly caught on, however, combined with the retention of Lombardic arcading. Detached bell towers known as campaniles and baptisteries also offered scope for such rhythmic surface decoration and sculptural embellishment. Bologna Cathedral has fine portal sculpture, in French fashion, added around 1400 by Jacopo della Quercia whose work is, however, more properly considered part of the Renaissance. Siena Cathedral's sculpted façade was begun between 1284–97 by an artist whose work epitomizes Italian Gothic – Giovanni Pisano (born c. 1245).

Nicola and Giovanni Pisano and Italian Gothic Sculpture

Nicola Pisano (c. 1220/5–before 1284) and his son Giovanni transformed the sculpture of central Italy, introducing a classical naturalism and a northern sense of emotive content. It is thought that Nicola may have originated in Apulia where, during the first half of the thirteenth century, Holy Roman Emperor Frederick II had fostered a revival of interest in the antique sculptures that littered his kingdom of Naples, recognizing the usefulness of such imperial Roman allusions in bolstering those of his own regime. Nicola studied the sarcophagi and other Roman sculptures he encountered and based some of his own figures and technique upon them. His pulpit in Pisa Baptistery, which he dated 1260 (1259, modern dating) is perhaps his greatest work – a hexagon supported on marble columns surmounted by personifications of the Virtues, the central column surrounded by grotesque figures and animals at its base. The side panels illustrate New Testament scenes, culminating in the Last Judgement. The figure style is classicizing and some of the figures in the Presentation in the Temple scene were modelled upon pagan personae on an antique vase outside the cathedral.

A masterpiece of Italian Gothic art: *Presentation* panel and overview, Pisa Baptistery pulpit, carved by Nicola Pisano in 1259 for Pisa Cathedral Baptistery.

184

During the 1260s Nicola was also awarded the important commission of carving the shrine of St Dominic for Bologna, in which members of his workshop also participated. One of these assistants was Giovanni, who collaborated with his father around this time on another pulpit for Siena Cathedral. This was octagonal, allowing more narrative panels, and here the New Testament scenes contain sequences of events and fuse the classical style with the emotional content of northern European Gothic and the style of French portal sculpture – the serene, triumphant Christ of the Pisa pulpit being here replaced by a tortured human form with horrified onlookers. This influential father-and-son team also worked on the exterior of Pisa Baptistery, introducing architectural sculpture to Tuscan art, and Giovanni carried their experiments further on the lower stages of the façade of Siena Cathedral, where the Prophets include Aristotle and Plato in their number.

Giovanni went on to carve two pulpits of his own for Sant'Andrea, Pistoia, and Pisa Cathedral. The number of scenes, the complexity of their content and their emotional impact continued to increase, although the first-hand observation of antique models persisted too. His figure of Temperance on the Pisa pulpit is based upon the Capitoline Venus.

Siena Cathedral pulpit, carved by father and son team Nicola and Giovanni Pisano, 1260. Siena Cathedral.

Italy, Crucible of Byzantine and Gothic Art

Illuminated manuscripts continued to be produced throughout the period, among the most notable of which are those painted in Bologna with its university dedicated to the study of law. Its output included not only large illustrated tomes of canon law but also liturgical and devotional books illuminated by artists who were experimenting with the depiction of the human form and the use of perspective, with foreshortening of figures and quirky views. Notable amongst them was Niccolo da Bologna. Painting in Italy during the Gothic age remained largely dominated by conservative Byzantine regional traditions. And yet it was in the fusion of these with incoming northern European artistic influence and an engagement with the substantial forms of monumental antique art that the transition to early Renaissance art lay.

The physical form of Byzantine icons, painted in tempera on wooden panels – some intended to be movable and to be displayed in various locations and carried in procession – and the tendency for icon writers to be named may have played a part in the rise of the concepts of 'the painting' as artwork and the rise of the artistic persona.

The work of Italo-Byzantine mosaicists also continued to influence artists who worked in other media, such as the Florentine Cimabue (c. 1240–c. 1302). The only work that can definitely be attributed to him is a mosaic of St John, dated 1302, in the apse of Pisa Cathedral, but he is best known as a painter and is applauded as a founder of the Renaissance, laying the foundations of 'modern' art. Cimabue combined the monumental iconic tradition and iconographies of Byzantine art with the softer emotional appeal of Gothic art. This can be seen in works usually attributed to him, such as the heavily restored enormous suspended crucifix at Sta Croce, Florence – an icon writer's interpretation of the monumental carved roods of northern Europe – and the large *Santa Trinità Madonna*[1] of c. 1285, in which the Virgin and Child can be perceived to enjoy a tender relationship (although this was not by any means alien to the Byzantine tradition, despite the distinctions that are often drawn between it and Western art, as we have seen). Other works attributed to Cimabue include: the Pisa Madonna; a crucifix in San Domenico,

Sta Croce Crucifix, attributed to Cimabue, late thirteenth century, Sta Croce, Florence.

186

Arezzo, and frescoes depicting the same theme; the life of the Virgin and evangelists, and apostolic and apocalyptic scenes in the Upper Church at Assisi; and an altarpiece of the Virgin and Child with St Francis in the Lower Church.

The Influence of International Gothic Art

Pisanello and Gentile di Fabriano (c. 1370–1427) subsequently played important roles in the importation into Italy of the International Gothic style, with its courtly naturalism. It can be seen in works such as: Gentile's *Adoration of the Kings*[2] for the

Adoration of the Kings, Gentile di Fabriano, painted for Sta Trinità, Florence, 1423.

Florentine bankers; the Strozzi, in paintings by Lorenzo Monaco; and sculptures by Ghiberti. The Sienese artist Simone Martini's time working in Avignon, from around 1334, for the exiled papal curia and its circle also served as a valuable two-way stylistic conduit between France and Italy. His San Caterina altarpiece[3] is the first 'micro-architectural polyptych' favoured by trecento painters, with a number of small, lively scenes set within a many-panelled architectural frame. Altarpieces with more than two wings needed to be lifted clear of the altar to open properly. The base became a valuable area for additional images and became known as the predella, the first dated example of which was Simone's St Louis of Toulouse[4] of 1317. Simone also worked in fresco and in miniature, illuminating a frontispiece for a copy of Virgil's poems for his friend, Petrarch.

The leading Sienese artist of the period, in the annals of art history, was Duccio di Buoninsegna (active c. 1278–c. 1319), a colourful character whom records

show being frequently fined for anti-social behaviour, getting into debt and refusing to acknowledge civic authorities. This contrasts with the calm and substance of his figures in works such as the *Rucellai Madonna*[5] (probably commissioned in 1285 for Sta Maria Novella in Florence), the *Madonna of the Franciscan*,[6] and the Siena Cathedral high altarpiece the *Maestà (Virgin in Majesty)* – now divided between Siena, New York, Washington and London – completed in 1311. This influential work, which also carries on its reverse an extensive and iconographically innovative series of scenes illustrating the Passion and post-resurrection events, transcends the Byzantine and Gothic traditions that had informed it to unify the figures of the Virgin and Child with attendant angels and saints in one single unified spatial composition. Duccio is not known to have worked in fresco. His use of colour and line is characterized by a serene lucidity, and yet emotional content is also conveyed – for example, when the Christ child squirms in his mother's arms in his

determination to reach out and bless the diminutive Franciscan friars who adore him.

The International Gothic vogue for portraiture can also be seen influencing the work of Cimabue and his assistants in the frescoes of the Upper and Lower Churches at Assisi, where the portrait of St Francis, in particular, combines the intercessory power of the icon with the naturalistic realism of northern European art. Nonetheless, it is to a pupil of Cimabue's that the laurel wreath passed, in the eyes of contemporaries and of subsequent art historians, for making the leap from the art of the Gothic into that of the Renaissance – Giotto.

Duccio di Buoninsegna,
Maestá, Siena, 1308–11 (back).
Siena Cathedral, New York,
Washington and London.

Christian Art and the Italian City-State

Dr Griffith Mann

On 9 June 1311, church bells pealed out over the Commune of Siena as its citizens poured into the streets to commemorate a landmark moment in the life of their city, the installation of a massive panel painting known as the *Maestá* (1308–11) on the high altar of their cathedral. The monumental, double-sided altarpiece had taken three years to complete. Its front prominently featured the enthroned Virgin and Child in the company of saints and angels, and a detailed Christological narrative covered the back of the painting. The front of the altarpiece asserted Siena's special relationship to the Virgin Mary, whom the Sienese had recently adopted as their primary advocate and protector. The serial narrative on the back, with its enlarged image of the crucifixion, offered a rendition of sacred history that called attention to the immediacy of Mary's participation in her son's Passion. This prestigious civic commission had been awarded to the painter Duccio di Buoninsegna, whose signature can still be discerned along the foot of the Virgin's throne: 'Holy Mother of God, be the cause of peace for Siena and life for Duccio because he painted you thus.' In scale, scope and ambition, the altarpiece was without equal in the city and its surrounding territories.

The imposing bulk and stunning execution of the *Maestá* must have created an impressive sight as it was paraded slowly through the city streets. A fourteenth-century chronicler described the festivities that marked the painting's journey to the cathedral:

'On the day on which it was carried to the Duomo, the shops were locked up and the Bishop ordered a great and devoted company of priests and friars with a solemn procession, accompanied by the Signori and all the officials of the Commune, and all the populace. All the most worthy were hand in hand next to said panel [painting] with lights lit in their hands; and then behind were the women and children with much devotion; and they accompanied it right to the Duomo making procession around the Campo, as was the custom, sounding all the bells in glory, out of devotion for such a noble panel as was this. Which panel, Duccio di Niccolò, the painter, made and he made it in the house of the Muciatta outside the gate of Stalloreggi. And all that day they remained in prayer, with much alms, which they gave to poor persons, praying to God and his Mother, who is our advocate, who defends us through her infinite mercy from every adversity and every evil, and guards us from the hands of traitors and enemies of Siena.'

The painting's position on the high altar of Siena's mother church firmly established its status as one of the pre-eminent images in the ceremonial life of the city. Standing at the end of the nave, the altarpiece united the urban congregation with the heavenly court and its celestial queen. Behind the high altar, the serial narrative of Christ's life engaged its audiences in the commemoration of sacred history, absorbing them in the unfolding drama of Christ's Passion with cinematic immediacy.

In Florence, the completion of an equally innovative painting, the *Rucellai Madonna* (1285), was similarly celebrated with a public spectacle in which a painting played a central part. Created nearly thirty years earlier than the *Maestá*, the

Duccio di Buoninsegna, the *Rucellai Madonna*, the epitome of the serenity and substance that this important early Renaissance artist achieved in his work, probably commissioned in 1285 for Santa Maria Novella in Florence. Florence, Uffizi.

CHRISTIAN ART AND THE ITALIAN CITY-STATE

Rucellai Madonna was commissioned by a Marian confraternity, a company of laypeople that gathered together to sing hymns in honour of the Virgin in the Dominican Church of Santa Maria Novella. As the sixteenth-century artist and writer Giorgio Vasari recalled, the impressive novelty of the painting caused such a stir among the populace that it was borne in solemn procession with trumpets and great rejoicing from the workshop where it was produced to the church. In its location near the high altar of Santa Maria Novella, the painting offered the Laudesi of Santa Maria Novella a brilliant backdrop for their daily recitation of Marian hymns, which honoured and praised the work's central subject. Illuminated by the candles that burned before it, the painting offered its audiences the novel spectacle of an enthroned Virgin and Child lowered to earth by a choir of six angels.

As products of a trend that American historian David Herlihy has characterized as an emerging 'civic Christianity', these two paintings embody many of the new currents in Christian art that emerged in Italy at the end of the Middle Ages. They not only participated in public ceremonies where civic and religious aspects of communal life intersected, they were a central part of their public expression. In Florence and Siena, the patronage of governments, families, guilds and confraternities produced a remarkable range of church architecture, murals, altarpieces and works of art in other media. Central public buildings such as cathedrals, neighbourhood churches, and town halls were seen as outward expressions of municipal pride. These edifices, many of them constructed with public assistance, provided opportunities for major civic commissions of sculpture, frescoes, and altarpieces. They also offered unprecedented opportunities for artistic patronage by private citizens, who had amassed fortunes in international banking and trade. In mendicant churches especially, where private burial chapels often flanked the high altar, prominent families commemorated their dead with liturgical vessels, sculpted tombs and pictorial decoration. These new classes of patrons, like the Scrovegni in Padua, and the Bardi and Peruzzi in Florence, enlisted leading artists to decorate their family chapels, creating spaces that asserted their special status.

Filled with both corporate and familial altars, these buildings also served as centres for the performance of the liturgical and para-liturgical ceremonies that punctuated the Christian calendars of Italian cities. At such moments, panel and mural paintings played a constitutive role in the religious experience of both lay and clerical communities. Though the textual sources of Christian images were important, the visual language of their realization – their figural composition, surface treatment, and relationship to the architecture of their setting – were equally central in enhancing the devotional experiences of their audiences. The lighting devices, costly textiles and liturgical accessories that accompanied Christian images helped in the performance of the scriptural subjects they depicted. Civic celebrations, like those that marked the completion of the *Maestá* and the *Rucellai Madonna*, directly engaged citizens in the commemoration of salvation history, uniting the sacred past with the devotional present.

At the same time, however, such accounts of the reception of Christian images must be reconciled with literary sources that evoke images of public worship that were far less orderly. In early fourteenth-century San Gimignano, for example, communal statutes outlawed parishioners from striking the benches and walls of their churches with rock hammers or staffs during masses celebrated in the Lenten period. Another banned citizens from throwing frogs and breaking ceramic jars against the walls of local churches during the celebration of Holy Week masses. The existence of such legislation indicates that, at least in some Tuscan communes, town governments attempted to shape the behaviour of worshippers by banning customs considered incompatible with Christian worship. Perhaps more important, however, such regulations also provide a telling reminder of the participatory nature of religious devotion in Late Medieval Italy. Ultimately, these sources offer an image of worshippers actively engaged in the celebration of sacred history.

This concept of lay piety, with its emphasis on experiential devotion, is key to understanding the inventive character of Christian art produced in the age of the Italian city-state. The increasingly participatory character of religious devotion in thirteenth- and fourteenth-century Italy was heavily indebted to the rise of the mendicant orders, particularly the Franciscans and the Dominicans, which significantly expanded the range of devotional forms available to the laity at the end of the Middle Ages. Having established houses in some of the fastest growing neighbourhoods in cities like Florence and Siena, these new orders set to work instructing an urban public in the mysteries of the Christian faith. They emphasized the humanity of Christ and of Mary, and the need for intense personal engagement in their veneration. In their attempts to connect new audiences with sacred history, the mendicants relied on theatrical performances and vernacular sermons, and stressed the importance of emotional and imaginative faculties in cultivating the interior experience of the worshipper.

One consequence of this development was a new emphasis on a personal, spiritual conception of Christian worship, in which the visual arts played a central role. As early as 1240, legends of the life of St Francis (1181/2–1226) describe how Christ spoke to the young St Francis while he knelt in prayer before a painted crucifix in the ruined Church of San Damiano. Similarly, Margarita of Cortona (1247–97) vividly experienced the pains of Christ's Passion while meditating on a crucifix hanging above the altar in her local church of San Francesco. By the middle of the thirteenth century, literary and pictorial narratives of Christ's life provided lay audiences with accounts of the Passion enriched with descriptive and emotional details. The Franciscan author of the *Meditations on the Life of Christ*, a text long thought central to the development of the increasingly naturalistic depictions of Christian art in Late Medieval Italy, stressed that his readers needed to harness their imaginative faculties when meditating on Christ's life. In conjuring mental images of Christ's suffering, he advised, the creative faculties of the worshipper would bring the images to life.

Indeed, the formal devices used by Late Medieval Italian artists and the authors of devotional texts betray a similar concern with arousing the compassion of their respective audiences in order to foster a more visceral engagement in sacred history. This trend suggests a new attitude toward the traditional Medieval dictum that pictures were 'Bibles for the illiterate'. Far from being visual summaries of scriptural subjects, pictures were increasingly recognized for their ability to appeal to the senses and to arouse the emotions. The Franciscan theologian Bonaventura, whose attitude toward sacred history paralleled that of the author of the *Meditations*, claimed that one of the primary justifications for pictures resided in their ability to incite empathetic devotion:

'On account of the slowness of devotion they were similarly introduced, namely so that men, who could not be excited to devotion in these things for which Christ acted for us, not yet by that perceived by the ear, at least they shall be excited while they shall discern those same things in figures and pictures made present before their bodily eyes. More than that also our devotion shall be excited by that which we see, than by that which we hear. Wherefore Horace: "Less vividly is the mind stirred by what passes through the ears than by that which is brought before the trusty eyes, and that which the spectator can see for himself."'[1]

The extent to which Late Medieval Italian painters incited the emotions of their audiences is demonstrated by the gashes that occasionally disfigure the faces of Christ's tormentors in panel and mural paintings of the Passion. Such examples offer dramatic testimony to a painting's ability to elicit a visceral response from its beholder.

As the fourteenth century progressed, Italian painters became increasingly skilled at articulating the tension between human and divine aspects of the sacred figures they depicted. The gold backgrounds of their magnificent altarpieces were especially suited to candlelit interiors, where their glimmering surfaces evoked the splendour of heaven. The solid, three-dimensional forms of their figural subjects, however, responded to new ideas about the importance of human experience in sacred history. Particularly in central Italy, artists experimented with novel painting styles to connect worshippers with the sacred subjects they depicted. The results of these experiments can be seen in the exploration of the themes of Mary's role as mother, in the human drama of Christ's Passion, and in a more aggressive pursuit of details derived from the direct observation of nature and the physical environment of Italian cities. In both private and public spheres, therefore, artists increasingly engaged their audiences in the unfolding drama of sacred history by playing directly on emotions. At the same time, the technical language of Italian painting, which retained the brilliant surface effects of metalwork, continued to assert the extraordinary status of its sacred subjects. The resulting synthesis of terrestrial and celestial realms is perhaps the greatest achievement of Christian art in Italy during this period.

193

The Cultural Life of the Italian City-States

Humanists, Artists and the Rise of the Renaissance

It was Dante Aligheri in his *Purgatorio* who first linked the names of Cimabue and Giotto to illustrate the premise of one man's fame being eclipsed by another. For Giotto di Bondone (c. 1266/7–1337) soon became the thinking man's artist, a role subsequently confirmed by the critic Giorgio Vasari (1511–74), who represented him as the initiator of Renaissance art.

Humanism and the Renaissance

The Renaissance was the most intellectually sustained and influential of a number of 'renascences' (rebirths) of the culture of Graeco-Roman Antiquity. Like its Insular, Carolingian, Macedonian and Early Gothic counterparts it was nonetheless imbued with a character unique to its age, and one which reflected its own agendas. During the fourteenth and fifteenth centuries – or *trecento* and *quattrocento* as they are known in Italian – an intellectual movement called humanism took root in a number of Italian cities, each of which formed the nucleus of its own state, ruled by the civic dignitaries of its commune and by a number of princely dynasties that emerged. The economic wealth of cities such as Rome, Mantua, Urbino, Ferrara, Siena and Florence, home of the Medici bankers, and the cultural aspirations of their urbane inhabitants, coupled with the availability of Roman art and rediscovered texts and an influx of Greek materials from Byzantium, made them ripe for an assertion of their own identity and heritage, which was presented by some as a liberation from northern Gothic control.

Commencing in the circle of the Florentine scholar-poet Petrarch (died 1370), a neo-classical literary elite emerged, committed to the study of the grammar, rhetoric, oratory and style of the authors of Classical Antiquity – the humanists. This was in no guise a rejection of the Christian faith in favour of an earlier paganism or an espousal of a purely human set of values and agendas, as the term tends to signify today. It was, rather, an affirmation of human intellect and creativity, but in the service of God. The Medieval mind had only rarely perceived anything unchristian in studying the works of Antiquity, acknowledging it as a past age prior to the coming of Christ, which had not yet been enlightened by his teaching. Paganism per se was condemned, but not necessarily the works of earlier pagan authors, or their art. One of Petrarch's friends and fellow humanists, Collucio Salutati, gives an intriguing insight into contemporary views on such matters:

> '*I think Caecilius Balbus' [a classical author] feelings about the Romans' religious images were no different from what we in the full rectitude of our faith feel about the painted or carved memorials of our Saints and Martyrs. For we perceive these not as Saints and as Gods but rather as images of God and the Saints. It may indeed be that the ignorant vulgar think more and otherwise of them than they should. But, since one enters into understanding and knowledge of spiritual things through the medium of sensible things, if pagan people made an image of Fortune with a cornucopia and a rudder – as distributing wealth and controlling human affairs – they did not deviate very much from the truth. So too, when our own artists represent Fortune as a queen turning with her hands a revolving wheel very fast, so long as we apprehend that picture as something made by a man's hand, not something itself divine but a similitude of divine providence, direction and order – and representing indeed not its essential character but rather the winding and turning of mundane affairs – who can reasonably complain?*'[1]

Petrarch said something similar of a panel painting of the Virgin and Child by Giotto in his possession – that only the cognoscenti could truly appreciate its meaning and beauty. The rise of connoisseurship and of art criticism was underway.

The Rise of the Artist

The Medieval makers of works of art on Christian themes had been motivated by their dedication to serving their faith, acting as evangelists via their art, or by the commercial imperative of commissions from those who wished to demonstrate their piety. The latter did not, of course, preclude a sense of spiritual dedication and endeavour on the part of either craftspeople or patrons. In the milieu of the Italian city-state, however, the artist was increasingly recognized as a member of a cultural elite, a valuable component within the upper echelons of the citizenry. The humanists played a key role in developing this attitude and, as in so many things, drew upon the inspiration of the ancients and their approach to the arts. Filippo Villani, Chancellor of the Republic of Perugia, wrote in his *De Origine*, dealing with the origins of Fiesole and Florence, of the new honour due to the painter:

> *'The ancients, who wrote admirable records of events, included in their books the best painters and sculptors of images and statues along with other famous men… These most wise men thought, so I infer, that imitators of nature who endeavoured to fashion likenesses of men from stone and bronze could not be unendowed with noble talents and exceptional memory, and with much delightful skill of hand… along with the other distinguished men in their annals they put… Praxiteles, Myron, Apelles of Cos… So let it be proper for me, with the mockers' leave, to introduce here the excellent Florentine painters, men who have rekindled an art that was pale and almost extinguished.*
>
> *'First among whom John, whose surname was Cimabue, summoned back with skill and talent the decayed art of painting, wantonly straying far from the likeness of nature as this was, since for many centuries previously Greek and Latin painting had been subject to the ministrations of but clumsy skills, as the figures and images we see decorating the churches of the Saints, both on panels and on walls, plainly show.*
>
> *'After John, the road to new things now lying open, Giotto – who is not only by virtue of his great fame to be compared with the ancient painters, but is even to be preferred to them for skill and talent – restored painting to its former worth and great reputation. For images formed by his brush agree so well with the lineaments of nature as to seem to the beholder to live and breathe… painters are of a talent no lower than those whom the liberal arts have rendered magistri, since these latter may learn by means of study and instruction written rules of their arts while the painters derive such rules as they find in their art only from a profound natural talent and a tenacious memory. Yet Giotto was a man of great understanding even apart from the art of painting, and one who had experience in many things. Besides having a full knowledge of history, he showed himself so far a rival of poetry that keen judges consider he painted what most poets represent in words. He was also, as was proper to a most prudent man, anxious for fame rather than gain. Thus with the desire of making his name widely known, he painted something in prominent places in almost every famous city of Italy.'[2]*

One cannot help thinking that such authors were projecting their own rhetoric and perceptions onto the artist. Their knowledge of art history was also unformed. We have seen that Byzantine artists had made a great contribution to keeping the art of painting alive, while the illuminator, in both East and West, had taken it to new levels even if in miniature format. There were also well-understood guidelines on technique and materials, not least those fostered by the trade guilds.

The illuminator would continue to play an important role in Renaissance art, for many of the humanists were not only authors but also scribes who 'published' their own works. These often contained a species of plant decoration known as 'white vine' – vine-scrolls with white or uncoloured tendrils, based on twelfth-century northern Italian illumination. This complemented the scripts used which were based on those that the humanists considered antique but which were actually Carolingian – namely Caroline minuscule, which now became known as humanist book script (*littera humanistica*), and an elegant cursively written version of it, known as 'cancellaresca', with Roman square and rustic capitals for display purposes. These capitals were often copied from the epigraphic monuments of the Roman past, which littered the cityscapes and which were studied and collected, along with other antiquities, by the humanists. One such student of the past was the gifted Paduan artist-scribe Bartolommeo di Sanvito, who also worked in other Italian cities. He, and other illuminators such as Attavante degli Attavanti, also copied classical motifs such as *putti* (cherubs), trophies, laurel wreaths, floral swags and the like. These adorned copies of the classics and humanist texts, prayerbooks and theological treatises alike, sold by *cartolai* (stationers) who might also be humanist scholars in their own right, notably Vespasiano di Bisticci.

One work by Giotto, in particular, was applauded by the early humanists as the epitome of painterly perfection: the *Navicella*, a depiction of Christ quelling the storm that threatened the apostles' fishing boat, not in paint but in mosaic in the atrium of St Peter's, Rome. This has been restored so many times that it is difficult to detect Giotto's original work. It was drawn by many subsequent artists who were inspired by it and by the high repute attached to it by the humanists. It seems that what most recommended it to them was the composition, a concept that they were the first to express in words, equating the artist's placing of parts in relation to the whole with their own rigorous methods of constructing verse and rhetorical argument.

Giotto was not the only artist favoured by the humanists. Pisanello (c. 1395–c. 1455) is also praised for the naturalism of his works. This gifted draughtsman, painter and medallist worked with Gentile da Fabriano on frescoes for the Doge's Palace in Venice and the Lateran in Rome, succeeding Gentile as the major exponent of International Gothic in Italy. The humanist writer Guarino of Verona

Giotto, The *Navicella*, a
depiction of Christ quelling
the storm that threatened
the apostles' fishing boat,
executed in mosaic in the
atrium of St Peter's, Rome.
This has been restored so
many times that it is difficult
to detect Giotto's influential
original work, which was
acclaimed by the humanists
as the perfect composition.

wrote of Pisanello's now lost painting of St Jerome in his study – a popular subject
with humanist scholars:

*'Why list your accomplishments one by one? Here as I write is their pattern: the noble
gift you have sent me, a picture of my beloved Jerome, offers a wonderful example of
your power and skill. The noble whiteness of his beard, the stern brows of his saintly
countenance — simply to behold these is to have one's mind drawn to higher things.
He is present with us and yet seems also absent, he is both here and somewhere else:
the grotto may hold his body, but his soul has the freedom of Heaven. However plainly
the picture declares itself to be a painted thing, in spite of the living figures it
displays, I scarcely dare open my mouth, and whisper close-lipped rather than let my
voice break loutishly in on one who contemplates God and his Kingdom of Heaven.'*[3]

Guarino spent the years 1403–09 studying in Constantinople, Rhodes and Chios and his approach is moulded by the scholarly Byzantine approach to the relationship between suppliant and icon.

Art appreciation gradually became a prerequisite of educated taste. But was it necessary to be able to practise art in order to properly pronounce upon it? Alberti, who wrote the most authoritative humanist account of painting, *De pictura*, was himself a painter – if a rather eccentric one – whereas Leonardo Bruni, who managed to get himself appointed to advise on the new bronze doors for Florence Baptistery by Ghiberti, was no practitioner but rather an informed critic. Design by committee was on its way. Lorenzo Ghiberti (1378–1455) won the commission in 1401 as the result of a competition and executed the second and third sets of doors for the baptistery. He made them his life's work, completing the third doors in 1452 and marking the arrival of the Florentine Renaissance proper.

The Third Bronze Doors for Florence Baptistery, the winning competition entry by Ghiberti, completed by 1452, Florence Cathedral Baptistery.

Florentine Art

Whereas the second doors feature panels of New Testament scenes with figures set in Gothic quatrefoil frames on blank grounds, in Ghiberti's third doors Old Testament subjects are treated more naturalistically within settings that are perspectively conveyed to create convincing depictions of space. Perspective had been pioneered by the Florentines Masaccio, Brunelleschi and Donatello, who also explored means of conveying genuine human emotion as well as space, and was here combined with the technique introduced by the Pisani of 'continuous representation' whereby several episodes could be conflated within the same image. Donatello (1386–1466) was a member of Ghiberti's workshop, where he learned the arts of the goldsmith and bronze caster. He worked in many media, contributing to the sculptures of Orsanmichele and Florence Cathedral and producing an influential series of marble and stucco reliefs of the Virgin and Child. He was capable of great expression in works such as the bronze Lamentation panel,[4] but perhaps his most intriguing and memorable work is his bronze of David, which originally stood in the courtyard of the Medici Palace and is now in the Bargello in Florence. The youthful David, the shepherd boy turned vanquisher of Goliath, upon whose severed head he rests his foot, is depicted as a vulnerable, almost languid adolescent and makes conscious reference to classical sculpture. Donatello may have had the opportunity to make a closer study of such earlier works during his visit to Rome in the company of his friend the architect and sculptor Brunelleschi. Other close associates included the humanist Poggio Bracciolini. Donatello's affair with Antiquity was evidently an informed one.

Ghiberti also designed stained glass for Florence Cathedral and wrote the first artist's autobiography, his *Commentarii*, in which he also discussed the art history of the Roman period and of Tuscany, and the principles of perspective and optics. The relationship between mathematics, geometry and music had been acknowledged in the classical syllabus of the liberal arts, which had been kept alive throughout the Middle Ages and now came to the fore, being extended to incorporate the visual arts. The humanist artist would need to be as familiar with the geometry of Euclid as with a paint brush. Principles of beauty were being rationalized, as revealed in a jocular comment by Alberti concerning composition and the views of an ancient Roman author, Varro:

'In my view there will be no painted narrative so filled with so great a variety of events that nine or ten persons will not be capable of acting them out quite fittingly; I feel that much to the point here is an opinion of Varro's, who, to avoid having a crush at parties, admitted not more than nine people to his table.'[5]

RIGHT: *The Expulsion*, Masaccio, c. 1425–28, Brancacci Chapel, Florence.

Giotto certainly measured up to such social and intellectual standards for his contemporaries. His influence on artists of the High Renaissance is attested by studies of his works in Leonardo's notebooks and Michelangelo's drawings after the past masters Masaccio and Giotto. His contemporary Dante and the sixteenth-century art critic Vasari both accorded him a primary significance. His work draws inspiration from a wealth of Antique, Byzantine, northern and Italian Gothic and contemporary sources (including the work of the architect/sculptor Arnolfo di Cambio). He is thought to have assisted Cimabue in the frescoes of the Basilica of San Francesco at Assisi, where the Legend of St Francis cycle in the Upper Church is usually attributed to him. However, his earliest certain commission was the series of frescoes in the Arena Chapel in Padua, painted between 1305–15. This simple little structure, built in a ruined Roman amphitheatre by Enrico Scrovegni, offered the perfect 'blank canvas' for Giotto's frescoes. It formed part of a growing trend to endow family chapels, a fashion started by leading Florentine families. Particularly splendid examples are those of the Peruzzi and Bardi at the Franciscan church of San Croce, both also decorated by Giotto who in the course of his work invented the fresco technique of painting in tempera on dry (*a secco*) rather than wet plaster. During the *quattrocento* it became de rigeur to rebuild or embellish local churches. Palla Strozzi paid for Gentile di Fabriano's altarpiece, *The Adoration of the Magi*, as part his reconstruction of the sacristy of the Vallombrosan monastery of San Trinità, while Felice Brancacci, his son-in-law, had his family chapel in the Carmelite friary of San Maria del Carmine decorated by Masaccio and Masolino in 1425–28. Masaccio's weighty image of *The Expulsion* in the

Brancacci Chapel is the epitome of regret, in which Adam covers his face in shame while Eve raises her anguished visage to heaven.

Giotto's Arena Chapel cycle narrates, in three tiers of scenes, the life of the Virgin and of Christ, culminating in the Last Judgement. His excision of extraneous detail, his airy compositions with their consistent directional lighting and substantial yet ethereal figures, the lightness of touch of his modelling, his emotive empathy for human experience and his virtuoso use of trompe l'oeil (eye-deceiving) architectural features combine to produce memorable images that produce a supremely serene, spiritual space. He went on in 1310–15 to paint works such as the *Ognissanti Madonna*,[6] which displays a clear debt to Cimabue's *Sta Trinità Madonna* and Duccio's *Rucellai Madonna*. Together, they gave birth to the *Sacra Conversazione* ('sacred conversation'), a theme beloved of *quattrocento* and *cinquecento* artists in which the Madonna is shown in an intimate moment of exchange with the Christ child and attendant saints. The Medieval polyptych had been replaced by the Renaissance painting.

202

The Ognissanti Madonna,
Giotto, c. 1310–15,
Florence.

Manuscripts, Humanism and Patronage in Renaissance Florence

Dr Mark Evans

203

During the second half of the fifteenth century Florence stood comparison only with Ghent, Bruges and Venice as a principal European centre of de luxe book production. One of the richest cities in Europe, its wealth stemmed from the cloth industry, trade and banking, augmented by a highly developed craft tradition. By the 1420s its one hundred richest citizens owned one sixth of the state's wealth, with a further 50 per cent distributed between some 3,000 households: a remarkably even distribution for the time. Patronage was traditionally communal and corporate, rather than aristocratic and private. The major artistic projects during the early fifteenth century were commissions of the ruling guilds to enrich their churches: Brunelleschi's dome at San Maria del Fiore financed by the *Arte della Lana*, Ghiberti's baptistery bronze doors sponsored by the *Arte di Calimala*, and the statues on the exterior of Orsanmichele, each commissioned by individual guilds.

By 1400 Florence was already a major centre of book production. Rome had ceased to be a focal point during the exile of the papal court at Avignon. The largest Italian university, Bologna, generated a local demand for legal codices and secular texts. Venice did not yet have a significant school of illuminators, its pictorial traditions remaining indebted to Byzantium until c. 1400. From around 1380 Milan emerged as an important centre of manuscript production, under the rule of Giangaleazzo Visconti (1351–1402) and his heirs. The painters of Siena were Florence's main competitors during the first half of the fourteenth century, but the smaller city never fully recovered from the Black Death.

In the fourteenth and early fifteenth centuries, most Florentine illuminated manuscripts were choir books: missals, antiphonaries and graduals for ecclesiastical use, frequently decorated by artists in religious orders who also worked on a large scale. Around 1315–20, the Master of St George, the leading Italian illuminator of his time, decorated graduals for the Cistercians at Badia a Settimo, near Florence. He later produced his finest work for Cardinal Jacopo Stefaneschi – patron of Pietro Cavallini, Giotto and Simone Martini. The Olivetan community that took over San Miniato al Monte in 1373 required a complete set of new choir books, and others were made for lay confraternities such as the Compagnia di Sant'Agnese at the Carmine. An important scriptorium was based at the Camaldolese monastery of San Maria degli Angeli, where the artists Don Silvestro dei Gherarducci (1339–99) and Lorenzo Monaco (c. 1370–1423/4) produced manuscripts. Fra Angelico (c. 1400–55) was a Dominican living in Fiesole. He painted manuscripts, panel paintings and frescoes for a wide range of patrons, ending his days at Rome working for Pope Nicholas V.

Between the early fourteenth and mid-fifteenth centuries Florentine manuscripts balanced pictorial imagery and Gothic script, but after 1450 they were transformed by a new kind of decoration. Its self-consciously classical aspirations are celebrated by an epigram in praise of the illuminator and *cassoni* painter Apollonio di Giovanni (c. 1416–65) by notary and humanist Ugolino Verino (1438–1516), who likened his work to the poetry of Antiquity:

'Once Homer sang of the walls of Apollo's Troy burned on Greek pyres, and again

MANUSCRIPTS, HUMANISM AND
PATRONAGE IN RENAISSANCE FLORENCE

Virgil's great work proclaimed the wiles of the Greeks and the ruins of Troy. But certainly the Tuscan Apelles Apollonius now painted burning Troy better for us.'

The crucible of such new illumination was provided by humanistic script, known as *littera antiqua*, which emerged between 1400 and 1430. Encouraged by the Chancellor of Florence, Coluccio Salutati (1331–1406), a number of students of classical grammar and history, led by Poggio Bracciolini (1380–1459) and Niccolò Niccoli (c. 1364/5–1437), sought to reform handwriting by imitating Romanesque texts, themselves based on earlier Carolingian manuscripts. Such enthusiasm for the classics did not meet with universal approval, as demonstrated by the Florentine patrician Cino Rinuccini who, some time before 1417, scornfully characterized the humanist avant-garde as:

'... a chattering flock who, in order to appear highly literate to the crowd, proclaim in the square how many dipthongs the ancients had and why only two are known today; which grammar is better, that of the time of the comedian Terence or that of the heroic Virgil corrected; how many feet the ancients used in versifying and why nowadays we use only the anapest of four unaccented syllables'.

Littera antiqua was initially disseminated by the humanists through their ambitious campaign to rediscover and copy classical texts, and was subsequently taken up by humanists in northern Italy and professional Florentine scribes. With the new script came decoration known as 'white vine-stem'. By the late 1420s, the libraries and scribes of Florence constituted a unique scholarly resource, humanism supplementing rather than conflicting with its traditional Christian context.

The second, decisive phase in the development of humanist script was ushered in by the arrival in Florence in 1434 of Pope Eugenius IV, who sought refuge at San Maria Novella from the recalcitrant Council of Basle and rebellion in Rome. This brought together the two principal centres of humanist learning, whose classical agenda gained considerably in prestige from the Council of Florence in 1439. This ecumenical council of the Eastern and Western churches was attended by the Byzantine emperor, the Patriarch of Constantinople, the Pope, and countless other international clerics and scholars. This gathering provided an international platform for *littera antiqua* and confirmed Florentine dominance of the Italian book trade, which endured until the appearance of printing. In 1442 the influential bookseller Vespasiano da Bisticci (c. 1422–98) first appeared. The election of one of his clients as Pope Nicholas V in 1447 strengthened the role of humanism at the papal curia, his books providing the nucleus of the Vatican Library, formally established by Sixtus IV in 1475.

The arrival of Eugenius IV was closely followed by the return from exile of Cosimo de' Medici *il Vecchio* (1389–1464). The Medici, bankers to the papacy, retained control of the city until 1492. From 1417–18 Cosimo had demonstrated a precocious interest in rediscovered classical texts, and in 1419 he and his father contributed generously to the commission of Ghiberti's bronze *Saint Matthew* for the bankers' guild at Orsanmichele. He spent freely on building at the family parish church of San Lorenzo, at San Marco, and the Augustinian Badia at Fiesole, and began the Medici Palace designed by Michelozzo. In 1456–64 he commissioned from Vespasiano a library of over 200 volumes for the Badia and assembled one of the principal Florentine libraries for himself. He was not a major patron of illumination, but one of the pioneering humanist bibliophiles. Cosimo's sons Piero (1416–69) and Giovanni (1421–63) were the principal collectors of illuminated manuscripts in Florence during the 1450s and 1460s. They favoured fine, richly decorated humanist manuscripts, establishing a standard for later princely libraries.

One of the most accomplished fifteenth-century Florentine illuminators, Francesco d'Antonio del Chierico (1433–84), carried out much work for Piero de' Medici and his son Lorenzo. Training as a goldsmith probably conditioned his taste for cameos, candelabra, and other decorative motifs that populated his witty miniatures. Francesco worked extensively for Federigo da Montefeltro, and was in charge of the decoration of the Urbino Bible, the most splendid Florentine manuscript, which was made between 1476–78.[1] This project pooled the talents of many fine miniaturists, including the Master of the Hamilton Xenophon, Francesco Rosselli (1445–1513) and the young Attavante degli Attavanti (1452–1520/25).

The library of over 900 volumes that Vespasiano assembled for Federigo was the largest and most spectacular project of its kind in Italy between the late 1460s and early 1480s. Similar princely endeavours included the library acquired from Vespasiano by Alessandro Sforza (1409–1473), Lord of Pesaro, and his son Costanzo. Another prominent humanist patron was King Matthias 'Corvinus' of Hungary (reigned 1459–90), husband of Beatrice of Aragon, daughter of King Ferrante of Naples. After the death of Federigo in 1482 he became the major patron of Florentine illumination. Francesco Rosselli, who illuminated choir books for Siena Cathedral, spent the years 1480–82 in Hungary, where he decorated the psalter of Beatrice of Aragon.[2] During the 1480s Matthias' librarian Taddeo Ugoleto resided in Florence, supervising the copying of manuscripts for his master. Twelve are signed by Attavante degli Attavanti. His mature pictorial style resembles that of the fresco painter Domenico Ghirlandaio (1449–94), with whom he collaborated. His early masterpiece is the missal of Thomas James, Bishop of Dol in Brittany, dated 1483.[3]

The brothers Gherardo (1446–97) and Monte di Giovanni del Fora (1448–1532/3) also produced major works for Matthias 'Corvinus', of which the most notable include the frontispieces to a large bible.[4] These combine great originality with a remarkable sense of scale, reflecting their experience as painters on panel and designers of

Francesco d'Antonio del Chicrico, Initial 'I' containing creation scenes, from the Bible of Federigo da Montefeltro, 1476–78.

205

mosaics. Gherardo was a lay member of the Dominican community at San Marco, with literary and musical interests, and an associate of Leonardo da Vinci. The monumental character of Monte's work is apparent in the full-page miniatures of 1509–10 from the baptistery missal, which includes a spectacular image of *St John the Baptist*, which resembles an altarpiece or processional banner. Like the frescoes of Ghirlandaio, Monte's miniatures include landscapes and minutely observed details.

The expulsion from Florence of Lorenzo's son Piero in 1494 terminated the princely patronage

206

that had kept the demand for quality manuscripts buoyant between the 1460s and 1490s. The situation was similar elsewhere: hand-painted frontispieces and initials added to de luxe printed books published in Venice were superseded by woodcut illustrations from the 1490s. Only in Rome did the demands of popes and cardinals, most famously Giulio Clovio's patron, Cardinal Alessandro Farnese, perpetuate the making of hand-written and decorated service books through the sixteenth century.

The professional scribes included, in addition to notaries and clerics, humanists from a similar class to their clients. Some copied primarily for their own libraries: Alessandro da Verazzano was a member of the Florentine *Signoria* in 1488, while Sigismondo de' Sigismondi was a Count Palatine. Of fifteenth century painters, only Gentile Bellini was similarly ennobled. Scribes' earnings and social status were concordant with the cost of copying – between three-fifths and two-thirds of the total cost of a book: the annual earnings of Francesco d'Antonio del Chierico were about the same as the cost of a copy of Pliny's *Natural History* requested from Vespasiano in 1460. Scribes and stationers/booksellers (*cartolai*) generally had more direct contact with patrons and purchasers than did illuminators. Occasionally, there was a slight overlap between the roles of scribe and painter; a handful of illustrations have been attributed to the scholar-scribe Bartolomeo Fonzio (c. 1446–1513). Most miniaturists worked as sub-contractors to the booksellers, although Gherardo and Monte di Giovanni were themselves *cartolai*, and Attavante probably helped organize the production of manuscripts for King Matthias.

While humanist script expressed the preoccupations of the Florentine avant-garde, painting – whether monumental or miniature – was a response to the taste engendered. Painters and sculptors exerting the greatest influence upon Florentine miniaturists included Pollaiuolo, Piero della Francesca and Verrocchio, while echoes of individual works by Donatello, Benedetto da Maiano, Benozzo Gozzoli, Perugino, Botticelli and Ghirlandaio are discernible. That Florentine Renaissance illumination was not especially derivative is indicated by its comparative immunity to imported German engravings, which increasingly influenced north Italian miniaturists and Florentine panel painters.

Text and images are both bearers of meaning, and Horace's maxim '*Ut pictura poesis*' ('as is painting so is poetry') from the *Ars Poetica* was a favourite humanist topos. Some contemporary criteria for a successful work of art appear in Leonardo Bruni's recommendations (c. 1425) for the third set of bronze doors for the Florence Baptistery:

'It is my opinion that the twenty stories… should mainly have two qualities; one that they should show splendour, the other that they should have significance. By splendour I mean that they should offer a feast to the eye through the variety of design; significant I call those which are sufficiently important to be worthy of memory…'

By the middle of the fifteenth century humanists increasingly interpreted 'Magnificence' as a virtue, utilizing the Aristotelian argument: '… great expenditure is becoming to those who have suitable means … for all these things bring with them greatness and prestige'. This applied as much to the bibliographic projects of the Medici and Federigo da Montefeltro as to their lavish architectural undertakings. The boom in the Florentine book trade during Vespasiano's career was caused by the princely fashion for libraries of humanist character. Local demand for choir books, already evident in the fourteenth century, continued unostentatiously, and was catered for by Monte di Giovanni and Attavante into the 1500s. On account of their personal character, books of hours were ill suited to printed editions, and de luxe manuscript copies continued.

The manuscript culture of humanism, itself largely a creation of the Florentine bourgeoisie, fuelled the process through which the civic elite of Renaissance Italy promoted a new sense of status, distinct from the feudal model. As citizens and *de facto* rulers of Florence, the Medici linked this urban milieu with that of the Italian aristocracy, whose taste for opulent decorated books may be traced back to Giangaleazzo Visconti, founder of the renowned Milanese ducal library. However, by the 1470s printed text availability and widening disparity in price rapidly confined the manuscript trade to the de luxe market, for a few mainly aristocratic patrons, precipitating the rapid demise of Florentine illumination after the expulsion of the Medici in 1494.

16

The Italian High Renaissance

Madonnas, Popes and Princes

During the 1430s to 1440s Florentine painters such as Fra Angelico and Domenico Veneziano explored the *Sacra Conversazione* format. It was extended to Milan by Piero della Francesca's Brera Altarpiece of c. 1475 and to Venice by Giovanni Bellini and his circle. But it was Raphael who brought it to Rome and fully realized its artistic potential. He and Leonardo da Vinci elevated the painted panel to the status of 'the painting', an artwork that could be appreciated in and of itself, regardless of context, whether in a church, an office, a domestic interior or a gallery.

The Didactic and the Devotional
in High Renaissance Art

The saintly Dominican Fra Angelico (or Fra Giovanni da Fiesole, active 1417–55), a member of the Florentine school, was famed by commentators such as Vasari and John Ruskin for his spirituality, which pervaded his painting. His Dominican training had imbued him with a well-developed sense of art in the service of faith. A native of Fiesole, he also worked in Florence, Orvieto and Rome, where he attracted several papal commissions including a chapel in the Vatican for Pope Eugenius IV, dedicated to Sts Stephen and Laurence. His work displays simple, didactic iconography and a tenderness of style. Although he is documented as a practising painter before joining the Order and also undertook administrative offices while in it, he devoted his talents to the service of the gospel and, unlike most Renaissance artists, only painted Christian themes for Christian contexts. His most extensive oeuvre consists of the frescoes and altarpieces for the new Dominican house of San Marco, Florence, where he actually resided, which were

Deposition, Fra
Angelico, 1440s,
Dominican Convent of
San Marco, Florence.

designed to aid the meditations of his brethren. Andrea da Firenze, who
encapsulated Dominican theology in encyclopedic fashion in his frescoes for the
Chapter House (Spanish Chapel) of Santa Maria Novella, Florence, commissioned
in 1365, was also devoted to embodying doctrine in art. Another Dominican who
was attracted to the Order by the preaching of Savonarola (1452–98) – whose stance
against worldly materialism led to the 'bonfires of the vanities' in which books and
art were burnt, and who initially therefore felt compelled to give up art – was Fra
Bartolommeo. He subsequently returned to painting to become one of the most
successful Florentine artists, producing works such as the *Mystic Marriage of St
Catherine* for San Marco, Florence, painted around 1511 and now in the Louvre.

Apparently secular subjects could also be imbued with religious meaning of
significance for faith, of course. Ambrogio Lorenzetti's ambitious fresco on the
themes of the causes and effects of good and bad government for the Palazzo
Publico in Siena, c. 1338, was an old Medieval theme, found in manuscript

A vividly tormented vision of the Last Judgement (to complement the ceiling above painted by Fra Angelico), completed by Luca Signorelli for Orvieto Cathedral, 1502.

illumination from at least the Anglo-Saxon and Carolingian periods onwards. The theme was obviously of relevance to a society that purported to espouse Christian ethics. Regardless of its earthly governors, however, Siena never really recovered its prominence after it was decimated by plague in 1348.

Among Fra Angelico's most challenging commissions was the huge fresco cycle depicting the Last Judgement in Orvieto Cathedral, on which he worked in 1447 and which was completed in 1502 – as the city's thank-offering for deliverance from a passing French army – by Luca Signorelli (c. 1451–1523), who also worked on the Sistine Chapel under the direction of Perugino. They were both pupils of Piero della Francesca, whose work is distinguished by its calm monumentality and its interest in accurate anatomical depiction – an interest shared by Signorelli, who preferred to explore energetic movement. His extension of the Last Judgement iconography to include the signs of the end of the world and of the antichrist (said to be based upon Savonarola, who had been condemned as a heretic) gave full reign to this predilection, while the *Resurrection of the Flesh* features unnervingly realistic cadavers. Signorelli's demons are not the comic caricatured grotesques of the Medieval tradition, but decaying human forms with sadistic intent. The influence of this awesome vision can be seen in Michelangelo's treatment of the same theme in the Sistine Chapel.

Piero hailed from Sansepolcro in Umbria where he executed a fine fresco of the resurrection, the differing receptions of humankind to this defining moment typified by the barren earth to one side and the burgeoning flora on the other, and by one Roman guard who stares in awe and the other who cowers and shies away. His major work takes the form of imposing hieratic frescoes narrating the Legend of the True Cross, based on accounts in the Medieval hagiographical compendium the *Golden Legend*, painted in 1452–59 in San Francesco, Arezzo. Another of his figures that imprints itself upon the memory is that of the *Madonna del Prato*, the heavily pregnant Virgin bearing the hope of the world – an unusual iconography more

The Queen of Sheba, from the Legend of the True Cross, Piero della Francesca, 1452–59. San Francesco, Arezzo.

familiar in Iberia – that presided over a little funerary chapel at Monterchi, near Arezzo, where Piero's own mother may lie buried. Piero was deeply influenced by Alberti's writings on perspective and himself wrote and illustrated a treatise, *De prospective pingendi*, which had a devotional as well as practical intention, enabling him (in his *Flagellation* in the Ducal Palace in Urbino) and others to more accurately depict challenging subjects such as the geometric pavement of Pilate's Judgement Hall upon which Christ was scourged – the Lithostratos (Hebrew *Gabbatha*), a portion of which still forms a pilgrim station in Jerusalem. The preoccupation with perspective could be taken too far, however, and attracted the criticism of Vasari upon Paolo Uccello (1397–1475). His *St George and the Dragon* and *Nativity*[1] present compelling but sterile compositions in which the figures seem trapped within their precisely composed grounds, even if they are imbued with a chilly elegance.

Andrea Mantegna, applauded as the leading Italian painter at the time of his death in 1506, is best remembered for his nine huge images of the Triumphs of Caesar (now in Hampton Court Palace). But his devotional images included some major early frescoes (1459) illustrating the lives of Sts Christopher and James in the Church of the Eremitani in Padua – which were among the many artistic casualties of the Second World War – in the iconic tradition, and *sacra conversazione* such as the *Madonna of Victory*,[2] painted in 1496, and his San Zeno altarpiece. He was also instrumental in pioneering the art of engraving, bringing his work and a familiarity with the antique inspiration that underpinned the Renaissance to a wider European audience: his work inspired northern artists such as Dürer. A devotee of Donatello's work and a relative by marriage of Bellini's, the young prodigy Mantegna also became the artist to the court of the Gonzaga in Mantua. His ability to imbue highly emotionally charged scenes with a sense of epic import and solemn commemoration can be seen in his *Dead Christ*[3] of 1480, in which Christ is lamented by the Virgin and Holy Women and is seen lying on a stone altar from the unusual viewpoint of his feet; and in his three versions of the martyrdom of St Sebastian, who was often evoked at times of plague. In the first, painted in 1459 and now in Vienna, the saint is depicted as the epitome of beauteous manhood in its prime (a theme later pursued by Derek Jarman in his treatment of the same subject in his film *Sebastiane*) – in superb physical condition, save that his perfect form has been pierced by a volley of arrows. A trickle of blood stains his loin, but he is otherwise unsullied and gazes stoically heavenward, his brow drawn in intense supplication. Two of his murderers engage in a banal conversation, only their heads visible in the lower right of the composition. Sebastian's marble-like form echoes that of the fragments of classical sculpture that litter the scene and he is tied to a carefully observed classical column, part of a ruined edifice in a fantastic landscape redolent of ancient Rome. His own body has become a pillar of faith and his muscular form

RIGHT: *St Sebastian*, Andrea Mantegna, 1459. Vienna, Kunsthistorisches Museum.

recalls that of the judge Samson, who brought the halls of paganism tumbling down around him, while the pillar recalls the scourging of Christ. Mantegna's final engagement with the theme, in the version painted in 1490 and now in the Ca' d'Oro in Venice, however, shows Sebastian tortured by the agonies he suffered and accompanied by the inscription, 'Only the divine is firm, the rest is smoke' – the response of an older, more experienced man.

Other artists who found the printed medium an exciting way of communicating their art were the two Pollaiuolo brothers, Antonio and Piero, who throughout the second half of the fifteenth century ran a successful Florentine business covering painting, engraving, embroidery, sculpting and goldsmithing – an indication that it was not only prominent figures such as Leonardo who were 'universal' in their range of skills and of how many strings it was necessary to have to one's bow to make a good living as a 'Renaissance man'. Antonio also introduced the model for papal tombs with his bronze effigies of Popes Sixtus IV and Innocent VIII (both in St Peter's, Rome).

The vigorous draughtsmanship practised by Mantegna and Pollaiuolo was also

213

adopted by one of the leading Florentine painters of the day, Sandro Botticelli (1445–1510). His work is permeated by the sweetness of earlier Florentines such as the Carmelite Fra Filippo Lippi (c. 1406–69), a pupil of Masaccio's, with whom he studied. He adopted Lippi's fascination with the *sacra conversazione* format and spent much of his career producing half-length or *tondo* format depictions of the Virgin and Child. These, such as the *Madonna of the Magnificat*,[4] are among his best-loved paintings, although he also produced portraits, altarpieces on other themes (such as his San Barnaba in the Uffizi), a number of small narrative figural panels, his famous allegory of Spring, *La Primavera*, and what has become an icon of Renaissance classicism, the *Birth of Venus*, for patrons such as the Medici. His style can appear somewhat dry and flat, however serene and beautiful the figures and their composition, for he did not favour oil glazes unlike some of his late contemporaries. He also left a series of drawings on parchment illustrating Dante.

Tondo known as the *Madonna of the Magnificat*, Sandro Botticelli, late fifteenth century, Florence.

Renaissance Illumination

The most stunning illustrated early copy of Dante's works, however, is the copy of the *Paradisio*[5] in the British Library illuminated by Giovanni di Paolo (c. 1399–1482), a Sienese painter and illuminator. His vision of paradise is an elegant, courtly one, inspired by the International Gothic style of Simone Martini and Gentile da Fabriano conflated with the Renaissance styles of Fra Angelico and Sassetta. The service books of Renaissance churches were finely illuminated and each city cultivated its own style; these are oversize tomes, designed so that the members of a choir could all read from the one book, with enormous historiated initials containing images that are the vellum counterparts of the panel paintings of the age.

Books of hours also continued to be commissioned by princes and merchants alike. One of the most lavish is the *Sforza Hours*,[6] illuminated in the 1490s for Bona Sforza, who presided as duchess over the glittering court of Milan, by the court artist Giovan Pietro Birago. His elegant and well-proportioned figures, inspired by those of contemporaries such as Leonardo, who was working in the court and city

vi gran da miration ma ozamuro
comio trifcenda quefti corpi leui
ndella appilo oun pio folspiro
gluochio onizo uer me conquel fenbiante
che madre fa foura figluol deliro

at the time on important commissions such as the *Virgin of the Rocks* and the *Last Supper*, inhabit colourful courtly interiors and rocky fantasy Renaissance landscapes. The borders of the pages are adorned with sumptuous jewels, antique trophies, *putti* and emblems, such as Bona's ermine. The work was stolen while in progress and the clerical thief, Fra Jacopo, finally tracked down. In the interim, Birago had placed an insurance valuation on the work that far exceeded that of Leonardo's *Virgin of the Rocks* – an indication of the value of such exquisite work, even in miniature. The unfinished book was inherited by another woman, related by marriage, Margaret of Austria, regent of the Spanish Netherlands, who had the work completed by a leading northern Renaissance artist, Gerard Horenbout. In the pages of this one book the interface between Italian and northern Renaissance is clearly displayed. If the painter's art traced its origins from that of the miniaturist, the most grandiose of artistic ambitions might be transported back into the miniature. The Croatian illuminator Giulio Clovio, whose visage is carved in relief on his funerary monument in San Pietro in Vincoli, Rome, near to Michelangelo's tomb of Julius II, was known by the nickname 'the little Michelangelo' for his attempts in the early sixteenth century to equal the grandeur of vision of the Sistine Chapel's decorative scheme in his illuminations for works such as the *Stuart de Rothesay Hours*.[7]

Dante and Beatrice ascend to the ninth Heaven of Paradise, the *Primum Mobile* (Plato's 'prime mover'), depicted as Christ in a ring of golden cherubim, set against a mappemonde (world map). Illustrations to Dante's *Paradisio*, illuminated in Tuscany by Giovanni di Paolo for the King of Naples, 1445.

Painting on ceramic was also a traditional skill that reached new heights in the West during the Renaissance. Majolica (tin-glazed) chargers and vessels bear Christian and classical mythological images in bright Mediterranean colours, while the arts of the painter and the sculptor are combined in the elegant terracotta panels with their delicate blue and white glazes by the firm of the della Robbia family, also patronized by the Medici. The material was suitable for ecclesiastical or domestic settings, interior or exterior use, and casting techniques meant that, like the smaller bronzes of the period and engravings, images could be easily and economically mass-produced. The faithful could increasingly possess their own devotional images, as well as viewing great public and church artworks, even if the Virgin had to share space on their walls and tables with Venus.

Leonardo da Vinci

A skilled practitioner of the goldsmith's, sculptor's and painter's arts was Andrea del Verrocchio, a Florentine whose pupils included Perugino, Lorenzo di Credi, Ghirlandaio and Leonardo da Vinci (1452–1519). A *Baptism of Christ* for the monastery of San Salvi, now in the Uffizi, which is attributed to him also features an angel holding clothing in the bottom left that Vasari said was painted by Leonardo – one of the earliest appearances, around 1472, of the hand of one of the greatest figures in art. Leonardo rapidly moved away from the dry linearity of Verrocchio's workshop, experimenting with improvised sketches of his own, featuring informal compositions. Gradually he freed himself from the influence of models and compositional types favoured by his predecessors and contemporaries and in 1482 he moved from Florence to Milan to pursue his broadening interests under Sforza patronage. In 1483 he was commissioned by the Confraternity of the Immaculate Conception to paint an altarpiece – the *Virgin of the Rocks*. Two versions survive: the earlier, in the Louvre, was sold elsewhere by Leonardo and his associates; the second, in the National Gallery in London, is the later of the two and was not finished until 1508. The composition, with the Virgin holding two children – Christ and John the Baptist – and attended by the angel Uriel (named in apocryphal sources), is based on a pyramid and the figures are connected by a series of gestures and glances. They, and the rock-strewn landscape they inhabit, are also bound together by colour and light effect, with Leonardo perfecting his experiments in the use of *chiaroscuro* (light and shade). The linear depiction of form and perspective gives way here – and in other later works such as the cartoon of the Virgin and St Anne[8] and the portrait known as the Mona Lisa[9] – to atmospheric recession in landscapes, smoky (*sfumato*) outlines and tonal variation. The effect is complex and compelling.

Baptism of Christ, Andrea
del Verrocchio, c. 1472–75,
Florence.

In 1495–97 Leonardo undertook another of his great Milanese commissions, to
produce a fresco of the Last Supper on the end wall of the refectory of the
Dominican Convent of San Maria delle Grazie, which enjoyed the support of
Ludovico Sforza. Leonardo's obsession with experimentation led him to devise his
own technique and this has unfortunately meant that the work is in a sad state of
preservation, although it can still be appreciated and many sketches survive. The
composition of Christ and the apostles seated at a long trestle table, facing the
viewer, was a traditional one that can be found in Gothic art. However, with his
distinctive mastery Leonardo introduces tremendously enhanced psychological and
emotional effect through the body language and faces of the figures. Christ, having

Virgin of the Rocks, Leonardo da Vinci, 1490s–1508, an altarpiece commissioned by the Confraternity of the Immaculate Conception in Milan in which Leonardo perfected his experiments in composition and *chiaroscuro*. London, National Gallery.

just announced the cataclysm of his imminent betrayal, remains calm; Peter is outraged; John, the apostle beloved of Christ, takes his usual youthful unbearded form, almost resembling a girl, and receives the news with visionary resignation; Judas is distinguished as the betrayer only by his physiognomy and posture, and we are left to ponder whether the prophecy of his subsequent actions triggers the intent, or vice versa.

In 1500 Leonardo moved back to Florence and from there to France where, from 1516, he enjoyed the protection of King François I, in whose fond arms he died at Amboise in 1519. He left behind him several volumes of collected working notes. One, containing his inventions to enable human flight, now belongs to Bill Gates – a latter-day figure of 'universal' interests. In another, the Arundel Codex in the British Library, there are drawings relating to the effect of the phases of the moon upon tides, bird flight, the use of mirrors to power industrial kilns (part of a quest for a 'green' energy source that we would do well to resume today), and plans for an ideal city, Rosmarantin, for the French king. His notes to the latter include another radical idea: that when the king and court were not in residence, the ordinary folk of the field should be allowed to enjoy it. Needless to say, it was never built.

The Last Supper, Leonardo da Vinci, 1495–97, fresco painted for the refectory of the Dominican Convent of Santa Maria delle Grazie, Milan, in which Leonardo employed new techniques which have caused the work to deteriorate.

Leonardo approached art as the 'science of painting… the grandchild of nature… related to God', and his work in this sphere was intimately bound up with his studies of optics, mechanics and anatomy. He asserted that nature was the 'mistress of all masters' and found it more profitable to study her works than those of other artists. In his letter to Ludovico Sforza of 1482 he listed his abilities in engineering and the sciences, citing painting as last in the list. This was a pitch for work, however, to design civil engineering projects, military hardware and stage designs for a Renaissance prince. Yet it is Leonardo whom we revere as 'Renaissance man', awed by his range of skills that united the sciences and the arts in a joined-up vision of creation. It is as a creator himself, primarily of art and beauty, that we remember him.

Michelangelo Buonarroti

Leonardo was the illegitimate son of a Florentine notary and a peasant girl. This may unfortunately have played some part in the animosity between he and his greatest rival, Michelangelo Buonarroti (1475–1564), scion of a family of minor Florentine nobility. Michelangelo was apprenticed in 1488 to the workshop of Domenico Ghirlandaio, then engaged in supplying the fresco cycle for the choir of San Maria Novella in Florence, but then transferred to that of Bertoldi di Giovanni in the gardens of the Medici who, along with the papacy, would become his major patrons. Before long he added sculpture to his repertoire and his first signed work (1498–c. 1500) was the magnificent marble *Pietà*, commissioned by a French cardinal who specified a northern Gothic theme of the dead Christ lying on his grieving mother's lap. Michelangelo's solution to the problem that had beset previous artists of how to represent convincingly the dead weight of a man's body cradled by the lighter female form was to use her draperies to create a marble bier. His study of antique sculpture and of the works of his true masters, Giotto and Masaccio, had prepared him for articulating the body of Christ, while the Renaissance tradition of depicting the Madonna led him to portray her as a tender young woman, ennobled by grief as she had been by the joy of new motherhood. This attracted adverse contemporary comment, for the Virgin should have been shown in her later years. Michelangelo, still a young man of 25, countered this by advancing a theologically based argument that sin corrupts and ages and that the immaculate Virgin would not, therefore, show her mortality in this way. Such underlying theological and spiritual motivation pervades the work of Michelangelo, who later counted among his acquaintances Ignatius Loyola, founder of the Jesuit Order.

FOLLOWING SPREAD: Sistine Chapel ceiling, Michelangelo Buonarroti's greatest and most arduous commission (from Pope Julius II), 1508–12, Sistine Chapel, Vatican. Here Michelangelo has irrevocably appropriated the idealized figural art of pagan Antiquity for Christian use.

It is instructive to recall that around the same time he was working on his sculpture of Bacchus, now in the Bargello. Upon his return to Florence in 1501, Michelangelo produced another monumental vision of classicizing beauty – the enormous marble figure of David, completed by 1504 for the Florentine Republic and symbolizing its fortitude, self-confidence and latent energy, about to erupt into action.

This productive period also saw the birth of his Bruges Madonna, figures for Florence Cathedral and probably the Taddei Tondo.[10] He also painted the Doni Tondo.[11] In 1504 the Florentine Signoria commissioned him to paint a large battle scene on the walls of the Palazzo Vecchio, a job that he shared with Leonardo. It was never completed. Michelangelo ridiculed Leonardo for his assertion that a work was never finished, and for his track record of incomplete projects. However, in 1505 he travelled to Rome to accept a commission from Pope Julius II for his tomb. The 'Tragedy of the Tomb', as it was dubbed by Condivi, his

Pietà, carved by Michelangelo Buonarroti for St Peter's, Rome, 1498–c. 1500. Michelangelo was only about 25 when he worked on this compelling piece, which displays the influence of both classical sculpture and the work of earlier Renaissance masters.

pupil and biographer, was to dog the rest of his career. The relationship between artist and patron was a key one, and these two powerful personalities were perhaps a little too alike. Michelangelo's artistic ambitions for it – with forty figures planned – were too great, as can be seen from his astounding figure of Moses which is virtually all that he eventually contributed to the incomplete monument which was finally erected in San Pietro in Vincoli in 1545, over thirty years after Julius's death. The figures of slaves emerging from the living stone which he also intended for the tomb are now in the Louvre.

Michelangelo absconded to Florence and Bologna to pursue other commissions, but returned to Rome in 1508 to realize another of Julius II's grand projects – the vault and upper walls of the Sistine Chapel in the Vatican. Michelangelo planned to organize a team to undertake this mammoth task, but no one measured up to his expectations and he completed most of this physically gruelling work with his own hands in a remarkably short period (1508–12). The iconography features scenes from the creation to the thanksgiving sacrifice offered up by Noah after the flood. The spaces between the windows are occupied by monumental figures of the enthroned Old Testament Prophets and Sibyls who prophesied the coming of the Messiah, accompanied by the ancestors of Christ and by naked male figures (the *Ignudi*), symbolizing humanist ideals of beauty. It is as if the gods of Classical Antiquity have left Mount Olympus to become heroic human enactors of God's will. Michelangelo has effectively appropriated the visual rhetoric of the classics; principles of idealized human beauty need no more be primarily the cultural currency of pagan classicism.

The figures are foreshortened, with the exception of the *Ignudi*, and contained in a painted architectural framework – architecture become liquid paint. In the corner spandrels are four scenes of divine intervention and salvation: Moses and the brazen serpent; David and Goliath; Esther pleading for her people against the conspiracy of Haman; and Judith and Holofernes – types and antitypes. This new work complemented the scenes of the lives of Moses and of Christ, the old and new dispensations, painted on the chapel's walls in 1481–82 by a team including Botticelli, Ghirlandaio and Perugino. Along with the tapestries commissioned from Raphael (1516 onwards) illustrating the Gospels and the apostolic mission, designed to cover the lowest parts of the walls, the scheme was intended to theologically link Genesis and Exodus, the Gospels and Acts – the coming of the Word and its dissemination – and those who prophesied their inter-relationships. All that was needed to complete the vision was the Second Coming, and this is what Michelangelo was commissioned to paint on the altar wall of the chapel – the *Last Judgement*.

RIGHT: *Last Judgement*, Michelangelo Buonarroti, 1536–41, Sistine Chapel, Vatican. This work was commissioned by Pope Paul III from Michelangelo, who was now in later life and whose art had entered a more 'mannerist' phase.

224

In the intervening twenty-nine years Michelangelo's outlook had changed.
After the fame and reputation that the Sistine ceiling brought him, he had returned
to work on the Julian tomb and had become embroiled in the struggle between the
Medici and the Florentine Republic, siding with the latter, enduring the besieging

and capitulation of the city (1529–31) and then having to seek a rapprochement with the reinstated dukes. Rome had been sacked by Emperor Charles V (1527), Protestantism was on the rise – as was the Counter Reformation – and a prudery was setting in that demanded that the nudes he was painting be omitted or over-painted. They were thankfully permitted and later given loin-clothes, now removed in painstaking recent restoration. This has also revealed the vibrancy of the original colour, which complements the vigour and movement of the multitudinous figures. Beauty gives way to profound spiritual experience and an underlying pessimism. Around the dynamic central figure of Christ, the dead struggle out of their tombs, the tortured martyrs cry out for justice, and the elect are welcomed into heaven while the damned are pushed, poked and prodded to their doom by demons and by a figure popularized by Dante – Charon, who ferries the dead across the River Styx and beats off the damned with his oars. The gaping mouth of hell awaits them, just above the altar, which mediates Christ's redeeming sacrifice and humankind.

Michelangelo was now in what was conventionally seen as old age and a similar mood pervades his later works, such as the Crucifixion of St Peter and the Conversion of St Paul, frescoes commissioned for the Capella Paolina (1542–50) by Pope Paul III, who had also commissioned the Sistine *Last Judgement*. The self-conscious emotion and energy of such works have led to the application of the term 'Mannerist', a style that Michelangelo helped to pioneer and with which he inspired subsequent artists. A large marble group of the Entombment is thought to include a self-portrait of the artist as the Pharisee Nicodemus, intended for his own tomb. He was also a gifted poet and wrote some of his finest verse in old age. However, Michelangelo was to live for many more years and, ironically, it was largely the ill-fated tomb of Pope Julius that led to his involvement in one of his greatest projects and his mastery of yet another skill – architecture. He was given the immense task of completing St Peter's, Rome, which had been begun by Bramante, and gave the world one of its greatest domed buildings. He began work in 1546 at the age of seventy-one and was still coming onto site until his death in his late eighties (as Christopher Wren, whom he inspired, would later do at St Paul's, London), working unpaid but sustained by his faith and his unerring vision.

Raphael

Between the building campaigns of Bramante and Michelangelo a younger artist, whose métier was that of painter rather than architect, had been called to work on the St Peter's project – Raffaello Sanzio (1483–1520). Raphael, as he is known, had studied initially under Perugino (c. 1448–1523), producing polite altarpieces in his popular style, charaterized by a sugary balletic grace, and small panels on courtly themes such as the *Dream of a Knight* and *St George*. Perugino's own work, and those turned out by his workshop, was often formulaic and he gained a reputation for plagiarizing his own work for what were supposed to be new commissions. Vasari wrote that he was 'of little religious faith, and was quite unable to believe in the immortality of the soul, so that, in words suited to his pig-headedness he obstinately rejected all good ways of life. All his hopes lay in wordly gain and he was willing to do anything for money'. Such devalued currency would later cause artists such as the Pre-Raphaelites to seek inspiration in earlier art, which they saw as purer in content and intent.

Raphael's artistic training had begun with his father, who was court painter to Guidobaldo da Montefeltro, Duke of Urbino. His urbane manners, cultivated at the court, opened doors and in 1504 he arrived in Florence, armed with letters of introduction from people in high places. He applied himself to mastering the Florentine aesthetic requirement of movement, emotion and narrative, studying the work of Donatello, Leonardo and Michelangelo. During his four years in the city he produced a series of portraits and paintings of the Virgin and Child, including *La Belle Jardinière* of 1507, which echoes the composition of the *Virgin of the Rocks*. In 1508 he moved to Rome to serve Pope Julius II and remained there until his death. His first commission, the frescoes of the Pope's library, the Stanza della Segnatura, revolved around its classification system, featuring Theology, Poety, Philosophy and Law, including his masterly *School of Athens*, inspired by the Sistine ceiling – popes might evidently also count themselves among the philosophers. Further works in the Vatican before 1519 included the decoration of the Stanza d'Eliodoro with action-packed scenes of God's intervention to save the church, such as the *Repulse of Attila*, and the *Stanza dell'Incendio* and the *Loggia* for Pope Leo X, featuring stuccowork and Old Testament scenes on its vaulting. In order to expedite the work Raphael assembled a team, which included Giovanni Francesco Penni and Giulio Romano, working from his sketches. In 1515–16 he also designed the tapestries for the Sistine Chapel (some of the cartoons for which are now in the Victoria and Albert Museum, London), which were woven in Brussels, Flanders which, along with France, had specialized in the art since the Gothic age.

Another of Raphael's key patrons was the Sienese banker Agostino Chigi, who commissioned paintings on secular and religious subjects. The latter included frescoes of the Prophets and Sibyls for the Chigi chapel in San Maria del Popolo (1512–15). Michelangelo's influence is immediately apparent, but his Sistine idealization of male beauty is here replaced by its feminine counterpart. Such charms also characterize Raphael's Roman altarpieces, such as: the *Sistine Madonna*[12]

Madonna di Foligno,
Raphael, 1512, Vatican
Museum. Here Raphael
introduces Venetian light
and colour into his work.

of c. 1512–14; the *Madonna di Foligno* of 1512 for the Franciscan San Maria in Aracoeli, with its introduction of Venetian landscape, light and colour, stimulated by his contact with Sebastiano del Piombo; and his tondo of the *Holy Family with Palm Tree*,[13] in which the *sacra conversazione* is transformed into an intimate scene of family life and subtle inter-relationship. That same year he painted an important portrait of Julius II in which the psychological introspection of the aged man is in sharp contrast with the sensual fabrics of his costume of office. This demonstrates an insight, subtlety and control of emotion that is also present in Raphael's many Madonnas, but which is easy to overlook in the face of the proliferation of the genre by subsequent lesser artists.

Like Leonardo and Michelangelo, with whom he established the 'High Renaissance', Raphael was a consummate draughtsman and prolific drawer. His collaboration with the Bolognese printmaker Marcantonio Raimondi disseminated his work throughout Europe, reproducing his paintings and some specially designed works for print, such as the *Massacre of the Innocents*. Raphael died young at thirty-seven, unlike his two major peers, but he won fame in his day and was subsequently extremely influential – although from the nineteenth century onwards, when his work was presented as a watershed by Ruskin and the Pre-Raphaelite Brotherhood in England, he has been seen as inaugurating an age of religiosity and mawkish sentimental piety, which is belied by contemplation of his own images.

229

Brazen Images and Sounding Brass: The Significance and Use of Bronze in Christian Contexts

Dr Victoria Avery

Bronze, an alloy of copper and tin, was prized in the ancient world both for its aesthetic qualities, with its warm tonality and glamorous reflective surfaces, and for the great skill involved in its manufacture. It was also recognized as having certain advantages over more commonly available and cheaper materials such as wax, clay, gesso, wood, stone, marble and ivory. For bronze has great inherent tensile strength that permits the casting of objects with complex, open forms; it is resistant to the elements and can therefore be used for objects intended for outdoor settings as well as for ones destined for close contact with water or other liquids and fire; and it is very hard and therefore durable, and when struck resonates with a pleasant tone that carries over long distances. Given its great costliness, bronze became a signifier of wealth and status, and the preserve of the elite. Thanks to these unique characteristics, it was used in ancient Greece, Etruria and Rome to make all manner of sculpture and functional artefacts destined for use in imperial residences and patrician homes, as well as important temples and shrines. As the material of choice for votive statues and statuettes of pagan deities (subsequently viewed as idols by the church because of the injunction in the second commandment against the making and worship of graven images of false gods), bronze came to be regarded as a material with particularly strong pagan connotations. As a result, in the Byzantine world and during the Middle Ages in western Europe, bronze was hardly ever used to make free-standing figures of the Godhead or other Christian subjects.

That said, the use of bronze in Christian contexts was justified by several passages in the Old Testament that refer to items in brass (more properly either copper or bronze) being made for the Temple, at the direct command of either the Lord God or one of his agents. For example, at the Lord's command Moses ordered certain parts of the altar of burnt offering and its associated vessels to be made from copper/bronze (Exodus 38:1–20, 29–31); Solomon ordered two enormous bronze pillars and other items for the Temple porch (1 Kings 7:13–47); and King David ordered brass cymbals to be used by the Levite choir when they sang their joyful hymns before the ark of the covenant (1 Chronicles 15:19). Clearly the Lord God was not adverse to the employment of bronze in his service, for he inspired a number of craftsmen with the knowledge of the art of bronze casting, including Bezalel, son of Uri, and his assistant, Aholiab, son of Ahisamach (Exodus 35:30–35; 38:22–23) as well as Hiram of Tyre (1 Kings 7:13–14). Moreover, he famously commanded Moses to make a brazen serpent and raise it on a pole, which the disobedient Israelites had to look at in order to be saved from lethal snake bites (Numbers 21:4–9).

These biblical precedents meant that bronze could legitimately be used to make functional objects for Christian settings whether in the Greek East or Latin West. Its strength and durability meant that it was the perfect material from which to construct entrance portals, tombs, pulpits, altar-complexes, lecterns and bishop's stools, while its imperviousness to water meant that it was often used in the manufacture of holy water stoups, baptismal fonts, aspersoria, acquamaniles, and lavabos. As a poor conductor of heat, bronze was the ideal material for thuribles and light-holders (chandeliers, altar-candlesticks, floor-candelabra and paschal candlesticks), while its pleasant ringing tone meant it was used to make bells of all shapes and sizes.

During the Middle Ages, three-dimensional images of Christian subjects had been made but were rarely wrought in bronze and were normally incorporated within an architectonic structure. With the advent of the Renaissance, freestanding figures in bronze became acceptable. Small-scale bronzes with Christian subjects were made for both sacred and secular settings. Significantly, however, very few bronze statuettes of isolated female saints were commissioned and those which were tended to be fixed on altars or fonts inside churches. This was presumably because the majority of small-scale figural bronzes made in the Renaissance portrayed erotic and/or pagan subjects and were intended for intimate handling and close scrutiny by male collectors in private studies and, as a result, the bronze statuette had connotations that made it an inappropriate format for the portrayal of chaste female saints.

Life-size bronze figures of Christian subjects were also made when funds and space permitted. Given their expense, such bronzes were only ever destined for places of special importance, such as significant altars or the facades of key Christian buildings. They were normally conceived either as singletons or in pairs but occasionally multiple-figure complexes were commissioned, as proven by the High Altars in the Santo, Padua, and San Giorgio Maggiore, Venice. Moreover, on rare occasions, secular figures in bronze were made for sacred facades, such as the portrait-statue of Julius II that temporarily embellished San Petronio, Bologna (erected February 1508; torn down December 1511), and that of Tommaso Rangone that still crowns the entrance portal of San Zulian, Venice (1550s).

After prolonged ambivalence towards the material, the Roman Catholic Church adopted bronze whole-heartedly in the Post-Tridentine period as a splendid way to promulgate its message. Nowhere is this seen to better effect than in Bernini's Baldachin (1623–33) and Cathedra Petri (1657–66) in St Peter's, Rome.

The Northern Renaissance

Merchants and Mysteries

Humanism also found eager followers in northern Europe, among the urban mercantile middle classes or with their Medieval guilds or 'mysteries' and their religious fraternities. The role of illuminators – members of the guilds of limners – in transmitting the influence of the humanists and of Italian Renaissance art to northern Europe has already been touched upon. Painters in miniature upon vellum, such as Gerard Horenbout, Gerard David and Simon Bening, introduced perspective depiction of interiors, receding landscapes, portraiture and naturalism into their work, and some also painted on panels. Bening's multi-panelled *Stein Quadriptych*[1] may have functioned as a portable altarpiece and his landscapes outstrip their Italian counterparts, some of his miniatures effectively equalling small panel paintings. Roger van der Weyden is also thought to have been an illuminator.

Humanist Patronage in Northern Europe

Learned or aesthetically inclined royal patrons such as King Matthias 'Corvinus' of Hungary, François I of France, Emperor Maximilian I and, later, Elizabeth I of England, fostered the absorption of humanism into their nations' cultural lives. Albrecht Dürer and Hans Burgkmair pioneered the development of the woodcut, under Maximilian, introducing images into the new brand of books printed with movable type, introduced to the West by Gutenberg in the 1450s. Fine illuminated manuscript books continued to be produced for wealthy patrons, however, and much of the decoration in incunables (early printed books) was added by hand. What largely disappeared was the use of colour and ornament to enliven, articulate and help the reader to navigate the text.

RIGHT: *The Stein Quadriptych*, either intended to be attached to a wooden panel as an altarpiece or to form part of a manuscript, by Simon Bening, early sixteenth century, south Netherlands, Ghent or Bruges.

In the mercantile domesticity of the towns of the Netherlands, books of hours, vernacular prayerbooks and small portable altars or devotional images were de rigeur. Individual patrons, guilds and charitable confraternities commissioned altarpieces and other works for their favoured churches and are depicted themselves among the ranks of the saints.

The Ghent Altarpiece, carrying twenty scenes revolving around the Adoration of the Lamb, carries an inscription of 1432 attributing it to Hubert van Eyck and his brother Jan, who completed it, at the behest of Joos Vijd and his wife Elizabeth Borhaut, for the Church of St John the Baptist (later St Bavo), Ghent. The donors are portrayed on the wings kneeling in prayer, and their endowment provided for a daily Mass to be said at the altar it graced. Jan van Eyck became court painter both to John of

The Ghent Altarpiece, Hubert and Jan Van Eyck, c. 1432, a Flemish masterwork, painted for St Bavo, Ghent.

234

Bavaria, ruler of Holland, working in The Hague, and Duke Philip the Good of Burgundy, relocating to Bruges around 1425. Philip also used him in diplomatic missions and entrusted him to paint the likeness of his prospective Portuguese bride. Like many of his Italian counterparts, he was absorbed in the study of optics and perspective, and his works exhibit a detached observation reminiscent of that of Paolo Uccello – but with greater realism. His most famous work, the *Arnolfini Marriage*, produced for an Italian merchant living in Bruges, with its reflection of Arnolfini and his bride in the convex mirror hanging on the wall, is well known for such preoccupations. His images are full of minutely observed detail – a legacy of Late Gothic art but also designed to convey complex exegetical meaning, drawn from works such as Rupert of Deutz's *Concerning the Victory of the Word of God*. Like Italian masters, such northern masters had to diversify commercially and van Eyck also painted and gilded statuary for Bruges town hall. He experimented with oil paints and glazes in order to achieve the maximum amount of realistic detailing and was attributed, erroneously, by Vasari with the invention of the oil-based medium. He certainly pioneered the technique and won renown for his expertise as far afield as Italy.

Roger van der Weyden and Netherlandish Art

The breath of life, emotion and movement was added in the work of Roger van der Weyden (c. 1399–1464). He learned his craft in the workshop of Robert Campin in Tournai (Belgium, then in the Duchy of Burgundy) from 1427–32 and in 1436 became City Painter of Brussels. Around this time he painted perhaps his most influential work, the *Escorial Deposition*,[2] in which the figures are depicted with tremendous realism and charged with intense emotion, while arranged like sculptures against a blank wall – a device repeated in his treatment of the subject of Calvary, as if the statuary familiar from Gothic sculpture had finally come to life. His interest in anatomy, convincing though it is, is ancillary to his desire to convey the anatomy of grief.

In 1450 van der Weyden was in Italy, and the influence of works by Fra Angelico and of commissions for the Medici can be detected in his subsequent work. The Italianate device of having one figure gaze out of the picture directly at the viewers, to draw them into the scene, is exploited in his *Adoration of the Kings* triptych[3] via the maidservant in the Presentation scene on one of the wings, while in the central panel, behind the Magi, a long cavalcade of people recedes into the distance – another favourite Italian device. The procession is headed by a Jewish High Priest, who represents Christian hopes that the Jews might also one day come to accept Christ as the Messiah. Northern Gothic motifs are also incorporated, such as

The *Escorial Deposition*,
Roger van der Weyden,
c. 1435–37, a Flemish
masterpiece.

the ox and ass in attendance (a detail not recounted in the Gospels): the former, representing the New Testament, looks on expectantly, while the latter is absorbed with the trough. Another major commission was a huge altarpiece on the theme of the Last Judgement for Chancellor Rolin's Hospital in Beaune, dedicated in 1451. It stood at the end of the huge hall wherein the sick lay; a Doom (Last Judgement) was hardly guaranteed to lift their spirits but would certainly encourage them to tend to their souls, even if their bodies were failing. Van der Weyden has done what he could to soften the worst excesses of suffering traditionally incorporated into the scene.

In his *St Luke Painting the Virgin* (two versions, in Boston and Munich), he makes visual allusion to van Eyck's *Madonna* of Chancellor Rolin, but introduces the illusion of the artist painting the artist who is drawing the Virgin and Child on his sketch pad. The theme also alludes to the Byzantine tradition that asserted that the definitive image of the Theotokos was granted to St Luke in a vision and was a

genuine, immutable likeness. Van der Weyden's intriguing approach gives us another valuable insight into the psychology and self-perception of the Renaissance artist.

Hans Memling (c. 1430/1440–94) was among Roger van der Weyden's followers and again catered for both the local townsfolk and Italian merchants in Bruges, with light, airy landscapes and sweetness of demeanour amongst his figures. His later works also featured the antique ornaments of Italian art. The idealization and mysticism that he introduced into portraits, for example, his *Young Man at Prayer*,[4]

Young Man at Prayer, Hans Memling, second half of the fifteenth century, southern Netherlands.

THE NORTHERN RENAISSANCE

recommended him to nineteenth-century romantics such as the Nazarenes. Sacred portraits, in the form of intimate little panels of half-length Virgin and Child images, were a speciality of the Louvain workshop of Dirk Bouts (c. 1415–75). Such portrait-like figures were also treated in the round by sculptors such as Nicolaus Gerhaerts who worked in and around Germany, in towns such as Cologne, Trier and Strasbourg, and also in Vienna between c. 1462–73, perpetuating the legacy of Netherlandish sculptor Claus Sluter (c. 1350–1406). The influence of such Gothic / Renaissance fusion can be seen as late as the mid-fifteenth century in the corbels depicting the townsfolk of Sibenik in Croatia, which were carved by Juraj Dalmatinac (also known as Giorgio Orsini) around its cathedral's exterior.

Van der Weyden's true heir, in terms of emotional content, however, was Hugo van der Goes. The veristic realism of his portraits and his ability to capture the spiritual revelation to both noble and peasant alike may have helped to ensure his fame in Italy, as well as the southern Netherlands. Tommaso Portinari, a Florentine merchant, commissioned him to paint a massive triptych for San Maria Nuova, Florence – the *Portinari Altarpiece*[5] of c. 1475–78. Tommaso and his family are actually there, in the chilly winter landscape in which the shepherds adore the named Christ child, whose role as sacrificial victim is implicit in his vulnerable form lying on the ground. Ghirlandaio paid tribute to the piece in his *Adoration* of 1485 for San Trinita, Florence. Hugo's inner vision finally came to dominate him. He had become a lay brother of the Roode Kloster monastery, near Brussels, by 1478 and later sadly slipped into delusion and clinical depression, participating fully in the anguish of his figures in late works, such as the *Death of the Virgin*.[6]

Quentin Massys (c. 1465/6–1530) ran the leading Antwerp workshop, passing it on to his sons. His two great altarpieces, the *St Anne Altarpiece* of 1507–09,[7] and the *St John Altarpiece*,[8] conflate northern Gothic iconographies with Italianate settings and figure style. He also possessed a talent for juxtaposing beauty and the grotesque, studying Leonardo's abilities in this area, and helped to popularize a satirical, moralizing genre. This can be seen in works such as the *Unequal Lovers*,[9] in which a young prostitute cajoles an elderly lecher out of his purse, which she passes to a fool. These caricatures, parodying human folly, would become a feature of sixteenth-century Netherlandish art. Such images paralleled the satirical writing of the humanist scholar Erasmus, of whom Massys painted an empathetic little portrait, owned by the sitter's close friend, the English Chancellor and stalwart Catholic, Sir Thomas More, who resisted King Henry VIII's divorce and the onset of the Reformation, being sacrificed as one of its early martyrs.

Keeping Your Head in Times of Change

Reformation, Resistance and the Rise of Protestantism

In 1517, while Raphael was designing his tapestries for the Sistine Chapel, Martin Luther nailed his 95 Theses to the door at Wittenberg. Both were a call for the reform of papal and clerical abuses of power and laxity of spiritual and moral life, and had been triggered by the campaign of Pope Leo X to sell indulgences to raise money for the rebuilding of St Peter's in Rome – someone had to pay for all those papal artistic commissions, and more often than not it was the people.

The Spread of Protestantism in Europe

These protests, hence the term Protestant, lit a long fuse that had been waiting since the dissent of the twelfth century to fully ignite. Luther, condemned as a heretic, was so shocked by the fires of popular unrest that had been lit that he sided with the German princes against the Peasants' War, with its destruction and looting. The princes, and some civic authorities, in Germany and Scandinavia adopted a more methodical but equally effective approach to the despoliation of church property by seizing it and ceasing to financially subsidize Rome. Churches were still required and so it was the monasteries that fared worst.

In England, Henry VIII, thwarted in his attempts to beget a male heir and to divorce Catherine of Aragon, a staunch Spanish Catholic, in favour of Anne Boleyn with her Protestant leanings, launched the Dissolution of the Monasteries in 1539. Cartloads of ecclesiastical treasures – the bulk of the Medieval metalworkers' art – were brought to London for melting down and the Crown also acquired monastic lands. Henry, who had prided himself upon his image as the ideal northern Renaissance prince, had now become the Defender of the Faith and Supreme Head of the English (Anglican) Church, and those who failed to swear the Oath of Supremacy, such as Thomas More and John Fisher, Bishop of Rochester, were executed. England had already been experiencing religious unrest for over a century. A popular movement to translate scripture into the English language, a trend begun by the Anglo-Saxons, had been led by John Wycliffe and the Lollards, who had posted their articles of complaint on the West Door of St Paul's Cathedral, London, in 1406, and more recently copies of Tyndale's English New Testament, printed in Worms in 1526 for export to England, were seized and burned there. Both Wycliffe and Tyndale were condemned as heretics. Later in the sixteenth century, however, St Paul's would be the first English church in which copies of the Bible in English were freely available for public consultation.

In Switzerland the Protestant cause was championed first by Zwingli and then by Calvin, who by 1541 had introduced his own brand of theocratic rule to Geneva, to which all citizens were forced to subscribe on pain of exile. His influence spread to Scotland and gave rise to the Huguenots in France, while in Holland it launched a long and bitter struggle to throw off Spanish rule of the Netherlands.

Wars of religion and political intrigues plagued much of the sixteenth and seventeenth centuries. Much art was destroyed, as well as a myriad of human lives, and in England much of what had escaped the denominational *voltes faces* of the reigns of the Tudors – Protestant Edward VI, Catholic Mary and her Spanish consort Philip, and Anglican Elizabeth I – fell foul of the destructive iconoclasm of the Puritans during the English Civil War of 1642–49 and the military rule that followed. The walls of ancient churches were now whitewashed, their windows glazed with clear glass, carved idols (i.e. sculptures) defaced and their altars stripped of all save the Book and the cross – much as their Byzantine counterparts had been some 900 years previously. Many cathedrals, however, perpetuated a rather higher churchmanship and preserved some ritual elements. Those who did not subscribe to the new brand of state religion, known as recusants, were heavily fined and sometimes persecuted, with penalties against Catholics persisting until the Act of Emancipation of 1829. They played an important role in salvaging some church treasures, including illuminated manuscripts – certain of which are still surfacing from private family ownership today – also smuggling many items to the Continent. Chances of survival there were patchy but higher; the French Revolution of 1789 unleashed similar waves of destruction.

Domesticity and Portraiture:
Art and the Personal Nature of Faith

The art of the period reflects these events and trends. The vision of the twelfth-century Irishman Tundal, who summoned up from the depths of his being a horrific, fiery vision of hell that burns itself onto the viewer's heart, achieved renewed popularity around this time, and a French manuscript preserves a terrifying visual embodiment of Tundal's nightmare. The influence of such illuminated manuscripts, and of the grotesques that stalked their margins, and that were also the denizens of Renaissance grottoes, can also be felt in the work of Hieronymus Bosch (c. 1450–1516), who worked in the north Netherlands and knew of a Dutch version of Tundal's work. His mastery of the oil technique adds an inner luminescence to his paintings, which feature hellfire, sweeping fantastic landscapes and a weird array of hybrid creatures inspired by their medieval ancestors but given even stranger variety by the vivid, apocalyptic imagination of the artist. Profound insight into human psychology and folly is conveyed by means of simple, innovative iconographies, such as the vain young lovers in his *Garden of Earthly Delights*[1] triptych of c. 1504, who are so self-absorbed that they inhabit a bubble, resembling a carriage, that isolates them from the needs of the world, and which will soon become an eternal prison for their souls and their psyches in the aftermath of their lustful obsession. Bosch was a devout member of a religious confraternity – the Brotherhood of Our Lady – and

The Mouth of Hell, from the Vision of Hell by the Irish cleric Tundal, illuminated by Simon Marmion, Franco-Flemish, c. 1470, and owned by Margaret of York. Los Angeles, Getty Museum.

A startling and perceptive allegory of the cost of human self-absorption, *The Garden of Earthly Delights*, by Hieronymus Bosch, c. 1504, Netherlands.

his concern was to use art to impart spiritual and moral truths, drawn from the popular devotional literature and preaching of the day. Where other artists, such as Grünewald, might rely upon terror and the empathy of pain to achieve this, Bosch employed a subtler, more imaginative vocabulary that, like the satire of the Monty Python team in modern times, also recognized the value of humour and the witty pun.

In 1505 Lucas Cranach the Elder (1472–1553), sometimes hailed as the principal artist of the Reformation, arrived in Wittenberg to paint for the court of Frederick the Wise, Elector of Saxony, the protector of Luther whom Cranach befriended, each serving as godfather to the other's child. He painted several portraits of Luther, illustrated his German translation of the Bible and designed the

new Lutheran style of altar. He also helped to introduce a new portrait format of full-length figures and extended these to small 'cabinet pictures' – to be enjoyed erotically in the privacy of the patron's own room – featuring classical nudes in either pagan or Christian subjects, such as the *Judgement of Paris* or *Bathsheba*. He did not, however, favour classical proportions, in Italian fashion, preferring those of Late Gothic art. In the *Allegory of Redemption*[2] painted by his son, Lucas the Younger, in 1553–55, Lutheran belief is represented with the artist at the foot of the cross, Christ's redeeming blood spurting directly onto him without any priestly intervention, while the figures of Luther and John the Baptist attend – thus affirming Luther's teaching that only the sacraments of baptism and the Eucharist were valid and that salvation was by faith alone.

Many altarpieces continued to be made as foci of divine intervention, of which the most elaborate form was the German *Schnitzaltar*, a striking and influential example of which is the *Isenheim Altar*³ painted by Matthias Grünewald (c. 1475–1528) with sculpture by Nikolaus von Hagenau/Hagnower. Grünewald produced art and hydraulic engineering projects for successive archbishops of Mainz, but joined the Peasants' Rebellion in 1525 and had to flee to Frankfurt and then Halle. His great polyptych was completed in 1515 for the hospitallers of San Anthony at Isenheim and is renowned for the gruesome detailing of its iconography, emphasizing Christ's physical wounds and the burning skin disease (ergotism – St Anthony's fire) that

244

Allegory of Redemption, Lucas Cranach the Younger, 1553–55, Wittenberg. An embodiment of Lutheran theology, with Luther and the Baptist in attendance, illustrating Luther's teaching that only the sacraments of baptism and the eucharist were valid, with salvation by faith alone.

The *Isenheim Altar*, a harrowing evocation of suffering painted by Matthias Grünewald.

tortures the demon who tempts St Anthony and in the treatment of which the Antonites specialized. St Anthony and the plague saint, Sebastian, feature as painted trompe l'oeil sculptures on the outer wings. The proportions of the figures are distorted, their gestures and expressions emotionally exaggerated, and they stand out against the lowering darkness of the background, save for the lyrical panel depicting the Virgin and Child in a garden – an enduring refuge and place of calm in the eye of the storm.

Bosch's influence can be detected in the Antwerp workshop of the Bruegel family. Its founder, Pieter Bruegel the Elder (c. 1525–69) likewise favoured moralistic themes, for example in his engravings of the *Seven Deadly Sins* and his nightmarish painting of the *Triumph of Death*[4] (c. 1562–64), a protest against the harshness of Spanish rule in the Netherlands. In typical urban fashion, he used the rural peasantry as his vehicle to make his messages more palatable and humorous to his clients.

A humane and empathetic treatment of *The Woman Taken in Adultery*, Pieter Bruegel the Elder, 1565, Brussels.

However, the importance of landscape in his work and the emphasis upon the labour necessary to live within it is also a major consideration. Bruegel travelled widely in Italy and imbibed its heady influence. Where Lorenzetti might dwell upon the effects of good and bad government, however, Bruegel connects the spiritual life of the people with the well-being of their partnership with Creation and their ability to thrive or to fail, as in his series of paintings entitled *Netherlandish Proverbs*[5] (1559) and his *Big Fish Eat Little Fish*. Upon moving to Brussels in 1565 his subject matter becomes more overtly religious and introduces further Italian influence inspired by works such as Raphael's Sistine tapestry cartoons, which had travelled to that city as models during the weaving of the tapestries themselves. His compositions are filled with more monumental figures, introducing a different kind of psychological drama

– like the close-up in film, as in his *The Woman Taken in Adultery* of 1565.[6] He was less compassionate, perhaps, towards the contemporary female rulers of England, Scotland, France and the Netherlands, who may be parodied by his *Dulle Griet* (sometimes paraphrased as 'Mad Meg') of 1562 in which a woman rampages through the world, causing havoc with her ill-considered array of arms.

Bruegel married the daughter of the earliest northern print publisher, Pieter Coeck van Aelst, who helped to disseminate his work. However, the greatest artist of the woodblock and copper engraving was the painter Albrecht Dürer (1471–1528) of Nuremberg. Only Rembrandt rivals him in effectively translating his art into the printed medium, and neither of these masterly artists stops at this but also uses the medium in its own right to tremendous graphic and narrative effect. The medieval craftsman was now fully the artist, a role that Dürer also theoretized, along with his observations on techniques and on aesthetic principles ('kunst' as he termed them) in his writings. The calibre of his drawings can be judged by his famous study of

Praying Hands, by skilled German painter, draughtsman and engraver Albrecht Dürer, 1509.

Praying Hands[8] for the *Assumption of the Virgin*, commissioned for the Dominican Church in Frankfurt in 1509. In 1498 he cut both the text and woodcuts for the Apocalypse – the first printed book made entirely by an artist, thereby perpetuating a fine medieval tradition. Other series, focusing upon the Passion and the Life of the Virgin, proved similarly influential, as did single prints such as *The Knight, Death and the Devil* (1513), which symbolized the resistance of faith to mortal peril and temptation, spreading his fame to Italy where he influenced artists such as the mannerist painter Pontormo. He knew humanist scholars in his hometown and also travelled to Venice, where he became acquainted with the elderly Giovanni Bellini, whom he praised as 'the best painter of them all'. While there he painted the *Madonna of the Rose Garlands*[9] (1505–06, now badly damaged) as an altarpiece for the German community of San Bartolommeo, celebrating ecumenical devotion to the rosary and paying homage to Bellini in its rich use of colour. This, along with his self-portraits and his educated approach, convinced Italian sceptics of

KEEPING YOUR HEAD IN TIMES OF CHANGE

his artistry. He admired Luther and his teaching and met Erasmus, his frustration at the erudite scholar's moderation causing him to write in his diary, 'Oh Erasmus of Rotterdam, where wilt thou stop? Behold how the wicked tyranny of worldly power… prevails. Hear, thou knight of Christ!… Attain the martyr's crown… make thyself heard' – a call to the intellegentsia to abandon the ivory tower and to engage with both the world and eternity that echoes down the ages.

In Erasmus's defence, these were highly dangerous times in the fundamentalist Protestant climate of Basel, which erupted into an iconoclastic riot in 1529 and which he shortly left. His pronouncement in 1526 that 'Basel is a place where the arts are freezing' had proved prophetic. Returning there in 1528 from spells working in France and England, Hans Holbein (1497/8–53) found that the religious subjects he had painted and engraved earlier, such as his *Last Supper*[10] influenced by Leonardo were no longer favoured. In 1529 he accepted Lutheranism but remained doctrinally uncertain; in 1530 he is recorded as saying that 'he needed a better explanation of Holy Communion before he would go' and, shortly after, that 'he was among those who do not object, but want to conform to other Christians'. Yet even Holbein's desire for Christian unity could not be accommodated and in 1532 he moved to England for good, leaving his family behind – a sadness enshrined in his melancholy portrait of them – to serve the vanity of King Henry VIII and his court. He relinquished Christian themes for veristic portraiture, save for his frontispiece to the Coverdale Bible of 1535 depicting the king as the head of the church, and a miniature for this unwise ruler in which he doubles as Solomon.

Symbolism and Allegory

If the Reformation court and the interiors of Protestant churches and civic buildings left little or no room for sacred art, there was still some scope in the home, even if religious content had to be obliquely or allegorically conveyed. One method of doing this was through the inclusion of certain motifs that covertly signalled belief, rather as early Christians had done under pagan Roman rule. The inclusion of loaves of bread and glasses of wine in still life compositions carried immediate Eucharistic allusions. The moralizing *Vanitas*[11] still-life was an even more coded way of making such connections in thought, its seemingly banal arrangement of objects imbued with symbolic meaning. It arose in the Calvinist university town of Leiden during the seventeenth century, the term *Vanitas* being taken from Ecclesiastes 1:2 – 'Vanity of vanities; all is vanity' – and employed traditional *memento mori* motifs such as the skull, the hour-glass, the expiring candle, the moth and the fading flower. These were juxtaposed with items denoting vanity, such as the mirror, books, musical instruments or collectibles.

Vanitas, an allegory of human mortality by Dutch artist Harmen Steenwyck, 1640.

Among the major practitioners of the genre were W. C. Heda, Jan de Heem, Harmen Steenwyck and, in Spain, Antonio Pereda and Juan de Valdés Leal. Holbein even predicted the genre, and linked it back to its medieval roots, in his *Ambassadors* of 1533, with its inclusion of a distorted skull (a false perception of mortality?) among the tools of the politician's trade. Some of his portraits also draw on a pre-existing medieval tradition of symbolism to convey coded messages concerning the sitters. For example, when portraying Luke Reskimer,[12] Page of the Chamber to Henry VIII, around 1534, Holbein introduces plants against his characteristic blue background: the vine and the fig, the former symbolizing faith and the latter good works – a fundamental source of theological conflict during the Reformation as the preferred routes to salvation of Protestant and Catholic factions respectively. The belief of Reskimer and, perhaps, of the artist that both were necessary and inextricably entwined in Christ is discretely signalled. Another portrait, of Sir Brian Tuke

(c. 1533–35), Henry VIII's Treasurer of the Chamber, is more overt. He wears a large gold cross bearing the five wounds of Christ and holds a piece of paper bearing the words of Job 10:20, 'Are not my days few?', presumably a comment upon the danger in which his continuing espousal of the old ways of faith placed him. It is also a meditation upon the inconsequentiality of the brevity of human life and its perils in relation to eternity, and the immutability of faith and conscience. The very fabric of the work may contribute to this, for Holbein's usual intense cobalt blue background, with its traditional celestial associations, has on this rare occasion corroded (it must have been a copper-based pigment) to a verdigris-brown. Might the artist have intentionally experimented with what we now term 'process art' (in which the technique used engenders a gradual physical change in the work's appearance) to contribute to the work's role as a *memento mori*, with its very substance decomposing before our eyes?

Playing it Safe?

Holbein has attracted some criticism for a perceived failure to use his talents to promote an art of the English Reformation, in favour of the safety and commercial gain of the court portrait. But these were times when it was easy to lose your head – literally – when most believers preferred to bide their time and hold their own counsel in respect of their faith; some to save their skins and some to preserve Christian unity and avoid further fuelling the fires of Smithfield that consumed their more outspoken peers. Holbein offered those caught in the maelstrom a dignified means of witnessing to their dilemma through the empathetic medium of that most psychologically revealing form of art – the portrait. If this offered a safely ambiguous insight into the interior psyche of the sitter, the interiors of buildings offered even more secure subject matter to painters. Some, notably Dutch artist Pieter Jansz Saenredam (1597–1665), would specialize in depictions of the stripped altars and austere, tranquil interiors of Protestant churches – often older Gothic structures with whitewashed walls and clear glass through which an even, all-illuming light penetrates like the rational intellect. The celebration of the virtues of puritanical domestic life would also lead to the genre of Dutch domestic interiors by masters such as Leiden painter Jan Steen (1626–79), whose works often conveyed a moralistic theme, as in *The Effects of Intemperance*,[13] or included biblical subjects such as Samson and Delilah. While working in Delft he consorted with other great genre artists such as Pieter de Hooch (1629–83) and Jan Vermeer (1632–75), whose œuvre includes not only the allegorical insights into private life for which he is renowned but, early in his career, larger history paintings including *Christ in the House of Martha*[14] and a late work, *The Allegory of Faith*,[15] in which Catholic doctrine is symbolically explored – for the Reformation by no means triumphed completely, even in the Netherlands.

In 1520 Dürer had also converted to Lutheranism, even though its puritanical tastes aborted some of his final works, including an altarpiece he intended to present to his hometown. Nor did his new faith prevent him from attending the coronation of the staunchly Catholic Emperor Charles V, successor to his former patron Maximilian I, and continuing to accept an imperial pension. But then, he had ever an eye to success and status. In one of his letters from Italy he had written, 'How shall I long for the sun in the cold; here I am a gentleman, at home I am a parasite.' His interests were wide and he was not averse to designing armour, as well as prints on knightly virtue, to support them. During his final tour of the Netherlands in 1520–21, accompanied by his wife Agnes who marketed his prints, he was struck by both the van Eyck Ghent altarpiece, the *Adoration of the Lamb*, and by Charles V's collection of exotic pre-Columbian objects, given to the Conquistadors by the Mexican Emperor Montezuma – or seized by them. He recorded the impact of the latter in his diary, writing 'I have seen nothing that rejoiced my heart so much as these things, for I saw amongst them wonderful works of art, and I marvelled at the subtle ingenia of men in foreign lands. Indeed I cannot express all that I thought there.' The world was becoming a much bigger place and the art of the Aztecs would soon be melted down and replaced, in its homeland, with a folk art version of Christian art, worshipped by an indigenous population that was unfamiliar with the white God and saints of the Spanish soldiers who exploited them and of the missionaries who, however pure their intentions, brought with them not only the Word of God but also an assortment of decimating plagues and a yoke reminiscent of those endured by the people of Israel under Pharaoh.

251

The Dispute on Images During the Reformation and Counter-Reformation

Professor Iole Carlettini

The vast and often dramatic debate that took place in the sixteenth century on the nature and aims of images is an issue that goes beyond art history and cuts to the very core of the Reformation itself. The accusation of 'idolatry' resonated for a long time in Europe, not only against the world of art, but also against the whole devotional and religious system of Catholicism. Images, or rather idols, were considered by some, along with works of art, relics, altars – and, in the most radical cases, the Mass and the Eucharist itself – to be part of that complex symbolic apparatus that had supported the Catholicism cult for centuries. The saints in particular were considered to be idols, as in growing numbers they appropriated the worship proper to God, creating a form of 'parapolitheism' in which images played a fundamental role.

The Reformation Stance

The crucial importance of the dispute concerning images is significantly demonstrated by the fact that the occasion for the 95 Theses, affixed by Martin Luther to the doors of Wittenberg Church on 31 October 1517, was provided by the impudent campaign to sell indulgences carried out in Germany to finance the renovation of St Peter's Basilica in Rome – the most significant element of the 'iconographic policy' pursued by the papacy at the beginning of the sixteenth century. This custom was stigmatized as 'most trivial' in one of the Theses: Luther's condemnation struck at the foundation of Late Medieval devotional practice – the belief in charitable acts as a means of gaining salvation, which was the main point of contention in his argument with the Catholic Church. In spite of this, and even though Luther had previously condemned the abuse of images, he never rejected figural art. It was his Wittenberg University colleague, Andreas Bodenstein von Karlstadt, who expanded the controversy to include the rejection of images and symbols in a broad and radical sense: from the image itself to holy water, to the denial of transubstantiation – the belief that Christ is physically present in the consecrated bread and wine used in the Eucharist. Karlstadt's ideas gained ground and found favour with Wittenberg City Council, which approved the reformation of the Mass and the abolition of images, and with the populace who, between the end of 1521 and the beginning of the following year, repeatedly destroyed altars and pulled down paintings and sculptures in the churches.

This social disorder induced Martin Luther to leave the Wartburg castle belonging to the Elector of Saxony, Frederic, where he had been hiding since his return from the Diet of Worms, and return to Wittenberg. On 9 March 1522, on the occasion of the Feast of Orthodoxy which celebrated the victory over iconoclasm, Luther delivered the first of a series of eight sermons, in which he frequently mentioned the theme of images. In the theologian's view, they were 'unnecessary, and we are free to have them or not, although it would be much better if we did not have them at all'; they were 'those things which for God are neither commanded nor forbidden'. Luther viewed images as *adiaphora* – that is, matters not regarded as essential to faith, but nevertheless permissible for Christians – thus disempowering them, 'just as when the poison has been removed from a snake'.

Luther's authority brought peace to Wittenberg, but it could not stop the wave of iconoclasm. Big

Lucas Cranach, *Altarpiece*, 1547, Wittenberg, Christ Church.

cities such as Strasburg and Basel emptied their churches of their iconographic apparatus, while a new and solid theological school of thought on such matters was developing, headed by Ulrich Zwingli in Zurich and above all by John Calvin in Geneva. In their writings the theological significance of the issue of images is evident: the two reformers, convinced that '*finitum non est capax infiniti*' (the finite cannot contain the infinite), both refused the representation of the sacred and the belief in the real presence of Christ in the consecrated bread of the Eucharist. This contrasted with the position of Luther, who never ceased to consider the sacraments as 'corporeal signs' of the presence of God in the church and to allow images in the churches. This ideological rift led to real differences – in 1620 Lutherans in Prague still fought against Calvinist iconoclasm – and paved the way to two different modes of figuration.

In the Protestant world the situation of art changed radically, both in places where iconoclasm was accepted as well as those where it was not. As early as 1526 Erasmus, who had also contested the abuse of images, lamented that in Zurich, where the ecclesiastical authorities methodically provided for their removal, 'the arts do freeze'. Many painters closed their studios or moved, such as Hans Holbein, who went to England. Where their walls were not bare, Calvinist churches such as the Huguenot Temple of Charanton, like their eighth-century Byzantine counterparts, were covered with inscriptions celebrating the centrality of the Word of God in the new religion.

In the opposite faction, once the didactic purpose of sacred art had been reaffirmed, it fell to Luther himself to conceive a series of images appropriate to reformed churches, based on the representation of the acknowledged sacraments and on the exaltation of the cross. The altarpiece of Wittenberg Church, commissioned from Lucas Cranach, can be considered a manifesto of this position. Alongside allusions to baptism and Holy Communion, the importance of preaching – together with the founders and spiritual fathers of the Reformation, Luther and Melanchthon among them – is affirmed. The portraits of prominent Lutherans became fundamental features of Reformation iconography, with curiously idolatrous consequences, for Luther's portraits were held to be wonder-working and incombustible.

The spread of new ideas was facilitated by the recent invention of print, allowing widespread circulation of texts and a rich pictorial output, based on the biblical representations and polemical images adopted in anti-papist propaganda. The limitations imposed on Reformation painters led, on the other hand, to an extraordinary flourishing of secular painting, often with a didactic-moralistic purpose, which soon developed into specialized genres – notable among which are the splendid reproductions of the bare, still interiors of Calvinist churches, in which the Dutch artist Pieter Jansz Saenredam excelled.

The Response of the Roman Catholic Church

The official position of the Roman Church was enunciated in a decree of the twenty-fifth session of the Council of Trent (3–4 December, 1563). The cult of icons of Christ, the Virgin Mary and the saints was legitimized on the grounds of the Second Council of Nicaea (787 CE): 'the honour paid to an image traverses it, reaching the model'. Other images were attributed with the function of educating the illiterate in line with the teaching *litterae laicorum* (in images the laity read), proposed by Gregory the Great (590–604 CE). All things considered, the conciliar fathers could have said, as their Nicaean predecessors had, 'We neither diminish nor augment, but simply guard intact all that pertains to the Catholic Church,' confirming the value of unwritten tradition. In the absence of any scriptural reference, bishops were entrusted with safeguarding orthodoxy: it was their task to lead the faithful towards a correct use of images, to check upon their conformity to evangelical provisions and norms of decorum, and to intervene in suspicious or dangerous cases.

Once the lawfulness of the cult of images had been established – in fact, it had never seriously been called into question – the debate shifted to consider their abuse, a matter that, even before the Protestant dispute, had raised no few doubts and anxieties even among those who would remain Catholic. Erasmus's polemics against the superstitious overvaluation of the power of religious images are well known, but even in Italy, replete with the triumphs of the Renaissance, an instance of denouncing the superstitious use of images can be found. The Dominican Bartholomew of Crema reproached 'ceremonial Christians' as guilty of indulging in the emotional effects of liturgical celebrations that were too full of the sensory seductions of light, music and images. Also of particular significance was the condemnation of the formal excesses of modern painting – a debate which focused upon the *Last Judgement* in the Sistine Chapel. The audacious iconographic choices (the presence of the pagan Charon, the wingless angels) and the extensive use of nudes violently heightened the deep sense of spiritual anxiety, which was far from the triumphant acceptance of doctrinal truths expressed in Raphael's rooms nearby. Michelangelo's masterpiece seemed to incorporate all the 'errors' that a painting solicitous for the viewer's devotional growth should avoid.

The responsibility that the Council had attributed to bishops generated a large number of treatises from which Cardinal Gabriele Paleotti's contribution stands out. Consultant on the matter of images at the Council of Trent and Bishop of Bologna, he wrote his *Discorso intorno alle immagini* (*Discourse upon Images*), published posthumously, after much authorial elaboration and a first circulation limited to a restricted circle of cultivated people and

254

prelates. Inspired by the need to implement the Tridentine decree on images, the treatise aims to guide art towards the exact mediation of the truths of faith. Paleotti's proposal is part of a broad historical and conceptual framework in which formal needs are completely neglected: indifferent to the dispute that divided mannerists and classicists, the Cardinal advocates painting in which theological content of assured orthodoxy is unambiguously transmitted to the believer. Paleotti's zeal led him in the last years of his life to plan a Latin translation of his work that would have allowed it to reach every corner of Catholic Europe, promoting a set of laws regulating images in the way that the *Index librorum prohibitorum* did for books. None of these projects was fulfilled: the Roman Church was not interested in stressing the potential danger of images and thereby confirming indirectly the criticism from the Protestant sector. The need for an operative control on images was satisfied by more direct means: the extremely successful *De picturibus et imaginibus sacris* by Jan Van der Meulen (Molanus), published soon after the end of the Council, and disseminated up until the nineteenth century – an ultimate guide for the definition of correct iconographies, above all those of the saints.

With regard to figurative language the Cardinal's proposals were more successful, promoting simplified images that empathically activated an honest devotion, as embodied in the works of Scipione Pulzone, in which several traditional elements, wisely combined, cancel each other in a neutral, timeless language. Similarly, the work of the Carraccis in Bologna gives the impression of that 'devoted truthfulness' sought by the Cardinal.

Artists' responses to the religious tensions of the sixteenth century seem to have varied considerably. There is no doubt that in its more extreme forms the intense work on the nature and purposes of image, with its large quantity of prescriptions, prohibitions and limitations, had called into question the autonomy of the artist, which some critics viewed as having given rise to almost heretical ideas and concepts among artists such as Michelangelo, Lorenzo Lotto and Pontormo – whose frescoes in the Choir of San Lorenzo in Florence have been interpreted as the visual epitome of the *Cathechism* by Juan de Valdés. More innocent were the liberties that brought Paolo Veronese to trial in generally tolerant Venice. Accused of not having followed the evangelical rules in his illustration of the Last Supper, which he transformed into the *Feast in the House of Levi*, the painter was forced to defend before the Inquisition his right to *inventioni*. If Veronese championed the artist's independence, it was Bartolomeo Ammannati who made public amends for the 'pagan' excesses of the sculptures of the Medicean Florence and exhorted the members of the Florentine Academy to refrain from erring: a testimony to the tragedy artists were subjected to by contemporary spiritual investigations.

255

19

Venice the Serene

Mercantile Meditation and the Cost of Sublime Art

Worshipping God and Mamon; Bellini, Giorgione, Veronese, Tintoretto and Titian; the light and colour of the lagoon; trade and the reception and dissemination of cultural influences. For the northerner Dürer, at the dawn of the sixteenth century, which is usually thought of as ushering in the modern age, the laurel wreath of the artistic muse was bestowed not on Rome, where the 'big three' (Leonardo, Michelangelo and Raphael) were busy working, but upon Venice and Bellini. Its special status in the annals of the history of art warrants separate consideration.

The Origins of Venetian Art

The magical city floating in the lagoon was founded in the post-Roman period when the invasions and warfare besetting Italy made it worth risking its water-borne diseases. The region was occupied during prehistory and an earlier Roman settlement existed on and near what was to become the island of Torcello, named after its church tower which links the low-lying earth to the heavens. On the internal west wall of this Romanesque church, the Basilica di San Maria Assunta founded in 639 CE by the Exarch of Ravenna, is a large and imposing mosaic of the Last Judgement, of thirteenth to fourteenth-century date, a provincial example of the Byzantine mosaicists' art that packs a powerful punch. It links the scenes of Crucifixion at the top, the Harrowing of Hell, the Resurrection, Christ in Majesty and the weighing and judgement of souls at the bottom, with the seven deadly sins, culminating in a paradise landscape of lagoon reeds. Its Christ is a dynamic redeemer, its demons scintillate in black and red tesserae, classical influence can be

RIGHT: Mosaic of the Last Judgement, thirteenth to fourteenth century, Torcello Cathedral, Torcello. Venice Lagoon.

seen in the figures of the little children who are welcomed into heaven, and the dead rise not from the ground but from the lagoon, which finally gives up the bodies of the drowned and is itself personified as a river deity, in antique fashion. Above the doorway is depicted the Virgin, her arms open in welcome. The imagination and the range of influences it displays already indicate a distinctive well of creativity. This is reflected also in the mosaics that adorn the Basilica di San Marco on the island of Venezia itself. These, which date from the eleventh to nineteenth centuries, indicate the depth and longevity of an artistic tradition which began under the influence of Byzantine and classical art. From the Renaissance onwards, however, the mosaic medium, made with glass tesserae manufactured on Murano, whose specialist glassblowers were confined on the island, was used to emulate the appearance of paintings of the day; a virtuoso display of technique, but perhaps a rather sterile one. The mosaics added to the decorative scheme for the dome of St Paul's Cathedral in

258   The Pala d'Oro, 976–1345, the high altarpiece of San Marco's, set with Byzantine enamels, San Marco Cathedral.

London during the second half of the nineteenth century would use Murano tesserae set by the Venetian Salviati to designs by British artists.

Upon San Marco's façade are set the Horses of San Marco, monumental bronzes either from classical Greece or from the fourth-century Roman empire, here imbued with Christian meaning as the Quadriga of the Apocalypse, a role belied by their gentle faces and sensitively quivering nostrils. Such works were among the booty brought to the city in the aftermath of the sack of Constantinople in 1204 – the maritime power's tribute money for shipping across the Crusaders who were diverted from their goal in the Holy Land by the prospect of despoiling the wealth of the greatest Christian city, the New Rome. The treasury of the new San Marco, reconstructed with five Byzantine domes in the eleventh century and given Gothic portal sculpture in the thirteenth, is crammed with amazing examples of metalwork, gems and worked semi-precious stones. In its high altar lie the relics of St Mark that were stolen from Alexandria by merchants in 800 CE and enshrined in the new basilica in 832 CE as patron of Venice, a role traditionally foretold by an angel. His symbol, the winged lion, is its emblem. Above it stands the glittering Pala d'Oro, a remarkable large golden polyptych set with figural enamels and jewels, first commissioned from Constantinope in 976 CE and remade several times between then and 1345, but always in Byzantine fashion. Venice was ruled by Byzantium under a leader known as a *dux* (duke or *doge*). San Marco is still nominally a partriarchate. By the ninth century the *doge* had already achieved enough independence to treat with the Carolingian emperor. The arrival of the Dominicans and Franciscans in the early thirteenth century brought the aspects of Gothic art to the city. The impact of Islamic architectural influence combined with that of Byzantium and of Lombardy and the northern Gothic style to form the distinctive, finely decorated façades of civic buildings and private palaces, such as the beautiful Ca' d'Oro built around 1424, that are reflected in its canals.

Power and Wealth

Venice was always a meeting place of peoples and influences. The Jewish ghetto originated in the city, an island within the island where ballistics were manufactured (from the Venetian dialect word *geto* for mortar manufacture). This was the first specifically designated area of Jewish residence, assigned to them in 1541. Not until the nineteenth century were the restrictions relaxed. In the early eighteenth century the island of San Lazzaro, a former leper colony, was granted to the Order of Uniate Armenian monks; the stelae in its cemetery differ little from the katchkars of the medieval period. Relations with neighbours were not always easy, especially from around 1500 when its mainland empire was in competition with the Holy Roman empire and Rome, and voyages to the New World and to India via the Cape of Good Hope lessened its trading supremacy. Proximity to the Balkans and Greece led not only to trade with the Turks but also to struggles with them for control of eastern Mediterranean mercantile centres such as Cyprus. These escalated after Constantinople fell once more in 1453, this time to Turkish forces rather than Westerners led by the Venetian *doge*. The tension culminated in the maritime Battle of Lepanto of 1571 at which a joint force of the papacy, Spain and Venice, defeated the Turkish fleet – an event in which the novelist Cervantes participated and which he judged the most important in history. It was painted by several Venetian artists, including Michieli (in the Doge's Palace) and Veronese, who included in his composition Venice,[1] personified as a virgin, presented to the Virgin by intercessory saints. Art can be a powerful vehicle of propaganda for political agendas masquerading under the guise of faith.

Venetian motivation was always mercantile, if not downright mercenary, and the wealth generated was immense. Its political espousal of the Republic meant most commissions were by the state or the confraternities, although contest for office ensured that all leading dignitaries felt it encumbent upon them to display an appreciation of art, contributing to the rise of collecting, connoisseurship and art trading in Venice from the sixteenth century onwards and to a rise in patronage among important patrician families such as the Grimani and Corner.

The Burgeoning of Venetian Art

Venetian painting, practised by artists such as Paolo Veneziano, remained firmly in the Byzantine tradition until around 1400, when International Gothic and Italian Renaissance influence began to be introduced when Gentile di Fabriano, Pisanello and the Paduan Guariento were employed to decorate the Doge's Palace with frescoes (destroyed by fire in the sixteenth century and subsequently redecorated). They influenced the *quattrocento* primitives such as Jacobello del Fiore, Michele Giambono (who also favoured orientalizing influence), and the Vivarini family working on Murano. The sixteenth century, however, witnessed the true flowering of Venetian art, producing innovative musicians, influential printers such as Aldus Manutius, sculptors and architects such as Buon, Palladio, Sansovino and Sanmichele, and painters such as the Bellini family, Lotto, Carpaccio, Giorgione, Titian, Tintoretto and Veronese. The seventeenth century saw Venice embrace Baroque architecture, with sublime buildings such as San Maria della Salute, and the eighteenth their adornment by painters such as Piazzetta and Tiepolo. Painters of purely secular and genre subjects, such as Guardi, Canaletto and the neo-classicist Canova, also flourished before the state finally fell to Napoleon in 1797.

Giovanni Bellini (c. 1430–1516) belonged to a family of artists and also exchanged influences with his brother-in-law, Andrea Mantegna. He combines Florentine form with the realism and technique of the Netherlands in a number of religious subjects; for example, his *Virgin and Sleeping Child* in the Accademia which predicts a nearby *Pietà* in which the tender, aged Mary holds her dead son in a manner recalling that of her young motherhood. But Bellini was especially dedicated to exploring infinite, subtle variations on the theme of the Virgin and Child, part of a Venetian tradition of *Madonnieri*, emphasizing the incarnation of the Word. Franciscan teaching also inspired him and these works are characterized by a serenity and a meditative quality that both involves its viewers, inviting them into the scene, and compels them to kneel in humble veneration. His study of relief carving imbues his figures with a monumental, static quality, while his mastery of the oil technique (perhaps inspired by his contemporary Antonello da Messina, who had studied its use in Flanders) and the depth and luminosity of his colours is striking and complements the reflected light of the lagoon with which his images are suffused.

261

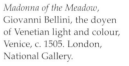

Madonna of the Meadow, Giovanni Bellini, the doyen of Venetian light and colour, Venice, c. 1505. London, National Gallery.

The same light permeates the work of Vittore Carpaccio (1455–1526), whose compositions are as crowded and as full of incidental details drawn from contemporary Venice, with its exotic orientalizing elements. Parrots, palm trees and turbans reintroduce the East into the biblical narrative, enacted in its Western Renaissance settings in works such as his *Legends of St George and St Jerome* for the Scuola di San Giorgio degli Schiavoni.

Giorgione (Giorgio di Castelfranco, 1475–1510) took the whole world as his stage. Human figures are put into proper perspective in relation to nature in works such as *The Tempest*,[2] which encapsulates the ephemeral transience of life's brief span

– and Giorgione's own life was indeed a brief whirlwind of creativity. His works, of which few are firmly attributed, exude a humanist love of philosophy, literature, music and the visual arts. The resulting sensuality has led him to be viewed as a pioneer of 'modern' art.

In 1573 Paolo Caliari (or Veronese as he is better known, after the place of his birth, c. 1528–88) completed a large painting, of fresco proportions, for the refectory of the monastery of Santi Giovanni e Paolo (or San Zanipòlo, as it is known locally) to replace a Last Supper by Titian that had been destroyed by fire. Its subject was a radical one, the *Feast in the House of Levi*,[3] depicting Christ socializing with the tax

Feast in the House of Levi, Paolo Veronese. The artist was charged with suspected heresy for setting the scene in a contemporary Palladian interior and peopling it with social outcasts.

collector and other undesirables, including the courtesans for which Venice was famed. All this in an architectural setting based on the local summer palaces of the Brenta Valley designed by Palladio. This was all a bit too close to home and Veronese was summoned before the Sant'Uffizá for suspected heresy and given three months to correct it at his own expense. The Dominicans advised him on how to solve the problem by the simple and irrefutable expedient of inscribing upon it his authority – Luke's Gospel chapter 5: 'and Levi made him a great feast in his own house'. This is an outright challenge to venal Venice to do likewise.

Subject matter that dealt with the inclusion of those considered socially unacceptable also appealed to Il Tintoretto (Jacopo Robusti, son of a dyer, hence his sobriquet, 1518–94), even if in the proselytizing service of the state. In *St Mark Freeing a Slave*[4] (1547–48), Venice's patronal saint intercedes on behalf of a slave who was to have his legs broken and his eyes put out for visiting the saint's shrine without his master's permission; the figures are influenced by those of Michelangelo. In *St Mark Saving a Saracen*[5] (1562–66), a Muslim is saved from a storm at sea when he prays to the saint. Tintoretto's greatest achievement, however, was the series of forty large paintings for the rooms of the Scuola di San Rocco, the opulence of which is breathtaking. The Scuole were the major patrons of art in Venice, after the state. They were devotional confraternities of wealthy non-patrician laymen, convened to support one another in their spiritual and working lives, under the patronage of a saint. Like the guilds of northern Europe, they might protect the interests of a particular profession. San Rocco, dedicated to the fourteenth-century plague saint, Roch, whose relics rested in the brotherhood's adjacent church, was one of the six Scuole Grandi and the only one to have survived Napoleonic suppression and to still function. After the great plague of 1528 Roch was proclaimed co-patron of Venice, alongside St Mark, hence the prominence of the building and of Tintoretto's commission. This was opened for competition in 1564, and Tintoretto snatched it from others who submitted drawings, including Veronese, by donating a ceiling panel of St Roch in glory as a mark of his

Crucifixion, Tintoretto, c. 1575–81.
Scuola Grande di San Rocco, Venice.

own devotion – how could he then fail to be appointed? He spent the next twenty-three years working on the scheme with his son, Domenico, in fulfilment of that devotion, perhaps never leaving Venice and never achieving great fame or wealth in a lifetime spent depicting ordinary people participating in great events.

The Sala dell'Albergo is dominated by a large crucifixion, which greets you upon entering the door. It bursts with dramatic action, its crowd of figures bathed in an ethereal luminosity that unites them as they pursue their own self-absorbed responses or rejections of the central (or rather, off-centred) moment of Christ's sacrifice. Light emanates from him and is complemented by a pool of light on the ground that moves in and out of the composition on diagonal axes, converging upon the foot of the cross and flooding out from it to light the world. In the background the opalescent light of dawn begins to suffuse the land, heralding Christ's second coming from the East. The Sala Capitolare, or chapter room, has at the centre of its ceiling the Old Testament parallel and prophecy of Christ's redemptive sacrifice, the brazen serpent of Numbers 21:4–9. This passage relates how the Israelites were plagued by serpents on their

journey and complained against God and Moses. When they sought forgiveness, the Lord instructed Moses to erect a fiery serpent of bronze upon a pole, so that whoever was bitten might live when they beheld it. This remarkable, simple visual analogy, encountered only infrequently but effectively in art, neatly encapsulates the theological complexity of the human condition and susceptibility to temptation, and of God's empathetic response in adopting human form and sharing in that condition, while triumphing over it and offering humankind the ability to do likewise.

Next door stands the Franciscan church known as the Frari, containing treasures such as Bellini's Frari Madonna and suffused with the light from Titian's early masterpiece, *The Assumption of the Virgin* (1516–18), with its unnerving red and yellow draperies. Unlike Giorgione, some of whose works he completed, Tiziano Vecellio (c. 1485–1586) enjoyed long life; and unlike Tintoretto he knew great worldly success, he and his fame travelling around Europe to the courts of Italy, France and Spain. Trained by Bellini in the classical style, and inspired by Raphael, he engaged in a brief affair with mannerism before developing the dignified and somewhat mystical style of his late maturity. He revitalized a taste for large altarpieces, imbuing them with a monumental harmony of composition achieved by dramatically contrasting areas

The uplifting and colourful *The Assumption of the Virgin*, Titian, 1516–18. Church of the Frari, Venice.

of colour arranged without undue regard to symmetry. The effect is exciting, uplifting and, at its best, transcendental. He and his contemporaries inspired future generations of artists, including the Venetian mannerists Palma Il Vecchio and Palma Il Giovane, Paris Bordone, Pordenone and Andrea Schiavone.

Venetian Baroque and Rococo

During the seventeenth century, Venetian art experienced a decline, eclipsed by the light of the preceding century's achievements and overshadowed by Roman Baroque. The eighteenth century and the age of the Enlightenment, however, brought a new burst of energy and a frenzy of entertainment. This carnival atmosphere even

Glorification of St Dominic, in which he is shown receiving the rosary, a devotional aid ascribed to him, painted by Giambattista Piazzetta on the ceiling of San Zanipòlo, Venice, early eighteenth century.

pervaded Venetian churches, their interiors echoing the opulent excess of the palazzo. Giambattista Piazzetta (1682–1754) triggered a fashion for massive painted ceilings, soaring to dizzying illusionistic heights, inhabited by figures viewed from every conceivable angle and employing every optical and perspectival conceit. Perhaps his finest was that depicting the *Glorification of St Dominic* in San Zanipòlo, which exhibits the influence of Caravaggio in its dark tonality that emphasizes the dramatic impact of light. His *Crucifixion* in the Accademia uses this to great effect and employs a vertiginous perspective resembling that later used by Salvador Dali. Piazzetto had a number of followers, including the female painter Giulia Lama (1681–1747), whose *Judith and Holofernes*[6] uses a brutally harsh light to illumine the moment of prayer in which Judith dedicates herself to the rejection of evil before beheading Holofernes.

Piazzetto's reputation was soon overtaken, however, by that of Giambattista Tiepolo, whom he had inspired to paint ceilings and altarpieces on a heroic scale. His work epitomizes Venetian Baroque, while at the same time moving into the lighter, more decorative style known as Rococo. Christian and mythological iconographies vie with one another in expansive trompe l'oeil universes, airily bathed in a celestial golden light. This ethereal quality has much to do with the fact that, unlike most artists of the age, Tiepolo was equally at home working in the oil and fresco media and was able to conflate the tonal contrasts and depth of the former with the lightness of the latter. That which hovers above the interior of the Church of the Gesuati, San Maria del Rosario on the Zattere (not the Jesuit church, but one belonging to an Order devoted to the Rosary), takes as its theme *The Institution of the Rosary* (1738–39), flanked by the *Glory of St Dominic*. The Virgin bestows upon the faithful the devotional use of the rosary or 'rose garland' – the ancient devotional aid of enumerating a cycle of prayers using a string of stones or flowers, or a prayer wheel as in Buddhism, popularized in a Christian context by the Dominicans. This is a powerful visual assertion of popular Catholic piety, and one of the last to be created in Venice, whose arts, like those of much of Europe, soon became devoted to the purely decorative: to views – to portraits and to genre scenes from everyday life, the precursor of the banal panacea of today's reality TV. In 1762 Tiepolo left Venice to paint his last religious subjects on the ceilings of the Royal Palace in Madrid. For Spain was one of the final bastions of Counter-Reformation art.

From Counter-Reformation to Baroque: Aspects of the Arts in Rome

Professor Daniela Gallavotti Cavallero

The twenty-fifth and last session of the Council of Trent, convened on 3–4 December 1563, decreed that the role of art in support of the Counter-Reformation should be solely pedagogical. The Council's ruling limited artists' creativity for the first time, both in terms of contents and iconographic expression, taking away their autonomy of invention and transforming them into manual executors of pre-ordained themes. The rules inaugurated by the Council constitute the basis of a vast literature conceived by authoritative churchmen, aiming at supplying a detailed case-by-case analysis of the concise Tridentine regulations.

The censure of Michelangelo's *Giudizio universale* by one such churchman (Giovanni Andrea Gilio) in 1564 is well known: this was due to his non-canonical representation of Christ as young and beardless, to the unusual posture and nudity of the saints, and to iconographic contamination from Dante's *Divina Commedia*, which led to Daniele da Volterra's pictorial censorship on the orders of Pope Paul IV (1555–59).

As a consequence of the Tridentine statutes several other paintings also underwent censorship. In Venice, for instance, Paolo Veronese was summoned to appear before the Inquisition (18 July, 1573) because of the unconventional presence of characters considered inappropriate and incorrect by the authorities – soldiers, a dog, a joker – in the large canvas commissioned to represent *The Last Supper of Christ and the Apostles in Simon's house*. To save his work and himself, the painter was forced to change the title of the subject to the less sacredly explicit *Feast in the House of Levi*, a title which is still employed.

Theological literature on the Tridentine statutes on art, although varied in nuance, agrees in identifying painting as the best propaganda tool in helping to re-establish Roman Catholic primacy, which had been weakened by the Lutheran Reformation. According to these statutes, images should be composed by imitating nature in order to acquire a teaching function, moving the faithful with representations of the sufferings of the early martyrs. This premise excluded the representation of abstract concepts, such as Truth, Vices or Virtues, and allegories or symbols – as well as everything of non-narrative content. Painted stories should serve as universal teaching aids for those unable to read or to follow sermons, and in particular for the crowds of foreign pilgrims who flocked to Rome on jubilee years.[1]

The latter years of the pontificate of Gregory XIII (1572–85), and more markedly those of Sixtus V (1585–90) and Clement VIII (1592–1605), witnessed the full implementation of the Tridentine rules, with pictorial representations frightening onlookers because of the variety and cruelty of their martyrdom scenes. This was the case in the churches of Saint Stefano Rotondo, the frescoes of which follow the canons of popular realism (1572–85), and of Saint Vitale (1600), in which a more detached approach to reality is adopted. Indeed, the key concept of decorum prescribed that, while suffering should be faithfully represented, the sacred figures should keep composed and resigned attitudes, their nobility designed to enrich the observers' souls. Caravaggio's paintings, deeply rooted in Lombardic naturalism, were repeatedly rejected for their lack of decorum by Roman ecclesiastical patrons, as in the case of the *Virgin's Death*[2] which was refused by the church of Saint Maria della Scala (1601–1605/6), or of the first version of *Saint Matthew and the Angel*[3] in the Contarelli Chapel in Saint Luigi dei Francesi (1600). Caravaggio entered the Roman scene when the Counter-Reformation had already undergone a formal evolution, abandoning the late Michelangelesque legacy in favour of a renewed interest in Raphael. The order and spatial equilibrium of his compositions fulfilled the requirement for a dignified representation of reality.

It was, in fact, Caravaggio's first Roman employer, Cavalier d'Arpino, who represented the most faithful, and most boring, instance of adhesion to Raphael's language. His ability to clearly depict the stories of Christianity elevated him to the title of papal painter during Clement VIII's papacy. The pope himself gave him the commission to decorate the transept of Saint Giovanni in Laterano – the so called Clementine

'nave', where Arpino painted in fresco an *Ascension*, faithfully inspired by Raphael's *Transfiguration*[4] (1518–20). The symmetrical interplays in it are excessive, producing a mechanical, cold composition. The cycle in the transept, which the Pope wanted as a manifesto for the 1600 Jubilee, can be taken as representative of Counter-Reformation painting at its highest point. After the Jubilee, and after more than three decades of assiduous visual propaganda, Roman Catholicism could be assumed to have defeated heresy and re-established its primacy.

This was also due to the shrewd political actions of Clement VIII, during whose pontificate the traditional Franco-Spanish hostility faded: Philip II of Spain remained the faithful ally of the Holy See, and the Calvinist Henry IV had forsworn his beliefs, drawing closer to the Pope and re-establishing Catholicism in France. From a doctrinal point of view Clement VIII remained intransigent, personally attending the Inquisition Tribunal, which in 1600 sentenced to the stake Giordano Bruno, extradited from Venice by direct papal request.

The new strict discipline and rules established, and even personally applied, by the Pope were backed by the revision activity that the Oratorian Caesar Baronius applied to events from Christian history, to provide them with an irrefutable historical foundation. His twelve-volume *Annales Ecclesiastici*, begun in 1588 at the behest of St Philip Neri but left incomplete at his death, were the direct answer to the *Magdeburg Centuriae*. They proved Catholicism's conformity to the very foundations of Christianity, thus becoming the fundamental reference work for artists, because their contents described events from Christian history for which the cardinal was considered to have found historical evidence. Uncertain facts were expunged, like the celebrated Donation of Constantine (which purported to record the emperor's conferral of dominion over all Italy and primacy over the eastern patriarchates upon the Pope), the content of which was reduced to his gift of gold and silver artefacts for the Lateran basilica altars and represented as such in one of the transept frescoes in the Jubilee cycle of 1600.

Ascension, Cavalier d'Arpino,
early seventeenth century,
San Giovanni in Laterano, Rome.

As a cardinal, Baronius held the titles (*titula*) to the churches of Saints Nereo and Achilleo and Saint Gregorio al Celio. He promoted the conservation of artefacts, mostly in marble, such as the openwork screens (*transennae*) and balustrades (*plutei*) of his paleo-Christian churches, along with relics that he considered to be materials directly related to the ordeals of the first martyrs. He is to be credited with the restoration of the apsidal paleo-Christian mosaics, for which he commanded interventions conforming to the original style and figurative culture of early Christianity. In this respect, Cardinal Baronius's cultural approach paralleled the phenomenon of the rediscovery of the hypogean (subterranean) paleo-Christian cemeteries and of their frescoes and sculptures. As custodians of the 'holy bodies', catacombs and crypts were subject to veneration and the piety of the faithful and provided doctrinal strengthening for the ecclesiastic hierarchies.

Paradoxically, Saint Peter's basilica did not originally have a crypt. Nevertheless, starting from Gregory XIII's pontificate (1572–85) the thin gap under the nave between the Constantinian basilica and the floor of the sixteenth-century building was proposed as a funerary site. Monuments – many of popes – began to be laid there after their removal from the ancient basilica that had already been demolished. To these *Grotte* Clement VIII added an annular path under the apse, through which Saint Peter's tomb could be seen and reached out to. The whole complex became a large crypt and the importance attributed to the transferred sculptures and paintings, which was not just devotional, is witnessed by their 1618 catalogue.[5]

At the beginning of the seventeenth century the construction of the new Saint Peter's basilica had changed from the centralized plan by Bramante and Michelangelo to the hybrid, but elongated form designed by Carlo Maderno which added two *campate*, with the façade completed in 1615. After a long interruption, in the last two decades of the century an intense debate between the cardinals of the *Congregazione per la Fabbrica* developed about the necessity of extending the new nave to cover the Constantinian basilica's area.

Saint Peter's is not an example of Counter-Reformation architecture because it does not have a single large nave like, for instance, the Gesù. But the early seventeenth-century additions stem from that culture, while the enormous inscription on the façade, celebrating Pope Paul V Borghese (1605–21) rather than the church itself or the apostle Peter, goes against all prescriptions of humility and overcomes allegiance to the Counter-Reformation, giving way to a new glorification of the patron, the head of Roman Catholicism.

It was Gian Lorenzo Bernini who interpreted at the highest level the figurative representations of the newly triumphant church, and who conceived the new language that was destined to overtake any remaining mannerist tendencies. His first religious work was the *Saint Bibiana* statue, created on the occasion of the 1625 Jubilee under the patronage of Pope Urban VIII (1623–44). Following a typical method of the Counter-Reformation period, the restoration of the small church was prompted by the declaration that the intact body of the martyr had been discovered – as had already happened in the 1600 Jubilee to justify the restoration of the churches of Saint Cecilia (whose intact body is represented in the celebrated statue by Stefano Maderno, 1600), Saint Prisca, Saint Balbina and several others.

Bernini had studied classical statuary and his *Bibiana* has the monumentality of an ancient sculpture, which becomes Christianized through the saint's languid gaze towards heaven, or in fact towards the natural light flowing from the window above, identifying natural and divine light in the onlooker's perception. However, it is in the *Saint Longinus* statue in one of the pillars of the crossing of Saint Peter that Bernini achieved the full expression of Baroque language (1628–40). The wide gesture of Longinus's open arms removes the spatial boundaries of the sculpture, establishing its communication with the surroundings and, in particular, with the light descending from the dome, which therefore becomes an element of the narrative. Natural light striking Longinus's visage at certain hours of the day becomes divine – the same divine light that gave him back his sight when blood from the chest of the crucified Christ dripped onto his eyes. For the first time, in this statue, Bernini attributes to drapery an autonomous spatial function, departing from its traditional flow along the body. The clothing thus increases and complicates the spatial structure of the figure and, from a psychological point of view, helps to stress the emotion and pathos of the character.

With the *Saint Longinus* Bernini achieved the extraordinary effect of merging into a single statue a complete narrative story, at a time when narrative cycles were becoming less frequent in churches and

were being replaced by grandiose altarpieces. Bernini's narrative language reached its peak in the funerary chapel of the Cornaro family in Santa Maria della Vittoria. As in a theatrical representation, in the space above the altar the *Ecstasy of Saint Teresa* (1647–52) becomes real while the light from the aperture above (which Bernini's biographers called *camera di luce*) makes the descent of divine light upon her a physical reality. The decoration of the chapel as a whole is conceived as a unity, representing a celestial vision: high clouds open up wide in the vault, the saint lies on lower clouds, while other clouds are on the sides of the *Ecstasy*.

The *Saint Peter Cathedra* (1656–66) in the basilica's apse – with its explosion of light within which the dove symbolizing the Holy Spirit appears, the Constantine (1564–71) on a *Scala regia* floor opening onto the atrium, and the *Colonnade* (from 1656) – adheres in various ways to the principle of magnifying the church and celebrating their patrons. Bernini's ability to weave these factors into a variety of contexts made him cherished and irreplaceable to seven popes.

The orgasmic *Ecstasy of Saint Teresa*, 1647–52, sensuous sculptural masterpiece of the Counter-Reformation, by Gianlorenzo Bernini, for the Cornaro chapel, Santa Maria della Vittoria, Rome.

Protestantism and the Catholic Counter-Reformation

Domestic Piety, Mannerism and the Theatricality of the Baroque

An altarpiece by Tiepolo in the Gesuati, Venice, depicts the Virgin with a trio of female saints, the Dominican Rose of Lima, Catherine of Siena and Agnes of Montepulciano. They adopt attitudes like those of a group of leading ladies on a stage, in an architectural setting resembling the proscenium and viewed as if from the seat of a theatre. Just as the theatrical tableau vivant sought to emulate art in life, so the moment is transported back into art. The Virgin is enthroned above, listening to the song of a bird, and has handed charge of the Christ child to the Christian graces below, who fondly dandle the rosy boy, their roses and the rosary. Christ's Passion is foretold by the crown of thorns and a large wooden crucifix borne by one of them. Sacrifice, devotion and charity are here embodied as the Christian virtues inspired by the Virgin and Christ. Such works characterize the theatricality of the Baroque, the artistic vocabulary of the Counter-Reformation – the Catholic response to the Protestant Reformation.

The Virgin with St Rose of Lima, St Catherine of Siena and St Agnes of Montepulciano, Giambattista Tiepolo, 1748. Santa Maria del Rosario (Gesuati), Venice.

High Baroque

In 1512–17 the Fifth Lateran Council initiated some internal reforms that were carried further by the Council of Trent (1545–63), the rulings of which prevailed until the 1960s. New Orders were also formed to combat Lutheranism – notably, from 1540, the Jesuits. Their subtle intellectualism and deep Ignatian spirituality was complemented by an emphasis upon the emotive conduits of art and music that revitalized them from the mid-sixteenth century onwards and engendered the Baroque, sometimes referred to as the 'Jesuit style'. The *Spiritual Exercises* (1548) by St Ignatius Loyola, founder of the Order, stress the need to visualize the subjects of meditation, such as the suffering of Christ and the martyrs. In churches architecture, sculpture and painting were to work in unison to achieve this dramatic effect, combining classical naturalism with exuberant ornament. High Baroque was centered in Rome and epitomized by the architectural and sculptural work of Gian Lorenzo Bernini (1598–1680) and the painting of Michelangelo Merisi di Caravaggio (1571–1610).

Michelangelo Buonarotti's legacy inspired mannerist sculptors such as Giambologna (1529–1608), whose work for his Medici patrons – most of which treated classical mythology – included the imposing garden ornament, *Samson and the Philistine*[1] (c. 1560–62), while the self-publicizing Benvenuto Cellini translated the style into opulent smaller works in precious metals and gems. It was Bernini who heightened its dramatic impact in truly Baroque fashion, after one of his Barberini patrons became Pope Urban VIII in 1625 and appointed him architect to St Peter's, where he erected the massive *baldacchino* over the saint's tomb and inserted a huge statue of St Longinus into one of Michelangelo's piers beneath the dome. Other of his works in Rome include the famous *Four Rivers* fountain in the Piazza Navona, with the streams of living water of Paradise depicted as antique river gods. His *Ecstasy of St Teresa* (1645–52) in the Cornaro family chapel in Santa Maria della Vittoria in Rome uses the whole architectural space, surface articulation and lighting to build up to the crescendo of orgasmic intensity experienced by the swooning figure of the visionary Spanish mystic and Carmelite reformer, St Teresa of Avila (1515–82), as, in response to the intense practice of personal prayer that she advocated, she is pierced by an insight into the enormity of

Bronze of *Samson and the Philistine*, Giambologna, c. 1560–62.

274

God's love, symbolized by the attendant figure of an angel. The angel also serves to relate this new iconography to the traditional one of the Annunciation to the Virgin and the Conception of Christ. Divine radiance illuminates the scene from the amber glass of a hidden skylight and marmorian members of the Cornaro clan occupy theatre boxes carved in relief on the walls, joining the viewer as spectators of the great dramatic mystery. Bernini's inner vision had evidently profited greatly from one of his favourite books – the Ignatian *Spiritual Exercises*.

Caravaggio and His Influence

Caravaggio rebelled against his training in the jobbing workshops of Rome which practised the effete popular mannerism of Zuccaro and others, churning out sentimental religious works, portraits, still lives and genre scenes. The mannerist tendencies of Michelangelo's work had been carried to the extreme in the work of artists such as Parmigianino (Francesco Mazzuola from Parma, 1503–40), in whose later compositions the elegant attenuation of his figures becomes so exaggerated that his horses resemble giraffes, as in his *Conversion of St Paul*[2]; and his Madonnas might more appropriately be regarded as the progeny of Leda and the swan, so stretched are their necks, as in the unfinished *Madonna of the Long Neck*[3] (1534–40). They raise questions concerning Parmigianino's own psychological state. He was taken hostage during the siege of Rome in 1527 but seems to have been almost oblivious to the fact, so absorbed was he in his art. Having returned to Parma in 1530 he became obsessed with alchemy and the pursuit of the philosophers' stone, reputed to turn mercury into gold. His physical appearance grew wild and unkempt and he was sued by the ecclesiastical authorities for breach of contract over failed commissions. He died of fever during his ensuing flight.

Although Caravaggio's character would also lead him to live beyond the pale, only the more serious and meditative work of the Caracci of Bologna, among his peers, inspired the young artist in his quest to inject real substance and content into his work. The prevailing taste for mawkish or amusing scenes from the supposed lives of peasants or the urban poor did, however, combine with his personal familiarity with the seamy underbelly of the city, enabling him to create new iconographical solutions of his own with which to depict traditional biblical and hagiographical subjects. He imbued them with a new realism to which people could actually relate their own experience: it was all too easy to imagine oneself being rooked by his *Cardsharps* or transported by his *Lute-Player*. The emotional impact of his first church commission, scenes from the life of St Matthew for the Contarelli Chapel in San Luigi dei Francesi, Rome, shot him to immediate fame. This social

275

Death of the Virgin,
Caravaggio, 1606.
Caravaggio's personal history
is as dark and dramatic as his
compelling images, yet they
have inspired a deep
devotional and aesthetic
response across the centuries.

realism was an approach also favoured by St Philip Neri, founder of the Oratorian Order, in his preaching to the people of Rome and for whose own church of San Maria Nuova Caravaggio painted the *Entombment*.[4] The Oratorians were great patrons of art and music, the concerts they staged giving rise to the 'oratorio'. The Order spread to France in 1611 and was introduced to England by John Newman in 1848, focusing upon a grand church by Herbert Dribble in Neri's favoured Baroque style – the Brompton Oratory, London. In accordance with this spirit, in Caravaggio's

Death of the Virgin[5] (1606), the mother of Christ dies in a dingy backstreet room, attended by a helpless group of uncouth peasant-apostles. It was rejected by the church for which it had been commissioned; indeed, four of his six ecclesiastical commissions in Rome were rejected or required modification.

Caravaggio's use of *chiaroscuro* – the play of dark and light – was remarkable and imparted tremendous substance and gravitas to his work, but it was the exploration of the darker side of life that really drew him like a moth to a flame. His sexuality and violent disposition brought him a stormy existence, played out in the dangerous backstreets of Rome, Naples and Sicily. In 1606 he killed Ranuccio Tomassoni in a gang-fight and fled Rome, being sentenced to death in his absence. A year later he left the sanctuary of Naples, where he had painted his masterly *Seven Acts of Mercy* for the Pio Monte della Misericordia, for Malta, seeking to become a knight of the Order of St John, an ambition which he achieved in return for his *Decollation of St John the Baptist*[6] (1607–08). This sombre work captures the range of standard human responses to atrocity through the gruesome realism with which the execution is depicted: the callous indifference of the prison governor; the passivity of the maidservant sent to fetch John's head; the disempowered horror of an elderly woman onlooker; and the bloodlust of John's fellow prisoners. Caravaggio signed his own name in the blood pouring from the wound. By the end of 1608 he had spilled more blood himself, quarrelling with another knight, and fled to Sicily. He was expelled from the Order in his absence, before his own altarpiece of John's sacrifice. The works that he painted at this time, such as the *Raising of Lazarus*,[7] are suffused with tension and dark bleakness. By 1609 he was back in Naples, getting disfigured in a bar room brawl and focusing upon depictions of martyrdoms and execution. Caravaggio had looked death in the face and was supremely qualified to capture its likeness and the depth and variety of emotions it unleashes. Hearing of his imminent pardon by the Pope he headed for Rome, but was detained in prison and finally collapsed, pursuing his own belongings. The baggage of his own torrid life had finally caught up with him. Caravaggio was undoubtedly more sinner than saint, but he strove for something ennobling, as his ambitions to become a knight of St John demonstrate. It was through his work, however, and his honest attempts to connect the gospel message with the harsh realities of life in a violent age and environment, that his own remorse and redemption were pursued.

Hard-hitting as it was, his work was not so popular in Italy, other than Naples, from where artists such as Caracciolo and Ribera helped to transmit its influence to Spain, where it inspired Velázquez, Zurbarán, El Greco and Murillo. His principal followers in Rome were Orazio Gentileschi (1565–1659) and his daughter, Artemesia (1595–c. 1652), who picked up on his earlier style but perhaps with greater integrity

Decollation of St John the Baptist, Caravaggio, 1607–08.

than those whom Caravaggio despised for aping his work, such as Guido Reni and Manfredi. The Gentileschi achieved international repute: Orazio worked for Marie de Médicis in Paris and became, in 1626, court painter to King Charles I of England, for whom he painted an allegory of *Peace and the Arts Under the English Crown*[8] (1638–39), on the ceiling of the neo-Palladian Queen's House in Greenwich constructed by Inigo Jones. Artemesia's significance as a woman artist of unparalleled success for the age was further increased by a very public court case in 1612 surrounding her rape by her father's artistic collaborator, and her drawing master, Agostino Tassi. It must have taken immense courage to contest the case, against not only her assailant but also the public opinion that this was only to be expected if women tried to operate in a man's world. Artemesia does not appear to have allowed such trials to distort either her art or her personality, though. Unsurprisingly, her work, conducted in Rome, Florence, Naples and, briefly, in London where she painted a compelling *Self-Portrait as an Allegory of Painting*[9] (c. 1630), features heroic women in situations of conflict, such as *Judith and Holofernes*[10] (1613–14), which reverses the protagonists in the act of violence – the righteous woman here destroying an oppressor. In *Susannah and the Elders*[11]

THE LION COMPANION TO CHRISTIAN ART

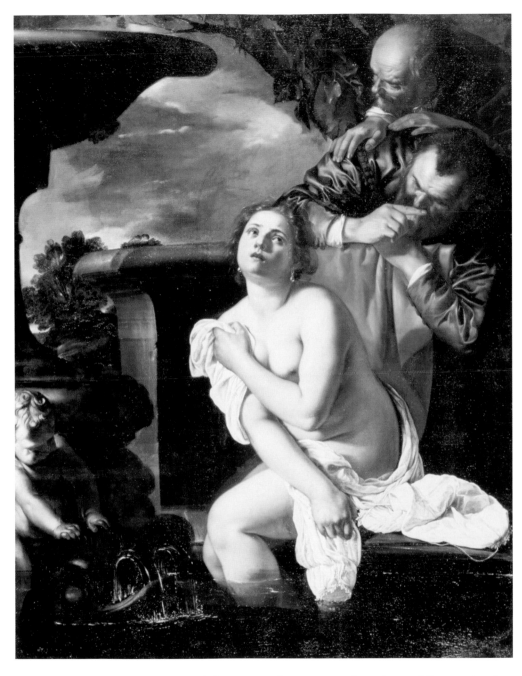

(1622), she explores the theme of the wronged woman undergoing public scrutiny by a corrupt misogynistic male hierarchy, but manages to do so without rancour, even instilling the theme with a gentle sensuality.

 In 1608 Rubens, 'Painter of Princes and Prince of Painters' (see p 289), visited Rome where he worked for the Oratorians, and imbibed the heady influence of Caravaggio. Rubens would carry the Baroque vocabulary to other parts of the Netherlands that still espoused Catholicism, such as Antwerp, where he painted the

Susannah and the Elders, 1622, an examination of hypocrisy and exploitation, painted by the female artist Artemesia Gentileschi, herself a victim of rape.

ceiling of the Jesuit church. Caravaggio's work also influenced the Catholic Utrecht school of artists (ter Brugghen, van Honthorst and van Baburen), some of whom worked in Rome and specialized in candlelit genre scenes that also appealed to a northern market. Caravaggism thereby extended its influence to the great Protestant artist Rembrandt Harmensz van Rijn (1606–1669).

Rembrandt

The Prodigal Son or Self-Portrait with Saskia, his wife, by Rembrandt van Rijn, 1635.

280

Protestantism did not greatly favour art in its churches, nor did it promote the saints and martyrs as role models. The emphasis was upon the authority of the Bible and strict adherence to and illustration of its texts, and Rembrandt excelled at inventing new iconographies with which to do so. The son of a wealthy Leiden mill owner, Rembrandt served his apprenticeship with Pieter Lastman, who specialized in the still-life and history genres, and supplemented his own early career as a history and portrait painter by exploring religious themes: the *Stoning of St Stephen*[12] (1625); *Judas Returning the Silver Pieces*[13] (1629); the *Miser from the Parable*[14] (1627); a cycle of Passion scenes purchased by Prince Henry of Orange[15] (1633–39); *Balshazzar's Feast*[16] (c. 1635), in which the *dextera dei* ('hand of God') inscribes glowing letters in the air; and the *Blinding of Samson*[17] (1636). All are executed in Baroque fashion, with Caravaggio's dramatic lighting and *chiaroscuro* forms, the subtle physiognomies of portraiture and the attention to costume and detail of the history painter. Any emphasis upon holy personages is achieved solely by means of such effects and devices such as haloes are noticeably absent.

His treatment of the themes of the Virgin and Child or the Nativity may seem simply an extension of the genre of scenes of everyday domesticity, as are the portraits of his family. His series of autobiographical self-portraits chart his own life journey, a particularly enigmatic example being his *Prodigal Son* or *Self-Portrait with Saskia*[18] (1635), his young wife, in which they are shown lustfully carousing. Was this a flaunting of conventional bourgeois values or a confession of personal sin? We can only surmise; it is a long way from the respectable self-image of the successful artist, collector and art-dealer of Amsterdam that he painted in 1640.[19] His brutal treatment of the *Blinding of Samson* however, also captures the impact of sins of the flesh. The fleshiness of his nudes is, to say the least, an ambiguous reaction to puritanical morality, as is the earthiness of his art in general. A prolific draughtsman, Rembrandt also recognized the value of the print medium in exploring the parameters of his work and in disseminating it, picking up the gauntlet cast down by Dürer. One of his most popular was the *Hundred Guilder Print*[20] of c. 1642–49 (named for the astronomical price it already commanded

281

The Blinding of Samson,
Rembrandt van Rijn, 1636.

PROTESTANTISM AND THE CATHOLIC COUNTER-REFORMATION

collectors of etchings in 1700), in which he deftly conflates the contents of Matthew chapter 19 (containing Christ's teachings, including 'suffer the little children to come unto me' and the rich young man and the 'eye of the needle') into one busy scene with Christ as its centre. Earlier, in *The Risen Christ Appearing to the Magdalene*[21] (1638), he had similarly applied a new treatment to the illustration of John 20:14–17, in which her burning tears of grief momentarily blind her to Christ's identity, mistaking him for the gardener. This meditative flavour also pervades later works, such as the *Christ at Emmaus*[22] (1648), created after the death of Saskia in 1642 and his ensuing quiet domesticity with their one surviving child, Titus, and his housekeeper and lover, Herndrickje Stoffels. Bankruptcy and a falling off of patronage fostered further introspection, revealed in his late self-portraits, the intense self-scrutiny of which seem intended for an audience consisting solely of himself and his God.

The Art of Royal Authority

The Baroque otherwise received limited attention in the Protestant North, but found an enthusiastic audience in the Catholic parts of Germany, Austria and Hungary. France employed its grandiloquent rhetoric to great effect, through the work of figures such as Perrault, Le Vau and Lebrun, but to venerate the *Roi du Soleil* – Louis XIV – rather than God. Although the Sun King had summoned Bernini to France in 1665 to discuss art, he was granted few commissions and Italian influence was largely resisted by French artists (other than the Caravaggesque painters Leclerc, Bellange and de la Tour) in favour of an evolving national decorative style known as Rococo. The rulers of England were not above using Baroque glitz to bolster their reigns, either, to varying effect. King James I commissioned Rubens to paint the ceiling of the new Banqueting House in Whitehall designed by Inigo Jones in Renaissance Palladian style. In 1649 his son, Charles I, was beheaded on a scaffold erected outside its windows by the representatives of a country lacerated by civil war triggered by the attempts of him and his wife, Henrietta Maria of France, to reintroduce Catholicism to England, and by their lavish expenditure on luxuries such as architecture and art. Within a century, the Protestant rulers William and Mary had commissioned James Thornhill to paint their apotheosis on the ceiling of the banqueting hall of the Naval College at Greenwich designed by one of the greatest architects of the Baroque, Sir Christopher Wren.

Wren was also given the task of rebuilding the cathedral and churches of the City of London after it was destroyed by fire in 1666, following the Restoration of the Monarchy under Charles II. His commission to design St Paul's Cathedral, a comparative bastion of Anglican high churchmanship and ritual, was fraught with controversy and committee intervention. His ambition to construct a modern building, in the European Baroque idiom, was dogged by a conservative affection among Londoners for the earlier Gothic structure, which had been one of the largest and grandest in Europe, and by a mistrust of the visual allusions his projected great dome made to that of Catholic St Peter's in Rome. Compromises were made, but Wren's final Warrant Design was saved from the worst of these by the intervention of Charles II, an enlightened monarch who shared Wren's passion for integrating the arts and sciences – the architect was also a founder of the Royal Society, dedicated to promoting scientific studies. For at its best, the Age of Enlightenment that was being ushered in did not exile faith but, rather, promoted a greater vision in which the 'how' was addressed without excluding the 'why'.

Wren appointed an unknown carver of ships' figureheads, the Dutchman Grinling Gibbons, to adorn his quire with some of the finest wood-carvings of the post-medieval West, with swags of exotic fruits and flowers (brought back from voyages of discovery), classical *putti* and angelic musicians. Wren had intended that the interior of his dome be adorned with mosaics, like some other great European Baroque buildings, but this was too much for the Ecclesiastical commissioners who could not countenance such 'popery'. They did, however, accept James Thornhill's designs for a scheme of paintings depicting the life of St Paul, executed at the start of the eighteenth century in a restrained but supremely elegant monochrome 'grisaille' technique (of medieval orgins), resembling engravings, against a subtly shimmering gold ground. They depict St Paul's conversion, the punishment of the sorcerer Elymas, the cure at Lystra, the conversion of the gaoler, preaching at Athens, the Ephesians burning books, Paul before Agrippa and the shipwreck on Malta. Much of the sculptural detail and statuary that adorns the building was by Francis Bird. These include his exuberant depiction of the conversion of St Paul on the road to Damascus which enlivens the pediment above the west portico, resembling that of a Roman temple, and the statues of Paul and other saints and prophets who crown the exterior. As Britain's commercial empire and its territories expanded, so the symbolic role of St Paul's Cathedral grew, leading it to be described as 'the parish church of the Empire'. The people and their leaders gathered here to seek God's protection, or to give thanks for peace, during the many conflicts of the period – the Counter-Reformation struggles surrounding the 'Glorious Revolution', the deposition of King James II and the Jacobite Rebellion, the shock of the French Revolution, the rival imperialism of the Napoleonic era, and the Boer and Crimean Wars.

'El Greco' and Iberian Baroque

Spain and Portugal both embraced the Baroque with alacrity, although in Portugal it combined with lingering Gothic influence to form the delightfully robust anomaly of the purely local Manueline style that features Gothic sculptures carved in exaggerated mannerist fashion amid a froth of ornament. One of the greatest mannerists of them all came to Spain to ply his trade: Domenikos Theotokopoulos – better known as 'El Greco' (1541–1614). Born on Crete, he pursued a successful career there as an icon writer, already favouring a fluid, attenuated figure style in his attempts to imbue them with a transcendental spirituality. By 1568 he had moved to Venice, where he absorbed the influence of Titian and Tintoretto, and in 1570 to Rome, where he criticized Michelangelo's Sistine nudes and allegedly offered to repaint his *Last Judgement*. He later recorded, in annotations to his copies of Vasari's *Lives of the Painters* and Vitruvius's *Ten Books on Architecture*, that he had absorbed the '*colore*' of Venice and the '*disegno*' (draughtsmanship) of Rome.

By 1577 he had settled in Spain, in the city of Toledo, where he remained, despite an abortive attempt to gain the patronage of Philip II with his highly-strung *Martyrdom of St Maurice and the Theban Legion*[23] (1580), which the king rejected. There he explored his characteristic anti-naturalistic style, with its elongated molten figures, quivering emotion and violently contrasting acidic colours, based in part upon the Byzantine practice of complementary shading (modelling in darker tones of a colour from the opposite side of the spectrum). The effect verges on the supernatural and reflects the mysticism of contemporary Spanish spirituality. Among his most significant commissions were the altarpieces for San Domingo el Antiguo and the *Espolio* or disrobing of Christ (1577–79), which was declined by its clerical commissioners, the multi-picture altarpiece for Nuestra Señora de la Encarnación, Madrid (1597-1600), and the *Burial of the Conde de Orgaz*[24] (c. 1580). In the *Assumption of the Virgin*[25] (c. 1607–1613), he gave the fluid brushwork he learned in Venice full rein. His compositions soar heavenward, nearly always favouring a tall vertical format. His portraits included great patrons of the arts, such as the *Portrait of a Cardinal*[26] (c. 1600), probably Bernardo de Sandoval y Rojas, and fellow-artist Giulio Clovio[27] (c. 1570–72). He and his workshop also churned out a line of popular subjects: saints, apostles, Christ crowned with thorns, the Holy Face (Vernicle cloth) and the Adoration of the Shepherds (some in *tondo*, or roundel, format and featuring the large heads of the ox and ass in the foreground). El Greco immersed himself in Loyola's *Spiritual Exercises*, meditating deeply upon the Passion. It is salutary to note that the spiritually charged vision that they evoked in him did not appeal to royalty or to some ecclesiastical authorities; it did, however, have a popular appeal as an aid to devotion.

Velázquez

Another popular form of art was the genre scene. One of its earliest exponents in Spain, who favoured Caravaggio's tenebrist use of light, was Diego de Silva y Velázquez (1599–1660) of Seville. Never before had an *Old Woman Frying Eggs*[28] (1618) recommended itself as a suitable subject for art, especially to a member of the minor nobility. He effortlessly translated the realism of such genre scenes into themes such as the *Feast of Bacchus* and the *Adoration of the Magi* alike. In 1621 Velázquez joined the court of Philip IV in Madrid, where he met Rubens in 1628 and subsequently travelled to Italy. Upon his return, his art was largely used in the service of the Spanish throne, adorning royal palaces and celebrating the royal family through classical imagery and portraits, such as his renowned *Las Meninas*[29] (1656), which conflates genre scene and portrait and is viewed from the startling perspective of the royal sitters. His few paintings on Christian themes include a massive *Christ on the Cross*[30] (1631–35), for the nuns of San Plácido in Madrid and *St Anthony Abbot and St Paul the Hermit*[31] (1634-35), for the hermitage of Buen Retiro, in which light and landscape reflect his experience of Italy.

One of his most intriguing works conflates a traditional Christian iconographic theme with domestic genre painting: *Christ in the House of Martha and Mary*[32] (1618). In the foreground a peasant girl, to all intents and purposes a contemporary of the

LEFT: *Assumption of the Virgin*, c. 1607–13, by El Greco, a Greek icon painter whose work was transformed by his studies in Italy and his employment in Spain, where he became a leading master of the Baroque.

artist's, prepares a meal, her face already grown sorrowful and sullen from her labours. An old woman stands at her shoulder and touches her arm solicitously. On the wall hangs a painting, set like a window into the scene it contains of Christ teaching, based on Luke 10:38–42, with one woman sitting attentively at his feet and another standing, her arm raised as if in remonstrance. Velázquez's adroit challenge to conventions of viewpoint has provoked much debate. Is Christ's visit to the sisters' house simply a pious image hanging on a wall in a scene from seventeenth-century Spanish life, or is the Master actually teaching in the next room while Martha toils to feed him and his listeners, including her sister Mary? A more complex and multivalent reading might also be proposed, however. The two sisters had become Christian allegories of the active and the contemplative life. The image of Christ instructing recalls the source of this meaning and his injunction to Martha that, much as her practical care for others was valued, Mary had chosen the better part in attending to his teaching (Luke 10:42). The young cook – a latter day Martha – stares out at the viewer, resenting her lot, although it is her labour that will give the flavour to the meal of fish (traditional Christian symbol) and eggs (redolent

Christ in the House of Martha and Mary, 1618, an eloquent and moving examination of the relationship between the active and the contemplative, by Spanish court painter Velázquez.

286

of the Paschal sacrifice). Good works and the service of others is a means of following the Saviour, but unless it is inspired by love and joy the act of self-sacrifice becomes empty and thankless. The older woman (her older self?), whose deeply lined face speaks of her own travails and of profound reflection, sympathizes and empathizes with her junior, but her careful touch seems to recall her to the recognition of the underlying purpose of her work, as does the adjacent image of Christ's own exhortation to base the active Christian life upon a firm basis of scriptural teaching and love. This complex image thereby embodies some of the deepest theological debates of the age: was redemption based solely upon grace or could the believer work to assist their own salvation? The artist seems to answer that it is the synergy between the two stances that offers the greatest potential but that the mystery lies beyond the reach of such man-made dialectic.

287

Spanish Monasteries and Missions

Shortly after Velázquez left Seville in search of fame and fortune at the court, Francisco de Zurbarán (1598–1664) settled there and spent his career painting religious subjects, becoming the favourite artist of the Spanish monasteries. The Franciscans of Seville received a cycle of images of the life of San Bonaventura, while some of his most powerful works focus on single figures that achieve a sacramental, transcendental effect through their intensity and *chiaroscuro*, such as his *St Francis in Meditation*[33] (c. 1635–40). Towards the end of his life Spanish taste was hankering for less plain fare and more sweetness and Zurbarán moved to Madrid in his turn, to die in poverty there. More suited to the new age was the work of Bartolomé Esteban Murillo (1617–82), also from Seville and a follower of Zurbarán and the Herreras, who painted tender images of the holy family for the cloister of San Francisco. He helped to popularize in Spain the iconographies of the Virgin and Child and of the *Immaculate Conception* with the Virgin standing upon the globe or moon and stars, one of his finest treatments of the latter being that of c. 1678[34] for the Hospitál de los Vulnerables in Seville. Another unusual subject that he introduced was that of the Two Trinities, with the divine Trinity shown above the human trinity of Mary, Joseph and the child, Jesus. Exposure to the court brought him into contact with Italian and Flemish art and his work became airier, with more dramatic light effects, and serene, soft figures with colourful draperies, as in his *Birth of the Virgin* painted for Seville Cathedral in 1660. He also experimented with genre scenes, such as the *Boy Killing Fleas*[35] (c. 1646–50), stimulating an enduring Spanish love of such themes from peasant life. Hard-working to the end, Murillo died as the result of a fall from his scaffolding while painting an altarpiece for San Catalina in Cadiz.

St Francis in Meditation, by Spanish artist Zurbarán, c. 1635–40.

The imperative of religious art persisted in Spain and although one of its greatest later masters, Francisco Goya (1746–1828), is better known for his portraits, nudes and political subjects of a patriotic bent, his early works were altarpieces, such as San Bernadine of Siena for San Francisco el Grande in Madrid, frescoes including Mary, Queen of Martyrs, for San Maria del Pilar, Saragossa, and cartoons for tapestries.

From Iberia the Baroque style spread to the colonies of South America, Mexico and California and to Portuguese Goa in India, giving rise to provincial regional variants. St Francis Xavier (1506–52) carried the Jesuit mission to Goa, Ceylon, Japan and China, from where his body was brought back to Goa and a series of silver reliefs commemorating his missionary work set up in its cathedral. At its grandest, the Baroque style could produce the many-tiered altarpieces of the eighteenth-century mission churches of El Camino, the route that runs the length of the Californian coast. At the most popular level it bred with native beliefs and folk art to give birth to effigies that found their modern counterpart in the besequinned cowboy-clad baby dolls of the Holy Child venerated at the New Mexican shrine of Chimayo. Hard though it may be for some to take such dolls seriously, they are held in great affection by the locals and find their equivalent in the traditional 'black Madonnas' of European regional Catholicism, with their flamboyant textile clothing and their blackened veneers enhanced by centuries of the holy smoke of incense and votive candles, and the modern plastic and plaster Virgins and the images of Christ whose eyes follow you round the room.

Rubens and the Theatre of the Counter-Reformation: Biblical Imagery made Flesh

Professor Michelle P. Brown

Peter Paul Rubens (1577–1640) was a native of Antwerp who, by his mid-thirties, had become the most successful commercial artist of his day, widely acclaimed as 'painter of princes, prince of painters'. He was born in Westphalia as his father, a protestant lawyer, had fled persecution in Antwerp – once an international trading centre and latterly the heart of the Counter-Reformation in Flanders. After his father's death, Rubens' mother and her offspring returned, having reconverted to Catholicism. His entry onto the international stage began in 1600 when the 22-year-old travelled to Italy to study the great works of Antiquity and the Renaissance, and those of contemporaries such as Caravaggio. This eight-year self-imposed apprenticeship took him to Venice, Genoa, Padua and Rome and was only curtailed by his mother's illness and death. On his return to Antwerp the heroism, energy and flamboyance that pervaded his work secured him the patronage of wealthy burghers and ecclesiastics alike, his popularity necessitating the establishment of a prolific workshop. The year following his return witnessed his appointment as court painter to the governors of the Spanish Netherlands, Archduke Albert and his wife, Isabella. Antwerp had returned to Catholicism in 1585, when Rubens was a boy, and the triumphalism of the Counter-Reformation shaped his vision of art, along with a love of things Roman, and of the light and numinous colour of Venice. He also

Peter Paul Rubens, *The Descent from the Cross*, 1611–14, painted for Antwerp Cathedral.

inherited a fluency of draughtsmanship, conveyed to the brush, and of a pride in the mastery of the oil-painting tradition of his native Netherlands.

The role of the church as a prospective patron must have been an important factor in the way in which Rubens shaped his career. He secured several major ecclesiastical commissions whilst in Italy: the crypt chapel of St Helena in Santa Croce in Gerusalemme and the area around the high altar of the Chiesa Nuova, both in Rome; three paintings for the Gonzaga family of Mantua; and a high-altarpiece for the Jesuit Church of Sant'Ambrogio in Genoa. Here he learned the art of pleasing informed Counter-Reformation taste, for the Chiesa Nuova's lay congregation of Oratorians, founded by the reformer Philip Neri, were not satisfied with his first attempt and demanded a second. As a result, he was already famed as a religious artist when he returned to Antwerp, where he was commissioned to paint massive triptychs of *The Raising of the Cross* (for St Walburga's on Antwerp's harbour-front, 1610) and *The Descent from the Cross* (for Antwerp Cathedral, 1611–14). The latter piece was particularly influenced by Caravaggio's *Entombment*, with which he had become mesmerized during his work at the Chiesa Nuova. These key commissions, along with those he left behind him in Italy, secured him the role of leading painter of the Counter-Reformation.

Early works and sketches demonstrate Rubens' fascination with the naked human body and with the epic, dynamic compositions of scenes of conflict. He voraciously imbibed idealized classical principles of anatomical depiction, embodied in the sculptures of Graeco-Roman Antiquity that he observed on his travels and in works by Michelangelo. To these influences he added a careful study of écorché figures – flayed human corpses arranged in poses that clearly articulated the mechanics of their musculature and underlying skeletal frame – enabling him to rise magnificently, if sometimes rather gruesomely, to his themes.

His most powerful depiction of mass struggle and contorted conflict is not a battle-scene of the conventional sort but *The Massacre of the Innocents*,[1] which was only discovered in 2001 in an Austrian private home. We know nothing of its origins but its style suggests that it was executed soon after his return from Italy. Its scale suggests that it may have originated as a private commission and its technique has a freedom and energy also seen in some of his oil sketches. There are no surviving preparatory studies

Peter Paul Rubens, *The Massacre of the Innocents*, c. 1611-12, in which the full dramatic potential of Counter-Reformation art is realized.

290

RUBENS AND THE THEATRE OF THE COUNTER-REFORMATION

292

for this work and Rubens chose not to translate it
into a print (a form of reproduction that he favoured
for many of his works), reinforcing the impression
of a spontaneous and emotive, if carefully thought
out, act of creation. The frenetic mêlée of writhing
semi-clad flesh at first sight recalls classical scenes
of the battle of the Amazons or the rape of the
Sabines; but here the desperate struggle for life is
being fought between the brawny militaristic
'heroes' of King Herod's guard and the civilian
women who claw, gouge, scream, plead and offer
their own bodies as living shields for the tiny,
vulnerable frames of their baby boys.

The opalescent light of a tranquil urban dawn
breaks upon this powerful freeze-frame scene in
which the beauty of monumental, translucent
human flesh and swirling, sensuous drapery
initially occludes and then enhances the awesome
horror of the events in motion. King Herod, his
paranoia triggered by the Magi's reports of the birth
of a new 'king of the Jews', has ordered the
slaughter of all the male babes-in-arms. The apex of
the triangular composition that veers towards its
tragic culmination in the right-hand foreground is
the arch-backed doll-like form of an infant who is
swung violently above the head of a Herculean

male, who is about to dash its brains out against the sharp marble corners of a pillar-base. It is already richly veined with the blood of the innocents, whose lifeless corpses litter the ground, some already tinged with a cold blue pallor (a veristic detail perhaps reflecting contemporary experiments concerning blood circulation). The frenzied pleas of the incredulous young mothers who throw themselves at his feet will not avail against his blind obedience to the orders of Herod – who watches the mayhem he has unleashed from the safe distance of an upper window. The flimsy justification for the perpetration of such atrocities – 'I was only obeying orders' – has not availed in trials of war crimes in recent times; nor, Rubens seems to say, will it be allowed to stand in eternity, whenever the crime was committed.

At the heart of the composition sways the still-vibrant, succulent white flesh of a living babe, the fate of which is contested by another naked soldier and the infant's mother. Her own luscious pale flesh resembles that of her son. Her shimmering golden hair is delicately coiffed and, along with her dishevelled blood-red satin gown, proclaims the high social status of this beautiful young matriarch. The highest altar of human society is being defiled. She is not the Madonna and the infant she clasps is not the Christ-child – but what if they had been? Her free hand claws the cheek of the assailant, as she fights like a tigress in defence of her young. An older woman – one of the crones who fulfil a range of functions in Rubens' compositions, some benign others malevolent – tries to shield the bodies of her darlings with her own. Her visage already assumes the aspect of the corpse, its mouth prised open by the vice-like fingers of another virile man of violence. She grasps the sharpened blade of his sword, directing it towards her own breasts, one of which hangs heavy and pendulous, its nipple distended in recollection of the babies she has herself suckled as a nurse. Behind them a fourth soldier, this time clad in shining plates of polished armour, in sharp contrast to the yielding flesh and drapery, yanks the hair of two young mothers from its roots as they attempt to flee with their bawling babes. In the background further figures lament or run, some to plead for mercy at Herod's gate.

Visual tributes to other masterpieces can be detected in the poses of some figures: the woman clad in white on the left recalls the classical pose of the Crouching Venus and some of the children cast

upon the ground seem almost to slumber, in tribute to the marble *Sleeping Children* that Rubens so admired in the Borghese Collection. The vigorous male swinging the baby above his head has been likened to a Michelangelo sketch of the Resurrection – the similarity of his pose to that of the risen Christ contrasting brutally and poignantly with the difference in intent, but perhaps serving to emphasize that the innocent will be the first recipients of Christ's compassion and redemption. For the innocent are always the victims of conflict, but they will receive justice at the end time and, unlike Herod and other worldly authorities, God will not be deaf to their pleas.

Rubens was himself the father of a young child at the time that he painted this disturbing work. Two years later he would capture in loving, fluid paint-strokes the translucent innocence of his own firstborn, the five-year-old Clara Serena Rubens. His *Massacre of the Innocents* frames the perpetual human question 'Why does God allow the innocent to suffer?', and proclaims in reply that it is not God but Man who wreaks havoc and slaughters innocence – but that it is God, the font of justice and mercy, who ultimately redeems and reconciles the irreconcilable.

Another of Rubens' greatest and most successful works, *Samson and Delilah*,[2] treats once again of the destruction of innocence. This time it is romantic, sexual love that is about to be brutally crushed. The Old Testament hero Samson, who was renowned for his colossal strength, is about to be betrayed by his lover, Delilah, and shorn of his hair, the source and visible sign of his vigour. Outside the door lurk the guards who will seize the enfeebled hero, blind him and imprison him, until he brings the pillars and the edifice of power crashing about them – and the corrupt secular authority they represent. In the two oil-sketches in which Rubens planned the work it is the furore of the guards in the act of seizing Samson that is portrayed, but here, in the final work, it is the psychology of betrayal rather than the physicality of action that is explored. The muscular frame of Samson lies spent and exhausted by his sexual exertions and emotional release. His sleep plumbs the depths of corporal and sensual gratification. He trusts, but his trust is misplaced. As the sculptures of Venus and Cupid in the wall-niche above and the flagon of wine and glasses that shimmer in the background graphically betray, he has worshipped at the altars of love and wine, rather than that of his

293

God. Indeed, the weight of his head and torso still rest upon the living altar of his idolatry – the lap of the temptress Delilah. She represents forbidden fruit, bait placed by the enemies of the Lord God to ensnare this descendant of Adam, and it has (predictably) been suggested by some commentators that she may even have been a prostitute. The uncontrollable, urgent passion that she must have unleashed in Samson is conveyed by her clothing, for she remains largely clad – although her breasts spill from their binding cloths (a detail copied from Michelangelo's Sibyls in the Sistine Chapel). Her décolletage, her fine, elegantly dressed golden hair (Rubens excelled in his treatment of women's hair), her wine-coloured satin gown and white chemise recall those of the central figure of the beautiful young mother in the *Massacre of the Innocents* and was perhaps based on the same model. But her role here is very different. She betrays trust rather than battling to defend it. She cradles the sleeping hero's head while a man-servant stealthily shears his locks with assiduous delicacy and care, assisted by an aged crone who holds a candle to illuminate the act – age abetting the folly of youth. And yet, there is a look of almost maternal tenderness and regret upon Delilah's lovely face as she contemplates her lover's vulnerability and her hand rests reassuringly on his back. Does she really believe that she is acting in their best interests, in the self-absorbed way that lovers do, or is she essentially detached from the implications of her actions and merely touched by a fleeting compassion for the human condition? The light that spills into the canvas from the brazier and candle on the left, defining the diagonal composition, likewise stills and caresses the figures as they play their parts in the drama that is about to unfold and which will destroy the fragile, intimate domesticity of the scene.

This unusual visual meditation upon the destruction that misdirected passion and energy can wreak and on the illusion of human physical gratification and contentment was well suited to its context. For this painting was commissioned by one of Rubens' friends, the connoisseur burgomaster of Antwerp, Nicolaas Rockox (who also helped finance his two great Antwerp altarpieces), to hang above the fireplace in his own home, where it would have attracted much attention from his influential guests. The light-sources and composition of the painting have been carefully designed to complement this location, with a window to the left and the

flickering flames of the fire below. It is both an erotic and a comforting evocation of post-coital languor and domestic intimacy (Rubens was himself a happy newly-wed, having recently married his first wife, Isabella Brant, in 1609) and a warning against seduction and entrapment by its lures – unless there is also due recognition of the divine source of true contentment and of the God-focused work to which human energies should be devoted.

Unlike the *Massacre of the Innocents*, Rubens saw to it that *Samson and Delilah* was quickly engraved (by Jacob Matham) and circulated to publicise his name and his style. The same applied to another of these great works painted soon after his return from Italy, his *Ecce Homo*. This smaller canvas is dominated by the half-length figure of Christ, who is displayed to the crowds baying for his blood by a soldier, and Pilate, who announces 'Behold, the man' (*Ecce Homo*), before he is rejected and taken away to be crucified. The proximity of Christ to the viewer personalizes the scene, implying complicity and inviting scrutiny of the conscience in respect of one's own response – how do we acknowledge the truth that is revealed to us? Christ's torso is bathed in light and its pose is based upon that of an antique sculpture of a centaur that was drawn by Rubens when in Rome. Christ's likewise bridled posture conveys a sense of triumph and impending victory (recalling some early medieval stylized depictions of the triumphant crucified Christ). But this is belied by the crown of thorns that pierces his brow and the blood that trickles from these wounds and from the weals caused during his flagellation that seep from his back onto his neck and upper arms. A further ingredient in this invitation to self-examination of conscience is the expression upon Christ's face. For he shies away from the hurtful, invasive gaze of the beholder and from the act of his captors. He is wounded at a far deeper level than the purely physical, by human acts that continue to scar and blemish a perfected creation.

The beauty of his body and the way it is revealed by the drawing apart of drapery may be intended to presage the tearing asunder of the curtain of the Holy of Holies at the point of Christ's death. It also recalls the compositions and reactions of the protagonists in Rubens' paintings of *Susannah and the Elders* and conveys a similar impression of humankind's violation of innocence, reinforcing the traditional iconographic significance of Susannah in symbolizing the church, triumphant in the face of persecution.

294

Following Isabella's death in 1626, Rubens acted as a secret agent for the Infanta and then served as a diplomat, promoting peace in Europe and the reunification of the Netherlands. This work took him to Spain and England where he fulfilled important commissions, including the ceiling of Inigo Jones's Banqueting Hall in Whitehall, completed in 1634 for King Charles I of England – who was soon to be executed there as the price for his suspected plans to return England to the Catholic faith. Many of the mythological subjects painted by Rubens in this period reflect his exploration of the themes of war and peace (such as *Minerva Protecting Peace from Mars*,[3] also painted for Charles I). From the time of his marriage to Helena Fourment in 1630 her magnificent Junoesque form dominates much of his work, which increasingly conveyed Rubens' concern for his homeland and international affairs and a retreat into painting for personal pleasure rather than public profit.

Yet perhaps most powerfully of all, the earlier 'Italianate' works by Rubens provide a graphic insight into the way in which an influential part of northern European society that retained its adherence to the Catholic faith of Rome framed its response to the emergent theology and arts of Protestantism. Rather than returning to a traditional medieval mode of expression it sought the inspiration of the Italian Renaissance and its classical sources of inspiration and made them its own by exploring new modes of heightened expression and personal emotive response. An appeal to the senses was made in which human experience and the fallibility of the flesh were fully exploited as a conduit for traditional theological thought. The iconographic themes portrayed may not have been new, but the way in which such art extended an invitation to act as participant, or spectator, at the theatre of the Counter-Reformation certainly was.

295

The Age of Enlightenment

Rationalism, Neo-Classicism and the New Imperialism

The seventeenth century also witnessed the rise of a new means of viewing the world – through the lens of rationalism, held up by French thinkers such as Descartes, Pascal and Corneille. Neither the opulence and the ambiguous *chiaroscuro* of the Baroque nor the intellectual and spiritual sophistry of the Jesuits suited a mindset that favoured the absolutism of 'facts' and the clarity of direct, bright light. This dichotomy of two parallel thought-worlds is thrown into stark relief on the canvases of Georges de la Tour (1595–1652), a leading French realist influenced by Caravaggism.

French Rationalism and Realism

De la Tour's work divided into two strands: daylight pictures, suffused with life, light and colour, generally depicting secular scenes of everyday life, such as the *Musician's Brawl*,[1] and nocturnal works, in which candlelight and shadow define quieter, subtler scenes from scripture, such as *The Penitent Magdalene*.[2] In a late work, his *St Sebastian tended by St Irene*,[3] he has managed to eliminate movement, achieving a stillness of meditative contemplation that is rarely encountered in art. The use of candlelight for dramatic effect was not a device employed by Caravaggio and may have been borrowed from Netherlandish artists, but de la Tour's fascination with its effects may have had much to do with contemporary forays into experimental sciences, including the optical effects of light, by the academies that were springing up in leading cities. These included academies of art, and among the foundation members of the Académie Royale in Paris were the three brothers Le Nain, Antoine, Louis and Mathieu, whose work enjoyed success there during the 1630s to 1640s.

Their subjects include overtly Christian themes such as the *Adoration of the Shepherds*[4] and the *Supper at Emmaus*[5], but they are best known for their genre scenes depicting the life of the poor. Such subject matter was rare in French art and may have been stimulated not only by its popularity in some Italian, Spanish and Netherlandish art, but also by debate concerning society's treatment of the poor initiated by the clergy of San Sulpice, in which parish the Le Nains lived. Christian art did not have to treat only biblical, hagiographical or exegetical themes – it could address the underlying message of the Gospels too. By the eighteenth century this hard-hitting social realism, with its implicit moral challenge, had been replaced by Chardin's blooming milkmaids and Marie Antoinette's fantasies of life as a shepherdess, played out in the gardens of Versailles.

Integrating science and the optics of light with the subject matter of faith, *St Sebastian tended by St Irene*, Georges de la Tour, c. 1650.

Neo-Classicism and the Rise of Imperialism

Another theological response to the challenges of the day was that of the Jansenists, a movement founded by Cornelius Jansen, Bishop of Ypres (Flanders) whose *Augustinus*, published in 1640 two years after his death and subsequently condemned, took a dour, almost Calvinistic line and was anti-Jesuit in flavour, denouncing their moral permissiveness. The Cistercian convent of Port-Royal in Paris became its focal point in France and it was there that one of its nuns, the paralyzed daughter of the Flemish painter Philippe de Champaigne (1602–74), was miraculously healed by the community's prayers. Champaigne commemorated this blessing in a double portrait of 1662.[6] The Rubenesque nature of his earlier works, such as his portraits of Cardinal Richelieu,[7] began to harden, under Jansenist influence, into a more rigid style, seen in works such as *The Crucifixion*[8] (1674). This paralleled the neo-classicism introduced in landscape painting by Poussin, whom he had met. Both painted landscapes with biblical themes.

Nicolas Poussin (1594–1665) left France for Rome in 1624. A brief flirtation with painting altarpieces in the Baroque grand manner, such as his *Martyrdom of St Erasmus*[9] for St Peter's, demonstrated his unease with strong emotion and gesture and, after an illness restricted his physical energies (1629–30), he focused on smaller works for learned middle-class patrons, including the influential civil servants, Cassiano del Pozzo and Chanteloup, for whom he painted two series of canvases of the *Seven Sacraments*[10] which explored the human life journey and sacramental rites of passage. At their height, his talents were largely devoted to classical scenes and

The Crucifixion,
Philippe de Champaigne, 1674.

landscapes, some imbued with an allegorical significance that extends into the Christian sphere, and some dealing with unusual biblical subjects such as the *Return from the Flight into Egypt*[11] (c. 1628–29), in which the Christ child has a vision of an angel carrying a cross as the family embark on a ferry, and the *Worship of the Golden Calf*[12] (c. 1636–37). He also painted several Madonnas, such as the *Madonna on the Steps*[13] (1648), and Annunciations. His response to his subjects was a highly composed and cerebral one – the essence of classicism – which was admired by the

Return from the Flight into Egypt by Nicolas Poussin, c. 1628–29.

299

arch-mannerist Bernini, with whom he worked at St Peter's. His great ability was to connect imaginatively with the past, whether that of Classical Antiquity or of biblical times, and to perceive an integrity in beauty of form and to use it to convey human virtue and harmony within nature. Claude Lorraine (c. 1604–82) also introduced both classical and biblical scenes into his poetic landscapes in order to lend an emotional and compositional focus to his idealization of nature. Ovid and Virgil might serve as an equally valid source of inspiration for such rural idylls as the book of Exodus did for his *Landscape with the Adoration of the Golden Calf*[14] (1653), and Pope Urban VIII and his cardinals were among his foremost patrons for such works.

As the decorative ephemerism of the Rococo took hold on French society during the late seventeenth and eighteenth centuries, so an antiquarian neo-classicism was fostered by English phlegmatism and the passion of its aristocracy for Italian classical and Renaissance art gained during the 'grand tour'. This also captured the artistic imagination of French artists such as Jacques Louis David (1748–1825) and the Italian sculptor Antonio Canova (1757–1822), and dispelled both the careless Rococo and the vapid neo-classicism of Boucher and Vien, which toppled along with the heads of Louis XVI and Marie Antoinette. David's early studies in Rome led him to experiment with the fusion of influences from antique sculpture, Raphael, Caravaggio and Poussin, producing works on traditional religious themes, such as *St Roch Interceding for the Plague-Stricken*.[15] His extreme political views meant that he devoted the traumatic decades of the 1780s to 1790s to painting scenes from Roman history in support of the nascent Republic and led him to become embroiled in the Terror that followed the French Revolution, supplying iconic images of the new martyrs of the state in works such as *The Dead Marat in his Bath*[16] (1795), celebrated by Baudelaire as a modern secular *pietà*. The latter part of his career, and that of his peers, was likewise spent employing classical themes and style to eulogize the rise of a new emperor – Napoleon. Both would later die in exile.

The academies of art, in both Paris and London, may have encouraged study of the style and technique of the Old Masters, but they did not favour the same religious iconographies. History, portraiture, political allegories, and contemporary scenes of the life of those in high society, their children, horses and dogs were the order of the day. Popular piety was satisfied by the visual focal points of religious prints, crucifixes and rosary beads. Symbols also abounded, including the sacred heart, *nomina sacra* (sacred names) such as 'IHS', the contraction of *Ihesus* (Jesus), and the Titulus nailed above the crucified Christ, 'INRI' (*Ihesus Nazarenus Rex Iudeorum*, Jesus of Nazareth King of the Jews). One of the last exponents of a neo-classicism now bordering upon romanticism was Eugène Delacroix (1798–1863). He was not

Jacob Wrestling with the Angel,
Eugène Delacroix, 1853–61.

301

himself a Christian, although his first works were provincial altarpieces and he undertook a number of commissions on Christian themes throughout his career, such as the *Pietà*, and a late series of murals for San Sulpice, such as *Jacob Wrestling with the Angel*[17] (1853–61). His later works also embody his feelings concerning the fate of the artist condemned by critics, featuring scenes of martyrdom, such as that of St Stephen, the first martyr, whose body is carried away by his mourning disciples in a small work painted in 1862. Baudelaire commented that he was the only artist who 'in our faithless generation conceived religious pictures'.

302

Most medieval objects served piety, belief and devotion, having been intended to confirm, clarify and 'make visible' Christian doctrine. Modern scholars consider them sacred works of art. Some medieval works of art, however, emanated from and functioned primarily within the mundane (secular) sphere of medieval life. Within these societies such distinctions between ecclesiastical and secular jurisdictions were often vague, thus the materials they produced also often defy strict classification or may have functioned in different spheres at different times. Indeed, art historians have tended to use these classifications loosely without carefully defining them. Objects made for non-ecclesiastical use often depict quotidian subjects: hunting, sport, science and technology, commerce and trade, personifications, imperial ceremony, chivalry, military campaigns, and topography. The traditional division of artworks dating from the Middle Ages into categories of sacred and secular appears too rigid to accurately reflect the multiplicity of messages that most of these objects convey. Just as there is no clear dividing line between sacred and secular medieval texts, neither can such a boundary be established between objects. The roots of secular/sacred division may be traced to the Middle Ages, however.

The accumulation of objects produced throughout the Middle Ages by monastic or cathedral workshops, or received as gifts from secular patrons for the decoration of ecclesiastical foundations, for liturgical use or for preservation in their treasuries, represent the first segregation of sacred medieval works of art. Church treasuries, like the splendid examples still in the cathedrals of Trier, Cologne, Sens, and Hildesheim, were often repositories representing great ecclesiastical wealth and power. They comprised many types of objects, including reliquaries, textiles, manuscripts, paintings and sculptures. Medieval inventories of church treasuries, like those of secular, primarily royal, collections that emerged in the fourteenth century, reveal little interest in classification except by function and material, and no distinction between religious objects and others.

The Early Modern Vision

Long before the mid-nineteenth century when art history became an academic discipline, a small group of Christian archaeologists in Rome, where classification of certain medieval objects as sacred seems to have originated, took an interest in the study and collection of medieval antiquities. Beginning in the mid-sixteenth century, during the Catholic Counter-Reformation, these archaeologists, unlike other contemporary humanists, valued the tangible vestiges of Christian Rome (*Roma antica cristiana*) on a par with those of the classical past (*Roma antica*). This new breed of archaeologist sought to reconstruct the lives of early Christians by examining textual sources in conjunction with material artefacts. They began to explore the catacombs, derelict and forgotten during the later Middle Ages, and other Christian monuments. From these sites they made drawings of inscriptions, frescoes, sculptures, and metalwork from early Christianity, attempting to construct a material history of the church and of its cult of early saints and martyrs. At the same time, they focused attention on the relics and shrines preserved in medieval church treasuries to inspire renewed reverence and devotion. These works of art became powerful ammunition for Catholic polemicists to contradict Protestant arguments in support of iconoclasm. For Catholics, the paintings in the catacombs, especially, provided incontrovertible evidence that the first Christians used images in their sacred spaces.

Surveys of early Christian monuments yielded sacred objects that now found a home in the 'cabinets' of private collectors. Such assemblages of sacred objects resonated with current Catholic needs, serving as assertions of the ancient presence, continuity and authority of the Church of Rome and as reminders of the heroic faith of Christians demonstrated in the face of earlier persecutions.

By the end of the sixteenth century and continuing through the seventeenth century, sacred monuments and objects, used together with textual evidence, had become a principal tool for historians, as demonstrated in works such as the *Martyrology of Roman Saints* (1586) and *Annales ecclesiastici* (1588–1607) – twelve volumes with inserted engravings in which the influential Catholic scholar Cardinal Cesare Baronio (1538–1607) traced the historical continuity of the church through to 1198. Around the same time, Alfonso Ciaconio (1530–99), a Spanish Dominican in Rome, assembled a museum to house pagan and Christian antiquities, including copies of paintings from the catacombs. The Vatican librarian, Cardinal Francesco Barberini (1597–1679), commissioned watercolours documenting medieval paintings and sculptures in Roman churches; he and others such as Cassiano dal Pozzo (1588–1657) created virtual museums-on-paper of medieval religious art. During the final decades of the seventeenth century a key figure in Roman intellectual circles, the Christian archaeologist Giovanni Ciampini (1633–98), took a keen interest in early medieval and Byzantine antiquities, especially mosaics like those in the churches at Ravenna. Clerics throughout Italy made drawings of these monuments, which Ciampini collected and then had engraved for publication in the five volumes of his *Vetera Monimenta* (1690). One purpose of such collections of sacred art, the Italian painter Giovanni Baglione wrote in 1639, was to 'revive in the memory of the faithful the dress and the rites of the early Church'. Reclaiming the material culture of early Christianity provided a conduit for re-constructing and, thus, re-imagining the practices of early Christians as part of Rome's religious rebirth during the Catholic Counter-Reformation.

The Eighteenth-Century Enlightenment

Consistent with the Enlightenment imperative to provide a systematic philosophical dimension to the collection of objects, the early eighteenth century brought the first institutional museum of sacred medieval art. Pope Clement XI (1700–21) appointed Francesco Bianchini (1662–1729), one of the most learned men in Rome, to form a Museo Ecclesiastico in the Vatican Cortile. Bianchini collected early Christian and medieval inscriptions from the surrounding gardens and from churches and monasteries throughout Rome. At the same time, he marshalled many of these works and others as 'proof' for the historical narratives in his many scholarly studies.

It was not until the mid-eighteenth century under the patronage of the erudite and cultured Bolognese pope, Benedict XIV (1740–58) – who had already established several academies for the study of antiquities and the history of the church – that the systematic assemblage of scattered and neglected medieval objects, and relics of early Christianity, including sarcophagi, glass, inscriptions and bas-reliefs, was revived within the Vatican Library. A museum of the Christian Church, the Museo Sacro (also referred to as the Museo Cristiano), opened in 1757. In a single gallery, the Vatican's Museo Sacro combined several important private collections. The inscription over the entrance refers to the objects in the 'new museum' as 'sacred monuments of Christianity', preserved there to provide historical confirmation of the origins of the religion and to prevent their dispersal. On the ceiling, the *Triumph of the Church* and the *Triumph of the Faith* paintings by Stefano Pozzi convey the overriding message of the assembled objects below. Somewhat later in the eighteenth century, beginning in around 1772, the epigraphic scholar Gaetano Marini (1742–1815) undertook to install hundreds of ancient inscriptions in a corridor of the Vatican by systematically dividing the Christian examples on one side from the profane on the other, in the tradition of the Enlightenment. This classification of medieval Christian objects and inscriptions as separate from all others reveals the priority of the earliest and most important institutional collector of medieval artefacts, the Vatican, to preserve sacred objects as material evidence of the early history of the church.

303

The Nineteenth Century

As excavations of the catacombs continued throughout the nineteenth century, the number of sacred objects (especially sarcophagi, mosaics and inscriptions) in the Museo Sacro, then under the direction of the most distinguished Christian archaeologist of his generation, Giovanni Battista de Rossi (1822–94), grew to such an extent that a second museum of the same name was opened in the Lateran in 1854. Added to these excavated works were medieval liturgical objects and reliquaries made of various precious and non-precious materials. Largely due to de Rossi's efforts, the field of Christian archaeology, which examined medieval artefacts as sacred documents of a 'great age of faith', blossomed into a 'science' in the mid-nineteenth century. De Rossi's comprehensive study, *Roma Sotterranea*, published in three volumes between 1864 and 1877, included a ground-breaking examination of the sacred symbolic character of early Christian art. De Rossi's travels to confer with scholars, as well as his publications, including the *Bulletino d'archaeologia cristiana*, which he inaugurated in 1863, ignited interest throughout Europe in Christian medieval archaeology and artefacts.

Concurrently, in France, a group of scholars seeking to revive religiosity – led by the archaeologist and journalist Adolphe-Napoleon Didron (1806–86) and followed by the archaeologists Fernand Cabrol (1855–1937) and Henri Leclercq (1869–1945), and the amateur art historian/theologian Emile Mâle (1862–1954) – embarked upon iconographic studies of the sacred art of the later Middle Ages. These scholars systematized the study of medieval Christian symbolism, stressing its didacticism.

Periodicals that prominently featured specifically sacred medieval objects appeared in the mid-nineteenth century. In the 1840s and 1850s, Christian archaeological journals, often supported by the ecclesiastical hierarchy, who feared the momentum of secularism, sprang up all over Europe. These were followed in the later nineteenth century by a second wave of journals dedicated to religious art, much of which was medieval. The latter publications constituted a response to what was viewed as the de-sanctification of medieval art posed by study of these objects by an emerging group of art historians. Not surprisingly, these religious publications focused on sacred medieval objects, their iconography, and their theological meanings, as did a new breed of 'Christian' museums that emerged primarily in Germany. Many of these museums were connected to dioceses (*diocesan museum* in German), like one in Cologne that had a particularly rich collection of sacred paintings and metalwork. One of the most significant collections of medieval art was formed, also in Cologne, by a canon of the cathedral, Alexander Schnütgen (1843–1918). During the last third of the nineteenth century, Schnütgen assembled hundreds of medieval artefacts to trace the development of various types of sacred objects (such as chalices, patens and vestments) and Christian representations like the Crucifixion and the Madonna and Child. The goal of this collection was to visually preach Catholic values and impart a sense of the imposing history of Catholicism.

At the same time, there also developed, primarily among a small group of professors within the German-speaking academy, the discipline of medieval art history. Unlike their colleagues in Christian archaeology, art historians such as Adolph Goldschmidt (1863–1944) and Wilhelm Vöge (1868–1952) strove to arrange medieval works of art into an empirically based systematic narrative sequence. Following methods adapted from the study of the natural sciences, they employed, among other approaches, iconographic analysis and careful scrutiny of the formal properties of an object – a method dubbed 'connoisseurship' – to classify medieval objects historically, nationally, regionally and chronologically. For medieval art historians, works of art served the same aim of presenting 'objective' proof of chronological and geographic ordering that documents provided for contemporary historians in constructing their narratives.

Mysticism and Romanticism Reborn

Blake, the Ancients and the Art of Nonconformity

In eighteenth-century England, the refinement of the society portraits by Royal Academicians such as Reynolds and Gainsborough and the monumental tranquillity of Constable's rural landscapes spoke more of faith in what it meant to be English than in God – however much he was viewed as the guarantor of that happy state. Life for the rural and urban poor was a far cry from such idealization, however, with dislocation of the populace as the Industrial Revolution forced more and more people into the towns and the 'dark, satanic mills' of Blake's poem 'Jerusalem'. Their plight was highlighted in the writings of Swift and the paintings and engravings of William Hogarth (1697–1764). In 1728 he painted his first version of John Gay's popular operetta, *The Beggar's Opera*. His *Gin Lane* (1751) is as unsettling as any medieval vision of hell and graphically portrays the plight of those cast to perdition in the here and now. In the background towers the pyramidal spire of St George's, Bloomsbury, one of the Baroque London churches by Nicholas Hawksmoor, 'the devil's architect' (as he was known for his predilection for pagan classical ornament). The slippery slope of the temptations of fashionable life was likewise the subject of his *Rake's Progress* (1733–34), in which gambling and debauchery ruin the life of the carefree, careless socialite and his *Marriage à la Mode* (1743) – a cutting insight into the cynicism and ennui of society marriages of convenience. The morality of Bunyan's *Pilgrim's Progress* and Milton's *Paradise Lost* could evidently still find a place in the fashionable London world of political satire and in what Hogarth himself described as his 'modern moral subjects', which he ensured were affordable and not just for the connoisseur's print room.

A son of 'trade', Hogarth's concern with social reform also expressed itself in his involvement with charitable institutions such as Thomas Coram's Foundling Hospital. He donated his work and encouraged other artists to make it a venue for the display of contemporary art and to benefit from admission charges to view. He also painted biblical murals on the staircase of St Bartholomew's Hospital, without fee, and, concerned at the values (or lack of them) of 'high art', established his own alternative academy of art in St Martin's Lane (1735), which is still stimulating contemporary art, and debate on art, in London. Another controversial artist from the ranks of London's trading class, Joseph Mallord William Turner (1775–1851), devoted his art to the exploration of atmosphere, colour and light through the medium of landscape, but likewise expressed his philanthropic concern for others by leaving his works to the nation[1] and his fortune to establish almshouses for destitute fellow-artists – ambitions that came to fruition despite his family contesting the will.

Nonconformity and Dissent

The eighteenth century also witnessed the continued growth of religious nonconformity and dissent. In the mid-seventeenth century George Fox had founded the Society of Friends, or 'Quakers' (named, like another group, the 'Shakers') for their shaking movements when immersed in prayer during worship. Clergy and ecclesiastical hierarchy were eschewed in favour of meeting houses and collective lay ministry. William Penn led the colony of Pennsylvania to where members of the Friends had emigrated. Art was generally disapproved of by such nonconformist groups, although the virtues of honest craftsmanship and hard work were valued and gave rise to a distinctive Shaker style of domestic interior. The best-known example of Quaker art is the *Peaceable Kingdom*[2] by Edward Hicks (1780–1849), an American Primitive who nonetheless wrote that painting 'appears to me to be one of those trifling, insignificant arts which has never been of any substantial benefit to mankind'. For artistic philistinism can often accompany extreme evangelical expressions of faith, fostered by a reaction against mainstream religion and perceived excess. Hicks's illustration of Isaiah 11:6–8 is nevertheless a touching and uplifting vision of harmony within creation, and reconciliation enabled by Christ taking human form as a vulnerable child. It is effective in its close adherence to the text:

> '*The wolf shall live with the lamb, and the leopard shall lie down with the kid:*
> *and the calf and the lion and the fatling together; and a little child shall lead them.*'

Peaceable Kingdom, a vision of peace and reconciliation throughout creation, inspired by Isaiah 11:6 8, by American Quaker Edward Hicks, with William Penn concluding his peace treaty with the native Americans in the background, 1845–46.

In the background of the image, in its many reproductions, is usually depicted a group of Native Americans concluding a treaty with Penn – a literal application of the symbolism to near-contemporary events – or of a group of Quakers bearing banners proclaiming 'peace on earth and good-will to men'. The simple morality of early American folk artists such as Hicks and Erastus Salisbury Field (1805–1900) was to be perpetuated into the twentieth century by Grandma Moses (Anna Maria Robertson, 1860–1961), a New York County farmer's wife and self-taught primitive painter on canvas and ceramics, and by Duncan Wood's iconic *American Gothic* (1930), in which the artist's dentist and his sister pose as a midwestern farming couple set against the backdrop of a Carpenter Gothic farmhouse. This is a work imbued with nostalgia for the rural past, in the face of the Depression, with a celebration of honest toil and also with a disturbing puritanical austerity.

Another leading nonconformist faith that took shape during the eighteenth century was Methodism, founded in Britain by the charismatic preacher John Wesley (1703–91). Its austerity and integrity appealed particularly to those familiar with the world of work and those in demanding environments, such as the mining communities of Cornwall. Such groups, with their emphasis on lay ministry, offered particular scope for active participation by women, including the artist Maria Spilsbury (1777–1823), whose works included the sentimental but touching portrait of the toddler Elizabeth Julia Angerstein attended by her equally young guardian angels (1805).

William Blake and Samuel Palmer

William Blake (1757–1827) was a nonconformist by nature as well as in his religious leanings. His rebellion against high art and the tyranny of the academies expressed itself in his rejection of the oil medium in favour of tempera, which he termed 'fresco', and his revival of the integrated text and image of the illuminated manuscript – but translated by him onto engravings in which words and pictures were carved together in relief on copper plates and hand-painted in watercolour, forming his own distinctive illuminated books, such as his *Songs of Innocence* (1789) and *Songs of Experience* (1794). Their protest against materialism was complemented by prophetic political books, such as *America: A Prophecy* (1795). His love of Gothic sculpture and of engravings of Michelangelo's work helped to shape his dynamic, monumental style. Heroic figures inhabit timeless voids and his *God Judging Adam* (1795) is an obvious allusion to *God Creating Adam* on the Sistine Chapel ceiling. His vision is prophetic and is also given voice in his poetry. Blake's mysticism and religious fervour led him to question an emergent belief in the absolutism of science, embodied in his *Newton Creating the Universe*[3] (1795) in which he challenges a rationalism that purported to supplant God, rather than acting as an agent of divine will.

In 1824 Blake was introduced, via the artist John Linnell who commissioned his *Book of Job* (1825), to a promising young artist, Samuel Palmer (1805–81), who drank deeply of his influence and, along with Edward Calvert, gave the elderly visionary the audience he craved, despite his High Anglican views. An intense and moving self-portrait, sketched by an adolescent plunged into an abyss of grief by the death of his mother, prophesies the depth and force of Palmer's own inner vision. Basing himself in beautiful Shoreham by the North Downs of Kent (1826–35), Palmer created his own Valley of Vision: trees in luxuriant leaf, and long vistas across high, rolling fields, illumined by harvest moons. Occasional human figures occupy an Elysian realm free of the ravages of mechanization and urbanization, inspired by scripture, Virgil's Bucolics, Milton and Bunyan. Palmer's politics were conservative, Tory in complexion, and he seems to have perceived the countryside and its hub of the parish church as the social anchor in a rising tide of unsettling modernity. Such views found expression in Wordsworth's poems and, although he resisted allegorical

Newton Creating the Universe, 1795, a mystic's challenge to the usurpation of God by science by artist–poet William Blake.

interpretation of his work, is also echoed in Constable's *Salisbury Cathedral from the Meadows*.[4] Its spire recalls Wordsworth's 'silent finger points to heaven', pointing towards the rainbow of the covenant, embattled by a stormy sky and rising flood. Palmer's *Coming from Evening Church*[5] likewise features a Gothic church with spire which, along with the encircling hills, nurtures and protects generations of the young and old who issue from it into the world, sent out by the pivotal figure of their pastor, the rural vicar.

In Shoreham Palmer attracted a group of followers, forming an artistic brotherhood known as 'the Ancients', growing his hair and cultivating a conventional Christ-like appearance. Other fraternities had also recently been formed, united by a sense of equality and opposition to hierarchical authority of the academies – such as the earliest to appear, the Barbus, who emerged in the 1790s from David's Paris studio – and by their commitment to a spiritual quest through art – such as the Viennese Nazarenes who worked in Rome. Edward Calvert, himself an Ancient,

A romantic evocation of
rural life and devotion
by founder of the
English 'Ancients'.
Samuel Palmer, *Coming
from Evening Church*,
Shoreham, Kent, 1830.

wrote, 'We were brothers in art, brothers in love, and brothers in that for which art and love subsist – the Ideal – the Kingdom within.' Their ambitions to instil a new direction in British art were soon dispelled in the 1830s as financial necessity and the recognition of how much they still had to learn about art dawned on them. Palmer's marriage and protracted honeymoon in Italy, during which he painted more commercial landscapes to support the newly-weds' lifestyle, disrupted his artistic development, but the death of his son in later life recalled him to the contemplation of life, death and continued existence, embodied in the melancholic and elegiac etching *The Lonely Tower*.[6] Palmer worked in minute detail in pen and ink, watercolour and etchings (inspired by Blake's work), some rendered even denser by his experimentation with brown-hued glazes that enhance the elegaic autumnal appearance. This mystical eulogization of the English countryside echoed the refrain of Blake's 'green and pleasant land' (again, from the poem 'Jerusalem') and would continue to inspire twentieth-century neo-Romanticism, including the Brotherhood of Ruralists founded by Peter Blake (born 1932), whose love of fantasy also conjured the cover to the Beatles LP *Sergeant Pepper's Lonely Hearts Club Band* (1967).

311

Permission, Prohibition, Patronage and Methodism: A Denomination Engages with Art

Dr Peter Forsaith

Methodism is essentially a hybrid. Emerging as a revivalist, reforming group in the Church of England – generally acknowledged as Catholic in structure while Protestant in doctrine – Methodism is organizationally Protestant, yet its 'Wesleyan Arminian' theology has more than a tinge of catholicity. Down more than two centuries it has struggled with resultant identity issues. Prevailing attitudes to the arts, in British Methodism at least, rarely seem sympathetic and often appear puritanical or philistine.

Ambiguity about visual art is complicated by attitudes to culture more generally. Charles Wesley, brother to Methodism's founding father John Wesley, was perhaps Christendom's most prolific poet, penning some 9,000 hymns – a spectacular literary and musical achievement. Methodism was not only born in song but has lived and breathed through its music. If Methodists were reputedly thin-lipped killjoys, they were ever ready for a tune. While popular music or non-sacred literature could be censured (it was the Wesleys' associate George Whitefield who coined the phrase 'Why should the devil have all the best tunes?'), yet the movement has spawned composers from S. S. Wesley (Charles' grandson) to Andrew Lloyd Webber. Michael Eavis, progenitor of the Glastonbury festival, has attributed his love of music to singing Charles Wesley hymns in the village chapel.

Literary connections are less well pronounced: Methodists can at best directly boast a small crop of minor writers. Yet the Romantic Movement owes a great deal to Methodism at its roots, and the Brontës, George Eliot, Arnold Bennet and Rudyard Kipling all had Methodist connections.

But what of art? Methodist chapels are customarily plain; until recent times a cross on or near the communion table smacked of idolatry. While in its eighteenth-century formative years Methodism's links with the art world are reasonably clear, its nineteenth-century evolution into a nonconformist denomination engendered a hardening of the battle-lines between worldly corruption and holy church (in this case the 'connexion', as its network structure is termed). The twentieth century brought substantial theological and cultural shifts that changed the picture again.

One of John Wesley's executors burned his late Godfather's fine, annotated, edition of Shakespeare, so fearful was he that people might discover that Wesley appreciated Stratford's bard. Yet Charles Wesley, characteristically adroit, could weave Hamlet's pathos into a hymn on – of all things – mysticism:

> 'To do, or not to do; to have
> Or not to have, I leave to Thee;
> To be or not to be I leave:
> Thy only will be done in me...'[1]

At first sight John Wesley, more so than Charles, hardly seems a cultural figure. In his *Journal* he deprecated great houses with their furnishings, pictures and worldly owners. He felt ill-at-ease at his nephews' subscription concerts. Yet – and here is a root of the ambiguity – as an educated eighteenth-century Englishman he could hardly be acultural. Appreciation and understanding of the arts was written into his education and lifestyle; arts were a civilizing fact of life. He became accustomed to having his portrait taken, selected Caslon's aesthetic 'long face primer' type for his publications and encouraged the building of architecturally elegant, and egalitarian, octagonal chapels.

Charles Wesley moved readily within a cultural circle that included artists such as John Russell. Russell's pastel portraits brought him fame and wealth and his evangelical beliefs were for the most part tolerated by his patrons and sitters. His depictions of the moon embodied his theology. As the moon reflects sunlight, the church should reflect the glory of God; in its own firmament the church is an object as mysterious but as constant as the moon. So in his art Russell found a pulpit for his beliefs. Even his 'fancy pictures' of children carried moral and evangelical messages.

Russell was not alone in his time in expressing beliefs through art. Gainsborough's 'landskips' (and, later, Constable's) can be read as expressive of moral and spiritual values although Gainsborough, despite a wayward lifestyle, owed his religious tenets more to Dissenting, rather than Methodist, influence. Nevertheless, the engagement between Evangelicals and art, both at elite and popular levels, should not be overlooked. The minor artist Jonathan Spilsbury moved between the Methodists and Moravians; his daughter Maria Spilsbury / Taylor's art was likewise influenced by her faith. The sculptor John Bacon was an avowed 'Evangelical' at a time when 'Methodist' was coming to mean straightforwardly one of Wesley's followers.

Both Russell's and Bacon's sons abandoned fine art, perceiving it to contradict their faith. The hardening of religious boundaries in the early nineteenth century marked the onset of a mood of cultural prohibition. A psychological separation between art and Methodism became apparent. Yet one Methodist artist's name stands out in the early nineteenth century: John Jackson. As a slick and prolific painter of society portraits Jackson had few rivals; arguably his Methodist allegiance hindered him from fulfilling his talents as he sought to make his name, although his art is hardly an expression of faith. He contributed to Wesleyan Methodism by producing portrait prints of leading ministers for the monthly *Methodist Magazine* for over twenty years as well as a synthesized (and unsatisfactory) 1827 portrait of Wesley which, engraved, became perhaps the dominant image of the founder. As an individual, his friend John Constable wrote posthumously of Jackson:

...he had no enemies. He did a great deal of good, much more, I believe, than is generally known, and he never did harm to any living creature.[2]

Representations of John Wesley, especially as 'scene paintings', enjoyed a lucrative market by the mid-nineteenth century, and represented a safe hagiographic art form for artists with Methodist ties. Marshall Claxton, son of a minister, painted several dramatized scenes from Wesley's life. Perhaps these had especial propaganda value at the time of the High Church Oxford Movement. The Newcastle artist Henry Perlee Parker painted arguably the most famous such scene, pregnant with symbolism, of Wesley's 'miraculous' rescue from fire, aged six. The composition was suggested by James Everett, a leading minister of wide and considerable abilities, chiefly known for his celebrated expulsion from Wesleyan Methodism, who published some fine sketches.

F. J. Jobson, a leading minister, trained as an architect and brought his visual skills to bear upon chapel design; out went the classical and in came the Gothic. His friend James Smetham, another child of the manse, was a romantic associate of the Pre-Raphaelites. Prone to mental illness – perhaps because he lived when Methodism's cultural prohibition was at its height – he could not reconcile his faith with his art, which led to his final breakdown.

By contrast, James Clarke Hook was a lifelong Methodist whose landscape art sat comfortably within his prosperous, Wesleyan but politically radical lifestyle. The grandson of the Methodist leader and polymath Adam Clarke, he owed the start of his career to an introduction to Constable by John Jackson.

William Etty and, later, Stanley Spencer and Eric Gill (and, much later still, David Hockney) were among those who had roots in Methodism or associated denominations but who departed to pursue their art. By the mid-nineteenth century the divergent denominational factions (Wesleyan, Primitive, Free Methodists and others) were exercising strong social proscription. Being a Methodist was heavily solid and respectable; art could be subversive and artists whose names can be associated with Methodism during the later nineteenth century, such as H. E. Tidmarsh, were generally producing anodyne illustrations.

W. H. Y. Titcomb, while not a Methodist, almost alone among the 'Newlyn School' pictured Methodistical religious scenes from life in west Cornwall.

The early twentieth century brought an easing in prohibitive attitudes. Frank Salisbury was a devout Methodist (though a convinced ecumenist), portraitist and stained glass artist who apparently viewed himself as the heir of the English school and whose traditionalism was entirely at odds with prevailing trends in the post-Great War art world. The magnificent but old-fashioned portraits that issued from his Hampstead studio/mansion were something of an embarrassment to a Methodism that was re-uniting and re-shaping itself for new challenges.

While Methodist 'new money' in the nineteenth century could support Methodist artists, buying their works for their grand homes, patronage was rarely a Methodist attribute and artistic expression was generally limited to the architecture or decoration of chapels. Late in the day, however, patronage found its feet in the person of Dr John M. Gibbs whose support of arts in Methodism from the 1950s, as well as in his native south Wales, was notable. He and Douglas Wollen assembled an outstanding collection of Modern Art on Christian themes with the objective of changing the aesthetic perceptions of Methodist people. Artists represented in the collection – such as Edward Burra, Elisabeth Frink, Eric Gill, Patrick Heron, William Roberts and Graham Sutherland – include no Methodists; some are not Christians. Yet they painted biblical scenes in a modern idiom that spoke to them and to the viewer. The extent to which Gibbs and Wollen succeeded remains an open question, but the flowering of creative arts in Methodism – as in other British churches – in the late twentieth century is a sign that permission and prohibition have given way to the promotion of art.

In conclusion, throughout the life of British Methodism, which at first sight seems a barren place for art, it is possible to trace an ongoing flow of artistic activity. Running like an underground stream for much of its way, ignored and hidden, from time to time it emerges, bubbling, chuckling and sparkling to the surface, to reinvigorate its surroundings.

314

23

Faith and the Origins of North American Art

A New Eden

Nonconformity and the constraints of an English pragmatic approach to the consumption of art was to play a significant role in the early formation of the artistic traditions of the 'New World', which of course already had a plethora of vibrant native American artistic traditions. During the eighteenth and early nineteenth centuries the European settlers of North America experienced two divergent approaches to the visual arts in a faith context, which were essentially rooted within the Catholic and Protestant traditions and their various manifestations. The introduction of Catholicism to South America and its subsequent spread north-westwards was, as might be expected, accompanied by the ornate visual trappings of the Spanish Counter-Reformation. This was given a further boost by the immigration of Irish, Italian and other Catholic settlers during the nineteenth and twentieth centuries, who brought with them a taste for popular visual piety with its prints, rosaries, shrines and plaster effigies.

English Roots

The culture of New England Protestants, however, whether Congregational, Presbyterian, Episcopal, Methodist, Baptist or Quaker, reflected both its ultimately vernacular Lollard roots and the comparative paucity of artistic expressions in contemporaneous English religious life, inclining towards the more puritanical and nonconformist end of its spectrum. In England word and text assumed a primacy over the sense of sight (it may not have produced a Michelangelo or a Rubens, but it did give the world Shakespeare and Donne). The New England clergy considered themselves to be literary figures and, like the British artists William Blake and Dante Gabriel Rossetti, the Americans Allston and Cole wanted to be known as poets as well as painters. Where it was valued, art and design generally had more to do with the

FAITH AND THE ORIGINS OF NORTH AMERICAN ART

trappings and aspirations of a civilized, cultured lifestyle and with domestic well-being than with the aesthetics of high art. Porcelain was more likely to be imported and carefully transported across the interior of the American colonies than works of art. Accordingly, in emergent American culture, the visual arts served to confirm and support what was already known or believed, without particularly helping to inform them, although during the nineteenth century there was evidence of a growing public interest in art and of the accordingly enhanced role of the artist. If the quality of American art is not particularly high at this period it should be recalled that it was not an especially high point for art with a Christian orientation elsewhere either.

Shaping a Nation

The variety of American religious viewpoints reflected the composition of society at large and its composite cultural mix. During the nineteenth century this crystallized into participation in the international debate concerning the respective merits and appropriateness of neo-Gothic and neo-classical styles of ecclesiastical architecture, which contextually framed and set the tone for whatever art it might contain. In the process of creating a distinctively American visual expression of civil religion, subject matter with overtly religious themes (although seldom directly based upon scripture), treatment of nature, portraits and other depictions of religious leaders laid the foundations for public commissioning of Old and New Testament subjects. The role of art in general, and of religious art in particular, was to impart ideas of a moral, purposeful history and destiny for the new nation. It formed what Dillenberger has termed an 'epi-phenomenon' – a seismic reaction to the epi-centre of public mores and the body politic, developed in a religious culture but generally outside the church, or churches – for there was no single established State denomination – which were either austere or clad with the polychrome gilt trappings and devotional aides-mémoire of conventional Catholic piety. In the wake of the trauma and liberation of the two World Wars, art produced in the United States increasingly grew to form, rather than just reflect, cultural identity and perception as these in turn became more fluid and less focused or united. The visual arts could now stand alone – art for art's sake, rather than supporting unified cultural agendas.

Some of the earliest examples of North American 'Christian' art are portraits of clergymen which, like those of their secular counterparts, are a provincial reflection of a tradition stretching back into the Tudor and Late Medieval periods. They are no better or worse than those portraits that hung upon the walls of vicarages and country houses of their British counterparts. Not every eighteenth-century socialite, let alone those outside of English court circles, had their likeness painted by Gainsborough or

Reynolds. Thus John Smibert's study (painted in Newport during Berkeley's stay) of *The Bermuda Group – Dean George Berkeley and His Family*[1] compares favourably with its European peers as a group portrait, while Samuel King's *Portrait of Ezra Stiles* (1771),[2] a prominent Newport clergyman who became president of Yale, has a warmth and homeliness in its somewhat naïve simplicity; the cleric's gesture is one of heartfelt integrity, informed by the well-stocked bookshelves alongside which he sits and which attest to his knowledge of Judaism and of the Christian Dionysian theology of divine light. However, the calibre of such works was to a great extent still reliant upon that of artists attracted to North America from Britain.

Portrait of Ezra Stiles, painted by American artist Samuel King, 1771.

FAITH AND THE ORIGINS OF NORTH AMERICAN ART

The Influence of European Art

Under the influence of the Dutch settlement of the upper Hudson Valley, religious subjects began to be painted, alongside portraits, during the early nineteenth century. Of the thirty-eight such paintings some of the earliest have been attributed to Gerardus Duyckinck, who came from a Dutch family with a background as limners (illuminators or engravers) and who was an early member of the Hudson River School. His *Naming of John the Baptist*[3] is signed and dated 1713 and other of his subjects include *Esther and Ahasuerus,*[4] *The Four Evangelists,*[5] *Christ on the Road to Emmaus,*[6] *Christ at Emmaus and Christ Healing the Blindman.*[7] The sources for these and works by other limners working in America included the illustrated Dutch Bibles published in 1702–14 by the Keur family in Dortrecht and Rotterdam, and illustrated biblical episodes based on work by Nicolaus Visscher and Matthew Merian. They are imbued with the charm of the genre scenes of the Brueghels, coupled with an endearing naivety which complements the theme of the extraordinary encountered in the midst of the mundane and everyday. There is an easy domesticity to such art that well suited the context of its new home.

Records show that in 1721 a Swedish emigrant, Gustavus Hesselius, painted a *Last Supper* for St Barnabas Episcopal Church, Upper Marlboro, Maryland. It disappeared during the American Revolution and the work that now hangs in its place, if not the original, is a fine example of the sort of painting imported or produced by émigrés at this period, which still bore the traces of mainstream Italianate influence (the St Barnabas *Last Supper* recalling works by Leonardo and Andrea del Sarto), often absorbed through engravings.

There were other European influences at work too. Art figured in the religious life of French and Spanish settlements from their inception, although little has survived from before the mid-eighteenth century. Some examples imitate their European forebears: the Cathedral of St Louis the King, New Orleans, Louisiana, is richly decorated (if heavily restored) and features a mural above the high altar depicting St Louis, King of France, Announcing the Seventh Crusade; while on the nave ceiling Christ gives his charge of authority to St Peter. Less predictably, an early eighteenth-century altar frontal from Jeune, Lorette, Quebec, shows a Virgin and Child set in the wilds of nature and surrounded by Native Americans.

The crucifixion was not a favoured iconography, except amongst Catholic, Lutheran and some German faith communities, with the exception of the work of two major late-nineteenth-century artists, Thomas Eakins and John Singer Sargent. Eakins loaned his *Crucifixion*, in which Christ's youthful head is occluded by shadow, to St Charles Borromeo Seminary but it never graced its chapel, while Sargent's treatment of the subject formed part of a decorative cycle of frescoes in Boston Public Library. American artists seem to have experienced an unease concerning the depiction of Christ which is both akin to but different from that of earlier Byzantine or Puritanical iconoclasts. This ambiguity seems to have revolved more around the nature of Christ's role than whether it was acceptable to depict him in human form, however, and as a result those Christological subjects that do occur tend to be narrative depictions of biblical scenes rather than more symbolic iconographies mediating meaning. The influence of the English Protestant tradition is particularly apparent here, combining with the impulse of American Protestantism, which was more concerned with the results of faith and its practical application of the gospel to morality and mission than with the framework of its theological meaning and liturgical enactment. The resultant emphasis on sanctification rather than justification and on experiential faith meant, for example, that it was deemed more appropriate when considering sin and redemption to contemplate and empathize with human suffering than that which Christ endured on our behalf. Iconographic themes addressed therefore tend to be those with which the viewer can identify through their own experience and sentiment; thus the plight of the drowned in the deluge or the fate of Adam and Eve after the Fall offered greater attraction than those of the Creation, Crucifixion or the Last Judgement, for they enable the emphasis to fall directly on how the event emotionally effects us. This strategy is one that was also recognized and employed to great effect by Walt Disney and other American film makers.

Inured as we are to the public statuary of the late eighteenth and nineteenth centuries, it can be hard to appreciate the impact that works such as Hiram Power's sculptures *Eve Tempted*[8] (1842) or *The Greek Slave*[9] (1843) had upon the populace, which flocked to view them in special exhibitions. The vulnerability, beauty and sensuality of such works, their naked marble forms perfectly proportioned in accordance with the classical ideal, make them easy to identify with, and certainly attractive; they appear incorruptibly pure even at the moment of incipient corruption. Like her ancient Roman forebears, William Wetmore Story's *Salome*[10] (1871) could embody the essence of the young American society matriarch, reclining confidently and languidly in her chair, were it not for her brazenly exposed breasts; while his statue of *Saul*[11] (1882) could, save for his flowing robes and sandals, be a public worthy or a company director, stroking his flowing beard as he contemplates his own achievements and limitations.

319

Catholic Missionary Culture

Whereas the Catholicism of the eastern seaboard and the Midwest was largely reliant on mass-produced imported liturgical and devotional goods, such as the ubiquitous plaster statues of the pantheon of saints, the Spanish and Pacific North-west Catholic churches generally remained closer to the aesthetic ideals of the early missionaries of the seventeenth and eighteenth centuries and gave rein to indigenous craftspeople to interact with the artistic vocabulary of their new faith. At worst, like the religiosity itself, this could be an imposition rather than a super-imposition; but where the latter occurred the resultant religious art has a transcendental nature that elevates both native and missionary cultures to new heights of union, giving expression to both. The resultant art may be naïve in style but it is rich in content and in cultural and spiritual resonance. The effect of the interiors and sanctuaries of churches such as El Santuario, Chimayo (New Mexico) or San Juan Battista (California) is both simple and opulent, naïve and dignified, blending the reality of the human condition and the transcendental hope of things to come.

The basis of popular Spanish piety was largely visual and aural, rather than founded upon individual reading of scripture, and offered great scope for integration with pre-existing belief systems. Thus, rather as the Celtic deities of north-western Europe had transformed themselves into the Roman pantheon, becoming synonymous with their Mediterranean counterparts and, subsequently, merging imperceptibly with many a Celtic Christian saint, so the needs of the natives for protecting spirits and their images were transferred to the new guardians and heroes introduced by Jesuit and Franciscan missionaries. The colourful feathers that once gave status to Aztec kings now adorned the robes of the Queen of Heaven and a taste for the macabre found full vent in the Last Judgement and the festive frolics of the Mexican Day of the Dead. The oldest church to survive in the United States in essentially its original form is San Esteban del Rey Mission Church at Acoma ('Sky City') in New Mexico, which dates from 1629 (although the walls of San Miguel in Santa Fe date from c. 1610), where the Pueblo Indians incorporated signs from their culture into the decorative scheme to ensure that it might survive the cultural and political imposition of the new faith that they were compelled to accept. Today, the guides, drawn from the fifteen or so families who still dwell atop their tribe's ancestral stronghold, use the church as a didactic aid to instruct tourists in the injustices inflicted upon them by European missionaries and settlers who 'discovered' the ancient pueblos in which they had lived for centuries throughout the so-called unoccupied territories that they seized.

The earliest missions to the Americas were those of Jesuits, such as Eusebio

Francisco Kino and San Xavier del Bac, 'Apostle to the Indies' (they also served to popularize in the Americas devotion to Francis Xavier, Jesuit missionary to Asia). But by 1767 the impact of the expulsion of the Jesuits from Spanish territory had reached Mexico and the initiative passed to the Franciscans. The Jesuits continued to be welcomed in other parts of America into the nineteenth century however, and they were active in Kentucky, Louisiana and the Pacific North-west, where Jesuit artists such as the Belgian Nicolas Point, who worked in Montana, and the Italian Antonio Ravalli – whose work can be seen at the Mission of the Sacred Heart, Cataldo, Idaho – used their art to convey the rudiments of Catholic teaching (recalling Gregory the Great's injunction: 'in images the illiterate read'). In Point's case, he recorded native peoples and their way of life, drawing from and conveying inspiration through depictions of liturgical celebrations and the deeds of their nobles.

Other prominent churches of nineteenth-century date include the extension to the Conewago Chapel, the focus of Jesuit missions in Pennsylvania and Maryland, and the early Catholic churches of Hawaii (such as St Benedict's, Honaunau), decorated by Brother Michel, Fr John and Fr Evarist Gielen between the 1870s and the early twentieth century – all folk responses to the mainstream European classical tradition. Other distinctive traditions in a similar vein included that of the Moravians, or 'visible-wound Church' of Pennsylvania, a Protestant sect stemming from the Hussite and Waldensian traditions which retained its pre-Reformation roots and hung paintings in its altar-less churches. Their mystic absorption with the wounds (which they placed in Christ's left side, rather than the traditional right) and body of Christ can be observed in the paintings by John Valentine Haidt, such as his *Crucifixion*, 1757, and *Lamentation Over the Dead Christ*, c. 1760,[12] who joined the Moravians in 1740 and saw himself as preaching Christ's martyrdom through his paintings. Such an approach led even their patron and spiritual leader, Count Zinzendorf, to refer to the Moravian Brethren as 'little blood worms in the sea of grace'.

Missions spread throughout San Antonio, Texas, Tucson, Arizona, New Mexico and California throughout the eighteenth and early nineteenth centuries. The spirit of these early churches was Baroque, even if their construction favoured regional novelties such as the Mexican Churrigueresque style with its *estipite* columns of inverted triangles, and their altar reredos or *retablos* resemble the festooned tiers of a small theatre, with each box occupied by its own carved saint, sometimes clad in textile dress. The earliest mission art to have survived in North America dates from the mid-eighteenth century and is to be found in San Antonio, Texas, in churches such as Mission Concepción, completed in 1755, with its murals of faux stone panels, its Crucifixion and its Eye of God – a talisman for the protection of crops and children which is still popular with the Huichol people of

Mexico. Perhaps the finest example of Spanish Baroque in North America is also at San Antonio, Mission San José. Its elaborately carved façade with its hierarchy of garland-honoured saints proudly features the icon of Our Lady of Guadalupe, the famous painted icon in the pilgrimage shrine north of Mexico City, demonstrating the umbilical links back to 'New Spain'. The portable artwork of the Texan missions, however, was imported from Mexico or Spain (early examples including the figures of saints from the altar and chancel of San Juan Capistrano); whereas in New Mexico indigenous traditions of painting and sculpture flourished and absorbed earlier European Baroque influences to produce *santeros* art, with its doll-like effigies of saints, often dipped in gesso to give the impression of drapery. The adobe churches of El Santuario de Chimayo, built in 1816 and decorated by Molleno, Rafael Aragón and José Aragón, and of Santa Cruz are particularly fine examples of this exuberant style of religious folk art, which still inspires the prayers of flocks of pilgrims who come for healing from the earth, in age-old fashion, at Chimayo in the form of the inexhaustible pit of 'holy dirt'.

Particular saints or iconographies were favoured in the North American mission churches, as in other lands, such as Mary of the Immaculate Conception (La Purisima – her crown of stars and the crescent moon stemming from the Apocalypse), patroness of Spanish territories, whose popularity was established early on, and who was declared by Catholics to be the patroness of the United States in 1840, even though the Immaculate Conception was not declared dogma until 1854. God enthroned in Majesty, holding the globe (*orbis terrarium*) surmounted by a cross, his hand raised in blessing, is another favourite subject, while Fr Kino's teaching that the Virgin had prophesied to St James that he would enable Spain to convert the world led to the pilgrim's scallop shell of Santiago de Compostela reaching the art of the New World. José Aragón was one of the most sophisticated and Eurocentric of these local folk artists, but even his provincialism is stressed by his lack of awareness of contemporary Catholic teaching. His Holy Trinity (*La Santisima Trinidad*, early 1800s),[13] with its tritheistic resonances, represents his response to earlier art and his ignorance of the proscription of this iconography by Pope Benedict XIV in 1745.

Many of the statues, images and liturgical objects of the Californian missions were imported from Mexico or Spain, although paintings by Thomas Doak, an Anglo-American artist working in California during the early nineteenth century, are to be found at Mission San Juan Bautista. The murals at Mission San Miguel Arcangel (1816-21) are by a Barcelonan settler in Monterey, Don Esteban Carlo Munras. Native American work is also to be found at sites such as Mission San Antonio de Pala, the mission church to the Pala tribe, with its traditional saw-tooth patterns representing the waters of heaven, its helmeted heads, triangular shields/symbols of fertility and other native symbols integrated into the Christian repertoire.

Early Expressions of North American Taste

Popular piety expressed in folk art through emulation of the aesthetics of a European past, or the espousal of a puritanical simplicity in which 'art' found little place – although integrity of craftsmanship certainly did as Shaker aesthetics amply testify – were competing and/or complementary strands in the cultural composition of this 'New World'. There were also those who perceived virtue in the absence of an indigenous tradition – at least as far as those of non-Native American origin were concerned – and who celebrated the paradisiacal natural environment as a new Eden and the human impact upon it as the work of a new Adam and Eve. Timothy Dwight, a revivalist theologian / preacher and President of Yale during the late eighteenth to early nineteenth century, wrote of his travels through New England and opined that:

> 'Few of those human efforts, which have excited the applause of mankind, have demanded equal energy, or merited equal approbation. A forest, changed within a short period into fruitful fields, covered with houses, schools and churches, and filled with inhabitants, possessing not only the necessaries and comforts, but also the conveniences of life, and devoted to the worship of Jehovah, when seen only in prophetic vision, enraptured the mind even of Isaiah; and when realized, can hardly fail to delight that of the spectator. At least, it may compensate the want of ancient castles, ruined abbeys and fine pictures.'[14]

This American dream expressed a conventional view of Christian stewardship of the day, which is now increasingly perceived as rather too homocentric in its focus to be able to promote a sustainable integration and balance of humankind within the interwoven unity of creation. It did, however, promote a conceptual appreciation of natural landscape that coincided with and contributed to that of European Romanticism. Dwight and Lord Kames also wrote on the subject of taste as a constituent of religious and moral life, helping to unite human effort with the divine plan. Accordingly, those with the leisure and funds to do so were exhorted, male and female alike, to cultivate a taste for and proficiency in the arts. The creative voice of theologian Horace Bushnell, whose portrait, painted by Jared B. Flagg in 1847, now hangs in the Wadsworth Atheneum, Hartford, Connecticut, proclaimed:

'…the Gospel is, in one view, a magnificent work of art, a manifestation of God which is to find the world, and move it, and change it, through the medium of expression. Hence it requires for an inlet, not reason or logic or a scientific power so much as a right sensibility. The true and only sufficient interpreter of it is an esthetic talent, viz., the talent of love, or a sensibility exalted and purified by love.'[15]

His poetic framework for such expression owed much to the work of Samuel Taylor Coleridge. Other commentators, such as George Washington Betune, a Princeton graduate who was ordained in the Dutch Reformed Church and holder of pastorates including Philadelphia and New York, wrote that although it was fitting that art had not figured in the early Puritan phase of settlement, while the new Americans tamed (parts of) the wilderness and constructed a political and moral society, it was now time for an interest in art to assume its place in the body politic and religious life.

This view was also espoused by successful Protestant painter Emanuel Leutze (1816–68), whose best-known work, *Washington Crossing the Delaware* (1851), is a pinnacle of American history painting. It is one of a number of works in which he explored the origins of American political, intellectual, religious and artistic freedom. Another was *The Iconoclasts* (1846) in which he depicted a group of puritanical roundheads, during the seventeenth-century English Civil War, destroying the images in a medieval church. Leutze uses the lens of history most effectively to comment upon the approach to religious art still prevalent in much of American society, the puritanical tendencies of which he saw as potentially destructive to man's union with God and to human compassion, reflected in a rather condemnatory stance adopted towards Catholics and their devotional images. The exhibition of such works at venues such as the American Art-Union, the Pennsylvania Academy of the Fine Arts, and the Boston Atheneum helped to encourage the shift in the American public's perception of art and faith.

Collectors and Patrons

The accomplished American who was au fait with Occidental and perhaps even Oriental culture (fuelled by travels and reading) emerged on the scene, with appreciative skills based upon moralistic foundations. This phenomenon did not result, however, in a significant introduction of the visual arts into places of worship (with the notable exception of stained glass); but it could serve to inspire the creation of art collections by figures such as Elias Magoon, a Baptist clergyman active in

Virginia, Ohio, New York City, Albany and Philadelphia, for whom collecting formed part of his Christian vocation while still in his twenties. He wrote:

'Thirty years ago, without the first dollar that was my own and without one friend in the world who sympathized with my imagination, I set about gathering a collection that should illustrate human progress under and along the divine purpose, Christianity illustrated by its monuments.'[16]

His collection now belongs to Vassar Female College Art Gallery, which he was instrumental in founding, the Committee of which reported in 1864 that:

'Art stood boldly forth as an educating force, to have its first fair play in the history of education. Somebody, at length, had come to see that man's delight in God's work is the mightiest means of moral culture, and that such exactly is true art.'[17]

For such early collectors in the 'Age of Washington' art was seen to flourish, like political theory, in the free soil of America, its spirit reflecting that of the land and the people, the sublimity of which would soon be celebrated in the work of the Hudson River School. No wonder then that there is such a strong tradition in North America of art history and art appreciation, the seeds of which were subsequently strengthened by the influx of refugees from Nazi Europe, notably the Jewish intelligentsia of Germany and central Europe.

Among Roman Catholic clergy recognition of the role of images in the Christian tradition was usual if not necessarily informed. Several (including Archbishops John England, John Lancaster Spalding, John Hughes and James Cardinal Gibbons) took up the pen to preach against Protestant misunderstanding of the Catholic approach. Gibbons subscribed to a letter of Catholic bishops in Baltimore (1884), which stated that homes should be 'beautified with what will keep the inmates in mind of our Divine Lord, and of His saints, and with such other pictures of the great and good as will be incentives to civic and religious virtue'. Generally such devotional aids, whether for domestic or church consumption, were of a mass-produced commercial variety. Some prelates, notably Fr Isaac Hecker, founder of the Paulist Fathers whose mother church was St Paul the Apostle in New York City, were in the vanguard of ecclesiastical art and design; Hecker consulted prominent artists such as John LaFarge, a Catholic who otherwise usually received only Episcopal commissions.

Only in the late nineteenth century had Anglican churches in North America joined the Moravians and Catholics in patronizing the arts, however. Most of the first wave of American Protestant artists had trained in London under the history painter Benjamin West, who came from a Quaker background but joined the Anglican Church after settling in England. Edward Hicks, who has already been mentioned, was the leading North American folk artist of the first half of the nineteenth century. He became a Quaker as a young man, supporting his ministry along the eastern seaboard partly by painting signs and stage coaches. Despite producing around a hundred versions of his *Peaceable Kingdom*, Hicks remained uneasy, in Quaker fashion, with his own art and unconvinced of the need for painting in a world that was divinely created, if only it would continue to reflect God's image, writing:

> 'If the Christian world was in the real spirit of Christ, I do not believe there would be such a thing as a fine painter in Christendom.'

Also suspicious of the seductive, sensory dangers of art for religious life was another part-time painter during the first half of the nineteenth century, the Presbyterian Samuel F. B. Morse, inventor of the telegraph and Morse Code, a staunch and aggressive 'WASP' (White Anglo-Saxon Protestant) who wrote, after visiting Milan Cathedral, that Catholicism was:

> 'a religion of the imagination... architecture, painting, sculpture, music have lent all the charm to enchant the senses and impose on the imagination by substituting for the solemn truths of God's Word, which are addressed to the understanding, the fictions of poetry and the delusion of feeling'.

Still he justified his own painting, which seldom directly featured religious scenes, by the contrasting propriety of its use until, thwarted in his ambition to receive a commission for one of the Rotunda paintings in the Capitol, he finally abandoned art as a wanton mistress.

The Liberating Power of Art

Yet she was a mistress who could offer liberty, even to those enslaved. A passion for neo-classical sculpture offered scope for its production to women artists and to African Americans who acquired the sculptor's art through their labours as artisan stonecutters. One such was Eugene Warburg (1826–59), who was born a slave, became a monumental mason and settled in Rome in 1857 as a portrait sculptor in the classical Roman tradition. But the first African American sculptor to receive international recognition was a woman and a nonconformist, Edmonia M. Lewis (1845-1911), although her chosen subjects – African Americans and Native Americans – precluded her commercial success. In 1863 abolitionist William Lloyd Garrison provided her with a letter of introduction to Bostonian portrait sculptor Edmund Brackett, under whom she subsequently studied. She soon opened her own studio, achieved popularity through her busts of figures such as John Brown and Colonel Robert Gould Shaw, and travelled to Florence and Rome, where she joined what Henry James described as 'that strange sisterhood of American "lady sculptors" who at one time settled upon the seven hills in a white marmorean flock'. Lewis used the idealized neo-classical human figure to celebrate Christian ideals of redemption and human dignity: her *Forever Free* (1867), depicting two liberated slaves – man and woman – embodies both abolitionism and the salvation of Adam and Eve. Its appeal, if sentimental, was universal, accessible to the visually educated and to the general public, male and female, black and white. Moreover, the kneeling black female slave became for white women a metaphor for their unliberated condition, and Lewis is quoted as saying, 'I have a strong sympathy for all women who have stuggled and suffered.'

327

The idealism of neo-classicism soon gave way to paintings of rural and urban subjects. One of many successful genre painters was African American Henry Ossawa Tanner (1859–1937), whose father was a bishop in the African Methodist Episcopal Church. He studied at the Pennsylvania Academy of Fine Arts under Thomas Eakins (1849–1916), who pioneered the study of nude models and of photography in the United States. His first exhibition, held in Cincinnati in 1890, was sponsored by white Methodist Episcopal bishop Joseph Crane Hartzell and his wife, who also funded his travels to Paris where he spent much of his career. His studies of scenes from the lives of African Americans gradually gave way to biblical subjects, fostered by his friendship with French artist and Orientalist J. J. Benjamin-Constant and travels in the Holy Land funded by American patrons. His *Resurrection of Lazarus* (1896) won him a medal from the Paris Salon, rarely bestowed upon American artists. From then on his work focused on scenes from the Gospels and the life of Christ, including a contemporary reworking in 1898 of Fra Angelico's *Annunciation*,[18] with Mary depicted as a simple Middle Eastern woman and the archangel Gabriel as a shaft of light. Tanner wrote in 1913:

'I have no doubt an inheritance of religious feeling, and for this I am glad, but I have also a decided and I hope an intelligent religious faith not due to inheritance but to my own convictions. I have chosen the character of my art because it conveys my message and tells what I want to tell to my own generation and leave to the future.'

328

Annunciation, 1898, a daring reworking of a work by Fra Angelico by African-American artist Henry Ossawa Tanner, in which the Virgin is depicted as an ordinary Middle Eastern girl and the Archangel Gabriel as a shaft of bright white light.

By seeking to unite ancient biblical insights with contemporary experience in order to perceive something of God's will in the present, Tanner was reflecting a popular strand of African-American preaching. Like Lewis, he achieved acceptance and acclaim by excelling in an aesthetic that was popular both in North America and in Europe, rather than by seeking to establish a distinctively 'negro' school of art, for which he has attracted no little criticism. Tanner wished to pursue his artistic mission and to rank among the foremost American artists. During the twentieth century a new kind of black identity would emerge, finding expression in the figurative, the urban, the class-conscious and the African heritage. Modern black artists have found many ways of expressing their cultural similarities and dissimilarities, while works such as Vincent Smith's *Negotiating Commission for Amnesty* (1972), with its trussed figures suspended upside down like chickens, speak a universal language of morality that transcends categorization of race, gender, nationalism or faith.

At a less fashionable or radical level, folk art has also been able to offer a liberating and fulfilling form of expression. African-American stonecutter William Edmondson (1863–1951) spent most of his life in his birthplace, Nashville, Tennessee, where, at around the age of sixty, he began carving gravestones from offcut stone depicting 'critters' and biblical figures that struggle to emerge from the stone, like Michelangelo's Slaves. Edmondson also regarded his work as a sacred mission:

'This here stone and all those out there in the yard come from God. It's the work in Jesus speaking His mind in my mind. I must be one of His disciples. These here is miracles I can do. Can't nobody do these but me. I can't help carving. I just does it. It's like when you're leaving here you're going home. Well I know I'm going to carve. Jesus has planted the seed of carving in me.'

Religious Folk Art

Professor Virginia Raguin

Religion furnished the most consistent inspiration for centuries of autonomous image making in Europe and the New World. The Christian religion favoured images: as testimonials, as souvenirs of experience (such as a pilgrimage), and as acts of atonement or gratitude. Thus the impetus to own or create works of art was strong. With the advent of the printed medium in the mid-fifteenth century individuals could possess small works on paper. These were routinely displayed in homes, as exemplified by the woodcut of St Christopher tacked to the wall behind the Virgin Annunciate in a painting by Robert Campin.[1]

Colour entered these homey arts through reverse glass painting that gained popularity in the eighteenth century. The compositions were most commonly inspired by prints, themselves often derived from major paintings. Colours were bold in hue and the outline simple and uncomplicated, sometimes enhanced with metallic foil that evoked gilding in metalwork and frames. The craft was concentrated in the German-speaking lands of Austria, Bohemia and the Black Forest. Similar types of images emerged about the same time in equally pious communities of the south-west of the United States, Mexico and other parts of South America. In the New World, tin frames using reverse glass painting as a decorative embellishment were made to surround imported prints. The variegated patterns of colour with leaf or geometric designs surround black and white or chromolithographic commercial prints. Whether small-scale for home use or large-scale for display as Stations of the Cross, these objects present compelling juxtapositions of commercial and handcrafted product.

Many of these works served a testimonial purpose and are commonly referred to as *ex votos*. The high art tradition is rife with thank-offerings. Entire buildings were constructed after a victorious battle, or a cycle of paintings commissioned to give thanks for the avoidance of the plague. Individuals had similar desires, leaving tokens of gratitude, such as flowers, crutches, or a rosary, and, for many with significant circumstances of deliverance, a personalized image of the cure. Mexico supported a long tradition of paintings on tin of small dimensions, often around 7 x 10 inches (18 x 25 cm) for such purposes. Invariably the afflicted individual was shown – lying ill in bed, being gored by a bull, falling down a cliff – and the sufferer, or an intermediary such as a mother, wife, parent or child, praying to a specific devotional image. Thus the picture presents an image within an image, and was often meant to be affixed to the site of the miracle-working object. An *ex voto* constructed in 1881 to the Lord of Mercy of the Encarnación (El Señor de la Misericordia de la Encarnación)[2] demonstrates a typical formula. The inscription states that the petitioner 'invoked the Lord of Mercy that is venerated in the cemetery of the Incarnation who saved her life and restored her health: and in return she dedicates this'. A public display of sentiment validated the private emotion of gratitude.

Naïve painters in Europe and the United States have sometimes entered the domain of 'fine art'. Henri Rousseau's works such as the *Sleeping Gypsy* and *The Snake Charmer* have entered prestigious museums such as the Museum of Modern Art and the Musée d'Orsay. Edward Hicks (1780–1849), who produced some of the best-known images of modern Christian piety, also appears in collections of major museums. Hicks's painting of Niagara Falls[3] is a purposeful image extolling the glory of God and moral behaviour. The borders carry an inscription that praises the power of the falls 'with uproar hideous', ending with the injunction to 'kneel and Time's great God adore'.

Hicks was a Quaker and began his career as a decorator of carriages and sign painter. For a time he took up farming to distance himself from such worldly pursuits; unsuccessful, he returned to making images, which allowed him to maintain a non-remunerative career as a Quaker preacher. During the last forty years of his life he is thought to have executed some 100 paintings entitled the *Peaceable Kingdom*. Based on Isaiah 11:6–8, the images depict a world of reconciliation and peace under the rule of the Messiah (see p. 307).

Despite his untutored style, Hicks's concepts were quite sophisticated. The image of William Penn is taken from Benjamin West's *The Treaty of Penn with the Indians*[4] (1771–72), in itself after the image of Christ in the midst of his disciples from Masaccio's *Tribute Money*[5] (1426). Although textually based, the animals themselves relate the theory of the four humours of human personality traits: the wolf melancholic, the leopard sanguine, the bear phlegmatic, and the lion choleric. Hicks preached a sermon in 1837 explaining that under the influence of the Holy Spirit, which Hick's faction of Quakerism called the Inner Light, these wild animals became their domesticated selves. Thus in the version in the Worcester Art Museum, the lamb is next to the wolf, the kid lies behind the leopard, the cow grazes next to the bear, and the ox and lion command the centre.

As in Hicks's work, repetitious themes, even compositions, were common in popular images to commemorate the dead. Mourning pictures were a common subject in nineteenth-century England and the United States, frequently showing a tomb

monument, often with a classical urn, shaded by weeping willows and flanked by one or several mourners. The viewer empathizes with the pensive moment showing the inevitability of death. Similar to the context of reverse glass painting in Germany and the New World, the mass-produced print and the hand-made object again intersect. Prints of mourning pictures by companies such as Pendelton, Currier and Ives, and Kellogg could be purchased uncoloured or hand-tinted. Owners personalized them by writing specific names on the grave monument depicted. The same type of image was often the subject of needlework executed by girls in the Ladies Academies of the era. Catherine Willard, attending Mrs Rowson's Academy of Boston, embroidered a remembrance to William Henry Dorr, who died on 3 September 1809, aged twenty months, with the phrase 'Born just to bloom and fade'.[6] These objects, like samplers, were exercises that trained genteel girls for 'women's work', including the bearing of and mourning after children.

The modern world is now witnessing an interest in 'outsider' art. Often the terms for these works are varied and include intuitive, self-taught or visionary art. A clear criterion is that artists demonstrate little influence from the mainstream

Ex voto, Lord of Mercy of the Encarnación, an example of religious folk art, Mexico, 1881.

art world, and create from their own inner resources. Traditional folk art, however, was most often created within a specific community of artists and sought a targeted audience. The reverse glass painting of Austria, for example, was produced for a ready market of homes and distributed by itinerant merchants. The contemporary art market's interest in the individual and the value of originality has encouraged a professional interest in expressions of unique personal visions. In 2004, an exhibition entitled 'Coming Home! Self-Taught Artists, the Bible, and the American South', organized by the Art Museum of the University of Memphis, found a second venue at the Museum of Biblical Art, New York. The exhibition argued forcefully that the understanding of the art was inseparable from that of the cultural and religious climate of the American South. Among the themes were vivid visions of the Second Coming of Christ, as well as didactic text and image statements that gained a particular fervour around the year 2000. Evangelical belief had been tapped to reveal a wide variety of imagery in sculpture, pictures and the mingling of text and image.

As the globalization of society continues, tightly knit Christian communities with highly focused belief systems are becoming rarer. The availability of inexpensive commercial imagery lessens the need for local production. Folk art expressions, however, have been many and varied and will inevitably continue to transform as they have in the past.

Doll-like effigy of the Holy Child from the New Mexican shrine of Chimayo, a popular pilgrimage centre which has been given lots of votive folk art such as this.

Industrial Innovation, Aesthetic Nostalgia

Romanticism, Pre-Raphaelitism and the Rediscovery of Medievalism

The later eighteenth and nineteenth centuries witnessed a backlash to the rationalism and rampant secularism of the age of Enlightenment, as Europe was plunged into the turmoil of revolution, warfare and rapidly developing industrialization. Crowned heads were severed from their bodies, courtesy of madame guillotine (Louis XVI and Marie Antoinette were executed in 1793), while elsewhere in Europe new nations emerged (Victor Emmanuel II of Sardinia being proclaimed king of the newly unified Italy in 1861). In the interim Napoleon Bonaparte declared himself emperor (in 1804) and embarked on the conquest of much of Europe; Queen Victoria ascended the British throne (1837–1901) and made a political reality of the British trading empire; and the Franco-Prussian and Crimean Wars were fought. The tastes of aristocratic patrons and the ambition among artists to achieve fame and wealth through the recognition and advancement of the establishment and its hierarchy retreated in the face of popular radicalism and the rise of the bourgeoisie, whose artistic needs were satiated by mass produced consumables, including prints and illustrated books. Popular piety was once more on the rise, alongside a growing social realism and materialism.

Brotherhoods and the Art of Self

In the face of this many artists reacted by cultivating a heightened sense of self. This might assume the form of the radical bohemian (such as Courbet and Lautrec) or the suave flâneur (the fashionable man about town) and aesthete compelled by 'art for art's sake' (such as the Frenchman Manet, the American Whistler and the Englishman

Beardsley). Some chose to express their view of their place in society by forming artistic brotherhoods. These were often underpinned by a shared sense of spiritual commitment and vocation. One such was a group of Viennese artists who formed the Brotherhood of St Luke (*Lukasbrüderschaft*), better known as the Nazarenes (*Nazarener*, from the Nazarite sect referred to in Numbers 6:1–21), for their long hair and flowing garb, their simple lifestyles and their commitment to devotional art. They established themselves in the abandoned church of St Luke in Rome and embarked upon a quest to revive religion through art, bypassing the Baroque and emulating the Late Medieval and Renaissance styles that preceded Raphael's maturity. In this sense they were the forerunners of the English Pre-Raphaelite Brotherhood, but they were rather more conventional in their adherence to earlier exemplars. Their joint commissions in Rome included the *Life of Joseph in Egypt* and scenes from Dante for the Casino Massimo. Their principles are clearly expressed in a portrait of one of their founders,

Friedrich Overbeck, *Portrait of Franz Pforr*, 1810, Rome. A portrait of a founder of the Nazarenes by its co-founder, in late fifteenth-century fashion.

Franz Pforr,[1] by the other, Friedrich Overbeck (1789–1869). Painted around 1810, it is in a self-consciously Late Medieval / Early Renaissance style and is replete with iconographic allusions to the religiosity of the Middle Ages. Pforr's hair and dress are in period and he leans on a Gothic window ledge on which is carved a skull and a cross – a *memento mori* reminding him of his mortality as he gazes out in contemplation of his spiritual ideals. In the background is a church and a young woman reading a prayer book, in the attitude of the Virgin – an allusion reinforced by the accompanying lilies of purity. Eucharistic grapevines frame the scene and a cat and chained raven recall the need to guard against, and restrain, sin.

Even the solitary, unaffiliated, secular artist could be imbued with ideals of romanticism and ascetic spirituality. A depiction of *The Artist's Studio* painted in 1845 by the Frenchman Octave Tassaert (1800–74) presents the archetypal vision of the young impoverished bohemian painter suffering for his art in a dingy garret, with only a few potatoes to hold body and soul together as he crouches beside a dying fire, his palette discarded and empty of the pigments he can no longer afford. On the wall is pinned an engraving of a friar, his arms outstretched in benediction and welcome – or is it St Francis displaying his stigmata, the wounds he bore in emulation of Christ's suffering? The inference is that the self-inflicted vocational poverty of the artist, intent on bearing witness to beauty and his ideals, is akin to that of the mendicant orders. That same year saw the publication of the first installment of Henri Murger's influential collection of short stories, *Scenes of Bohemian Life* (the inspiration for Puccini's opera *La Bohème*), recounting the adventures of a small band of artists, writers and musicians (the term bohemian, for gypsy, was first used in this context by the playwright Félix Pyat in 1834). Murger wrote of the precarious liberation and public alienation of the artistic condition:

335

'Bohemia, bordered on the North by hope, work and gaiety, and on the South by necessity and courage; on the West and East by slander and the hospital.'

Discussion of art and politics, especially of the radical kind espoused by Courbet with its rejection of the establishment and of bourgeois values, was the principle diet of the artists who frequented the cafes and bars of Montmartre, however, rather than religion and spirituality.

Romanticism

Romanticism also held sway during the nineteenth century. Caspar David Friedrich (1774–1840) was the leading exponent of the German Romantic Movement (which also included Runge and Blechen), which adopted a spiritual approach to Nature and depictions of landscape. Direct observation combined in Friedrich's work with a melancholic all-pervading atmosphere, fuelled by German Romantic poets such as Goethe and the English nature poets such as Thomas Gray, and a rising sense of nationalism in the wake of Napoleon's invasion of Germany in 1806. His treatment of landscape was formal and symbolic: works such as *The Cross in the Mountains*[2] (1808) and *The Monk by the Sea*[3] (1809) explored spiritual revelation through the scenery of the North.

The American wilderness also evoked a transcendental spiritual revelation in artists, fuelled by the writings of authors such as James Fenimore Cooper, Henry David Thoreau, Ralph Waldo Emerson and Washington Irving. Studies of wildlife by Alexander Wilson and John James Audubon, and George Catlin's studies of Native American tribes and their lifestyles (a genre perpetuated by Albert Bierstadt) also served to inspire nineteenth-century American painters of the sublime natural landscape, such as Thomas Doughty, Thomas Cole, Asher Brown Durand, Frederick Edward Church and other members of the Hudson River School. Their attempts to capture the symbolic power of landscape reached a crescendo in Cole's *The Voyage of Life*[4] (1850). Their romantic realism in turn inspired those who subsequently painted or photographed the American West, such as William Hahn, George Catlin, John Gast, Eastman Johnson and Henry F. Farny.

The Power of Nature

Painting somewhat in the style of the Pre-Raphaelites, although seeking to emulate the art of the Renaissance, Abbott Henderson Thayer embodied contemporary ideals of domesticity and the submissive, 'trophy' role of women and children in his *Virgin Enthroned* (1891), modelled upon his daughters. But conventions were being challenged and, along with the fin de siècle urbane cosmopolitanism of the Eurocentric art of Whistler, Sargent and Cassatt, were rejected by artists such as Winslow Homer in favour of unsentimental depictions of the harshness of wresting a living from the New England seaboard and the wild Atlantic, and the trauma of the American Civil War. Philadelphian Thomas Eakins espoused a carefully observed sobriety and scientific accuracy in his portraits, with their psychological intensity and human vulnerability, and in his depictions of surgical operations – notably the *Gross Clinic*, which he declared one of his most important paintings. The 'rabbit in headlights' ineffectual immobility of his portrait of Catholic *Archbishop Domede Falconio* (1905), apostolic delegate to Canada, perhaps expresses Eakins's view of formal religion.

For nineteenth-century luminists such as John Kensett, Sanford Gifford, George Loring Brown and Fitz Hugh Lane it was the exploration of atmospheric light rather than scenic grandeur that served as inspiration. George Inness, Ralph Blakelock and Albert Pinkham Ryder preferred to imbue their landscapes with a mystic symbolism, extending the genre into the twentieth century, like Belgian Expressionist painter James Ensor (1860–1949), who was so inspired by the North Sea off the Flemish coast and who, in 1923, wrote:

> 'My friends, work of a personal vision alone will live. One must create a personal pictorial science, and be excited before beauty as before a woman one loves. Let us work with love and without fear of our faults, those inevitable and habitual companions of the great qualities. Yes, faults are qualities; and fault is superior to quality. Quality stands for uniformity in the

effort to achieve certain common perfections accessible to anyone. Fault eludes conventional and banal perfections. Therefore fault is multiple, it is life, it reflects the personality of the artist and his character; it is human, it is everything, it will redeem the work.'

During that troubled century photographers such as Anselm Adams (1902–84) and Alfred Stieglitz (1864–1946) used their art to explore both the natural and urban landscape, and a young group of painters known as 'The Eight', led by Robert Henri, espoused a gritty urban realism that gained them the sobriquet of Ashcan Realists. Urbanism also inspired the 291 artists (those who exhibited at Alfred Stieglitz's 291 Gallery in New York) such as Max Weber and Joseph Stella, but in others, notably Arthur Dove (1880–1946) and Georgia O'Keefe (1887–1986), it provoked a reaction that impelled them to acknowledge the power of nature through their art. Like the earlier wilderness artists and transcendentalist philosophers Emerson and Thoreau, they sought a personalized religious expression and spirituality through union with nature rather than through formal religious teaching and scripture. The desert, always a place of spiritual encounter, offered particular inspiration to O'Keefe, who was one of several modernist artists to stay at the Los Gallos artists' colony founded at Taos, New Mexico, by New Yorker Mabel Dodge and her Tiwa Indian husband, Antonio Luhan. Writers were also attracted to this ancient area with its compelling natural landscape and mixture of Pueblo Indian and Hispano-Catholic cultures. Artefacts from both cultures, including little icons of saints, figure in the work of Marsden Hartley, and Catholic symbols such as *Black Cross, New Mexico*, appear among O'Keefe's subjects. D. H. Lawrence wrote in 1931: 'The sky-scraper will scatter on the winds like thistledown, and the genuine America, the America of New Mexico, will start on its course again.'

Gothic Romanticism

For others, back in the 'Old World', it was the monuments of the past, rather than the untamed wilderness, that tended to inspire romantic and spiritual reflection. The romantic ruins of Gothic England, such as Tintern Abbey, had inspired eighteenth-century artists, but during the nineteenth century thought turned to their preservation. Augustus William N. Pugin (1812–52) and George Gilbert Scott (1811–78) led the trend for restoring, and building, medieval churches, while in France, Eugène Viollet-le-duc (1814–79) undertook a more thorough-going academic study of Gothic architecture, publishing a ten-volume *Dictionnaire raisonné de l'architecture française du XIe au XVIe siècle* (1854–68), which informed his restoration work on major monuments such as Amiens Cathedral and Notre Dame de Paris (1844-64), from the parapets of which his famous pensive demons still contemplate the follies of the tourists below. His anti-clericalism led him to espouse the Gothic style as representative of the rise of urbanization and secularism and to champion it as an early example of the architectural dogma of form suiting function.

The interior decoration of such buildings also occupied Pugin, Gilbert Scott and William Burges (1827–81), an architect who gained some major commissions from the Earl of Bute at Cardiff Castle and the nearby retreat of Castell Coch – a perfect little Gothic fantasy in which every surface, including furniture, was ornamented in medieval fashion and even the tableware was inspired by the metalwork of the Middle Ages. In Lichtenstein Germanic romanticism likewise conjured up the Disneyesque confection of the castle of Neuschwanstein, designed by Christian Jank for 'Mad' King Ludwig of Bavaria (died 1886).

For Pugin, son of a French émigré who had fled the Revolution, the Gothic Revival that swept through Victorian England was intimately bound up with his conversion to Catholicism in 1835. The following year he published *Contrasts: Or, a Parallel Between the Noble Edifices of the Fourteenth and Fifteenth Centuries, and Similar Buildings of the Present Day; Shewing the Present Decay of Taste* (1836), the first of his polemics in which he asserted that Gothic was the only true Christian and Catholic style of art. The Act of Emancipation of 1829 had finally lifted the penalties imposed on Catholics since the Reformation, and Pugin attracted leading Catholic patrons such as the Earl of Shrewsbury, for whom he designed Alton Towers, and the Catholic Church in Britain and Ireland which embarked upon a programme of new builds in medieval style, such as Ramsgate Abbey, next to Pugin's own home, from which he scanned the sea in search of victims of shipwreck whom he might rescue. He even collaborated with the architect Charles Barry on the new Palace of Westminster to accommodate the British Parliament, designing everything down to the wallpaper and tiles to ensure the complete Gothicization of the seat of democracy. The heightened ritual favoured by the Oxford Movement promoted the refitting of church interiors, replacing liturgical features such as the Rood Screen, which had been stripped out during the early Protestant centuries. Ironically, the Oxford Movement (1833–45), led by John Keble, John Henry (later Cardinal) Newman and W. G. Ward before they converted to Catholicism, was an Anglican High Church group 'against popery and dissent', which promoted a return to seventeenth-century non-puritanical principles emphasizing the essential catholicity of Anglicanism. Initially a leading Goth in the antiquarian High Church Cambridge Camden Society, which also championed the Gothic Revival, Pugin's views on Medieval Catholic exclusivity became so extreme that he was expelled in 1846 following his attacks on

338

Newman and the Oratorians who, since their order was only founded in 1564, favoured the Baroque for Gribble's Brompton Oratory and the classical style for that in Birmingham. His public rejection and crushing workload finally prompted Pugin's mental breakdown in 1851.

Gilbert Scott was also a member of the Cambridge Camden Society, despite his own evangelical background, but he had to leave when he designed a Lutheran church in Hamburg, and in 1856 he capitulated to Lord Palmerson in the 'battle of the styles', agreeing to design the Foreign Office in Whitehall in classical style. In 1864 he reverted to the Gothic idiom, however, for the Albert Memorial, which did not receive public acclaim. Stylistic vocabulary had become the language of contemporary politics. His son and grandson continued the tradition, culminating in Liverpool's Anglican Cathedral, begun in 1903 but only completed, on a greatly reduced scale, in 1980. Like Gaudi's Sagrada Familia in Barcelona, which still awaits completion, the impetus to build to the glory of God was overtaken by the conflagration of human conflict that unleashed the two World Wars.

William Morris and the Arts and Crafts Movement

The passion for 'improving' ancient buildings, often to the detriment of their original structures and fittings, led the Englishman William Morris (1834–96) to found the Society for the Protection of Ancient Buildings in 1877. He was supported in this endeavour by art critic and aesthete John Ruskin (1819-1900), whose passionate and polemical prose helped to form and inform Victorian taste. In his *Seven Lamps of Architecture* (1849), Ruskin championed Italian Gothic and denigrated the Renaissance as 'the Fall'; he admired Veronese and Tintoretto but despised seventeenth-century art; he also had little time for Pugin. His evangelical upbringing and absorption with the Bible did not deter him from, but rather attracted him to the study of Christian art and he was able to travel widely to broaden his familiarity. He also had a deeply rooted love of nature and of the British landscape, and in his five-volume *Modern Painters* (1843–60) he defended Turner's work and explored the relationship between nature, art and the divine. This led him to encourage modern painters, such as the Pre-Raphaelites whom he befriended, to work directly from their observations of nature and to idealize the Middle Ages as the antithesis of urban industrialization (which had, of course, been initiated by the rise of towns in Europe during the thirteenth century). Sadly, the highly charged psychological and emotional intensity of an over-absorption in 'art' and its religious implications, pursued to the detriment of personal relationships, probably contributed, as it had with Pugin, to Ruskin's mental collapse in later life.

William Morris's personal life may also have been a complex one, but his work ethic was rather more down to earth. His espousal of emerging socialist politics and his conviction that good design contributed to an environment that was beneficial to ordinary people led him to champion the value of handmade crafts over mass-produced industrial artefacts, and the foundation of the Arts and Crafts Movement, in which he was joined by male and female artists, including Edward Burne-Jones. The medieval tradition of craftsmanship was a source of inspiration and medieval religious and Arthurian themes pervade their work, including some fine ecclesiastical stained glass commissions in Britain and the US. The movement showed a growing interest in the pure and austere aesthetic of Japanese art too, as reinterpreted by the Japanese Mingei Folk Art Movement of the 1920s and 30s, which would later also inspire Bernard Leach and his St Ives Pottery. Stylistic reference was also made to the Christian primitivism and purity of line of Celtic – or, more correctly, Insular – art, stimulated by recent archaeological discoveries such as the Tara Brooch and the antiquarian rediscovery of the Lindisfarne Gospels and the Book of Kells. Arts and Crafts principles would go on to inform those of the decorative Art Nouveau style that emerged on the Continent, the Glasgow School, and the Omega Workshops established in London in 1913 by Roger Fry and other members of the Bloomsbury Group. Art Nouveau, or *Jugendstil*, although largely decorative, might also take Christian themes as its subject matter on occasion: Gustav Klimt's scintillating mosaic-like confections incorporate the biblical figure *Salome*[5] (1909). But, like the sensual linear illustrations of the same subject by Aubrey Beardsley, this had more to do with the writings of Oscar Wilde than with a religious impetus.

The Pre-Raphaelite Brotherhood

Morris also helped to inspire, and collaborated with, the Pre-Raphaelite Brotherhood. This was founded in 1848 – a year of unrest inaugurated by the socially reforming Chartist Movement – by William Holman Hunt, Dante Gabriel Rossetti and John Everett Millais (1829–96), and it was distinguished by its veneration of poetry, passion and piety, expressed in their journal, *The Germ*. They reacted against conventional academy art and what had become a debased currency of High Renaissance and Baroque imagery, heralded by the work of Raphael, which was copied in banal contemporary church fittings and the illustrations to religious tracts and 'morally improving' writings, carried by missionaries around an expanding British empire. In response they sought to create new biblical iconographies with high moral content, often expressed through allegory and myths such as those surrounding King Arthur and the Grail Quest, or by reference to literary works such as those by Dante, Shakespeare and Keats. Some subjects also focused upon social mores and the moral dilemmas facing the poor, such as Hunt's *Awakening Conscience*[6] (1853) and Maddox Brown's *Work*[7] (1852–65). This was complemented by an honest and detailed observation of nature colourfully expressed in carefully worked detail undertaken as a spiritual exercise. Less prominent Pre-Raphaelites included James Collinson, Frederick George Stephens and the sculptor Thomas Woolner and, in a younger generation, William Dyce.

Popular suspicions that they were setting themselves up to rival the great artists of the Renaissance in stature and those of a Romanist agenda, like the Nazarenes, led to criticism on the heels of the flurry of popularity of the 'new'. In 1850 Millais's *Christ in the House of His Parents*,[8] which depicted Jesus as a boy assisting in Joseph's carpenter's shop, and with red hair – the traditional sign of otherness – to boot, was attacked as blasphemous. But it was defended by Ruskin, who took up the young artist until he developed a relationship with his wife, Effie, whom he later married and with whom Ruskin had been unable to enjoy physical relations because of his obsession with the beauty of art rather than its reality.

Christ in the House of His Parents, John Everett Millais, 1850, England.

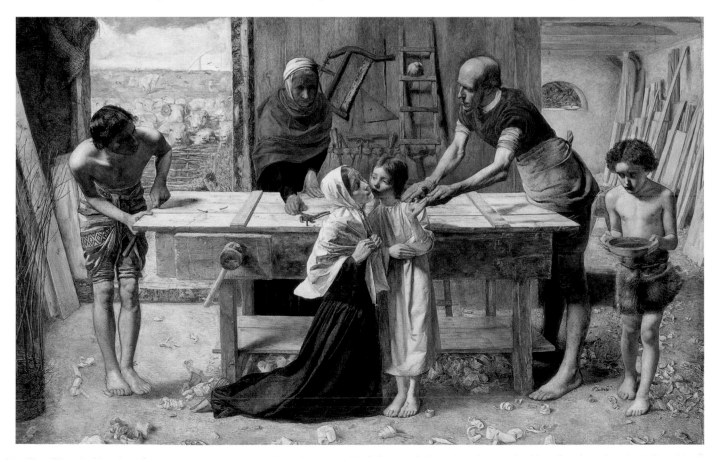

Ruskin's hopes that the brotherhood might 'lay in our England the foundations of a school of Art nobler than the world has seen for three hundred years' evaporated after 1853 as the founder members dispersed: Millais to join the Royal Academy and adapt his art to popular commercial tastes; Rossetti to immerse himself in chivalric and poetic themes, such as the *Blessed Damosel* in which his dead lover, Elizabeth Siddal, looks down from the heavens; and Hunt to journey to Palestine to inject biblical topographic authenticity into his work. There he painted the remarkable *Scapegoat*[9] (1854), the Old Testament sin-offering of a goat tethered in the desolate, scorching wilderness, serving as metaphor for Christ's sacrifice in which he assumed the burden of human sin. Perhaps his best-known work, however, is *The Light of the World*, of which he produced three versions,[10] in which Christ, bearing an Eastern-style lantern, knocks on a door in a nocturnal forest clearing. The door, which represents the human heart, is overgrown with foliage and can only be opened from inside to allow Christ to enter in. Some of his work, like that of his French counterpart, Tissot, is more in the nature of biblical topography. The poetic imagination of the Pre-Raphaelites was echoed in later Victorian art, such as the allegorical paintings and sculptures by George Frederick Watts (1817–1904), a famous example of which is *Hope*[11] (1886). He is commemorated at Compton, Surrey, by a gallery of his work and by an exquisite memorial chapel built and decorated by his wife and the villagers, forming an encyclopedia of revived Celtic, Arts and Crafts and Pre-Raphaelite motifs in terracotta, metalwork, mosaic and painted stucco angels.

Faith, Science and Art

During the second half of the nineteenth century the Dean and Chapter of St Paul's, prompted by complaints from Queen Victoria that Wren's Baroque masterpiece was a chilly mausoleum, started introducing artworks to alleviate its austerity. They began commissioning mosaics which span high Victorian art, the Pre-Raphaelite and Arts and Crafts Movement and Art Nouveau. These were designed by Alfred Stevens (the prophets – the first of which was installed in 1864) and George Frederick Watts (the apostles Matthew and John) and were completed by W. E. F. Britten in 1888–93. Britten's depictions in the Quire of the Benedicite, featuring the birds, beast and fish of creation, exhibit a great interest in the naturalistic depiction of species, in the wake of Darwin's *Origin of Species* and the violent debate it initiated concerning the processes and timescale of creation adopted by God. His flanking images of the creation, the annunciation and related biblical scenes include the first nudes (Adam and Eve) to be permitted in a Victorian church – a scandal in their day.

With some honourable exceptions, such as the work of Arthur Fleischmann, there has generally been a marked absence of imaginative attempts by Christian artists to engage with the reconciliation of faith and science and to treat visually, as well as theologically, the metaphorical ways in which scripture seeks to convey enormous concepts and the scientific mechanisms through which God's plan was implemented. We have yet to see an inspiring modern Christian treatment of the moment of creation celebrated in the cosmic context of the Big Bang, although medieval images of Logos wielding the compasses of a divine scientific geometry within a celestial vortex (as in the Holkham Bible Picture Book, made beside St Paul's in the 1330s) came close to conveying it symbolically – as did the visions of twelfth-century German mystic Hildegard of Bingen, who also expressed such conceptual mysteries through the science of music.

343

Art for a New Age

The Realists, Impressionists and Symbolists

During the nineteenth century, France once more embraced social realism and confronted the spectre of rural and urban poverty through the caricatures and political satires engraved by Honoré Daumier and Jean-François Millet (1814–75), who was himself of peasant stock. His *Angelus*[1] (1859), which shows a couple pausing in their labour in the field to pray along with the bell sounding the angelus in a nearby church, brought him both public acclaim and the criticism of intellectuals such as Baudelaire, who accused him of trivializing the plight of the poor – in which he shared. A friend of Millet's, Corot, although best known for his landscapes and portraits, also painted religious works for provincial French churches.

The popularity of Impressionism, with its liberating technique and plein-air pursuit, absorbed the energies of many artists during the second half of the nineteenth and early twentieth centuries. Scenes from everyday life were still de rigeur, but the plight of the poor gave way to depictions of bohemian life and to the quest to capture form through light and colour. This in itself could represent the pursuit of the sublime and a retreat from the ways of the world, just as Claude Monet (1840–1926) finally retired to Giverny in 1883 to create in plants and in paint a rural utopia. Many of his 250 tranquil studies of water lilies were executed during the horrific First World War.

Symbolism

During the 1880s the Romantic concept of the artist as one of the elect was reasserted by the Symbolists, who saw it as the role of the artist to reveal spiritual truths, combating the utilitarian materialism of bourgeois society. In Paris this led to the formation of the

345

Nabi brotherhood of painters, their name derived from a conflation of the Arabic and Hebrew terms for 'prophet'. The leader of the group, and its foremost seer, was Paul Sérusier, who was painted in 1894 by Georges Lacombe (1868–1916) as *Le Nabi à la barbe rutilante*.[2] His vigorous beard proclaims him a prophet, his hand is outstretched in blessing and his dress recalls the archaizing elitist rituals of the Nabi brotherhood. Other Symbolists also produced self-portraits depicting themselves in prophetic or Christ-like

A prophetic figure by Georges Lacombe, a member of the Nabi Brotherhood, *Le Nabi à la barbe rutilante*, 1894, Paris.

guise, such as the Swiss artist Ferdinand Hodler and the Italian Giovanni Segantini (1858–99), who in 1895 produced a monochrome image of his head, with flowing beard, set against a wilderness landscape. This was intended to resemble the *Vernicula* or Vernicle cloth – the visage of Christ miraculously imprinted upon the cloth with which St Veronica wiped his face during the painful journey along the Via Dolorosa.

Paul Gauguin and Vincent Van Gogh

The Nabi were inspired by Gauguin in their use of Symbolism and a colourful abstracted language to express their inner vision. Despite his somewhat decadent lifestyle and large sexual appetites, Paul Gauguin (1848–1903) was evidently beguiled by the simple, sustaining beliefs of ordinary folk, whether from Brittany or Polynesia.

346

Paul Gauguin depicts himself as Christ in the Agony in the Garden, 1889.

A number of his works, especially those painted during his time at Pont-Aven in Brittany, feature biblical subject matter, such as his *Vision After the Sermon: Jacob Wrestling with the Angel*[3] (1888). Like several of his peers he also identified with the messianic suffering of Christ, writing in 1890 to fellow artist Emile Bernard:

> 'Yes, we are destined (we searching, thinking artists) to perish under the blows of the world.'

In his *Agony in the Garden*,[4] painted in 1889, he even went so far as to depict Christ with his own features and the flaming red hair of his companion, Vincent Van Gogh (1853–90). Hailed as the leader of the Symbolists, his work often reflects a personal quest to discern and convey meaning in life, culminating in his 1897 work *D'où venons-nous? Que sommes-nous? Où allons-nous?* ('Where do we come from? What are we? Where are we going?').[5] The answers either eluded him or proved profoundly unsatisfactory, for having painted it he tried to commit suicide. He wrote to Daniel de Monfried from Tahiti in 1898, 'I have finished a philosophical work on this theme, comparable to the Gospels. I think it is good.' Perhaps he relied just too much upon his own intellectual and spiritual self-sufficiency.

Van Gogh himself was more preoccupied with depicting the sensations and insight he gained from nature and the small details of life among the working classes of the Netherlands and France, perceiving the face of God amongst the contemporary poor. He wrote to his brother, Theo, in 1888:

> 'I can very well do without God both in my life and in my painting, but I cannot, ill as I am, do without something which is greater than I, which is my life – the power to create... And in a picture I want to say something comforting, as music is comforting. I want to paint men and women with that something of the eternal that the halo used to symbolize, and which we seek to convey by the actual radiance and vibration of our colouring.'

Irritated by attempts by Gauguin and Emile Bernard to depict Christ's agony in the Garden of Gethsemane, he wrote to Bernard in 1889:

> '... one can try to give an impression of anguish without aiming straight at the historic Garden of Gethsemane; [that] it is not necessary to portray the characters of the Sermon on the Mount in order to produce a consoling and gentle motif.
>
> Oh! Undoubtedly it is wise and proper to be moved by the Bible, but modern reality has got such a hold on us that, even when we attempt to reconstruct the

ancient days in our thoughts, abstractly, the minor events of our lives tear us away from our meditations, and our own adventures thrust us back into our personal sensations – joy, boredom, suffering, anger, or a smile…'

He was profoundly shocked both by Gauguin's depiction of them jointly as Christ and by his discovery that during times of mental instability and confinement in the St Remy Asylum he believed himself to be God, even painting himself as Christ in his *Pietà after Delacroix*[6] in 1889. He once wrote that 'Only Rembrandt and Delacroix could paint the face of Christ.' In this disturbing canvas Christ's limp, red-haired body is cradled in the lap of a peasant woman virgin against the distinctive swirling paint-strokes of a bleak landscape and a turbulent sky, contiguous with those that form their broken bodies. It was painted after Van Gogh's mental breakdown which ensued upon his time working with Gauguin in Arles, when he inflicted his well-known self-injury, cutting off his own ear as an expression of his inner torture, in which he evidently identified with Christ's sacrifice – and the hope of his resurrection.

Auguste Rodin

For Auguste Rodin (1840–1917) it was in sensuality that both sin and salvation were most tangibly encountered. His sculptured torso of the author Balzac, clutching his large, erect penis, was the embodiment of creativity – of the masculine variety. Feminine attributes were also celebrated by him, but assumed a gentler, more passive form. He wrote:

'A gentle woman is the mighty intermediary between God and us artists.'

This encapsulated centuries of Marian theology – the gentle mother and Virgin as the channel of divine inspiration and salvation. Seemingly erotic forms such as his sculpture *The Kiss* accordingly celebrate not only the human bond between man and woman, but also the creative union of man and God. And yet, the destructive potential of such power was also enshrined in his monumental *Gates of Hell*, designed as the doors of the proposed Musée des Arts Décoratifs[7] and inspired by Ghiberti's *Gates of Paradise* for Florence Baptistry, which are adorned with the writhing forms of the damned from Dante's *Divine Comedy*, including the equally sensual, sensitive and poignant intertwined figures of doomed illicit lovers. As the volatile new century dawned they were not the only ones to be plunged into torment.

LEFT: Vincent Van Gogh depicts himself as Christ in his *Pietà after Delacroix*, 1889.

The Shock of the New

Mechanization, Expressionism, Spiritual Realism and the Origins of Abstraction

The opening of the twentieth century was already permeated with political and social tension, rapidly escalating mechanization and change. In the disturbing anti-Semitic environment of decadent fin-de-siècle Vienna, expressionist artists such as Egon Schiele (1890–1918) and Oscar Kokoschka (1886–1980) created tortured images revealing inner psychological and sexual turmoil. These may appear to have more to do with growing social neurosis, and an obsession with self and psychosis fostered by analysts such as Freud, than with any association with Christian ethos. However, revealingly they include self-portraits that echo a concept, expressed by artists from Delacroix to Van Gogh, that suffering was the fate of the artist and a source of creativity – themes that were inherently associated with the concepts of Christ's passion and the renewal of resurrection. Schiele's disturbing self-portrait, *The Poet* (1911), depicts the broken form of the Man of Sorrows, a white nimbus framing his Christ-like head. Another Viennese artist who identified himself with Christ was the Jewish painter Richard Gerstl (1883–1908). In 1904–05 he depicted himself in the guise of the baptized or risen Christ, his body swathed in a loin-cloth and set against a celestial blue background with a halo-like aura framing his head,[1] recollecting the commonality of the human condition and that Christ too was a Jew.

German Art and the Impact of the First World War

Exposure to the cultures and religious convictions of other peoples also impacted on the art and faith of German furniture designer, painter and graphic artist Emil Nolde

(1867–1956), a member of the Expressionist group Die Brücke, who began painting New Testament scenes with his agitated colourful brushwork in 1909 and who travelled through Russia, China, Japan and the South Seas in 1913–14, absorbing their influences. The Nazis later confiscated his work and prohibited him from exhibiting, forcing him to work in isolation in his farm at Seebull until 1946. His contemporary and fellow countrywoman Kathe Kollwitz (1867–1945) was born into a nonconformist socialist family at Königsberg and trained at the women's art schools in Berlin and Munich as a graphic artist and sculptor, becoming the first woman to be elected to the Prussian Academy of Art. In her life and work she championed the cause of the oppressed, especially the urban poor (her prints featured themes such as *The Weavers' Revolt*,

Richard Gerstl, *Self-portrait Against a Blue Background*, 1904–05, painted by a Jewish artist and intended to recall images of Christ's baptism in order to remind a dangerous new century of their shared humanity.

1895–97) and women, their stoic suffering which she graphically depicted recalling that of the Virgin Mary. Her work was expressive and conservative in style – her engravings, woodcuts and lithographs exhibiting the influence of Dürer, Rembrandt and Daumier – but her subject matter was radical, reflecting her faith, her left-wing politics and her pacifism, which was strengthened by her son's death in action in 1914. She and her husband are the grieving parents depicted in her sculpture at the entrance to the military cemetery at Roggevelt, Belgium.

Another artist whose work was transformed by the horrors of war was Max Beckmann (1884–1950). Initially a leading German Impressionist, he served as a medical orderly in Flanders during the First World War until he was discharged with a nervous breakdown. After this he worked in Frankfurt and was declared degenerate by the Nazis on account of the critical nature of his work (such as *Night*, 1918–19, protesting the murder of Communists Liebknecht and Rosa Luxemburg), which became increasingly expressionist in style. His work also addressed Christian iconographies and he described the aims of his work as 'transcendental objectivity'. In 1937 he moved to Amsterdam, having been forbidden to work in Germany, and in 1947 to the US, where he taught in Washington and New York.

Kandinsky and the Origins of Abstract Art

By contrast, Wassily Kandinsky (1866–1944) began his career painting scenes from folklore in his native Russia and the landscape of Bavaria around Murnau, near Munich. A fairytale-like beguilement with Moscow, the Impressionism of Monet and the tonal nuances of the music of Wagner helped to shape his approach to the arts, and over the next twenty years he became a pioneer of abstract art and an important figure in Modernism. He made a gradual but profound journey from figurative painting into abstraction and an exploration of the sensual and spiritual perception of form, line and colour. Kandinsky's progressive relinquishment of the observed material world brought him closer to what he considered a deeper spiritual reality. The analogy of abstract forms interpreted by contemporary musicians such as Schoenberg assisted him in this, and in his work, as with music, experimental abstraction was balanced with mathematical and geometric logic. As music was made up of sounds, so colours made a painting and had the same power to evoke response. In 1904 he wrote to his lover, Gabriele Münter:

'Should I succeed in this task, I will be showing [a] new, beautiful path for painting susceptible to infinite development. I am on a new track, which some masters, just here and there, suspected and which will be recognized, sooner or later.'

During the prelude to the First World War he was inspired by dream-like landscapes and apocalyptic imagery and became a founder of the Blue Rider (*Der Blaue Reiter*) group of artists, who published an Almanac, or art magazine, of that name. The figure of a blue rider that appeared in several of his works during these years symbolized both the horsemen of the Apocalypse and a belief in the healing power of art and of spiritual elevation, which could transform society and its ills.

The vestigal forms of the riders can still be detected in the foreground of his sketch for *Composition II* [2] (painted in 1910), along with the figures of those about to receive judgement and the landscape they inhabit. By 1913, when Kandinsky achieved his breakthrough into pure abstraction and produced the large canvas of *Composition VII*,[3] his underlying subject, once again the last judgement, was rendered as a pure distillation of sensation, emotion and elemental forces. The vortex of destruction and renewal swirls and bursts in a cacophony of colour, the only identifiable recollection of narrative being the outline of a black boat with oars in the lower left. Form has dissolved, leaving the spirit of the work and the feelings it inspires.

Wassily Kandinsky, *Sketch for Composition II*, 1910. A work of the Blue Rider group (its distinctive motif of the horse and rider, inspired by images of St George, can still be detected in the centre of the work) by the pioneer of abstract art.

354

Wassily Kandinsky, *Composition VII*, 1913. Kandinsky was inspired by his Theosophist beliefs and music by modern composers such as Stravinsky to explore links between the senses and spirituality through abstract art.

Kandinsky's own writings reveal that he wished the perception of his works to be primarily emotional, allowing the viewer to feel and 'hear' the inner sound of the colours and forms through the subconscious, rather than reading them iconographically and being constrained by an intellectual interpretation. His experimentation with colour's optical effects led him to assert that it produced a sympathetic vibration and a psychological response within the viewer. His 'impressions' are works based on observed events or places, encapsulating the impression they left upon him; his 'improvisations' have been characterized as analogous to concertos and his 'compositions' with symphonies. He and Münter had a long-term preoccupation with Theosophism and the occult, which inspired him to seek to achieve a 'second level' of reality perceivable by those with heightened spiritual sensibilities. His desire to convey the auras, thought forms and spiritual essence of entities was an underlying motivation in his quest to replace the representational with ethereal space occupied by manifestations of colour and form, related to Theosophist concepts of space and matter.

The rich, occult mysticism of Kandinsky's art might, in some respects, be seen to have emerged also from the Russian Orthodox tradition, contrasting with what has been described as the 'Protestant' reductionism of Piet Mondrian (1872–1944). The work of this Dutch artist was informed by his Theosophist beliefs and represents a quest to reflect universal harmony. He achieved this through what he termed neo-Plasticism: an uncompromising inter-relationship of linear geometrics and colour, from which all narrative, symbolism and naturalism were excised to leave a purity based on what in earlier centuries had been seen as divine geometry, as in *Composition with Red, Yellow and Blue*[4] (1937–42). His wish to extend such harmony into human environments led to his influence upon modern architecture and design and is expressed in his writings, *Piet Mondrian: Plastic Art and Pure Plastic Art*.[5] The Swiss artist Paul Klee (1879–1940) was also affiliated to the Blue Rider group and shared Mondrian's minimalist Calvinistic tendencies until he was influenced by Picasso, Rousseau and the colour theories of Delaunay, and a visit to Tunisia that injected a passion for colour into his work. In his lecture *On Modern Art* (1924), delivered to the Bauhaus in Weimar, Klee provides an insight into his essentially mystical philosophy of art, in which the artist acts as medium, transforming imagination and experience into an art that presents a valid alternative reality. In the lecture he stated, 'I do not wish to represent the man as he is, but only as he might be.' In his quest to do so he turned to the work of children and the mentally ill for inspiration.

An essay in Protestant reductionism by Dutch artist Piet Mondrian, *Composition with Red, Yellow and Blue*, 1937–42.

The figure of the rider that pervades much of Kandinsky's early work derived initially from that of St George trampling the dragon of evil in the icons of the Russian Orthodox Church; likewise the trumpeting angels and saints whose liquid forms inhabit some of his works containing vestigal figurative elements. Like several of his contemporaries, such as Diaghilev and Dostoevsky, the theme of resurrection was one that fascinated him and which was inextricably linked to their vision of cultural rebirth – the 'Russian renaissance' – in which the Russian Orthodox tradition and rural religious belief were reconciled with Western Modernism and science.

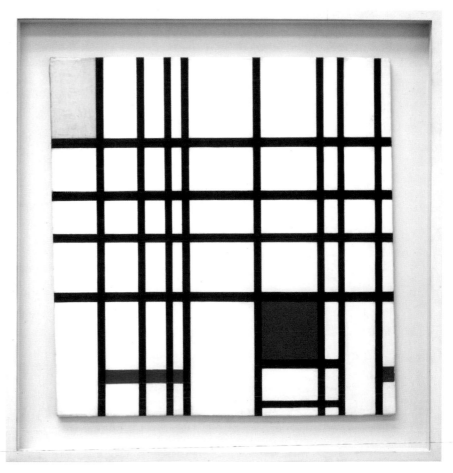

Kandinsky wrote on the subject of belief and art in a manner unusual among modern artists. He devoted a whole book to the topic, *Concerning the Spiritual in Art*, and in his *Cologne Lecture* wrote:

> '*Composition 2* is painted without theme, and perhaps at that time I would have been nervous of taking a theme as my starting point. On the other hand, I calmly chose the Resurrection as the theme for *Composition 5*, and the Deluge for the sixth. One needs a certain daring if one is to take such outworn themes as the starting point for pure painting. It was for me a trial of strength, which in my opinion has turned out for the best.'

With the outbreak of war in 1914 he had to return to Russia, where he contributed to the artistic and cultural policy of the new post-revolutionary republic and the Russian avant-garde, alongside artists such as the Constructivists Kasimir Malevich and El Lissitzky. Eventually, alienated by its hardening ideology and state control, he returned to Germany in 1921 to teach at the Bauhaus, where the linear and geometric increasingly dominated his work, with greater structure containing his more muted colours. His contribution to Modernism and Abstraction has been recognized and celebrated; his contribution to an understanding of the spiritual in art has been less so.

Nature and the Human Condition

An empathy with nature and the animal kingdom was apparent in the work of the Blue Rider group and also characterized that of Henri Rousseau (1844–1910), a Parisian customs officer and autodidact who drew special inspiration from his visits to the Jardin des Plantes and is famed for his stylized scenes of lush verdant jungles and rainforests, which he never visited in person. These are often considered naïve and largely decorative, but some betray a Darwinian concern with the question of origins and a refuge within the primordial from the harsh, over-evolved world of the city and its dark side, celebrated by artists such as Edgar Degas, Walter Sickert and Henri de Toulouse-Lautrec. Apes figure in many of his works, aping, as had their forebears in medieval manuscripts, Adam and Eve, who are tempted by oranges rather than apples; and analogies are drawn between their young and human babies. In *The Dream*,[6] which earned him the reputation as a precursor of Surrealism, Rousseau explored his own sensual and spiritual repression and liberation, the exotic figure of the snake charmer perhaps embodying his own fantasies and desires. Another artist who would take a more pessimistic view of his moral struggles with sexuality and residual guilt, seeing the subjection of self as a path to personal salvation, was the Norwegian Expressionist Edvard Munch (1865–1944), whose *The Scream*[7] (1893) epitomizes the experience of having stared into the abyss.

Rousseau's admirers included Kandinsky, Picasso and the poet Apollinaire. The theme of humankind's place in nature and in the urban jungle was also explored by a group of young German artists – Karl Schmidt-Rottluff, Ernst Ludwig Kirchner, Erich Heckel and Fritz Bleyl – who in 1905 formed *Die Brücke* ('The Bridge') as a link between the art of the past and that of the future. Their work was highly graphic and Late Medieval German woodcuts were among their sources of inspiration. Such concerns, along with the rejection of prevailing Impressionism and Realism, was shared by the French Fauvists ('Wild Beasts'), as they were termed by the critic Vauxcelles on account of their violent application of pure colour, straight from the tube, the significance of which seemed almost mystical. The international but French-based group, which was active c. 1898–1908, included Henri Matisse, Georges Rouault, Maurice de Vlaminck, Andre Derain, Georges Braque, Raoul Dufy and Kees van Dongen. Matisse and Rouault, in particular, would make valuable contributions to the corpus of art in a Christian context.

Each of these groups was influenced by the experimentation with the use of colour and its theoretization conducted by Robert Delaunay (1885–1941) and his Ukrainian wife, Sonia (1885–1979), from around 1906 onwards. Influenced initially by Pointillists such as Georges-Pierre Seurat and the Cubism of Braque and Picasso, they soon enabled colour to triumph over form, giving rise to what Apollinaire termed 'Orphism'. By their brushes even war-torn Paris could take on the radiance of hope and light.

Bathed in the Light: Modern Stained Glass

The metaphysical stimulus of colour and light continued to be explored, just as it had been by medieval commentators such as Suger and the makers of stained glass. Glass once more came into its own as an artistic medium, notably through the stained glass designs of Marc Chagall (1887–1985). Born to Jewish parents in Vitebsk, Russia, Chagall trained in St Petersburg and subsequently worked in Paris, returning to Vitebsk in 1914 on the outbreak of war to found an art school. He illustrated books, including Gogol's *Dead Souls* (1923–25), and designed for the Jewish Theatre in Moscow and, later, for Stravinsky's *Firebird* in the US, to which he had fled in 1941, returning to Paris after the Second World War. Much of his work, which ventured into Cubism and Surrealism but retained its own distinctive colourful fairy-tale quality derived from Russian-Jewish folklore, was intended to counter the rise of Fascism and anti-Semitism. It features iconographic references to both Jewish and Christian art, stressing their joint Abrahamic roots, as in his *White Crucifixion*[8] (1938), and a series entitled *The Bible Message*[9] (1955–56).

Jewish commissions included *The Blessings of Jacob and of Moses* and the *Twelve Tribes of Israel* (1974) for the Hadassah Medical Centre's synagogue, near Jerusalem, and tapestries of the *Creation, Exodus* and the *Entry into Jerusalem* for the Knesset in Jerusalem. The stimulus of Chartres inspired his work in glass: for the church at Plateau d'Assy (1957), for which he also designed majolica (tin-glazed earthenware) tiles depicting Moses parting the Red Sea; and for Metz Cathedral (1958–68) and Reims Cathedral (1974). In England he designed windows for Tudley Church in Kent (1966 and 1978) and a vitreous meditation on *Psalm 150* for Chichester Cathedral (1978).

Other prominent modern artists also designed glass to illumine sacred spaces: Georges Braque (1882–1963) helped to design that for Vence and for Varengeville-sur-Mer; Georges Rouault (1871–1958) made a colourful St Veronica window for Assy (1939–48); while Maria Elena Viera da Silva's stained glass for St Jacques, Reims (1966–76) adopted a more monochrome approach, highlighted with touches of red and yellow, recalling the late medieval silver-stain technique. Other parts of Europe and North America also witnessed a revival in stained glass, and Norman St Clair Carter began a modern tradition of its design in Australia, while the US and Canada had fostered fine traditions of their own since the nineteenth century. Glass tesserae also witnessed a revival in the mosaics designed by Fernand Lèger for the mortuary crypt of Bastogne (1949–50) and the façade of Notre-Dame de Toute Grâce at Assy (1946–49), featuring the head of the Virgin and traditional symbols associated with her, such as the 'mystical rose'.

Creating sacred space:
Le Corbusier, 1951–55, interior
with stained glass, Ronchamp,
the pilgrim chapel of Notre-Dame-
de-Haut.

    Apprenticeship to a stained glass painter was to prove a lasting aesthetic
influence on one of the foremost practising Christian artists of the modern age, the
French Catholic Georges Rouault. From 1891 he studied at the École des Beaux-Arts
in Paris under author-artist Gustave Moreau, whose symbolist-inspired works,
sometimes with religious themes, initially influenced him (as did Rembrandt's
works), until his strength of religious conviction led him to employ his art to
denounce the ills and injustices of the world. From then on the luminous colours and
black outlines of his training in glass were applied to depictions of prisoners, judges,
prostitutes and tragic clowns. In addition to these explorations of the human
condition he also produced sequences of overtly religious subjects – the *Holy Face,
Christ Mocked* and the *Crucifixion*. In 1906 he entered into partnership with the dealer
Vollard to disseminate his work more widely as prints. Age did not prevent him from
assuming a leading role during the Second World War in a group of French Catholic
patriot artists, Les Jeunes Peintres de la Tradition Française; nor did it cloud his
optimism – his post-war works being pervaded with colour and serenity.

    The interplay of light and space also beguiled the Swiss polymath Charles-
Edouard Jeanneret (1887–1965), who adopted the pseudonym Le Corbusier (derived

LEFT: Marc Chagall, *Psalm 150,
stained glass*, 1978, for Chichester
Cathedral, a work for a
Christian context by a Russian-
Jewish artist who explored both
Old and New Testament
iconographies in his art.

Decorating sacred space:
Henri Matisse, 1949–51,
murals and stained glass of
the Rosary Chapel of Vence.

from 'the Raven' on account of his physiognomy) to distinguish his professional life as an architect from that as a writer and artist working in the media of painting, drawing, lithography, book illustration, tapestry and furniture design. He acknowledged the artist's obligations towards society, as expressed by Morris, Ruskin and Nietzsche, contributing to the experiments in social engineering undertaken by many twentieth-century architects. His buildings include two churches: Ronchamp, the pilgrim chapel of Notre-Dame-de-Haut (1951–55); and the Dominican monastery of La Tourette, Évaux-sur-l'Arbresle (1953–63). Ronchamp features the use of areas of stained glass as part of the articulation of its walls, while the underground chapel at La Tourette introduced the light tube to capture the light and feed it down into the space. As a painter Jeanneret co-founded, with Amédée Ozenfant, Purism in which, as in his architecture, he abhorred excess and ornament.

The routes to distilling the essence of the role of art within modern conceptions of sacred space could be many and varied, however. The avowed aim of one of the founding Fauvists and one of the most influential of early twentieth-century artists, Henri Matisse (1869–1954), was to 'bring comfort and express joy' through his art. Colour and an increasing use of abstraction were his vehicles in achieving 'balance, purity and moderation'. The graceful, decorative quality of his work reached a crescendo in his late works, which included designs for the murals and stained glass of the Rosary Chapel of Vence, which were implemented in 1949–51. Another French artist who had studied with Gustave Moreau in Paris, alongside Matisse and Rouault, was Charles Milcendeau (1872–1919), who returned to his native Vendée to work on a number of church commissions, including *Le Flagellation* at Soullans. Its figures were modelled upon local inhabitants and Milcendeau's loving concentration upon this poor local community echoes that of earlier Dutch and Netherlandish art, including that of Van Gogh, and, even more significantly, that of Christ himself. This tradition was perpetuated in the work of Henri Simon and continues in the Vendée to this day.

The course of modern art therefore, although often considered secular, has been frequently underpinned by deeply spiritual motivation expressed through many stylistic languages – a Pentecost of paint and other media. It is also somewhat surprising to note the range of artists who accepted ecclesiastical commissions of traditional iconographic subjects, even if their treatment of them was entirely modern, the *liber vitae* of their names including Annigoni, Bonnard, Buffet, Denis, Fontana, Manzù, Messina, Minguzzi, Miró, Nevelson, Rauschenberg, Romanelli, Saetti, Severini, Shahn, Villon and Wolf. Even the arch Abstract Expressionist Jackson Pollock embarked upon an abortive collaborative project for a Catholic church on Long Island, for which he designed the glass.

Jewish Artists, Christian Themes

Emily D. Bilski

Western art is inconceivable without the lexicon of Christian imagery. For Jewish artists, subjects drawn from the New Testament and especially representations of scenes from the life of Jesus were often powerful themes through which they could express their personal struggles, as well as explore themes of Jewish history and identity. Yet, in part because of the heritage of Christian anti-Semitism, works of art on Christian subjects by Jewish artists have generated controversy. Such discomfort was manifested both in the negative reception of Max Liebermann's early masterpiece, *The Twelve-year-old Jesus in the Temple* [1](1879), by Christian critics and lawmakers and in the debate about the planned inclusion of Christian subjects in a retrospective exhibition of the Jewish artist David Aronson that was held at the New York's Jewish Museum in 1979. Despite these negative responses, Jewish artists' renditions of Christian subjects have an important place in art history from the nineteenth century until today. One of the most popular twentieth-century artists of Christian subjects was Marc Chagall, who is also generally considered to be the Jewish artist par excellence. Moreover, contemporary Israeli art is replete with examples of works that derive visual and emotional power from their references to Christian imagery.

With the onset of political emancipation in western Europe in the early nineteenth century, restrictions on Jewish life were eased, which made it possible for potential Jewish artists to obtain artistic training. Almost from the beginning of their activity as artists, Jews depicted Christian subjects. Initially, they depicted Christian themes because artistic competitions and commissions by Christian patrons required these subjects. However, Jewish artists were also attracted to subjects drawn from the life of Jesus for a variety of personal reasons. Jews were beginning to establish reputations as artists at the same time that western European Jews – as a consequence of acculturation and assimilation – were questioning the nature of Jewish identity. New Testament subjects provided rich contexts for exploring these themes. By thematizing such Christian subjects, Jewish artists were able to engage in a dialogue with the tradition of Western art.

The Russian sculptor Mark Antokolsky (1843–1902), in his life-size sculpture *Ecce Homo* [2] (1873), created what may be the earliest example of the 'Jewish Jesus'. Jesus is modeled with facial features that resemble the artist's and the side locks (*payyot*) and skullcap (*kippah*) of an observant Jewish man. He wears a striped garment suggesting the Jewish prayer shawl. Antokolsky depicted Jesus as a Jewish prophet and reformer whose mission was to preach to the Jews, and whose message of universal love could provide a counterforce to growing anti-Semitism in Russia.

In a letter to Vladimir Stasov he explained: 'I solemnly admit that He was and died a Jew for truth and brotherhood. That is why I want to present him as a purely Jewish type.' Anticipating negative responses from members of both religions, Antokolsky continued: 'Jews will probably say, "How is it that he made Christ?" And Christians will say, "What kind of Christ did he make?" But I do not care for this.'

That controversy would ensue when Jesus was

The Twelve-year-old Jesus in the Temple, 1879, by Max Liebermann. This veristic depiction by a Jewish artist of Christ as a Jewish child amongst the rabbis in a synagogue was met with anti-Semitic attacks in Germany.

depicted as a Jew became evident a few years later when German artist Max Liebermann (1847–1935) exhibited *The Twelve-year-old Jesus in the Temple* in Munich, which elicited anti-Semitic attacks in the press and prompted a debate in the Bavarian parliament. Liebermann's unidealized depiction of Jesus was criticized as 'the ugliest, most impertinent Jewish boy imaginable'. Liebermann presented Jesus in a clearly Jewish context without recourse to the generalized dress of Antiquity. The young Jesus speaks to an audience of rabbis dressed in traditional European Jewish garb, and in a setting modelled on the interior of a Venetian synagogue, the *scuola levantina*. Liebermann was influenced by Naturalism, which inspired artists to situate biblical scenes in contemporary surroundings, often with local peasants and farmers serving as models for biblical characters. Yet while other German artists were presenting New Testament scenes with contemporary realism, a Jewish artist's interpretation of this theme proved to be too much for many Germans to tolerate. In response, Liebermann altered the painting to make Jesus look less scruffy, less unkempt, and less stereotypically Jewish. He generally avoided biblical subjects for the rest of his career. By situating the young Jesus in a Jewish milieu, Liebermann was reminding his audience of the Jewish origins of Jesus, and was also claiming that Jews were inseparable from the mainstream of Western culture.

In contrast to Liebermann's Naturalist approach, Galician born Maurycy Gottlieb (1856–79) created monumental Orientalist paintings of episodes drawn from Jesus' life, with figures garbed in ancient costumes. Gottlieb's approach to history painting was influenced by his contact with the Polish history painter, Jan Matejko, by his exposure to Karl von Piloty, his teacher at the Munich Academy, and through his close study of Rembrandt. Heinrich Graetz's *History of the Jews* influenced Gottlieb's interpretation of Jesus as a devout Jew who sought to impart a positive message to his co-religionists. In *Christ Preaching at Capernaum* (1878-79),[3] which remained unfinished at the time of Gottlieb's premature death, Jesus is presented with a halo, yet dressed as a Jew with an open Torah scroll before him. Jesus speaks to a Jewish congregation in a synagogue, with women sitting separately, as is customary in Orthodox Judaism. Gottlieb included his self-portrait and

depictions of relatives and friends among the listeners, emphasizing Jesus' role as a preacher to his fellow Jews. Gottlieb's depiction of Jesus was at least partially motivated by Polish anti-Semitism and the artist's yearning for a rapprochement between his Polish and Jewish identities. As he wrote to a friend at the time he was working on *Christ Preaching at Capernaum*: 'How deeply I wish to eradicate all the prejudices against my people! How avidly I desire to uproot the hatred enveloping the oppressed and tormented nation and to bring peace between the Poles and the Jews, for the history of both people is a chronicle of grief and anguish.'

Mobilizing the image of Jesus as a stand-in for the struggles of the tortured artist who is plagued by society's indifference or his own emotional anguish is a known trope of modern art, as can be seen in the work of Paul Gauguin or Oskar Kokoschka. Modern Jewish artists also created self-portraits in the image of Jesus in order to express the idea of the artist as both victim and prophet. In *Descent from the Cross*[4] (1910–11), Austrian artist Max Oppenheimer (1885–1954) portrayed himself as Christ, with contemporary members of his circle as the figures gathered around his lifeless body. In 1911, the poster he designed to publicize his one-man show at Thannhauser's 'Moderne Galerie' in Munich caused a scandal with its depiction of the artist as Christ with the stigmata; the police forbade hanging the poster in public.

This occasionally solipsistic use of the suffering Christ as a representation of the misunderstood artist was transformed by Marc Chagall in a series of paintings of the crucifixion, in which he developed the figure of the crucified Jesus as a symbol of Jewish suffering. In the first of these works, *The White Crucifixion*[5] (1938), the crucifixion is set amid scenes of fleeing Jews, pogroms, ransacked homes, and a synagogue in flames. In the centre of the composition, the crucified Christ wears a loincloth that resembles a *tallit*, the striped and fringed Jewish prayer shawl. Amid the scenes of panic and destructive violence, the crucifixion and the candelabra beneath it – with a ring of light emanating from the candles that echoes Christ's

Marc Chagall, *The White Crucifixion*, 1938, in which Christ's Judaic background and his empathetic humanity and sacrifice are juxtaposed with scenes of the persecution of the Jews.

halo – are anchors of quiet stability. Scholars have identified the candelabra as the menorah – the lamp that burned in the ancient Temple in Jerusalem, which became one of the symbols of Judaism – although the traditional menorah has seven branches, and in the painting's present state, there are only six candles (a later reference to the six million victims of the Holocaust?). When the painting was first published in 1939, it had several specific references to the Nazi persecution of Jews, which Chagall later painted out, thereby changing what had been an immediate response to contemporary events into a more generalized meditation on Jewish suffering and on human suffering generally.

Contemporary Jewish artists continue to employ Christian imagery. It is striking how prevalent this phenomenon is among contemporary Israeli artists. Israeli works referring to episodes from the life of Jesus implicitly link life in contemporary Israel to life in the same geographical location in Jesus' time. Sometimes this relationship is explicit. In the performance work *Via Dolorosa* (1973), Motti Mizrachi (born 1946) walked in Jesus' footsteps in Jerusalem's Old City, supported on crutches and carrying his own Christ-like photographic portrait on his back. In one of the still photographs documenting this event, we see the artist, whose face is obscured by the oversize portrait, standing beneath a sculptural relief above a doorway that depicts Christ carrying the cross; two local Arab children watching the performance with curiosity are also captured in the frame. This juxtaposition of elements raises questions about the artist's place in Israeli society while echoing the complex and volatile mix of politics, religion and national identities that are at the root of tensions in the region. *Via Dolorosa* continues the modernist practice whereby an artist identifies his personal travails with those of Jesus; as Mizrachi explained: 'This is a story about a man in the Land of Israel who paid for people's reaction to what he said. Jesus' sufferings are mine.'

Christian imagery emphasizes the political message of the photograph *Aisha el-kord, Khan Younis Refugee Camp* (1988), by Micha Kirshner (born 1947). A work from Kirshner's intifada series, it depicts a Palestinian mother with her baby as a Madonna and child. Other artists refer to the Pietà motif in their works as a means of expressing loss and mourning. In an untitled wax and resin

sculpture (2001) by Gil Shachar (born 1965), two arms projecting from a wall support a body draped in a white sheet from which a limp arm hangs. The khaki sleeves visible on the supporting arms are the only topical references in a work that is otherwise generalized and mysterious.

The video work *El Maleh Rachamim* (*God Abounding in Mercy*; 2004) by Erez Israeli (born 1974) shows a woman struggling to hold upright the lifeless body of a young man. The formal similarity to Michelangelo's *Pietà* leads us to assume that she is the man's mother. *El Maleh Rachamim*, the Jewish memorial prayer asking God to grant 'perfect rest' to the soul of the deceased, is played at a very slow pace on the soundtrack. The allusion to Michelangelo's *Pietà* underscores the pathos of the scene. Here there is no hope of resurrection and redemption; only the finality of death and a mother's desperation to hold onto her son, which is reinforced through the repetition of the scene in a continuous video loop.

Adi Nes (born 1966) explores issues of contemporary Israeli society, such as the military and gender, via his series of painstakingly composed photographs. The blatant artificiality of his staging, combined with the many references to iconic images from the history of art, has resulted in works that seem timeless. One of the works from the military series depicts a soldier with stigmata-like wounds, lying in the arms of a comrade, a composition based on the *Pietà*. On closer inspection, the soldier in the Mary role is holding a make-up brush, as if he is 'touching up' the corpse, and the make-up palette rests on the dead soldier's waist. The reference to the *Pietà* is crucial to the image's irony and eroticism. Another one of Nes's photographs depicts a group of soldiers sitting at a mess table, in a recreation of Leonardo's *Last Supper*. Thirteen seated figures of soldiers are arranged in groupings that follow Leonardo's painting, with an additional figure standing at the left edge of the frame, as if about to leave. We are reminded that the Last Supper was a Seder service, part of the celebration of the Jewish festival of Passover. Since a Seder is a family celebration, it generally includes the participation of women and children; the Last Supper, with only male apostles present, was thus an anomaly from a Jewish perspective. Nes has created an all male Last Supper that makes sense in a contemporary Jewish context, a Last Supper of soldiers in the Israeli

366

army. The staged photo evokes the vulnerability of soldiers, their fear that any such meal might indeed be the last one.

Christian subjects depicted by Jewish artists can reveal some of the ways Jews understood their relations to mainstream Western culture, and how these Jewish artists situated themselves within the tradition of Western art. Perhaps these works of art also reveal additional dimensions of the Christian visual patrimony as they enrich this heritage as well.

The Impact of Modernity

Destruction, Creation, Abstraction

The Iberian taste for the supernatural, seen in the Mozarabic manuscripts of the Apocalypse and the ectoplasmic figures of El Greco's paintings, may have contributed to the extraordinary artistic vision of Pablo Picasso (1881–1975). He eschewed pre-existing conventions for depicting the perceived appearance of things in favour of conveying an inner reality, apprehended through the subjective response of artist and audience. His first large canvas was *First Communion*[1] (1896), and his images of maternity – some painted in his early, melancholic 'Blue Period' which followed the suicide of his friend and fellow-artist Casagemas, and others in the more classical style he adopted around the time of the birth of his son Paolo in 1921 – are steeped in traditions for depicting the Virgin and Child.

Conflict and Compassion

Picasso ranged widely in his sources of inspiration, from ancient Greek vases and African masks, through the Old Masters such as Vélasquez and Rembrandt, to Delacroix and some of his contemporaries, such as Braque with whom he developed Cubism. These were all brought into service when he summoned up every impulse he possessed to express his horror and outrage at the German bombing of the Basque town of Guernica in 1937 – a victim of Fascism during the Spanish Civil War, in which Picasso took the Republican part. His massive monochrome painting *Guernica*[2] (1937) uses his favoured semi-abstracted motifs of the weeping woman, the sacrificial bull and the dying horse to express empathy, atrocity, and the disgust and disgrace of the offence against God, nature and humanity that is war. On the outstretched hand of the fallen warrior can be seen the stigmata, recalling Christ's Passion. This detail also featured in an earlier outcry in paint against the murder of

369

Pablo Picasso, *Mother and Child*, 1921. Painted around the time of the birth of the artist's son, Paolo, this lyrical classical piece was inspired by images of the Virgin and Child. Chicago, Art Institute.

those defending the rights of ordinary people – Goya's *The 3rd of May, 1808*[3] (1814), in which a leader of the citizens of Madrid, facing the occupying Napoleonic firing squad, raises his arms in emulation of the crucified Christ and is illuminated by the lamplight that facilitates the dirty work of his executioners, thereby turning him into a premonition of the risen Christ and of the promise of new uprisings. In 1944 Picasso joined the Communist Party and attended Peace Congresses annually from 1948–51, and he was twice awarded the Lenin Peace Prize. His lithograph *The Dove* (1949), an iconography traditionally associated with the Holy Spirit, has become the international symbol of peace.

Scenes of destruction, representing the epic human struggle, also characterize much of the work of the Mexican painter David Alfaro Siqueiros (1896–1974) who, along with the other great Mexican Muralists Diego Rivera (1886–1957) and José

THE IMPACT OF MODERNITY

Clemente Orozco (1883-1949), explored the relationship between art, revolution and human rights in works such as Rivera's *Echo of a Scream*[4] (1937). Although achieved largely through depictions of scenes from Mexican history and of the labour of contemporary workers, it contributed to the visualization of emerging South American liberation theology, which seeks to free them from violence and oppression and works for social justice. Their work was also promoted as a model of community art by President Franklin D. Roosevelt and influenced a number of African Americans as well as the Abstract Expressionists. Some South American artists, however, perceive Christian religiosity as part of the problem rather than the solution, such as José Clemente Juárez and the 'la Riforma' movement, who adopt a stance of artistic anti-clericalism.

Abstraction and Freedom of Expression

The suppression of avant-garde art in Nazi Germany and Stalinist Russia brought many artists to Paris, which became a magnet for those interested in abstract art (from the Latin *abstrahere*, to 'draw out' the essence of something) during the 1930s. Many of them, including Kandinsky, Mondrian, Jean Arp and Naum Gabo became affiliated to a movement founded by Jean Hélion, August Herbin and Georges Vantongerloo known as Abstraction-Création, which was non-representational and non-figural and welcomed practitioners of all forms of abstraction. Members not resident in Paris included Barbara Hepworth (1903–75) and her husband Ben Nicholson (1894–1982), based at St Ives amid the rugged beauty of west Cornwall. Nicholson, who also pioneered Constructivism with Gabo and Mondrian, wrote that 'realism must be abandoned in the search for reality'. Their art and that of their associates in the St Ives School, including another of Nicholson's wives, Winifred, focused on abstraction from the surrounding awesome art of nature in order to capture its physical and metaphysical impact on humankind.

During the 1940s and 1950s a group of artists working in New York developed a form of art known as Abstract Expressionism (they also became known as the 'Action Painters'). Among them were: Arshile Gorky; Willem de Koonig, whose altarpiece for St Peter's Lutheran Church in New York City was later removed by vote of the congregation; William Congdon, who abandoned the American arts scene to live and paint in a Catholic community in Italy; Robert Motherwell; and Jackson Pollock, who sought to liberate the subconscious psyche from the constraints of rationalism through the use of automatic techniques that allowed it free expression, as in Pollock's *Cathedral*[5] (1947). Motherwell wrote: '…whatever the source of this sense of being unwedded to the universe, I think that one's art is just one's effort to wed oneself to the universe, to unify oneself through union.' Transcendent beliefs, derived from diverse traditions including Zen Buddhism and Christianity, played a part in the movement, especially in the work of Barnett Newman (1905-70) and Mark Rothko, and of Pollock, who was influenced by the teachings of Theosophist Jiddu Krishnamurti. Convinced that abstract art could convey profound metaphysical concepts, Newman, a professed anarchist, painted a series of massive canvases entitled *14 + 1 Stations of the Cross*[6] (1966) in which planes of black paint on white are used to convey the physical and psychological enormity of sacrifice, and of purity and innocence sullied by violence. The earlier works of Russian-born American Mark Rothko (Marcus Rothkovich, 1903-70) include the Abstract-Surrealist *Baptismal Scene*[7] (1945), although he is better known for his 'colour field' paintings, perhaps influenced by his work as a theatrical scene painter, which feature superimposed rectangles of stained colour (especially red, black and maroon) that have the power to convey great calm or menace. With Motherwell, Newman, William Baziotes and Clyfford Still he founded an art school dedicated to the quest for simplicity – Subjects of the Artist. He objected, on occasion, to the ethics of the boardroom for which some of his works were commissioned, refusing to install them in such a potentially immoral setting, and considered his masterworks to be the murals for the de Mesnil Family Chapel in Houston, now known as the Rothko Chapel (1967–69), in which he explored clarity of content and the creation of contemplative sacred space.

The legacy of abstraction has been a long one, and its use to convey the very essence of experience and sensation, rather than its depiction, continues to render it a fascinating vehicle for embodying the spiritual, the mystical and the unknowable. For it takes us beyond the confines of human intellect into a realm of the eternal and infinite, one that we apprehend through knowledge and transcend through intuition. Many abstract works can evoke such a reaction in the viewer, which they can interpret in a Christian context if they are so inclined. Although the trend in modern abstraction, under the influence of the American Abstract Expressionists, has been to avoid the interpretation of works by bestowing on them titles that convey artistic intent, some artists chose to imbue their creations with meaningful titles or to comment upon their motivation.

One such was Tony O'Malley (1913–2003), who formed part of the St Ives School in Cornwall from the 1960s to 1990s, before returning to his native Ireland to paint. One of his best-known series of works comprises a sequence of meditations on the crucifixion. Perhaps influenced by the cultural Catholicism of his homeland, from 1961 until 1999 he spent the time around each Good Friday producing a penitential work that addressed Christ's Passion. One of the most powerful is *Good Friday 1968*, a stark collage of charred splinters of wood, their sharp tips reddened as if by blood, set

against a cold slate ground.[8] During the 1990s, following formative visit to the Bahamas during the 1970s and 1980s, the mood lifted, as if in anticipation of a joyful resurrection, as the elderly artist – always so aware that every day of life and work counted – expanded his exploration of human suffering to embrace the celebratory nature of religious festival, introducing more colour and the resonance of gesture into pieces such as *Good Friday Painting 1999*. Others of his works again allude to an awareness of a cultural Christian heritage, his *Calvary 2* (1983) being inspired by and visually alluding to funerary monuments erected by the O'Tunney family in St Mary's Church, Callan. His *Shadowy Carvings of an Ancient Execution* (1992) is likewise imbued with the character of eroded petroglyphs (rock carvings) and half-forgotten truths, its figures and the instruments of the Passion fading into a pastel haze. O'Malley once remarked, 'I've always regarded painting as a sacramental thing. It's a great mystery, you know. You work on it day after day and then suddenly something happens, a revelation.'

Another innovative force in post-war painting in Britain is John Hoyland (born 1934), whose monumental canvases bear the overt stamp of the influence of American Abstract Expressionism but which challenge the modernist insistence on the two-dimensional reality of the surface in favour of a more traditional exploration of illusory space and inventive allusion. His imagination speaks through the works themselves, which are usually labelled only with a day/month/year formula. An intriguing exception is *Quas 23.1.86* (1986). Quas was a mythological fallen angel whose resonance is conflated by Hoyland with the quasar of astrophysics – an astronomical source of electro-magnetic energy. Cerebral knowledge gives way to an imagined evocation of a universe, or multiverse, saturated by creative intelligence and the conflict of good and evil in our post-modernist world, in which the language of quantum physics draws ever closer to that of theology and an artificial rift between faith and science, perceived by some for over a century, narrows. In this large canvas the golden splendour of the golden angel who, like Icarus, has flown too close to the sun, goes into meltdown against a black infinity, along with a blood-red molten sun. And yet, the forces of chaos are never allowed to triumph in Hoyland's painted cosmos, and to the upper right of this work is an optimistic burst of colour – purple and green – as a supernova is born, like the star that announced God becoming part of his own creation.

A fascination with the interface between science and faith can also be detected in the later works of Arthur Fleischmann (1896–1990), born in Bratislava to Jewish parents, such as *Homage to the Big Bang* and *Homage to the Discovery of DNA*. Fleischmann is better known, however, for his bronze sculptures from the lives of four popes, commencing with Pope Pius XII in 1939 and culminating with that of John Paul II in 1979 when the artist was 83.

Light could also serve as a vehicle for abstraction. The American Dan Flavin (1933–96) explored an abstract minimalism (or what he preferred to call 'maximalism') through the medium of fluorescent tubes of light in which optical effects are tested and less is more. Flavin wrote in his autobiography of the repressive effects of a strict Catholic education on his early creative development. He nevertheless went on to enter a seminary, whence he fled to pursue a secular life devoted to art. The industrial, commercial medium of fluorescent tube lighting was the chosen medium by which Flavin rejected the traditional conventions of art and religiosity in favour of building upon the more recent foundations laid by Russian avant-garde artists. This, he felt, offered scope for a 'concrete humanity' and a blank canvas of light against which personal experience could be exercised.

Some of his early works were inspired by the exhibition in New York of Orthodox icons, but they represent the substitution for their transcendent mysticism

Dan Flavin, *The Nominal Three (To William of Ockham)*, 1963. An exploration in neon by self-professed atheist Flavin of the nature of the Trinity through the teachings of a medieval English theologian who argued that entities should not be multiplied unnecessarily. New York, Guggenheim Museum.

of the modern electric icon, so redolent of its age. He disliked the romantic mysticism of Kandinsky's approach to abstraction, but admired that of Mondrian, which he viewed as rational – overlooking that artist's own preoccupation with Theosophy and Spiritualism. Flavin's theological training nevertheless informs his work, even as he reacts against it. In his *The Nominal Three* (To William of Ockham) of 1963 – which consists of one, two and three vertical tubes of bright white light – he paid tribute to the fourteenth-century English writer William of Ockham, who reacted against over-complex scholasticism and theology by asserting that reality is individual and universals are merely abstract signs, and also that entities should not be multiplied unnecessarily. Depending on your point of view, the work might be interpreted as an assertion of the visible and indivisible nature of the Trinity, in which three elements form one entity; or as the concept of the 'Three in One' as an unnecessary multiplication of the divine. However one does, or does not, chose to comprehend this piece, the ambience it creates is one of spiritual purity and intense meditative quiet, causing some viewers to whisper 'it's like entering a church'. Whatever Flavin's intentions, or absence of them, it has the power to create sacred space. However much Flavin might protest that his works were devoid of interpretative meaning and that they did not express any underlying spirituality, it is fascinating to note that one of his major commissions, commenced in 1996 on the eve of his death, was a light installation for the church of San Maria in Chiesa Rossa, Milan – an austere 1930s basilican structure by Giovanni Muzio which Flavin illuminated from within by inserting neon strips along key internal architectural elements and junctures to form planes of softly diffused colour – turquoise, rose pink and gold – which vary in intensity along with the penetration of natural light. An uncompromising, unforgiving, sterile space has become a baptism of light and an immersion into the spiritual dimension. This might well be seen as a rapprochement with religion, but Flavin always rejected attempts to imbue his work with spiritual meaning, maintaining that it was neutral in this regard and that the same installation might be conducive to religious experience in a religious context or to a secular one in a secular space.

Critical Analysis and Experiencing Modern Art

For the artist's intent alone is not what determines the nature of such work, but the opportunities for its reception in light of the viewer's personal experience. Such an engagement with art does not come easily to most people, however, and critics and art historians such as Herbert Read, Michael Fried (who espoused a metaphysical, intuitive approach to modernism), Clement Greenberg (who assumed a markedly secularist anti-religious approach), T. J. Clark and Irving Sandler have been of great significance in helping to educate the public in the reading of modern art and in liberating their own responses. The role of such commentators in mediating modern art has been a formative one and might be considered to have been a more critical factor in any mutual alienation of art and faith than that of the artists themselves.

Reacting to the intangibility of Fried's phrases such as 'Presentness is grace' and 'a distinct *realm* of the pictorial', Clark wrote:

'I do not mean to insinuate, finally, that a religious point of view is indefensible in criticism, how could I, with Eliot as a reminder? It may even be that a religious perspective is the only possible one from which a cogent defence of modernism in its recent guise can be mounted. But the view is not defended here, it seems to me, just noised abroad in an odd manner; and that is its usual status in such writing. If on the contrary a defence were offered, arguments about modernism, other than the name-calling kind, would be made much easier.'[9]

Perhaps the unwillingness of many critics and art historians of more recent art to force the hand of grey, politically correct secularism has likewise played a significant part in discouraging artists to engage with issues of faith.

The 'Modern Man' discourse, as articulated in Arthur Schlesinger's *The Vital Center* (1949), presented the freedoms of the West as entailing alienation and insecurity. The liberal intelligentsia turned to psychoanalysis to fill the void and to explain the irrational extremes of human behaviour with its personal and political manifestations. Pollock's psychic explosions of paint were compared to the atomic forces unleashed on Hiroshima, and nuclear technology and psychoanalysis were elevated as harnessing forces. Clement Greenberg, whose writings did so much to popularize Pollock's work, presented the Abstract Expressionists as moving away from the private consumption of the 'cabinet picture' to the social location and public consumption – although ironically many of their works were purchased for the private enjoyment or investment of wealthy capitalists, whilst those that made it into public locations or art galleries regained something of the accessibility of earlier ecclesiastical and civic art. The anarchic tendencies of such works were often balanced with a metaphysical enquiry akin to that of contemporaneous French art and the existential emphasis that Sartre and Ponty placed upon personal liberty and moral probity. Barnett Newman, who like Rothko was of Jewish background, wrote one of the most cogent rationales of modern art in *The Sublime is Now* in 1948:

'The failure of European art to achieve the sublime is due to [this] blind desire to exist inside the reality of sensation (the object world, whether distorted or pure) and to build an art within the framework of pure plasticity (the Greek ideal of beauty, whether that plasticity be a romantic active surface, or a classic stable one). In other words, modern art, caught without a sublime content, was incapable of creating a new sublime image, and unable to move away from the Renaissance imagery of figures and objects except by distortion or by denying it completely for an empty world of geometric formalisms – a pure rhetoric of abstract mathematical relationships – became enmeshed in a struggle over the nature of beauty; whether beauty was in nature or could be found without nature.

'I believe that here in America, some of us, free from the weight of European culture, are finding the answer, by completely denying that art has any concern with the problem of beauty and where to find it. The question that now arises is how, if we are living in a time without a legend or mythos that can be called sublime, if we refuse to admit any exaltation in pure relations, if we refuse to live in the abstract, how can we be creating a sublime art?

'We are reasserting man's natural desire for the exalted, for a concern with our relationship to the absolute emotions. We do not need the obsolete props of an outmoded and antiquated legend. We are creating images whose reality is self-evident and which are devoid of the props and crutches that evoke associations with outmoded images, both sublime and beautiful. We are freeing ourselves of the impediments of memory, association, nostalgia, legend, myth, or what have you, that have been the devices of western European painting. Instead of making cathedrals out of Christ, man or "life", we are making them out of ourselves, out of our own feelings. The image we produce is the self-evident one of revelation, real and concrete, that can be understood by anyone who will look at it without the nostalgic glasses of history.'

Perhaps influenced in part by the aniconic proscriptions placed by Judaism on the exploration of eternal truths by means of the human figure, Newman and Rothko sought spiritual gravity through an abstraction of coloured or monochrome planes and clouds of paint that perform the emotional functions of figures. For other Abstract Expressionists, such as Willem de Koonig and Arshile Gorky, the human form remained central to their work.

The liberation of intuitive art has been consciously pursued in the West since Odilon Redon explored the subconscious state of dream time in what is now termed 'suggestive art'. In 1948 Jean Dubuffet and André Breton founded La Compagnie de l'Art Brut which sought to explore and celebrate 'works executed by people free from artistic culture, for whom mimesis plays little or no part, so that their creators draw up everything from their own depths and not from the stereotypes of classical art or of modish art. We have here a "chemically pure" artistic operation'.[10] Such 'raw art', as Dubuffet termed it, produced by children, psychiatric patients and prisoners (such as schizophrenic prisoner Adolph Wölfli during the early twentieth century) is now known as Outsider Art, a genre epitomized in the US by the work of practising Protestant Howard Finster and which finds expression in communities as diverse as the southern states and cities such as Los Angeles and New York.

The Impact of the Second World War

Surrealism, Symbolism and the Resurgence of Figural Art

Abstraction was one form of artistic response to the curse of interesting times and the challenge of the new, but it was by no means the only one. Around the time of the outbreak of the First World War in 1914, an Italian artist, Giorgio de Chirico (1888–1978), was establishing a school of Metaphysical Painting (*la Pittura Metafisica*) inspired by a period working in Paris. Unrelated objects – including ancient marble statues and faceless mannequins – come together in a dreamlike space and pictures dwell within pictures, as in *Metaphysical Interior with Large Factory (1916–17)*.[1] The Futurists Carlo Carrà and Giorgio Morandi were among those who joined him and whose works influenced the Surrealists. Carrà wrote, in 1919: 'The painter-poet feels that his true immutable essence comes from that invisible realm that offers him a vision of eternal reality.'

The Rise of Surrealism

The obscenity of the First World War, perpetrated and condoned by 'rational' bourgeois societies, provoked both the optimistic response of the Futurists and the anarchic nihilism of the Dada movement. These also helped to stimulate the rise of Surrealism, as did individualist artists such as the Frenchman Odilon Redon, whose dreamlike lithographs, pastels and oils included both classical mythological and Christian subjects, such as *L'Apocalypse de St Jean* (1899). Surrealism (a term first coined by Apollinaire) was founded in 1924 by a group of Parisian intellectuals surrounding the poet André Breton, who had been involved with Dada, perpetuating its challenge to conventions. They sought a super-reality by conflating realism and logic with the unconscious and the dream state, as explored by Freudian psychoanalysis and automatism, exiling thought, control and any moral or aesthetic considerations.

The release of subconscious impulses could also include any spiritual imperative, however, as was soon demonstrated by the work of the Chilean painter Roberto Matta, whose apocalyptic vision was the heir of Tondal and Bosch, and one of the leading Surrealists, the Catalan Salvador Dalí (1904–89). In addition to works devoted to what he termed 'paranoia criticism', in which his neuroses found expression in a disjointed series of objects capable of multiple meanings, such as his dripping clocks and masks on props, he also painted subjects reflecting the long tradition of Spanish Catholicism and mysticism. His reworkings of traditional Christian iconographies include the *Corpus Hypercubus Crucifixion* (1954), in which the pristine body of Christ hovers above the surface of a cubic cross, as if held in suspended animation by a field of energy, and is contemplated by the serene figure of either the Virgin or St John, modelled upon Dalí's estranged wife. Dalí described his *Sacrament of the Last Supper* (1955) as 'arithmetic and philosophical cosmogony based on the paranoic sublimity of the number twelve… the pentagon contains microcosmic man: Christ.' Dalí is obviously out to impress, with his psychoanalytical jargon and his

Christ of St John of the Cross, 1951, a highly popular image by leading Spanish surrealist Salvidor Dali. The Burrell Collection, Glasgow Museums.

technical mastery of figurative conventions and the depiction of space, which he challenges through his manipulation of perspective and geometry. Sometimes he lets the mask with its waxed moustaches slip, however, to reveal an underlying legacy of centuries of Catholic faith. His *Christ of St John of the Cross* (1951) was inspired by a drawing by the Carmelite friar St John of the Cross (1542–91), recording his vision in which he looked down on the crucifixion. In it the viewer takes the perspective of God the Father and the Holy Spirit, and looks down on a monumental crucified figure of God the Son, in Baroque fashion, to the world below and the boat in which he charged his disciples to be 'fishers of men', modelled on the harbour of the place of Dalí's birth, Port Lligat. Mass-produced in poster form during the 1970s and 1980s, this became a modern icon, although art critics reviled it for what they saw as a retrograde step in the development of art, back into the figurative religious themes of the past – a notorious stunt of a flamboyant artist who recognized that a most effective form of rebellion could be the reassertion of the conventional.

As a supporter of Franco's fascist regime, Dalí's politics were notoriously right wing and reactionary, despite the self-proclaimed radicalism of his art. Meanwhile, in Britain the traumas of war stimulated both a reaction against and a revival of religious sentiment, and of personal artistic exploration and public and ecclesiastical commissioning of art with overt Christian themes as part of the fight against fascism. Dada and Surrealism being somewhat overstated for contemporary British taste, it sought recourse to a revival of representational figural art and the language of symbolism.

Jacob Epstein, *St Michael and Satan*, 1958, for Coventry Cathedral. The shared nature of the Archangel Michael and Satan is emphasized in this humane work which formed part of the new cathedral erected beside its bombed predecessor as a post-war symbol of hope and reconciliation.

380

Sculpture and Figural Art

Born in New York to Russian-Jewish parents, the sculptor and painter Jacob Epstein (1880–1959) studied in Paris and settled in London, where he helped to found the London Group in 1913. His expressionistic work, with its uncompromising nudity – his statue of Oscar Wilde that graced his tomb in Père Lachaise Cemetery later had a fig leaf placed over its genitalia for a while – often provoked controversy. His *Genesis* (1930), in the form of an enormous and exaggeratedly pregnant woman, was even displayed in a Blackpool sideshow. Epstein's church commissions included a powerful effigy of St Michael defeating Satan on the exterior of the new Coventry Cathedral (1958). This is remarkable in the way in which it departs from traditional iconographic formula and portrays the devil not as a dragon, serpent or demon, but as a vulnerable human form – a fallen angel who is both the antithesis and kin of the archangel. This ran counter to the convention established by artists such as Ninian Comper, in the wake of the First World War, of depicting St Michael in the guise of a soldier, defeating a two-dimensional caricature of evil.

Another New York sculptor of Jewish background, George Segal (1924–2000), originally a chicken farmer who painted nudes as a hobby, began sculpting his characteristic life-size painted plaster figures in 1958. Arranged with objects in tableaux they nonetheless convey a spiritual isolation when dealing with subjects such as *The Restaurant Window* (1967),[2] *Holocaust* (1982)[3] or, latterly, biblical subjects such as Abraham and Isaac. His work is sometimes considered representative of 'Pop' and 'Environment' art. American Jewish illustrator Leonard Baskin (1922–2000) likewise favoured the human figure, sculpted in wood or bronze, as a vehicle for conveying an isolated dignity of being.

A prominent British figural sculptor to address Christian themes was Eric Gill (1882–1940), also famed for his work as an epigrapher, engraver and designer of typefaces. Despite his voracious and indiscriminate sexual appetites, Gill converted to Catholicism in 1913 and became a Dominican Tertiary, although his beliefs were highly personal and incorporated elements of Indian mysticism and a faith in the creative energy of sex. He founded a communal artistic brotherhood at Ditchling, Sussex (later moving to an old monastery at Capel-y-ffin in south Wales), devoted to reviving a religious approach to art and craftsmanship, and with an emphasis upon artistic integrity and truth to materials that was indebted to Morris. Some of his finest graphic work, in the form of woodblocks, and lettering, were made in association with the Cockerell Press. His robust muscular sculptures, with their simplified linearity, reveal him wrestling with stone, the flesh and the ills of the age in commissions such as: the *Stations of the Cross* (1914–18) for the Catholic Westminster Cathedral, when humanity was undergoing its own Passion, having forgotten that of Christ; panels for the new museum in Jerusalem (1934–37); and the *Re-creation of Adam* (1935–38) for the League of Nations, which was trying to reconstruct society just as it was about to be plunged back into the cataclysm of war. A member of his artistic commune, London-born Welshman David Jones (1895–1974), was also profoundly affected by his experience of the First World War, which he wrote of in his *In Parenthesis*, converting to Catholicism in 1921 and becoming a gifted illustrator, engraver, painter and poet. W. H. Auden proclaimed Jones's *The Anathemata*, inspired by his views on the British Mandate in Palestine, one of the masterworks of Modernism. The subjects of his illustrations for St Dominic's Press and the Golden Cockerel Press included biblical themes such as David and Goliath, the Book of Jonah, and the Chester Play of the Deluge, while his drawings and paintings focused upon nature and wildlife.

Another of Gill's contemporaries, Stanley Spencer (1891-1959), devoted much of his career as a painter to creating a series of biblical scenes transposed into the daily life of his home village of Cookham, Berkshire, executed in a tragic-comical exaggerated figural style. These include *Christ Carrying the Cross* (1920)[4] and *Resurrection* (1923–27),[5] in which the villagers arise from their posthumous slumbers in Cookham Churchyard. His personal encounters with death while serving with the Medical Corps in Macedonia during the First World War surface in his murals for a war memorial chapel at Burghclere, Hampshire, which incorporates the altarpiece *Resurrection of the Soldiers* (1928–29). Another treatment of the theme, *Resurrection: Port Glasgow* (1945–50) focuses on the war effort in Port Glasgow. During the 1930s his work shows a preoccupation with eroticism, mirroring his own relationship, which he also constructively applied to religious themes. His *Christ Rising from Sleep*

382

in the Morning (1940) resembles a flamboyant vaginal flower, like those of American abstractionist Georgia O'Keefe, from which Christ arises, like a stamen, replete with the promise of new life. His work at this period also included the strikingly naïve and inflated figure of *St Francis and the Birds* (1935),[6] which caused him to resign from the Royal Academy when it refused to exhibit it. The style may have played a part in this decision, but so might the overtly religious content which was no longer the stuff of which Academy art was made.

Stanley Spencer, *Resurrection*, 1923–27, set in the
churchyard of his home village of Cookham.
London, Tate Britain.

Crucifixion and Resurrection: War and Reconciliation

Saturation bombing during the Second World War destroyed countless lives and also obliterated or imperiled many of the churches that had given them succour. In the aftermath of war and the processes of reconstruction it was all too easy to level what remained and start afresh. In a remarkable, positive act of optimism and faith some

Anish Kapoor, *Untitled*, 1995–96, stainless steel sculpture for St Peter's, Cologne, a medieval church restored, after bombing in the Second World War, as an act of reconciliation. The church is reinterpreted through its reflection in the disk.

cities and their people rose to the challenge of preserving what remained and transforming it into symbols of hope and of reconciliation.

One such programme that stands out is the rebuilding of a number of Wren's churches in the City of London, or the incorporation of their remains into new buildings, such as the tower of St Augustine's Church just east of St Paul's Cathedral, which had been a victim of the Blitz and was now incorporated into the new building for the Cathedral School. Even more enterprising was the rebirth of the twelve Romanesque and other medieval churches of Cologne, itself bombed in return, a town characterized for its rich ecclesiastical heritage. As the culmination of their rebuilding, 1985 was declared the Year of the Romanesque Churches, and the work of architects, artists, townspeople and clergy combined not only to reconstruct them but also to transform them into highly successful meeting places of the past, present and future by introducing new artworks and design solutions for liturgical fixtures, such as altar furniture and fonts. Instead of reconstructed heritage, these churches became living, vibrant places of worship in which the lessons and techniques learned and revived by craftspeople during the process were applied to the creation of new artistic expressions of faith. Artworks by leading artists have been installed, such as Alfred Menessier's stained glass for St Gereon (1964) and the *Untitled* works (1995–96) by the British, Bombay-born, sculptor Anish Kapoor for St Peter's. New churches were also built, such as St Maria-Königin, designed by Dominikus Böhm in 1954.

In 1961, out of the devastation of Berlin arose a new church and campanile on the site of the neo-Romanesque late-nineteenth-century memorial church to Kaiser Wilhelm I (Kaiser-Wilhelm-Gedächtniskirche), incorporating the ruins of the earlier structure and featuring glass by Gabriel Loire made in Chartres, which had suffered Nazi occupation. Those who died for freedom of conscience under Hitler's regime are commemorated in the Church of Maria Regina Martyrum, built in 1963 by Hans Schädel and Friedrich Ebert, its brutalist concrete relieved by the colourful engraved mural by Georg Meistermann. The *Stations of the Cross* by O. H. Hajek recall the victims of the concentration camps, while the sculptures by F. Koenig of the *Woman of the Apocalypse* and the *Pietà* link the themes of destruction, mourning and mercy. The work of German neo-Expressionist artist Anselm Kiefer (born 1945) embodies attempts to come to terms with his country's recent past, sometimes through the exploration of themes relating to German history and Nordic mythology. Keifer's recent works, notably *Jericho* – two tottering life-size watchtowers composed of casts of container crates and massive compressed books – and *Palm Sunday* evince an exciting and profound engagement with biblical themes.

Another vibrant symbol of the phoenix-like resurrection of the future from the ashes of the past and a testimony to the power of art to attest to healing and

385

Tapestry by Graham Sutherland, *Christ in Glory*, 1954–57, for the new Coventry Cathedral.

reconciliation was erected in Coventry, England, where the ruinous fabric of the medieval cathedral was likewise retained and a new building constructed adjacent to it, with which it enjoys a symbiotic relationship. At the heart of Basil Spence's building, behind the high altar, hangs a massive tapestry of *Christ in Glory* (1954–57), designed by painter and printmaker Graham Sutherland (1903–80). His prints were initially in the tradition of Samuel Palmer, but subsequent forays into abstraction led him to develop his landscape-based vision to incorporate what he termed 'imaginative paraphrase', inspired by the rugged Pembrokeshire coast in west Wales. During the 1930s he experimented with surrealism and in the 1940s served as a war artist, depicting the work of Cornish miners and the effects of bombing on London. He undertook a number of commissions on Christian themes, having himself converted to Catholicism in 1927, including a *Crucifixion* (1944) for St Matthew's Northampton, a painting of the resurrected Christ entitled *Noli Me Tangere* commissioned for Chichester Cathedral by Dean Walter Hussey, who did so much to construct its fine reputation for artworks, and the great Coventry tapestry. The former two pieces are permeated with the suffering of war and the latter with the stoical optimism of a victory hard won, and at tremendous cost to all concerned, and with the hope of reconciliation. Similar evocations of anguish and hope pervade Coventry Cathedral's imposing stained and etched glass windows by French Abstract Expressionist painter Alfred Manessier (1911–93), who became deeply spiritual following a Trappist retreat in 1943. Manessier also designed glass for churches in France, Switzerland and Germany, including that at Bréseux; the church of St-Pierre, Trinquetaille, Arles; the Chapel of Sainte-Thérèse de l'Infant Jésus et de la Sainte Face, Hem, Nord; the Unserer Lieben Frauenkirche at Brema, Germany; and All Saints church, Basle.

The striking edifice of the new Coventry Cathedral, built as an international act of collaboration and reconciliation in which the German people participated, became a shrine to the best that British post-war art had to offer and is replete with works that speak of the triumph of the spirit over adversity and grief.

New Churches, New Artworks

The twentieth century witnessed a spectacular growth in the practice of writing on art, with new journals appearing and new strands of theological and art historical criticism of sacred art developing. Dogmatic pronouncements on the liturgical role of art also resurfaced in a series of Vatican encyclicals. In Italy, following each of the World Wars, artworks were commissioned for churches. The more notable are: the reliefs illustrating the preaching of John the Baptist on the font and candelabra of San Babila, Milan, made around 1933 by Fausto Melotti; the encaustic roundels depicting scenes from the life of St Benedict, painted by Ferruccio Ferrazzi for San Benedetto, Rome, in 1949, and his frescoes for Santa Maria Assunta at Amatrice (1951–53) and in the crypt of the Mausoleo Ottolenghi at Acqui (1953), all featuring bold figures in expressionistic style; the dark and disturbing ceramic altarpiece of St Margherita Alacoque's vision of the Sacred Heart at San Fedele, Milan, designed in 1956 by Lucio Fontana, and his 1950s designs for Portal V of Milan Cathedral; and the monumental bronze doors – perpetuating the ancient Roman, Romanesque and Renaissance genre – known as la Porte della Morte in St Peter's, Rome, designed by Giacomo Manzù in 1961–63.

There was also a flurry of activity in the design of new churches, and also of synagogues. Many feature simplified sacred spaces in which lighting, stained glass, and surface treatments of walls and floors all play a pivotal artistic role in creating a contemplative ambience. The few remaining fixtures and furnishings are treated as artworks and designed both to perform their function and to make powerful symbolic and aesthetic statements. The Benedictine Order in particular commissioned many new abbey churches, several of them in Ireland and the US, such as Saint Meinrad Archabbey, Saint Meinrad, Indiana, which features the *Risen Christ* mural by Dom Gregory de Wit of Louvain. Among the most effective and affecting architects of such modern churches, in which architecture and art are fully integrated, are: Gio Ponti (1958, San Remo, Italy; 1970, Taranto, Italy); Charles Moore (1983, Pacific Palisades, California); Votjen Ravnikar (1990, Lubjana, Slovenia); Mario Botta and Enzo Cucchi (1990–96, Monte Tamarro, Switzerland); Marco Bagnoli (1994, Crypt of Beato Bernardo, San Miniato al Monte, Florence); and Tadao Ando, the interior of whose Church of Light at Ibaraki (1987–89, Osaka, Japan) is relieved only by the massive cross composed of light, in the form of window slits across its end wall – an epitome of Minimalism in which the ancient symbol of the cross transforms space into art. Despite lamentations of the decline of the formal Christian faith, new sacred spaces are being built and aesthetically equipped, such as the Anglican Centre in Doha Qatar (Diocese of Cyprus and the Gulf), designed by architect Tom Hornsby, who has commissioned artworks by Mark Cazalet and Nicholas Mynheer – the first church to be built in Qatar since the seventh century.

The interior fittings of such ecclesiastical structures take the form of integrated artworks, and temporary installations are also now increasingly to be seen inside churches, such as Anish Kapoor's *Untitled* (1997) for the Mausoleum at the Domkirche in Graz, Austria. Other examples include *Moon Mirror* by German installation and performance artist Rebecca Horn (installed in Berlin and subsequently in St Paul's Cathedral, London, in 2005), with its accompanying sound installation with its Sephardic desert resonances; and her terrifyingly pertinent vision of *Hell* (1994), which consists of a spiralling tower of iron bed frames, installed in the stark neo-classical interior of the Chapelle St Louis de la Salpêtrière, Paris, during 1995. Images of beds are usually replete with sexual overtones, but here their harsh forms and the descent from a dishevelled clothed bed to the stark, naked frames conjures up thoughts, not only of fall through acts of shame, but also of the spiraling decline into an abyss of illness and death experienced by the victims of war, and of dehumanized health provision and uncaring social care.

Meanwhile, in the Cathedral Church of St John the Divine in New York, situated between the vibrant campus of Columbia University and the colourful street life of Harlem and the West Side, 2004 and 2005 witnessed 'Season South Africa', the result of a partnership between the Cathedral and the Museum for African Art. This performing arts programme featured vibrant dramatic performances by Dimpho Di Kopane (South African Lyric Theatre Company) of works such as *The Mysteries* and the *Beggar's Opera* – conflating Zulu, Afrikaans, Xhosa and Dutch influences – and artworks by contemporary South African artists. Later in 2005, the same church, commenced in 1892 and still awaiting completion, hosted a very different series of large canvasses redolent of the austere mythological mysticism of the far north – *The Apostles*, painterly primeval effigies, recalling those of Easter Island and of Viking age art, by contemporary Swedish artist Michel Östlund.

Buildings intended for worship can also become installations themselves, such as Graeco-American artist Stephen Antonakos's *Chapel of the Heavenly Ladder*[7] (1997), in which a ladder leads from the tomb-like interior of a metal container-like structure to a calvary of crosses on its roof. The Chapel of the Saints at Rodi, Greece (1990s), is illumined by the metaphysical coloured fluorescent light emanating from behind large painted metal squares, also by Antonakos, who successfully conflates the Byzantine icon tradition with that of Flavin's electric icons to form timeless foci of prayer. The modern church, at its best, is a holistic artistic expression of faith and of sustained and integrated craftsmanship that is on a par in quality, if not in scale, with that of the medieval cathedrals.

Installing non-faith-specific artworks in a sacred space can also inspire different levels of reading and participation. During the 2006 City of London Festival, which celebrated 'Trading Places: London and Tokyo', three works by Japanese artist Yoko Ono were displayed in St Paul's Cathedral, having previously been shown in Portsmouth Cathedral: *Morning Beams*, *Cleaning Piece (Riverbed)* and *Wish Tree*. The first of these consisted of taut white ropes, anchored by wooden beams, that emulated a shaft of light – a Godburst – falling through the clear glass of a north transept window (above Holman Hunt's *Light of the World*, which entered into dialogue with it). The experience of light falling on simulated light at different times of day and night was a moving and mystical one. *Cleaning Piece* and *Wish Tree* extended the viewer's participative experience still further. The former comprised a meander of river-washed cobbles, flowing out from the anchor beams of *Morning Beams*, which those passing were invited to remove and to place upon facing cairns of sorrow and joy, as they felt fit – their ritual actions replete with prayer and praise. These silent intercessions took shape in words in the corresponding expressions of joy and sorrow that were written out by visitors – and staff – and tied to the *Wish Tree*. Thus the works metamorphosed and were continually co-created by their audience, fulfilling both the Surrealist Marcel Duchamp's assertion that 'No work of art is finished until completed by the spectator', and Nicholas Bourriaud's premise of 'relational aesthetics', in which the artwork becomes 'an opening to unlimited discussion', and its form ('poesis') is completed or transformed by its active reception and interaction ('praxis'). Ono's work is rooted in conceptual art, which places ideas above objects, and in the Fluxus movement that she helped to establish, and it speaks to everyone in a truly democratic fashion, transcending man-made barriers of tribe and creed. Their installation in a place of worship did not serve to appropriate them to a specific faith but, rather, increased its accessibility to all by offering a simple conduit for individual participation within collective communion.

390

The Millennium and Beyond: Exhibiting Contemporary Christian Art in Britain

Meryl Doney

It was 1999, the eve of the millennium, and the new sculpture *Ecce Homo*, by Mark Wallinger, was unveiled on the iconic fourth plinth in London's Trafalgar Square. A simple, lifelike, life-sized figure of Jesus, naked but for a halo of gold barbed wire and a loincloth, stood waiting for a verdict once again. The figure was, as might be expected, controversial. But I found it exciting that he was there at all. In this public space, a highly respected, contemporary British artist was unashamedly revisiting the most moving moment in the story of Christ – whose birth date we were marking with the millennium. Wallinger made it clear that his sculpture was not meant to be perverse or ironic. He said: 'I wanted to show him as an ordinary human being. Jesus was at the very least a political leader of an oppressed people and I think he has a place here in front of all these oversized imperial symbols.' The figure was at once a political statement and, I felt, an outstanding contribution to and continuation of the great history of Christian art.

Not long afterwards, I was asked to curate an exhibition for the 150th anniversary of *BibleLands*, a small relief and development agency working with medical, educational and development projects across the Middle East. It was to be a survey of attitudes towards the person of Christ. We decided on a series of linked exhibitions of contemporary art involving the work of some fifty artists in six cathedrals – Canterbury, Durham, Lincoln, Worcester, the Episcopal Cathedral, Glasgow and St Paul's, London. The series was eventually entitled *Presence: Images of Christ for the Third Millennium*.

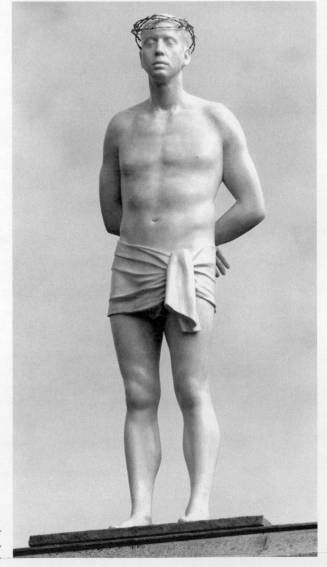

Mark Wallinger, *Ecce Homo*, 1999, with Christ portrayed as a prisoner of conscience. Britain (installed for a while in Trafalgar Square, London, as part of a changing installation on the 'spare' plinth).

The brief, with its focus on the person of Christ, was in some ways a narrow one – challenging artists, in some cases, to move outside their usual areas of concern. However, the project turned out to be a unique opportunity to ask some big questions about faith, belief, spirituality and meaning and to gauge their continued relevance as the new century dawned.

The first happy discovery was that some of the best practising artists were prepared to show work, keen to engage both with the unusual setting of an ancient cathedral and with the theme. The works included: Antony Gormley's *Rise* in Canterbury Cathedral; Nicola Hicks's *Sorry, Sorry Sarajevo* and *Chowl* and Mark Wallinger's *Angel* in Lincoln; Fenwick Lawson's stunning series of sculptures throughout Durham Cathedral; and Bill Viola's *The Messenger* in St Paul's Cathedral, London.

Another discovery was the dynamic that occurs when works of art are placed in sacred spaces. These surroundings are very different from the neutral, quasi-clinical setting of the white cube or the gallery. The beauty, age and sheer size of the spaces offered by a cathedral or church challenge and inspire the artist. And a building formed for, and inhabited by, a worshipping community adds its own resonance to any piece sited within it. To encounter Antony Gormley's *Rise*, for instance, on the flagstone floor of a place (the shrine of Thomas Becket) where many centuries of pilgrims have gathered, is to see the piece in a startlingly moving context. Contrastingly, try as we might to find a place for Mark Wallinger's *Ecce Homo* in St Paul's Cathedral, we could not. He simply did not fit.

It is always difficult hanging paintings in a church context, but in St Paul's Cathedral we solved the problem by mounting a single exhibition of pictures on stand-alone boards in the transepts. Each artist's take on the subject, of course, was different. Some, like Peter Howson and Iain McKillop, were happy to be overtly confessional. Others – like Tracey Emin, William Hamper (Billy Childish) and Maggie Hambling – referenced the rich heritage of Christian history and iconography. Mark Cazalet, Albert Herbert and Robert Hardy, on the other hand, chose contemporary settings. Yet others took a more tangential approach. Paul Martin's *The Restorer* showed a contemporary picture restorer on scaffolding in front of a fresco of the crucifixion, and Christopher Le Brun's *The Morning Watch* portrayed an evocative landscape

with an angel in the foreground.

As the title implies, *Presence*, as an entity, was less about representations of the figure of Jesus than about the presence of Christ himself. In this regard, artists working in some of the newer media were able to offer their different insights. Bill Viola's massive image of *The Messenger* endlessly rising through water offered a striking new take on baptism. The dramatic light installation *Vigil* (made for the Easter Fire service at Canterbury by Willie Williams) enhanced the Lenten themes of waiting and longing. *Iconography* by Mike Gough (in which an actor dressed as a clichéd representation of Jesus walked the streets of the City of London) explored ideas of encounter with Christ.

Artists were free to respond to the theme in any way they wished, but by far the most 'popular' subject was the passion of Christ, and particularly the crucifixion with its emphasis on Jesus' humanity and identification with humankind. The subject least represented was the resurrection. Perhaps for our times, the image of the resurrection is too much of a statement of 'belief' – too certain, too triumphalistic. As the Archbishop of Canterbury Dr Rowan Williams said in his introduction to the catalogue: 'The event of Jesus Christ is for the Christian tradition the unsurpassable enlargement of the world; nothing could take us further. It makes possible what had been impossible. And it does so without tearing the fabric of history and matter.' Put like that, it becomes clear why representing miracles is pretty hard, and representing the resurrection is the most difficult thing of all. This challenge was taken up by four painters exhibited in Worcester Cathedral: *Resurrection* by both Iain McKillop and Louise McLary; Adam Boulter's triptych *The Resurrection That Was, The Resurrection That Is, The Resurrection That Will Be*; and Mark Cazalet's *Ascension Day*, set in a quiet street in west London.

My experience of curating *Presence* has left me with an overriding conviction that faith and spirituality are still profound issues for today's artists and, by extension, to people in general. It has also inspired me to continue to look out for the work of contemporary artists exploring this territory. They may not be card-carrying, fully signed up members of a faith community, but their work contains important insights despite, or perhaps because of, that. I can only cite a few of these works here, but I set them out as examples of what I believe is a serious and important strand of contemporary art practice.

Damien Hirst, for instance, uses Christian reference points in many of his works. He alluded to Jesus and his disciples in *Romance in the Age of Uncertainty* at White Cube2 in 2003, eliding the worlds of religion, art and science in an exploration of the human experience of love, life and death. And more recently, *New Religion* repeats this practice by drawing attention to our reliance on the pharmaceutical industry to cure our ills.

Nicholas Pope's stunning installation *Apostles Speaking in Tongues* drew crowds at Tate Britain in 1996; while a controversial series of paintings housed in their own room at Tate Modern form Chris Ophili's response to the Last Supper.

On a broader spiritual subject area, Susan Hiller's sound installation *Witness* filled a disused chapel with small hanging speakers emitting recordings of people describing UFO encounters. Hiller sees this activity as related to older forms of confession, ways of placing fears into the public arena. Jonathan Jones, writing in *The Guardian* newspaper, described the work as 'drawing on the experiences and storytelling abilities of a huge range of people, hinting at broader spiritual gaps in contemporary society'.

Film, video or DVD, adding as it does the element of time, has, in the hands of contemporary artists, become a medium in which to explore profound spiritual realities. Many of Sam Taylor-Wood's video images have Christian reference points. Take, for example, her use of photography to create *Bound Ram* – an image with deep roots in the Judeo-Christian image of the scapegoat.

I have already mentioned Bill Viola. His many video pieces use the medium with consummate skill and intelligence not only to revisit the classic themes of Christian art but also to reinterpret their inner meanings and relationships.

Mark Wallinger is another artist who exploits the moving image to profound effect. In his video, *Angel*, Wallinger himself plays the part of a blind prophet or angel, standing at the bottom of a moving escalator and intoning the beautiful opening words of John's Gospel: 'In the beginning was the Word and the Word was made flesh…' As the 'prophet' speaks, people on either side of him move up and down the escalators, as though passing through life, oblivious to his words. In his *Threshold to the Kingdom* the artist simply takes his camera to the arrivals gate at an international airport and films travellers at the moment they come home. Filmed in slow motion, the video is silent except for Allegri's *Miserere*, a setting of Psalm 51. This piece was described by Norman Lebrecht in the *Daily Telegraph* as 'the most moving evocation of the afterlife created by an artist since Gustav Dore illustrated Dante's *Paradiso* in the nineteenth century'.

There is still a significant, albeit minority, body of artists either of self-confessed Christian faith or who are working specifically within the area of Christian art: painters such as Craigie Aitchison, Anthony Green, Albert Herbert, Peter Howson and the late Norman Adams; sculptors such as Peter Ball, Stephen Broadbent, Jonathon Clarke, Stephen Cox, Steve Dilworth, Fenwick Lawson, John O'Rourke and Victoria Rance; John Newling, who works with installation and conceptual pieces; and performance artist Bobby Baker. And there is, I am glad to say, a younger generation of emerging artists, working across all media and genres, who are at least interested in, and in some cases preoccupied with, exploring the spiritual. For a list of these artists, see the reference section at the end of the book.[1]

The experience of making *Presence* a reality in 2004 proved to be invigorating and encouraging. As one would hope at the end of one century and the beginning of a new one, I was inspired by the fact that so many artists are taking spirituality and meaning seriously. If, at the turn of the millennium, the figure of Christ can take his place in the public square where Britons traditionally come both to celebrate and to protest, I am confirmed in my belief that we have by no means come to the end of this story. In fact, we are simply turning over to a new page.

The Journey Continues

Earth Art: Landscape, Art and Eco-Theology

Around 600 CE an Irishman inspired by the coast, moors and mountains of these islands, St Columbanus, wrote of how nature was a second revelation, to be 'read' alongside scripture to deepen our knowledge of God:

> 'Seek no further concerning God; for those who wish to know the great deep must first review the natural world. For knowledge of the Trinity is properly likened to the depths of the sea, according to that saying of the Sage, "and the great deep, who shall find it out?" If then a man wishes to know the deepest ocean of divine understanding, let him first if he is able scan that visible sea, and the less he finds himself to understand of those creatures which lurk beneath the waves, the more let him realize that he can know less of the depths of its Creator.'

This represented a distinctive, non-mainstream approach to nature born, in large part, of its appreciation and celebration by the prehistoric Celtic peoples who inhabited much of Europe in the Iron Age and who, with the exception of the Irish, were conquered by Rome. It marks the beginnings of an alternative eco-theology, proposing what might today be considered a more creative form of Christian environmentalism than conventional theological views on stewardship and the assumption that we have been set above the rest of creation to do with it as we will. The interpretation of landscape and of natural forms and phenomena has always played a role in Christian art, but its non-faith-specific treatment by a number of modern artists lends itself particularly well to spiritual contemplation by those concerned with exploring our place in the natural world and how best to respect and care for it and contribute to its sustainability.

Land Art

During the 1930s a London-based group of artists came together in the 7&5 Society and Unit 1, English responses to Abstraction-Création and the more local stimulus of the work of Epstein and Gill. They included Barbara Hepworth, Ben Nicholson and Henry Moore (1898–1986), who developed a biomorphic abstract style of sculpture through which they explored both the human form and those formed by nature within the landscape, with rounded, interlocking and pierced forms. Their intention

Henry Moore, *Mother and Child*, 1984. The organic forms of nature inspired Moore to create this powerful image of the mother-child relationship which recalls the iconography of the Virgin and Child. Moore, an atheist, approved the installation of the work in St Paul's, where it remains. Henry Moore Foundation, on loan to St Paul's Cathedral, London.

may not have been religious – Moore was an avowed humanist – but their work is imbued with a deep spirituality born of a communion with creation. One of Moore's pieces, a marble *Mother and Child* (1984) – a theme also beloved by Hepworth – is a celebration of the universal parent-child relationship and of the nurture of nature, but centuries of iconographic imagery invites an immediate association with that of the Virgin and Child. Towards the end of his life, Moore himself agreed that it should be on long-term loan (from the Moore Foundation) and display at St Paul's Cathedral, London.

West Cornwall, with its clear, honest light, granite cliffs, rock-strewn beaches and heathery moors, drew Hepworth and Nicholson to join the St Ives School, which gave birth to the Penwith Society of Arts whose members, including Peter Lanyon, Patrick Heron and Terry Frost, continued to apply abstract principles to landscape in their paintings and, in Heron's case, stained glass (he contributed a vibrant window to the new Tate Gallery in St Ives; the Methodist Art Collection also includes his painting of a crucifix flanked by candles in a study); it continues to inspire the artists of the St Just School today. The monuments of Cambodia provoked a similar response in American artist Beverly Pepper, who was inspired to move from painting to sculpture as 'the way to explore an interior life of feeling. I wish to make an object that has a powerful presence but is at the same time inwardly turned.' Her large metal sculptures, such as *Zig Zag* (1967), installed within the landscape, do just that, opening up what she terms a 'third reality' of infinite space.

During the course of the twentieth century artistic interaction with nature also became increasingly interventionist. Bulgarian-born Christo (Christo Jaacheff, born 1955) and his wife, Jeanne-Claude, introduced *empaquetage* ('packaging') as a means of challenging perception of form, wrapping tin cans, cars, buildings (such as the Reichstag in Berlin, 1995, and the Pont Neuf in Paris, 1985), and a mile of coastline near Sydney (Australia, 1969). They also erected the massive *Valley Curtain* across Rifle Gap, Colorado (USA, 1972) and some 24 miles of fabric walling (inspired by the Great Wall of China) in Sonoma and Marin Counties, California (USA, 1976). Such installations require an impressive amount of collaborative endeavour, becoming themselves an act of collective faith and communion. The same applies to much of the Earth Art of American artist Walter de Maria, who employed the photographic medium to explore natural phenomena within landscape, as well as installations of his own conception, such as *Lightning Field* in New Mexico (1977). Here he erected a number of lightning conductors to channel electro-kinetic energy into a condensed area, with a little cabin at its centre within which one can stay, becoming part of a phenomenal piece of performance art in which nature is the lead player, humankind the participative audience, and divine energy the quickening force.

Such close encounters with the awesome power of the natural world may be novel to many Western consumers of art, but since time immemorial people living on the land have erected features of their own, emulating or enhancing the landscape – prehistoric standing stones, petroglyphs, artificial pools and the like. Contemporary Australian aboriginal artists, such as Berthe Kaline Naparrula, continue to explore the ancient mysteries of dreamtime – their timeless place of spiritual encounter – through their art, with its basis in colourful mosaic-like paintings of totemic fauna and topographic features. Roger Ackling (UK), Odd Nerdrum (Norway), Walter de Maria (US), Robert Smithson (US), James Turrell (US), Michael Heizer (US), Nancy Holt (US), Olafur Eliasson (Denmark), Richard Long (UK), Andy Goldsworthy (UK), Rachel Whiteread (UK), Paul Hodges (UK), and Andrzej Jackowski (UK) have all experimented over recent decades in land art, 'earthworks' and eco-art, rejecting commodification and investigating the relationship between transience, the ephemeral and the eternal. Goldsworthy and Long have revived the concept of journey though landscape – with its traditional cultural overtones of pilgrimage – as a creative process, sometimes contributing temporary installations of their own within the environment, such as cairns or river-like confluences of stones or strips of bark, and recording them photographically and through mapping. Words (poetry or prose) often complement image, creating a parallel distillation of experience and engagement of all the senses.

Odd Nerdrum (born 1944) has called his art 'an historical anarchist', saying, 'To be in my own time is too poor a thing… My time lacks too much and I will be checked, cheated and defeated. My time shall not direct my feelings for the truth.' In reaction to this perceived contemporary poverty of spirit his works suggest a primordial no-time of the imagination. In *Revier* (1985-86),[1] the Buddha-like figure of a prehistoric hunter sits brandishing a staff and gun in the centre of a protective circle of boulders in a desolate landscape. The image evokes the barren loneliness of the human heart, which is about to be illuminated by the coming of God with the light of the dawn that breaks beyond.

Seeing Things Anew

The American artist James Turrell, a practising Quaker, challenges the ways in which we perceive space, form and light through his art, whether through the trompe l'oeil effects of recessed, lit panels within internal walls, through his skyspaces or through his Christo-like ongoing treatment of the natural landscape of Roden Crater, Arizona. These are circular chambers with open roofs, within which the viewer lies, sits or stands to contemplate the changing kaleidoscope of the framed patch of sky above.

The experience can be highly conducive to a meditative, spiritual connectivity with the environment and one that transcends our usual temporal and spatial perceptions. They recall the words of the seventh-century Northumbrian hermit-bishop, St Cuthbert, who is reported to have said that if only he could build an oratory with walls so high that all he could see was the sky, he would still be afraid that the love of money and the cares of the world would snatch him away. This is exactly what he did build on his Inner Farne hermitage. The island he chose was not one of the more remote, however, but that closest to the beach beneath the royal citadel of Bamburgh. Whenever its genocidal king, Egcfrith, and his worldly courtiers looked out to sea they were presented with the symbolic presence of Cuthbert – an emaciated, vulnerable, indomitable Gandhi-like figure, reminding them of the responsibilities that accompanied wealth and power and of spiritual as well as material concerns. In accordance with contemporary Irish law the means of obtaining ultimate legal redress for an injustice was to fast outside the offender's door. Such an eremitic visual installation could be a powerful tool in achieving social justice. Turrell's skyspaces likewise offer a contemporary challenge to the ways in which we view our material world and create a contemplative context that stimulates active reflection.

During 2003–2004, *The Weather Project* by Danish artist Olafur Eliasson occupied the heart of Tate Modern. A mammoth, pregnant, blood-orange orb hung pendulously at one end of the Gilbert Scott turbine hall (converted by Herzog and de Meuron), once itself the creator of another pulsing energy. From wall niches dry-ice machines pumped a fine mist; instant, palpable atmosphere. Viewers were immediately transported to the primordial swamp, to 'dreamtime' and to the mythic Nordic realm of the all-day sun. This is the sort of encounter that prompts humankind to raise up standing stones – commemorating the all-pervasive enormity of the divine.

And yet, there is another way of reading this phenomenon. The rising sun is an ancient Judaeo-Christian symbol of the Second Coming, when the Redeemer returns from the East, bringing resurrection and eternal life. As if heralding this time to come, the golden orb releases us to play and to unselfconsciously be ourselves. By drawing energy from the sun – or in Christian terms, the Son – we are filled with energy which we can feed back into the 'grid' of life.

Antony Gormley recently explored themes of environmental awareness and sustainability in his *Waste Man*, in which he invited the culturally diverse peoples of Margate (a somewhat run down but interesting seaside resort on the south-east coast of England) to participate in constructing a huge human figure from discarded household waste and consumer goods. Its arm was raised, recalling the posture of the Statue of Liberty at the seaward approach to New York, and it was inspired by the book of Exodus and the pursuit of freedom. This massive effigy was then burned, recalling the ancient wicker men of Celtic prehistory – a deeply evocative image of shared anthropological memory, of community collaboration and of our profligacy of precious resources. Andrzej Jackowski offers a hopeful vision of care for the environment in his *Holding the Tree* (1988), painted after the Great Hurricane deprived southern England of many of its ancient trees. In this gentle, pastel work, redolent of the Orphic lyricism of Odilon Redon's work, the fragile tree survives, although uprooted, sustained in the caring hands of a giant human form. Jackowski's aspiration for his work is that it should 'serve as [a] key for people to unlock, or enter into, their own self'. This requires the viewer to unlock their openness to God's care for creation and their sustainable role within it.

399

Innovation and Tradition

Searching for the Spiritual in Contemporary Art

Since the 1950s there has been a growing reassertion of figural narrative and symbolism, revived by artists such as the English sculptor and illustrator Elizabeth Frink. More recently, Leonard McComb has explored the vulnerability and sublimity of incarnation in his golden sculpture, *Portrait of a Young Man Standing*, whose uncompromising, unflinching nudity – which so offended some of the clergy and their flock during its display as part of 'The Journey' exhibition in Lincoln Cathedral – and its closed and open fists, representing the active and contemplative, signifies complete surrender and trust in God. Emma Young's monumental sculptures of the heads of angels, set atop columns in the new arcade of offices and shops flanking the piazza in front of St Paul's Cathedral, London, perpetuate an iconography of the supernatural that commenced with the winged victories of classical art and the angelic litany of the Early Christian church. Mark Wallinger has used the classic depiction of the idealized human figure to tremendously powerful effect as a symbol of vulnerable humanity in his *Ecce Homo* (1999), in the form of the prisoner of conscience. Antony Gormley also concentrates on the human form in what he describes as 'an attempt to materialize the place at the other side of appearance where we all live'. His figures are often cast from his own body, for it is the 'closest experience of matter that I will ever have and the only part of the material world that I live inside'. For Gormley the body is a place, inhabited by the commonality of the human condition. It can take the form of the epitome of reflection and repose, inviting a hushed contemplative response, as in his *Sound II* (1986) – a life-size figure cupping its hands as if reading a book – which stands in silent meditation in the ancient crypt of Winchester Cathedral; or it can become the powerful figure of *The*

Antony Gormley, *The Angel of the North*, 1998, a massive protecting figure recalling the industrial heritage of the region and its early Christian legacy and their relationship to the individual human figure. Gateshead, north-east England.

Angel of the North (1998), which presides over the approach to Newcastle and Gateshead. Stretching out across the land and its people its massive protecting wings – their riveted metal span recalling the girders of the ships and bridges built in the region during its industrial heyday – it symbolizes regeneration built upon a bedrock of hope and faith. Also from Northumbria, Fenwick Lawson's organic figural sculptures of *St Cuthbert*[1] and *The Bearers* employ the hagiographical genre to tap into the regional identity of north-east England and its underpinning traditions of faith, stemming from its conversion during the seventh century. Peter Ball also features the organic forms of driftwood in his remarkable figural sculptures.

Sergei Chepik (born 1953), a former Soviet dissident who spent time working in its mental institutions and who now works in Paris, adopted a literal narrative approach in his paintings of Christ's life, *I am the Way, the Truth and the Life*.[2] Chepik's figural treatment of the nativity, public ministry, crucifixion and resurrection of Christ may seem out of step with current trends towards symbolism and abstraction within Christian and spiritually orientated art; but perhaps figural narrative also warrants reassertion in a place of Christian worship that is also a focus for international tourism, in an age when biblical themes are no longer widely understood and are rapidly falling out of general cultural cognizance. French painter

Jean Rustin likewise uses dark figural works to plumb the depths of human torment and divine compassion, and Cecil Collins (UK, 1908–89) spent much of his life painting images of the angel and the fool in an attempt to capture the incomprehensible image of the reality of life, passionately pursuing his conviction that 'all art is an attempt to manifest the Face of the God of Life'.

That face has become obscured for artist John Kirby, formerly a devout British Roman Catholic who served the poor of Calcutta alongside Mother Teresa, but whose work now displays a longing for what he no longer considers 'true'. And yet, it is through his storytelling and his elegiac empathy with the human condition that he continues to seek the truth, whilst having recognized what the poet Keats termed the ability to 'dwell in uncertainty'. His progressive alienation from religious dogma did not deter the Vatican from commissioning a Madonna and Child from him for an exhibition in the Pantheon, Rome, to celebrate Pope John Paul II's silver jubilee in 2005. Kirby's sense of injustice at papal pronouncements concerning homosexuality deterred him from submitting his work, however, which now hangs in Santa Lucia del Gonfalone in Rome – an abortive commission, nonetheless popular among the people, which poignantly recalls the experiences of Caravaggio and El Greco.

Ancient Iconographies, New Approaches

Meanwhile, symbols and iconographies imbued with two millennia of Christian meaning are once more in vogue. Craigie Aitchison uses the traditional Christian symbols of the cross and the *Agnus Dei* ('Lamb of God') in his bold, colourful naïve canvases that nonetheless also have tremendous appeal to non-Christian audiences and art collectors. Those commissioning artworks for installation in churches often find symbols particularly appropriate and accessible vehicles for conveying their beliefs. Jonathan Clarke's sculpture *The Way of Life* for Ely Cathedral, Cambridgeshire, is a simple and highly effective metal symbol of the cross, illumined by a dawn-pink light, from the foot of which flows a molten river of life, set against the stone of the medieval cathedral wall. Stephen Cox's winning entry for a competitive sculptural commission for St Nicholas Cathedral, Newcastle-upon-Tyne, uses the traditional materials of alabaster from the pharaonic quarries of Egypt and purple porphyry with its imperial connotations in a moving and monumental evocation of the Eucharist. The fractured alabaster symbolizes the Trinity and the breaking of the bread that represents Christ's body, and conjures up associations with a broken world, while the elliptical pool of polished porphyry below is simultaneously a pool of wine, the claret-red redeeming blood of Christ and the life-giving waters of the sea (1996).

American artist Bill Viola also used the cleansing waters of baptism and rebirth from sin as the basis for his enormous video installation, *The Messenger*, commissioned by the Diocese of Durham, in which a naked, bearded male is slowly submerged in water and emerges, recalling iconographies of John the Baptist, the baptism of Christ and his death and resurrection. Water is also of tremendous significance to photographer Elizabeth Williams, for whom it 'symbolizes survival through flexibility and strength through endurance' – a Taoist approach that is equally accessible to the Christian. Her *Nothing Covered or Hidden No. 1* of 3 (1989), the title based on biblical passages relating to our collective and personal encounter with God, depicts the human heart exposed to divine judgement not in traditional guise as a scene of judicial condemnation and elevation, but in the form of a beach, in which we are all united as grains of sand, washed clean by the gentle embrace of an infinite ocean.

The photo-paintings by Vija Celmin, who was born in Riga in 1939 and moved to the US in 1949, were preoccupied with violent images – fire, car crashes and the like – during the 1960s, but later works such as *Untitled (Ocean with Cross, no. 1)* produced in 1971 have exorcized such horror and achieved a serenity. Veristic copies in paint of photographic images also served as a powerful visual medium for British Conceptualist artist Terry Atkinson, who used them to explore class difference, warfare and other aspects of social history in his modern history paintings. One of these features his two young daughters standing amid war graves (*The Stone Touchers I*, 1984–85). They are captured and made implicit and complicit to their history, in which religion plays a part. The work is subtitled:

Ruby and Amber in The Gardens of their old Empire
history-dressed men

Dear Ruby and Amber,
Do you think God is a person?
If he is, is he a he?
If he is, is he black or white, or brown or yellow,
or pink or orange or blue or red, or green or purple…?
What if he's a she?
Do you think God is a dissident? Or is he a South African,
Or an Argentinian, or an Anglo-Saxon, etc.?
Do you think he's the best knower?

If he is a she do you think all the he's would admit
she's the best knower?

Man's attempts across the millennia to own the divine and recreate it in his own image are succinctly conveyed by this over-exposed image of innocents whose enquiries will be framed by the rhetoric of their cultural and political history.

Traditional symbols, with their associated histories, can cross sectarian boundaries as well as confirm them. At the dawn of the new millennium Polish-German artist Gabriela Nasfeter chose the ancient form of the pyramid as her motif for an installation that straddled continents and denominational divides – *Lichtpyramide: A catalogue of Art as a Document of an Ecumenical Adventure*. A meditation on the intersection of sacred and secular, heaven and earth, the installation undertook a pilgrimage around twelve churches of the Orthodox, Catholic and Protestant traditions, travelling from Ulm to Armenian Etschmiadsiam in Erivan, under the sponsorship of the German Protestant Churches' commission for the arts. The resonance of the sacred geometry of the pyramid stretched across time as its light illumined space, speaking a truly universal language. A triangle also provides the structure for American feminist artist Judy Chicago's *The Dinner Party* (1974–79). This perfect geometric form, with its symbolic Trinitarian connotations, serves as an equal-sided table set, ritually like the Last Supper, with embroidered runners, chalices and customized plates referencing the women who are invited, including Sappho, Boudicca, Emily Dickinson and St Brigid. The symbolism of the crucifixion was also appropriated by American Neo-expressionist Julian Schnabel in *VITA* (1984) in which a woman is crucified against a landscape of broken crockery, the shattered vestiges of the cross of domesticity she has had to bear. While for Krzysztof Wodiczko, a church building itself formed the canvas onto which he projected images of the hands of a migrant worker holding aloft the fruits of his labour and those of a businessman waiting to consume them with his aggressively held knife and fork (*Projection*, 1988).[3]

Modern Art Outside Europe

Around the world artists from different cultures interact with mainstream traditions of Christian art to produce distinctive syntheses – Chinese, Japanese and Indian woodblocks, Balinese batik, African sculpture – often with a distinctly ecumenical flavour and with a concern for social justice. While the art generated by European expatriate communities in South America, Africa and Asia was often a provincial reflection of the European mainstream or a flood of imports, it could sometimes engage with that of local society and contribute to integration and the promotion of social justice and equality. Such has been the contribution of Cecil Skotnes, born in 1926 of Norwegian and Canadian Salvation Army parents working in South Africa, who assimilated African influences into his paintings and carvings and who has helped to reintroduce black artists to their artistic heritage through the art school he founded in Johannesburg in 1948. His endeavours have helped to fuel the protest art and the subsequent post-Apartheid art of South Africa.

In 1978 the Asian Christian Art Association was founded to encourage the visual arts in Asian churches. At its first meeting of artists in Bali, the aims of the Association were expressed:

- To encourage artists to express Christian concern through their art in an Asian context.
- To coordinate the activities of individuals and groups in the Asian region who are working on indigenous art forms.
- To provide a means of communication and information.
- To work with churches, with the Christian Conferences of Asia and with other bodies seeking to witness to Christian faith in Asia.

It now promotes the work of artists such as: He Qi and Lu Lan of China, who work in a colourful graphic work, and Chiang Chao Ho who produces delicate paintings in the classical Chinese calligraphic idiom; N. M. Misera and Solomon Raj, who reinterpret traditional Indian techniques and styles; Yoshihei Miya from Japan, whose work is indebted to the techniques of the Impressionists and Expressionists; Lucia Hartini, a victim of domestic abuse in Java, who seeks to expresses the spiritual state of female survivors of suffering; Timur I. Poerwowidagdo, who explores through art the experiences of women raped during times of war; and Karl Gaspar, a prisoner of conscience in the Philippines. For Gaspar's fellow countryman, Emmanuel Garibay, the *Supper at Emmaus* (1997) takes the form of a convivial scene in which workmen relax and roar with laughter at a joke told by a Christ, who takes the form of a local woman – not someone who would usually find a welcome in their masculine enclave, except that she looks like a bar hostess. The stigmata of social stigma are imprinted on her hands. Garibay thereby captures both the joy and the elusive mystery of the resurrection experience, for as followers of the risen Christ we are called to live with and love not only those who are familiar and beloved, but also the company of strangers and of those otherwise rejected by society.

Among the prolific work of modern African artists, many of whom reflect ancient artistic influences from their regions as well as contemporary trends, are to be found: the oil painting of *Suzannah and the Elders* by Sudanese artist Taj S. M. Ahmed; a *Mother and Child* wooden sculpture by Vincent Kofi of Ghana; *Christ in the Manger* in oils by Francis Musango (Brother Francis) of Uganda; a *Head of Christ*, by Tanzanian

Emmanuel Garibay,
*Love Unknown: Emmaus,
Jesus Laughing and Loving* in
which workmen joke with a
woman in a bar, the stigmata
on her hands identifying her
with Christ despite the social
stigma of her métier, c. 2000,
the Philippines.

Elimo P. Njau (from the murals at Fort Hall Memorial Chapel, Kenya); a print of *Pilate Washing Hands and Feet* by Nigerian artist Jimo B. Akolo; and, also from Nigeria, a carved wood panel of the *Annunciation of the Angel to Mary* by Lamidi Fakeye, in which the Virgin is shown pounding meal rather than reading – as much a Martha as a Mary. African-American artists, such as Dean Mitchell and Anthony Armstrong, have also developed a wide range of popular expressions of Christian themes. Also out of Africa came the new shrine of St Chad installed in Lichfield Cathedral in 2000. This robust piece was designed and made by Ian Redelinghuys, Head of Fine Art at the Pretoria Technikon in South Africa, who has said of his work:

'The sculpture is mainly brass and, as you cannot really weld brass, I have used screws which is an allusion to the industrial past of the Midlands. It is not quite a Meccano set, but it has similarities! It combines modernism with a real sense of the spiritual history of the subject. Chad was a Saxon, but was trained at Lindisfarne by the Celtic church. I looked at Celtic spirituality and have created a sacred area in a circular shape. The circle is of seat height so that people can sit on it, as I am very much in favour of sculpture being something to be used.'

It is a remarkable testimony to the abiding bonds of the *communio sanctorum* (communion of saints) that a modern South African can still be inspired to create by a seventh-century saint from north-east England.

The Language of Art

The course of the history of art offers a Babel of lines of communication that can carry us deep into the heart of the meaning of being, allowing us to tap into universal and eternal truths. We all have our aesthetic and theological preferences, whether the primitive purity of the dawning anthropological quest for relationship with God, the humano-centric idealization of classicism, the theocratic complexity and mysticism of the medieval, the erudite humanism of the Renaissance, the emotive theatricality of the Baroque, the rational clarity of the Enlightenment, the retrospection and introspection of Romanticism, the psychological semiotics of Symbolism and Surrealism, or the meditative abstraction of Modernism. But we are of our time and it is the language of the present that speaks most volubly of the role of art in speaking of our inner life. Like our societies, our contemporary art is multi-lingual, multi-cultural and multi-referential. Such diversity can foster both innovative, many-faceted creativity and strident – or even sensationalist – shouting in order to be heard above the babble.

Language can also distort and misrepresent. When contemporary artists employ Christian themes and iconographies they are not always used to communicate their traditional meanings, but also to challenge and subvert them. The Monty Python team's film *The Life of Brian* uses the Gospel narratives as the framework for an effective satirization of established religion. It is fashionable at present to produce cartoon-like visual 'sound-bite' satires on religions as the common enemy and as a catalyst of conflict. Among the more amusing is Parisian artist Ben Boutin's digital image of self-professed Christian leaders, US President George Bush and UK Prime Minister Tony Blair, the co-authors of the Iraqi war, flanking a man wearing a T-shirt which bears the slogan 'Jesus is coming – look busy'. Wittier still is *Nus* by Remy Le Guillerm, a photomontage of a naked contemporary Adam and Eve pushing a shopping trolley loaded with apples, set against a Renaissance image of the Fall – a biting and timely comment on the dangers of consumerism and over-consumption which recalls that implicit in the Pop Art depictions of ranks of Campbell's soup tins, Coca Cola bottles and other icons of consumerism (including Marilyn Monroe) by practising Catholic Andy Warhol (1928–87).

Of similar weight to the latter is Damien Hurst's recent treatment of the Last Supper as a series of animal body parts and the *Crucifixion* as a triptych of beef carcasses. These bring to mind a 3D conflation of a composition first used in a painting by Rembrandt, who invited the parallel between a hanging carcass and the ignominy of execution on the cross, a theme explored further in *Man with Meat* and *Crucifixion* by Francis Bacon who, in these works and his *Screaming Pope* series inspired by Velázquez's portrait of Pope Innocent X, exposed the incipient psychosis often associated with extreme religiosity. Bacon was an avowed atheist who nonetheless painted a crucifixion each decade of his working life; through this subject, like his Roman Catholic friend Graham Sutherland, he plumbed the darker depths of the human condition during and following the Second World War. To treat of such Christian iconography need not betoken belief in its dogmas – but perhaps to perceive its potential as a route to deeper understanding of humanity is itself a path to communion. Significantly, they both also viewed classical Aeschylean tragedies as a different path to the same end. Hirst's animal parts, preserved in tanks of formaldehyde, may be an exploration of ancient traditions of the zoo-anthropomorphic in art, of the anatomy of sacrifice – bloody or bloodless – and of our relationship to other created creatures. Or might they in part represent a cynical commercial attempt to provoke controversy and to gain publicity by targeting expressions of a faith that will not retaliate? Or will it? In the US Senate in 1989 New York Senator Alphonse D'Amato destroyed as blasphemous and degenerate an image of Andres Serrano's *Piss Christ* (1987) – a photograph of a plastic crucifix suspended in a vat of urine – provoking subsequent restrictions which dangerously approach state censorship on recipients of National Endowment in the Humanities grants. This attack failed to connect with Serrano's artistic engagement with Catholic teachings relating to birth, sexuality and death, which often incorporated bodily fluids, or with his avowed interest in the aesthetic and symbols of the church. Like Bacon and Serrano, Hirst's work displays a recurrent preoccupation with belief, most recently conveyed by his treatment of our misplaced faith in the absolute power of science and the pharmaceutical industry – one of all too few artistic engagements with the relationships between faith and science.

In 1962 Francis Bacon told David Sylvester, in interview:

'I think that man now realizes that he is an accident, that he is a completely futile being, that he has to play out the game without reason. I think that, even when Velásquez was painting, even when Rembrandt was painting, in a peculiar way they were still, whatever their attitude to life, slightly conditioned by certain types of religious possibilities, which man now, you could say, has had completely cancelled out for him. Now, of course, man can only attempt to make something very, very positive by trying to beguile himself for a time by the way he behaves, by prolonging possibly his life by buying a kind of immortality through the doctors. You see, all art has now become completely a game by which man distracts himself; and you may say it has always been like that, but now it's entirely a game. And I think that that is the way things have changed, and what is fascinating now is that it's going to become much more difficult for the artist because he must really deepen the game to be any good at all.'

The nihilism implicit in this vision of life and in a meaningless yet obsessive absorption in the distraction of art may in itself contribute to the compulsion of some deep-thinking artists to keep treating of a faith to which they are unable to subscribe intellectually, but to which the inner fibres of their being nonetheless cry out and resonate.

Lapsed Catholic American feminist artist Kiki Smith has continued to pursue her enquiry into the sacred through her radical and often shocking treatment of traditional Catholic iconographies. Her body sculpture of the flayed figure of the Virgin Mary (1992), her arms nonetheless outstretched in compassion and humility, conflates traditional Christian metaphors of suffering and forgiveness as means of uniting the human and the divine. Loss of his Catholic faith has led her fellow countryman Jeff Koons to challenge its teachings concerning poverty and sexuality, through works such as his celebration of consumerism in his display of vacuum cleaners in the window of New York's Museum of Contemporary Art (1980) and his billboard posters, parodying those of Hollywood films, depicting him and his wife, Hungarian-Italian porn star La Cicciolina ('Little Dumpling'), making love, entitled *Made in Heaven* (1989). Yet more facetiously, those British icons of iconoclasm, Gilbert and George, have recently parodied religious superstition and festive consumerism in their exhibit 'Sonofagod'[4] (2006), in which their hallmark besuited self-portraits form part of a Christmas card-like confection of mawkish stained glass, crosses, ribbon bows and tree baubles.

Send-up or authentic protest at the devaluation of the visual currency of faith?

Artistic intent alone is not the issue. Such works can creatively challenge and stimulate some people of faith, and those of none, and can alienate, offend and – at worst – damage others. Art is, indeed, a powerful medium.

The Scribe Speaks:
Making the St John's Bible

Donald Jackson

When I was a nine-year-old, desire led me to copy ancient scripts and decorated letters. I loved the feel of the pen as it touched the page and the breathtaking effect of coloured ink as its wetness caught the light. Those sensations, which I still experience as I work, are what seem to direct the shapes and colours of my designs and letters. The quill and the brush, not my conscious thinking, make the choice.

The continual process of opening up and accepting what may reveal itself through hand and heart on a crafted page is the closest I have ever come to God.

The German artist Paul Klee, said 'Drawing is like taking a line for a walk.' Imagine dipping a goose-quill pen into ink and taking it on a journey letter by letter, gliding from hairline stroke to fat black, word by word, from beginning to the end of every chapter and verse in the Bible.

As a Lettering Arts student in London at the end of the 1950s (we called ourselves 'scribes' then), I dreamed of writing out and illuminating the Bible. Later, with a living to make, even when I spent most of my time doing calligraphy for others, angels had a way of creeping in unawares whenever I made time to create for myself. But for years after that the idea of creating a modern Bible was only an occasional topic of coffee-break conversation with colleagues. Until, in 1995, I proposed the idea of writing and illuminating the Gospels as a Millennium project to a member of the Benedictine Community of monks at St John's Abbey, Minnesota.

My dream was to make a Gospel Book which recaptured, in its own right, the value of its sacred contents and which truly expressed this as a work of art. It was to be a restatement of faith for the twenty-first century, a clarion call of conviction conceived on the scale of the great Bibles of the twelfth century. Each spread would measure a yard wide and be over two feet high when opened. The idea took root in the Community and before long grew to include the whole Bible – Old and New Testaments with included Apocrypha.

The St John's Bible will have over 1,000 pages of text, interpretive illuminations and highlighted text on 272 folios of calfskin (measuring 31¾ x 24½ inches or 80.6 x 62.2 cm), divided into seven volumes, bound between Welsh oak boards.

Volume I	*Pentateuch*
Volume II	*Historical*
Volume III	*Wisdom Books*
Volume IV	*Psalms*
Volume V	*Prophets*
Volume VI	*Gospels and Acts*
Volume VII	*Letters and Revelation*

The text is laid out in four vertical columns across each spread, fifty-four lines to a column. The writing has taken over six years to complete, starting with four scribes, later joined by two others during years four, five and six.

A Committee of advisers was formed: Old and New Testament scholars, theologians, art historians and artists; for the most part Roman Catholic but with input from other denominations and traditions. From the start they were actively open to the 'present tense'. They chose the NRSV (New Revised Standard Version) translation of the text. Widely used by non-Catholics, including Episcopalian and nonconformist churches, it incorporates up-to-date translations with notes and comparative interpretations and uses formal but inclusive modern language. One of the inspiring aspects of working with the St John's team is their obviously genuine wish to acknowledge and emphasize, where appropriate, the part played by women and the underprivileged in the Bible stories. They encourage an openness to the relevance and the inclusion of imagery found in global contemporary sources, modern science, recent astronomical discoveries and the natural world.

There is encouragement too for my inclusion of decorative elements and details which are obviously drawn from designs of other religious traditions, such as the fragments of a Buddhist cosmic mandala and arabesques inspired by Islamic manuscripts used in the Matthew Frontispiece. These are consciously included as a mark of respect for the beliefs of others. This was not an attitude current in 1501, when a German Benedictine Community commissioned from the scribe John Trithemius what must surely have been the last handwritten and illuminated Bible of its kind to be made for the next five hundred years.

The finished volumes of the St John's Bible contain technical and artistic input from places as far away from our Scriptorium as India, Israel, the US and Europe. Artists from assorted denominations within the Christian faith (including a Greek Orthodox iconographer) have made contributions, as well as Jewish, Islamic and Hindu craftsmen.

While the Committee prepared detailed briefs for each volume, the basic grid for a page layout and a script had to be created. I had a clear sense of what texture I wanted – strong enough when arranged in a two-column format to support powerful illuminations. It had to be rich and intricate enough to sustain the eye over the many pages where the writing stands alone without embellishment.

Deciding on the look of the script is very much a diaphragm-dictated exercise. We all have to have presence of mind but as artists we also have much presence of heart. Heads are useful for weighing up the virtues of this or that option, avoiding spelling mistakes and missed lines. But in the end such judgements are weighed in the heart.

Handwritten European Bibles of the past were written mostly in Latin for an educated and

411

exclusive readership who were familiar with a series of conventionalized abbreviations of commonly used Latin words. These options gave the scribe the freedom to expand or contract lines to help him or her justify the right-hand side of the column. The modern reader is less tolerant of such variations and the NRSV translation itself is extremely rigid in its requirements. The use of a dictionary of approved word-breaks is compulsory. Such constraints place high demands on the skills of both the typesetter and the modern scribe who has to follow his computer-generated copy sheets.

To produce printed copies of the wording that the scribes could follow, my original written 'texture' was imitated using a malleable computer font. Many experiments were made to try and hit a distribution of letters and spacing which would match the stride and rhythm of a handwritten model. Once the parameters were settled (they have been subtly amended several times since) the text was set and

Detail from Ecclesiastes Incipit. The presence of God is represented by a vertical rainbow baton of certainty in a whirling cosmos inspired by images taken from the Hubble Space Telescope. Scattered shapes of silver, Wisdom's (female) presence and the gold lines of a medieval astronomical diagram define order in an apparently disordered universe.

ROED Bathsheba בת שבע
DAVID דוד
RAHAB רחב
JESSE ישי
BOAZ בעז
SALMON שלמון
NAHSHON נחשון
AMINADAB עמינדב
ARAM רם

Naamah נעמה JOTHAM יותם
REHOBOAM רחבעם REKALIAH רכליה
Pharoah's Daughter בת פרעה UZZIAH עזיהו
JORAM יהורם
Azubah עזובה
JEHOSHAPHAT יהושפט
ASAPH אסף

Sarah שרה
ABRAHAM אברהם
Hagar *mother of ISHMAEL* הגר

412

Detail from Matthew Frontispiece. Gilded sections of the DNA double helix diagram accent the names of the men and women in the genealogy of Christ to symbolize the oneness of all God's creatures. Fragments of a Buddhist Mandala and a single name in Arabic (Ishmael son of Hagar) acknowledge the spiritual paths of those who are not Christian.

'managed' by computer from a disc provided by the copyright holders. It was 'flowed' from page to page within the column grid and around spaces chosen and shaped to receive the interpretive illuminations and highlighted quotations.

The subjects chosen for illumination by the St John's Committee of advisers reflect the theological concerns of a modern world. They created a schema setting out their priorities: which texts should be highlighted and which should have interpretive illuminations or incidental decorative embellishment.

In addition, I usually choose to include flora and fauna and insects from local woods and prairies. This serves to root the St John's Bible in its physical home, surrounded as it is by the lakes and prairies of Minnesota, and to emphasize the wonders of

God's works in every detail of the natural world around us. It is also quite useful to have a lovely butterfly 'alight' on the margin as a pause for the eye after a series of undecorated pages.

Briefings from the Committee can be just three paragraphs long or extend to a five-page 'discussion paper' on a quarter-page illumination. I read these one by one, along with the appropriate Bible sections and start highlighting what I feel are key 'action' statements. Between these briefings and my own reading of the Bible I am usually able to put my finger on a moment and on a series of visual elements that can help focus on the theological nub of a chosen passage.

Where do I get ideas/inspiration? My old teacher's advice was always to 'put the pen in the ink and start making marks'. So I usually start sketching with a large brush; I 'put it in the ink' and begin. From these marks will grow a feeling for the visual mood of the piece and its elemental themes. Into these I weave details which creep out of the woodwork. References can be from such places as my beloved 1938 edition of Arthur Mee's Children's

Encyclopedia or pictures of the unfolding universe downloaded from the Hubble Telescope. Whatever I light upon, I hope the results allow space for the reader to bring to my marks the spark of a desire to seek their own interpretations.

The artist sees with a magpie's eye and furnishes his 'nest' with a collection of baubles taken from his own visual experiences. He combines and recombines them to see what will happen next with all the excitement of a child playing with coloured building blocks or turning over stones in a rock pool. I suspect this was just as true of an eighth-century scribe at Lindisfarne when he first saw an enamelled Celtic brooch or marvelled at an intricately woven prayer mat brought back from the Middle East.

Today, I can walk into a museum and look at Assyrian temple carvings from Nineveh or take photographs of Philistine, Greek and Roman artefacts. I can manipulate these on a computer screen to recreate the four-headed creatures Ezekiel saw in his Vision at Chebar. So, I can base my designs on actual 'graven images', of the kind he could well have seen guarding the Temple doors of the oppressors of his people.

On the Internet I can source images of fractals that modern science suggests exist as structured order, even within an apparently disordered and formless void. At the click of a mouse I can find images of the earliest surviving rock paintings made by our ancestors, and use them to represent the symbolic daily steps of the Genesis creation story. Or call up magnified details of the streptococci bacteria and the AIDS virus to symbolize the horrors of plague and pestilence. The magpie's cup runneth over!

There is a downside to our instant access to information and the effect of modern communication on a project like the St John's Bible. A high media profile can create an excruciatingly

413

LEFT: Detail from Daniel's vision. The ten-horned monster in Daniel's vision spews out diagramatic images of intestines, bacteria and viruses inspired by scientific photographs.

RIGHT: Detail from Life in Paradise. Aboriginal rock paintings from Australia and the figure of a huntress painted on the wall of an African cave thousands of years ago inhabit a world of plenteous beauty. But the coral snake, locusts and firebugs hint at the plagues and pestilence that come after the fall of Adam and Eve.

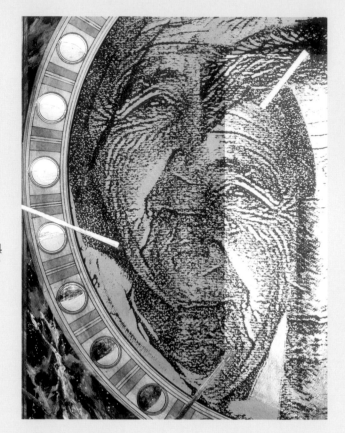

on the altar in a fanfare of colour and conviction.

During Easter Week in 2001 pages including scenes of the nativity, the raising of Lazarus and Pentecost with examples of paintings of natural historical elements were on display in St John's Abbey Church. The responses of different people were largely what one might expect. Some adored the butterflies; others were moved by what they saw in the interpretive work (some saw things I had no idea were there, but of course are); and all were touched and fascinated by the line after line of handwritten letters on the vellum pages. It was the first time I had seen these pages presented in an exhibition context. I felt my personal relationship with the work start to shift as I saw the pages displayed and selected pages were read by the Abbott. But when the crucifixion page was placed on the altar facing the congregation of over two thousand people – something like my original dream, I now realize – we caught our breath as the lights hit the gilded page and for that moment we were as one. That too was a response which one might well have expected; indeed it was planned and hoped for.

But there was also an experience that I had not foreseen. While the Abbot talked passionately about the Project to the congregation, the pages seemed to be speaking to us too. During that ceremony, for the first time, I saw the book begin to function – to become a reason in itself. The pages started to act in unforeseen ways. As our eyes and attention drifted between the gilded letters and images and the words spoken by the priest, the sacred texts seemed to be speaking for themselves as part of a duet, saying: 'The words in this book are those upon which our faith rests.' I felt then that we had indeed begun to create a Bible for the twenty-first century that did express the value of its sacred contents. It drew us to the words and to each other. The dream had become a reality.

difficult climate of expectation in which to create artwork; the public unveiling of the first page in the full glare of publicity at the Minneapolis Institute of Art was advertised weeks in advance of my first sketch design. So, when my hand is finally poised to make marks on an exquisitely prepared piece of vellum, I have a lot of invisible spectators leaning over my shoulder. That kind of pressure is always there, and it is a constant challenge to keep one's nerve and to create naturally and intuitively when every instinct is telling me to freeze. One of the many contradictions in an endeavour of this kind is that although we aim to create something which we mean to share with others, we make it first, in an intensely private way, for ourselves. Searching for images, staying open and ready to catch sparks of insight as they fly, is a lonely, selfish process. Even after that, it is only when the viewer is willing to bring something from within themselves that the work really begins to come alive.

From the start I had envisaged that each volume would be big – a statement of faith in itself – with a ceremonial function in which I saw all seven of them carried aloft by the monks down the length of St John's Abbey Church and placed, one by one, open

Detail from Wisdom Woman. The mirrored reflections of the face of Wisdom Woman are encircled by the waxing and waning shapes of the moon during her 28-day cycle and framed by Hubble Space Telescope images of the birth of stars. The silver batons move across the page representing Wisdom's (female) presence. They remind us of the responsibility we have to make wise choices throughout our uncertain lives.

Quo Vadis?

Where do we go from here?

Many pre-existing vocabularies have recently been called back into service both in the conception of contemporary art for Christian contexts and in the creation of spiritually orientated art of a non-religious character.

Reinterpreting Traditional Christian Art Forms

'Billy Childish' (William Hamper, UK) takes the modern icon as his vehicle, creating multi-media collages of cultural references. Nigerian-born sculptor Sokari Douglas Camp, who is based in south-east London and who has exhibited as far afield as New Zealand, draws deeply on her African roots in producing works such as her *Eleventh Commandment*, which are replete with care for the world and engagement with current affairs. Iain McKillop often reinterprets the figures and forms of medieval sculpture in his carefully worked paintings (such as that in Gloucester Cathedral, UK). Madrid-based Realist Antonio López Garcia perpetuates the Iberian vernacular of Goya and Picasso, exploring the tragedy and inevitability of mortal decay in works such as *Dead Dog*, and an elegaic Catholicism in some of his portraits of girls in their First Communion finery. Leading calligrapher Donald Jackson and his latter-day scriptorium in Wales perpetuate the craftsmanship, contemplation and artistry of the scribe and illuminator, painting with words and collaborating on the first handmade and illuminated copy of the Bible to post-date the advent of movable type in the mid-fifteenth century – the St John's Bible.

The Stations of the Cross, a liturgical ritual first introduced in Rome in the early eighth century – one of the most frequently encountered subjects for contemporary ecclesiastical artistic commissions – receive a new treatment at the hands of American artist Tom Faulkner in New York, with mundane everyday objects substituting for the usual figures. *Station two: Jesus Takes up his Cross* takes the form of a harshly lit dining table set with plates bearing bones in rusty mantraps, of which the artist comments:

> 'At what moment are we called to take up our cross in testimony to our faith?... The moment could be at home around the breakfast table when a parent is expressing prejudice against a particular ethnic group... Does a child's faith require a challenge to the parent when the child feels an injustice is being uttered? At what cost to the child? At what cost to the parent? The issue rarely is in not knowing Jesus' teachings, but rather in not having the courage to act upon those teachings.'

Station Four: Jesus meets his Afflicted Mother comprises cameras on tripods with children's books and snapshots scattered at their feet, of which Faulkner says:

> '... books mothers know well from bedtime reading which provide for a quiet bonding... On his way to crucifixion Jesus passed his beloved mother standing in the crowd. He must have seen a well of sadness in her eyes which no theology could comfort. Here was simply a mother and child, like so many throughout the ensuing centuries, joined together in inexpressible grief. No more stories to be told. No more joyous memories to be gathered and stored. No more images to be captured by the camera of the eye and treasured. It was over, and sorrow overwhelmed two hearts and all the universe.'[1]

This is a rather more accessible and humane interpretation than that of Mel Gibson's film *The Passion of the Christ*, although the cameras do introduce an element of voyeurism and of tension between the private and public in ministry and witness.

Other traditional skills such as textiles are once more being used to beautify churches. Vestment design is attracting renewed attention, along with other liturgical textiles such as the *Mildmay Altarcloth*, woven at the artistic community/college of West Dean, Sussex, for Chelmsford Cathedral, UK, and based upon a film-strip-like series of shots of landscapes and sites associated with its seventh-century founder, the Northumbrian St Cedd.

Artists are again becoming a little less reserved in sharing insights into their own spiritual life. Canadian painter Agnes Martin immerses herself in an ancient artistic asceticism in order to achieve an ultimate unity and horizontal infinity that transcends the material world, and which she characterizes as pure praise. Her paintings often comprise fields of white dissected by grids of fine lines, which offer a Zen-like calmness. Brice Morden (US) is supremely serious in his approach to artistic responsibility and its priestly function, insisting that 'he works to keep man's spirit alive' and the 'Painters are among the priests... worker priests of the cult of man – searching to understand but never to know.' The Welsh artist Margaret Neve applies herself to the labour of meditation – her work becoming an opus dei. The pointillism of her *Trees of Gold* (1989), with its benign vision of a blessed creation, recalls the stippled rosaries of dots, each one a prayer, on the incipit pages of the Lindisfarne Gospels and the attentive lyricism of Samuel Palmer's visionary vale. American artist Rebecca Purdum perpetuates the abstract Orphism of Delaunay in her atmospheric evocations of the 'wonderment' that she experiences in the face of the energy of New York, seen in works such as *N.Y.C. 264* (1989). Painting with her hands, to ensure absolute connection and immediacy, she writes, 'You become the paint, you become the form, you become the structure' – the artist's very self becomes living art, prayer and praise. British artist Maggi Hambling uses a similar language to express her wonder at God's gifts, expressed through abstract landscapes of light and colour that perpetuate the inspiration shared by Winifred Nicholson and the Orphists. Light and colour also pervade the abstract works of Chicago-born and based Robert Natkin, although he uses them to convey the mystery of what he terms the 'abyss', a holy otherness exemplified in *God's Way* (1988-90) – no black abyss of despair but one of sublime light to which we can surrender ourselves with complete confidence.

Faith and the Moving Image

In our multi-media age the role of the moving image, on cinema screen, TV screen or computer screen, is a powerful mode of communication. The oral, the aural and the visual are united in an inextricable symbiosis, engaging much of our sensory perception simultaneously. This has always been true of much sacred art: medieval sculptures came to life to the flickering light of candles, the dramatic performance of the liturgy and the chanting of its rhythms, and the painted ceilings and soaring altarpieces of the Baroque vibrated to the music of Handel and Mozart, their architecture becoming liquid music. Thus contemporary film, theatre and digitization make their own distinctive artistic contribution. Some explore overtly Christian subject matter, such as Hollywood's blockbuster biblical epics of the 1940s to 1960s, including *The Greatest Story Ever Told* and *The Robe*. The film that has won the greatest critical acclaim for having most faithfully encapsulated the Gospel teachings is Pier Paolo Passolini's *The Gospel According to St Matthew* (1964), made with the support of the Catholic Church. And yet, this complex neo-Realist poet-film maker was also responsible for the disturbing *Salò* (1975), based on *120 Days of Sodom* by the Marquis de Sade and still voted *Time Out*'s most controversial film of all time – a latter day Caravaggio.

Other notable contributions to the genre of Christian subject matter in film include: Franco Zeffirelli's *Brother Sun, Sister Moon* (1972), a lyrical celebration of the origins of the Franciscans and the Poor Clares; the film versions of the rock operas *Jesus Christ Superstar* (1973) by Andrew Lloyd Webber and Tim Rice, directed by Norman Jewson, and *Godspell* (1973) by Peggy Gordon and Stephen Schwartz, directed by David Greene, which gave a happy hippy spin to Christ's teachings; Derek Jarman's homo-erotic *Sebastiane* (1976); Martin Scorsese's controversial *The Last Temptation of Christ* (1988); and Mel Gibson's *The Passion of the Christ* (2004) which, like the wooden crucifixes of late medieval Spanish and German art, employed graphic depiction of torture and suffering to stimulate an emotive, sympathetic response in the viewer in an active call to repentance. And yet, as with modern art, works of a non-religious character can offer the greatest scope for spiritual reflection and empathetic insight into the mystery of being. Alfonso Cuarón's *Children of Men* (2006), for example, based on the P. D. James novel of the same name, takes an apocalyptic prophecy and turns it into a harrowing and yet ultimately optimistic meditation on the underlying fears, tensions and intolerances of contemporary society and the sustaining nature of love and hope. The focus and rallying point of these, as in much traditional Christian art and theology, remains the mother and child. At one pivotal point in the mayhem of destruction and human conflict all the protagonists, trapped in a situation over which they appear to have no control, pause in their trajectory of violence and self-destruction to acknowledge the inherent sacrality of life, in the form of the only new babe born to their expiring race, only to return immediately to its annihilation. What more searingly poignant contemporary evocation could there be of the Christian expression of the enduring need of a vulnerable sacrificial portal through which to enter into true reality, and of our continual quest to find it and our refusal to pass through it in the face of our own self-preoccupation?

Other directors whose films have dealt directly or obliquely with themes of faith include Eric Rohmer, Robert Bresson and Krzysztof Kielowski. In *Breaking the Waves* (1996), director Lars van Trier presents a courageous and heart-searing treatment of the tragic psychological and physical consequences that can be provoked by a rigid, repressive and judgemental patriarchal religiosity. It charts the process by which a young girl with learning difficulties, raised in the orbit of the strict Scottish Free Church in the Outer Hebrides, is impelled towards de facto self-sacrifice through guilt at her own innocent sexuality. The film explores her desire to appease a punitive God with her own death in order to save the life of her husband, with whom she has experienced physical union and delight, for which she has been led to believe they are being punished.

During recent decades video-installation artists have fused aspects of the painter's and film-maker's skills and perceptions to form a vibrant new art form. Northern Irish video artist Willie Doherty, for example, uses the medium to great effect to acquaint the viewer with the personal insecurity and anxiety generated by Ulster's religious and political doctrinal differences in his *The Only Good One is a Dead One* (1993), with its dual projections of surveillance cameras tracking a city street and a country road at night, and the accompanying Irish voice alternating between the viewpoints of aggressor and victim.

American Bill Viola, a lapsed Protestant, draws more positively upon the referential iconographic languages of several world faiths in his video explorations of human condition and spiritual journey.

Moving Passions: a personal response to Bill Viola's 'The Passions'

As contemporary art evokes personal experience and response, it seems appropriate to consider the work of leading video-installation artist, Bill Viola, through my own interaction with one of his major exhibits that has particular resonance for those drawn to art as a means of accessing the inner life of the spirit.

In an exhibition entitled 'The Passions', which was conceived during a fellowship at the J. Paul Getty Museum in Los Angeles and which was exhibited there and subsequently shown at the National Gallery, London, in 2003–2004, Viola presented a passage from an ongoing chronicle of self-discovery, stimulated at this stage by the loss of a parent and the birth of a child. It invites visitors to observe, to empathize and to participate: the audience becomes implicated in the work. It interacts with us through the very act of watching and we observe ourselves as assiduously as in a medieval *speculum* (moral mirror), reflected in the slowly evolving video-canvases of human experience. The collective experience of the human journey is – despite its varied forms and the curious uniqueness of those very events and emotions that are often experienced by us all – something that can speak across divides of belief: it is our common language.

On entering the exhibition *The Greeting* greets us – a monumental composition on large screen, recalling Pontormo and the stage sets of Renaissance and Baroque religious paintings. Three women come together, two heavy with child, the third the midwife delivering their encounter. One prospective mother is young and fair, serene and complacent in anticipation. The other is as old as time, of middle years, anxious, aware… weary. She feels excluded by the others' joyous greeting of one another, their sharing of a secret thing, until embraced by their expectant conspiracy, invited to participate, to play her part. The 'midwife' is revealed as prophetess. Older than

Bill Viola, one half of a video and sound diptych *The Crossing*, in which a figure is purified by immersion in water and fire, an ancient and enduring theme of many religions, from the installation *The Passions*, California, 2003.

the others she possesses an eternal youth born of hope – a hope soon to be fulfilled. Strange that, seen beside the vigour of youth, middle age seems older than the hills while the newly old, those who have crossed the Rubicon into the next 'age of man' and are content within their skins, seem young. To those versed in Christian iconography and art, this is the Visitation: the encounter between the Virgin-mother who brings life to the divine and her pregnant older kinswomen, Elizabeth, worn out beyond hope by the cares of this world but preparing the way for God to know what it is to be human. The prophetess, Anna, confirms and affirms them both and is, herself, delivered of the pregnancy of prophecy and fulfilled.

There follows a room that Viola has filled with icons drawn from cultural points of reference, all of meaning on his journey: a diptych from the fifteenth-century Flemish workshop of Dirk Bouts depicting the Mater Dolorosa and Christ crowned with thorns; a placid, fathomless mask from the Japanese Noh theatre; Bellini's painting *Dead Christ Supported by Angels*; a Japanese calligraphic ink sketch of the Buddhist sage Daruma; an Umbrian Virgin and Child and Man of Sorrows; a fiercesome Japanese wooden effigy of Fudo Myo-O (Buddhist defender and destroyer of ignorance and illusion); and Bosch's painting *Christ Mocked*. Viola's self-aware accompanying captions give vivid glimpses of the bearing of such pieces, and the ideologies they convey, upon his work.

The passivity of the Noh mask is transformed into a meditation on silence and solitude in Viola's five-screen predella *Catherine's Room*, which finds many parallels in *St Catherine of Siena Praying* by Andrea di Bartolo (1393). In it the same mature female figure performs ritual daily tasks – meditative exercise, sewing, study, preparation for sleep (or death) – within sparse monastic interiors, alike yet differently arranged, the foliage of the bough seen through the window and the light it admits changing with the seasons and the hours. A meditation on the ages, of humankind and of the world, it speaks of timelessness, of constructive internalization of experience, of the sustenance of the inner life and of opus dei (what Viola describes as 'the potential sanctity of ordinary tasks performed mindfully'). Viola, in the filmed interview shown at the exhibition's entrance / exit, reveals this as, in part, a tribute to the nun, the solitary, and to woman's ability to dwell within herself. Blessed is the woman 'who sees visions, who takes comfort within herself, who finds companionship in an empty room' – a tribute to Mother Julian and her like, and, potentially, to every woman.

One of Viola's captions contains a reference to an Islamic mystical Sufi concept likening the human soul to a drop of water within a bowl (the body). The bowl floats within a sea and gradually takes on more water (experience, empathy, wisdom) until it merges harmoniously with the whole: the bowl sinks, no longer necessary. Such notions are among those explored in several of Viola's works. *Emergence* takes as its historic visual point of departure a Renaissance painting, Masolino's *Deposition of Christ*, but transforms the entombment into a simultaneous image of resurrection as the pale body of the young man rises miraculously from the well / tomb with the life-giving waters that rush from it, the two attendant figures serving as mourners and as midwives to his rebirth. *Surrender* and *Silent Mountain* explore the endurance of extreme emotional pain. In the former the mirrored images of man and woman slowly dip their heads into the waters of their emotions and rise in pain, their figures gradually distorting into amorphous shapes reminiscent of Munch's *The Scream*. In *Silent Mountain* a diptych depicts the explosion of pent-up anger and anguish, the tortured figures of male and female actors writhing to release themselves and transcend the constraint of self, as Michelangelo's *Slaves* struggle to escape the marble of their substance. Here too we see the terrifying figure of Fudo Myo-O, seeking to cross the pain threshold of ignorance and illusion to free enlightenment and self-knowledge – 'to enter your own house you must break down the door'. The collective pain and trauma of the human condition is reflected back at us here, but the Sufi mystic's harmony has yet to be achieved. Viola's own recent experiences of life – of childbirth and the death of parents – has brought him so far on his journey into empathy, but joy needs to reassert itself within the equation more. Harmony is yet to come.

In *Dolorosa* Viola gives us insight into the devotional imagery of artists such as Dirk Bouts. Two slender video screens summon up the medieval diptych or portable altar. On one wing a female bust weeps gentle, free-flowing tears… no furrowed anguish, just the nobility of knowing acceptance and compassion. On the other a young man suffers quietly, heroically, questioning but embracing his lot. Almost imperceptibly the nuances of feeling and understanding pass across their visages and are reflected in our own. This tells us something about devotional art. We might spend as much as ten minutes gazing on a favourite artwork. For those who conducted their

421

daily prayer across the years, in times of tedium and in extremis, before such images their depth of assimilation and association would have altered over time. This is not only a flat mirror of human emotion but a medieval *speculum* in which we see ourselves, the image changing in response to our own shifts in feeling and perception.

The Crossing, a large video and sound installation, carries two opposing, complementary images on either side. A human figure advances toward the viewer and is engulfed, on one side by a deluge of water and on the other by tongues of flame, until it disappears and all is calm and emptiness. The figure raises his arms during the process to welcome his 'self-annihilation'. As in so many religions the purifying elements are used to symbolise death and renewal. Viola's captions and film interview reveal that, for him, the annihilation of self is 'a necessary means to transcendence and liberation'. Yet in his caption to the Buddhist image of Daruma he notes that the line between purification and annihilation is a razor-edge. Does achieving the goals of inner knowledge, of true empathy and integration with humanity and the Divine of necessity entail complete destruction of the self? Many religions have told us so. Is that then all there is – an endless sea in which we are all anonymous drops of essence and within which only our shared experience, tempered by suffering, qualifies us for inclusion? At one level it is a reassuring image and perhaps the only way in which our limited vision can conceive of true harmony. And yet, the sheer diversity of creation, the infinite variation on the finite surely betrays an artist's hand. Does a parent require children who are all clones of one another, created in self-image, in order to love them, or do their individual characters, limitations and potential render them pleasing in a parent's sight? The other aspect of this philosophy that holds me back is the innocent arrogance that proclaims that self-knowledge, self-purification, self-annihilation, self-transcendence is the key. However much I try I know that I cannot achieve it by and of myself, nor just by pooling my endeavour with that of the rest. For the spark of divinity that I feel lies within me, within us all, needs to respond to the spark of humanity in the Divine. It is that empathy that sustains me. God made human, joining us in our quest, nurturing us in it, forgiving us if we never achieve transcendental heights of self-abnegation – performing that miracle on our behalf.

The work that speaks to me most of all, within this remarkable exhibit / experience, is *Observance* – another plasma screen of Renaissance altarpiece proportions. A ragged queue of figures gradually advances to its head, like a communion line at the Christian services we attend. They advance in trepidation, for they know what lies ahead, and are reluctant but compelled to look upon it. One by one they come to gaze upon something, someone, who lies before the viewer's feet. Each in their own unique and personal way exhibits a shared response: intense sorrow, profound compassion and empathy, regret, repentance, witness. They share their collective grief, seek to comfort one another and are careful of each other's needs, yet each one is made to confront their own individual response on their own behalf. I gaze on it and weep – the unbidden, unforced, warm round tears that course naturally like water from a spring down the cheek and onto the breast. No shame in them, no anguish, no comfort. Just the only response possible, freely acknowledging love freely given and received, no matter what the cost. The work assumes an even greater intensity when one recalls that it was made in 2002, shortly after the Twin Towers were destroyed by acts of terrorism on September 11, 2001.

The experience has been an intensely personal one, and yet a collective, communal act. The silhouetted forms of others drift before the screens or can be sensed around you, each with their own space but becoming part of the very sensation of participating. In the darkness we've seen ourselves reflected and transformed, explored our place within the whole. My response is shaped by my Christian culture; other people's will be moulded by their cultural traditions – or their reaction against them. Yet somewhere herein lies the essence of faith. Take formal religions and religiosity out of the frame and the canvas still remains. 'Nothing' is not what confronts us, but 'Everything'.

423

Christianity and Contemporary Art in North America: The CIVA Case Study

Dr James Romaine

In 2004, Christians in the Visual Arts (CIVA)[1] celebrated its silver anniversary. That any artist-organized association should demonstrate such longevity is surprising; the fact that CIVA simultaneously continues to evolve in response to the developing needs of its artists and has had a documented impact on how Christianity and the visual arts are reconnecting is laudable. Although it is only one part of a much larger tapestry that is the emergent conversation between Christianity and the visual arts, the circumstances out of which CIVA originated and the issues that it has attempted to address make it a useful case study of an evolving, even flourishing, relationship.

A quarter of a century ago, a 'contemporary Christian artist' was regarded by many, in both Christian and artistic circles, to be a contradiction in terms. The flame of a two-thousand-year-old history of Christianity and the visual arts had, at least in America, been nearly extinguished. Up against some of the most iconophobic constituents of the Protestant tradition, overt religious art in America never gained a stronghold. Excluding folk and pietistic traditions of both Protestant and Roman Catholic varieties in which religious imagery has flourished, spiritual sentiment in American fine art has more often found non-overtly religious forms such as allegorical landscapes. With such shallow roots, any Christian presence in American fine arts struggled to withstand the secularizing efforts of Modernist critics such as Clement Greenberg. The visual silence of the Rothko Chapel (which opened in 1971) might have been the final exhalation of Christianity in American art.

As CIVA was founded, in 1979, Christians intent on making art that plainly reflected their faith were often anathemas of two worlds. They were likely to feel marginalized within their religious communities because of their artistic inclination. Tim Rollins, one of CIVA's most accomplished artists, recalled his experience growing up in a Baptist church in Maine saying, 'It was all right to sing, to dance a little, to play instruments, but the idea of making art, to paint an object and put it on the wall… was considered seriously close to idolatry. If you wanted to be an artist where I grew up, your spirituality was suspect, your personality was suspect, your mentality was suspect, and your sexuality was suspect.' At the same time, under the reign of formalism and Marxism, the art world has, at least officially, expunged content, especially religious content. Rosalind Krauss, a student of Greenberg's, wrote in 1985, '… given the absolute rift that had opened between the sacred and the secular… [religious emotion] is something that is inadmissible in the twentieth [century], so that by now we find it indescribably embarrassing to mention art and spirit in the same sentence'.

Against this historical backdrop, CIVA originated out of an experiment born of Eugene Johnson's curiosity as to whether there were other Christians in North America working as professional artists. As such, CIVA is and has been, primarily, a community of artists, geographically dispersed but united by common faith and artistic passions. Replacing their sense of isolation with the joy of fellowship, CIVA has developed as a network for artists to exchange encouragement, wisdom, resources (including trading works of art), and, most of all, friendships.

Today CIVA is a dynamic organization of some

Creation (after Haydn), by American artist Tim Rollins, 2005.

1,500 members, concentrated in the United States and Canada. This is the achievement of a devoted collaboration of artists of faith and vision.[2] Their art spans the aesthetic spectrum of contemporary art from realist and figural painting through abstract and conceptual installations to digital media. Some of their art is overtly religious and much of it is not. These artists recognize and celebrate their connection to a two-thousand-year tradition of faith realized in visual form that is, in the process of their working, creatively renewing itself into the present tense, and gives their art both historical context and present purpose.

Although the history of Christianity and the visual arts remains a potent resource for many CIVA artists, having contemporary colleagues and mentors is necessary as well. CIVA has functioned as a vibrant arena in which artists, across boundaries of age, artistic style, professional achievement and religious denomination, have been able to dialectically engage, with generosity and absence of rivalry or pretence, in exploring how their faith and creativity interrelate. CIVA's bold refusal to be ashamed of joining 'Christianity' and 'the visual arts' has given numerous Christians a mandate to integrate their faith and creativity in fulfillment of their spiritual callings and professional vocations, and a model for how to do so.

CIVA has also been marked by an ecumenical inclusivity that models, both for other Christians and for the world beyond the church, a spirit of Christian love. At a time when religion is as often a political weapon of division and violence, CIVA demonstrates what can happen when Christians build on a recognition that what they have in common (the love of the Father, the grace of Christ, and the fellowship of the Holy Spirit)[3] is more powerful than their differences.

CIVA is a movement as much as an organization. In what it has encouraged to be accomplished, CIVA has participated in a quiet, and for the most part critically overlooked, renaissance of art inspired by Christianity. Founded as a network of like-minded artists, mostly at Christian colleges and universities, CIVA's impact has resulted from the fact that it has consciously looked outside of itself, to both the church and the art world. From its inception, CIVA has aimed 'to foster intelligent understanding, a spirit of trust, and cooperation between those involved in the visual arts, the church, and society at large'. Through a worldwide community of scholars, patrons, and artists which it has encouraged, CIVA has contributed to the creation of a growing catalogue of resources, including books, journals, institutions, and local organizations that are available to artists of faith in their spiritual and creative journeys. In nurturing a community that encourages artists to pursue their own visions, CIVA has spawned developments that extend well beyond its own direct activities. Today there are countless local groups, many of them church supported, for artists of faith. Buttressed by their CIVA community, artists of faith have gone with greater confidence and competence into their religious and artistic communities.

CIVA has endeavoured to build bridges of mutual appreciation and acceptance between artists and their churches. Although artists, often nonconformists by temperament, may be wary of institutional authorities and dogmas, CIVA has always urged them to actively and gracefully participate in local churches and faith communities since artists, like all Christians, need theological instruction and validation. CIVA has encouraged artists not only to be engaged in their local churches to satisfy their own interests and needs, but also to look for particular roles of service in which they can participate in the church as 'the body of Christ'. Historically, artists have served the church in at least two ways. Whether they are placed in the sanctuary, gallery or home, works of art have often been aids for collective worship and private spiritual devotion. These works can bring new vitality to historic beliefs by translating them into the modern terms of present experience. Furthermore, because of its potential to transcend religious differences as it touches the mystery and meaning of our faith, art (when it is not being employed as a subject of division) has been a means of spiritual reconciliation, both within the church and between the church and the world.

CIVA's impact is evidenced in the amazing developments in the attitudes of an increasing number of American Christians toward the visual arts. Although the church in America has often been slower to embrace its own visual art history than artists who have no personal faith connection to Christianity, churches are increasingly recognizing the value of the visual arts to their purposes and presence in a visual media-oriented culture. There are signs everywhere, in Orthodox, Roman Catholic and Protestant denominations, of a revived appreciation of the value of creative expression, including the visual arts, within the personal and corporate faith experience. The hunger of contemporary Christians for visual arts that address their faith experience is reflected in the recent proliferation of church commissions, galleries and sponsored arts groups.

CIVA has also remained committed to engaging the discourse of the art world and challenging it to practise greater intellectual and creative open-mindedness. Partly as a result of CIVA's presence, the art world has demonstrated a greater interest in, not just tolerance of, but absorption with, Christianity-inspired art. A growing number of prominent American artists (by birth or residence) have, in only the past quarter century, made work that intentionally and considerately employs Judeo-Christian imagery, or was created for explicitly religious contexts.[4] Given the persistence in this country of the aforementioned suspicion of religious imagery, there have rarely, if ever, been so many prestigious artists using such imagery at any other comparable moment in the history of the United States.

Although we may be part of one of the most dynamic periods in the history of Christianity and the visual arts in North America, there is yet-to-be-realized potential. The two spheres might be compared to old friends once again re-acquainting themselves. There is the familiarity of shared past experiences, not all of them happy memories, and a level of scepticism. As brokers of this reunion, there is a vital need for artists of faith to know and embrace their own history. At least in the United States, there is a culture of amnesia in which the past is so often regarded as something to be discarded or, at a minimum, revised. The history of visual arts serves as a two-thousand-year tangible record of what Sandra Bowden, President of CIVA's board of directors from 1993 to the present, calls 'evidence that faith was alive in our times'. This begs the question, 'What realization of faith will the future see in the art of our times?'

Working within an expanding intersection between worlds of art and faith, a generation of artists is maturing.[5] For these artists, in contrast to artists of faith even one generation before, the question of whether one could be both a Christian and a visual artist has not been, or need not have been, a concern. Many of these artists refuse the term 'Christian artists', which they perceive as ghettoizing. This is not a rejection of their inheritance from the history of Christianity and art but rather signals a new period in that history, one in which artists of faith are, once again, no longer practising on the margins of the cultural plaza. As the art they create begins the next chapter in the history of Christianity and art, there is reason to expect that some of this tradition's brightest moments still lie in the future.

'Temporal' by Allison Luce, 2005, a hollow, handbuilt stoneware sculpture based upon the concept of clay as a metaphor for the body. It is part of a larger body of work entitled *Interminable Engagement*, a series about the ephemeral nature of our existence and the belief in the promise of eternal life. This piece is about a pre-occupation with our earthly lives in contrast with a concern for the eternal.

32

Some Concluding Thoughts

Modern art has demonstrated overtly what has been implicit all along: that everything that is open to human experience has the potential ability to speak of faith – and a corresponding inability to encapsulate it. Christian art is no longer a defined territory, delimited by the use of established symbol and narrative, but has transcended limitation and can be shared with and borrowed from those of other beliefs – and none – united in a shared quest for the exploration of the inter-relationship of the spiritual and the physical. Art has been opened up in new ways to the interplay of emotive, meditative, experiential and intellectual responses.

Can art now indeed provide a Utopian neutral ground for communication that does not need to take account of different backgrounds of faith, ethnicity and upbringing as a route to communion with one another and to union with the divine? And if so, is this multi-lane superhighway to infinity the only road? Or might the myriad highways and byways, which can help the individual to arrive there via an exploration of cultural landscapes that have been created over the centuries and that are steeped in varied local traditions, form an equally valid route?

There is certainly plenty of good art being produced in the traditional vocabularies of various faiths. There is also a lot of very poor imagery being generated, often of a figurative or symbolic nature. This has always been the case. For every outstanding example of Limoges enamelwork, of carved statuary, of paintings of the Madonna and Child, and of prints of biblical themes there are myriads of comparatively 'mechanical' counterparts, churned out to satisfy the needs of popular piety. They are none the less valid for that, for as American Professor David Morgan has said in his work on visual piety, 'the act of looking itself contributes to religious formation and, indeed, constitutes a powerful practice of belief'. A telling example of this for Morgan is the sincere devotional response of many believers in the American Mid-west to what are now considered rather sugary portraits of Christ and illustrations of Gospel episodes by one of the best known of early twentieth-century American artists, Warner Sallman (1892–1968). Born in Chicago, Sallmann was influenced by the work of Holman Hunt and other Victorian artists; his *Christ at the Heart's Door* is blatantly indebted to Hunt's *Light of the World*. In 1924, while working as a magazine illustrator and advertisement designer, he produced a charcoal sketch of the head of Christ which became so popular that, when he worked it up in oils, it was distributed by the Salvation Army and YMCA to servicemen en route to the front in the Second World War. The face portrayed is a sensitive and ascetic one, full of compassion, and doubtless offered tremendous solace to many; but it presents the archetypal Western fair-skinned, blond haired, bearded image of the Saviour which might enable some groups of people to identify with him more readily than others. After the war, groups in Oklahoma and Indiana conducted campaigns to distribute the image: one Lutheran organizer in Illinois said that there ought to be 'card-carrying Christians' to counter the effect of 'card-carrying Communists'. In 1994 Sallmann was pronounced by *The New York Times* to be 'the best-known artist of the century'.

Such popular images can serve to reinforce stereotypes and devalue the currency aesthetically, however, and in modern times much serious 'high art' has accordingly eschewed such figurative expressions, while the so-called 'secular age' has rendered faith-specific art unfashionable. There are green shoots of revival pushing their way through the concrete towards the light, however, leading some to speak optimistically of a post-secular era. Experimentation with overtly religious or spiritually orientated art is on the rise, and yet some of the most meaningful and moving contemporary works to sound a note of resonance among Christians are by no means so obvious. Perhaps we are, at last, getting better at seeing God in everything, penetrating to a more profound Christianity. Christian art – or rather art that speaks to Christians – no longer has to be 'Christian' in content, if indeed it ever has been.

It is increasingly trendy to opine that art galleries are the new cathedrals – and art and film the new modes of communion. As early as 1804 Goethe observed that 'art has consolidated its status as an independent cult, sometimes more flourishing than the churches themselves and Christian theology'. But can the 'cathedral of art' really become a non-faith or philosophy-specific meeting place of peoples that helps to connect them with something bigger than themselves? Or is this to ignore other sacramental and ritual needs that are deeply rooted within our socio-anthropological psyches – and our very souls? Art may help us to connect more fully with our inner selves and to reach out beyond to others and to the world – and even to God; but can it alone sustain us in times of dark despair, pain and loss, or consummate our utmost joy? Art is a *speculum* – a mirror – and if 'art for art's sake' can be an acknowledgement of our intuitive urge to create in response to God's gift of creation, it can also potentially represent a rejection of God in favour of a self-absorbed veneration of our own creativity, expressed and worshipped in art as well as in science and technology. Like ancient graven images, these vehicles can become modern idols, rather than reflections and conduits of the agency of creative power – what Christians call 'the Spirit'. Rejecting them, however, is to miss out, like former iconoclasts, on all that they bring to an appreciation of life and its meaning and all that they can help us to achieve. It all depends on how we view them.

These are big issues, and art itself will continue to help us to explore them. This book has added more ink to the process, but it is well to recall, in the face of such complexities, the words of Mel Bochner, one of the founders of Conceptual Art: 'There are thoughts and feelings that cannot be discussed or that are trivialized by talk.' Might the same be true of our attempts to capture and convey them visually, or does it indeed lie within the gift of the arts to transcend such constraints and enable us to express the otherwise inexpressible?

References

Introduction
1 Rowan Williams, *Grace and Necessity: Reflections on Art and Love*, Morehouse Publishing, 2005

Chapter 1
1 Eusebius, *Historia Ecclesiastica* 7.18.4
2 Eusebius, *Letter to Constantina*

Chapter 2
1 Oxford, Bodleian Library, Papyrus Bruce 96

Chapter 3
1 Sacramentary of Padua – Paduense, Introit, Hadrianum no. 690
2 *Ordo* XXIV

Chapter 4
1 British Library, Egerton MS 1139
2 Matenadaran, Erevan, Inv. No. 10675
3 Baltimore, Walters Art Museum, MS W.537
4 Tbilisi, K. Kekelidze Institute of Manuscripts (Georgia), H 1660, ff. 6v–7r
5 St Petersburg, National Library of Russia, Georgian new series 10
6 Florence, Biblioteca Medicea Laurenziana, MS Plut. 156

Chapter 5
1 Washington, Freer Gallery of Art, MS III, FGA 06.297, Matthew and John; 06.298, Mark and Luke
2 Coptic Museum, Cairo, Reg. No. 9962
3 New York, Pierpont Morgan Library, MS M.828

Chapter 6
1 Uppsala UB, DG I
2 Vienna, ÖNB, Cod. Theol. Gr. 31
3 Florence, Biblioteca Medicea-Laur., MS Plut. I.56
4 Brescia, Biblioteca Civica Queriniana
5 London, British Library, Add. MSS 5111–12
6 Dumbarton Oaks, Inv. 63.36.8–9
7 London, British Library, Cotton MS Otho B.vi
8 Oxford, Bodleian Library, Junius MS 11
9 London, British Library, Cotton MS Claudius B.iv

Chapter 7
1 John of Damascus, *On Holy Images*, c. 730 CE
2 London, British Library, Add. MS 39627, f. 3r

Chapter 8
1 London, British Library, APA, Add. MSS 22406–12

Chapter 9
1 London, British Library, Add. MS 5463
2 Florence, Biblioteca Medicea Laurenziana, MS Amiatino 1

Chapter 10
1 Paris, BNF, MS Lat. 1203
2 Epernay, Bibliothèque Municipale
3 Utrecht, University Library
4 London, British Library, Harley MS 2788; Vatican, Pal. Lat. 50
5 Paris, BNF, MS Lat. 1
6 Paris, BNF, MS Lat. 266
7 Aachen, Domschatzkammer Museum
8 Munich, Bayerische Staatsbibliothek, Clm 4456
9 Darmstadt, Hessische Landes und Hochschulbibliothek, Hs. 1640

'Words Passed Down'
1 Paris, BNF, MS Lat. 1
2 Rome, Vatican Library
3 Now in the monastery of San Paolo outside the walls of Rome
4 Translations of the captions in the San Paolo Bible are by Paul E. Dutton

Chapter 11
1 London, British Library, Cotton MS Tiberius A.ii
2 Oxford, Bodleian Library
3 London, British Library, Add. MS 4959
4 London, British Library, Harley MS 603
5 See Chapters 6, 8 and 9
6 London, British Library, Harley MS 2904
7 London, British Library, Cotton MS Titus D.xxvi–xxvii
8 Copenhagen, Kung Bibl. MS G1; New York, Pierpoint Morgan Library, M869; Cambridge, Trinity College, B.10.4; York, York Cathedral MS 1; Hanover, Kestner Museum, WMxxi036; London, British Library, Add. MS 34890 and Harley MS 76
9 London, British Library, Arundel MS 155
10 New York, Pierpont Morgan Library
11 London, British Library, Add. MSS 17739 and 11850

Chapter 12
1 Dijon, Bibliothèque Municipale, MSS 12–15
2 Rome, Vatican, MS Lat., 5279
3 London, British Library, Add. MS 11695
4 Cambridge, Corpus Christi College, MS 2, 3–4; London, Lambeth Palace, MS 3; Hildesheim Cathedral; Cambridge, Trinity College, MS R.17.1
5 London, British Library, Cotton MS Nero C.iii; Winchester Cathedral
6 London, British Library, Royal MS 2.A.xxii
7 Paris, Musée de Cluny
8 London, British Library, MS Add. 28106–07
9 Dublin, National Museum of Ireland

Chapter 13
1 London, British Library. Add. MS 28162
2 Paris, BNF, Lat. 11560
3 Vienna, Österreichische Nationalbibliothek, Österreich
4 London, British Library, Add. MS 18850
5 Château de Chantilly
6 London, British Library, Add. MS 74236
7 London, British Library, Add. MS 12531
8 London, National Gallery
9 London, British Library, Add. MS 42130
10 London, British Library, Add. MS 34309
11 London, British Library, Harley MS 4425
12 London, British Library, Add. MS 18852

Chapter 14
1 Florence, Galleria degli Uffizi
2 Florence, Galleria degli Uffizi
3 Pisa, Museo Nazionale
4 Naples Museum
5 Florence, Galleria degli Uffizi
6 Siena, Pinacoteca

Christian Art and Italian City-State
1 Bonaventura's commentary on the *Sentences* of Peter Lombard, lib. III, dist. ix, art. 1, q. 2, in *Opera Omnia*, vol. III, Quaracchi, 1887

Chapter 15
1 Coluccio Salutati, *De fato e fortuna*, Vatican Library, MS Vat. Lat. 2928, ff. 68v-69r, quoted from M. Baxandall, *Giotto and the Orators*, Oxford, 1971
2 Filippo Villani, *De Origine*, V, quoted from M. Baxandall, *Giotto and the Orators*, Oxford, 1971
3 Guarino of Verona, *Epistolario*, XI, quoted from M. Baxandall, *Giotto and the Orators*, Oxford, 1971
4 London, Victoria and Albert Museum
5 Alberti, *De pictura*, quoted from M. Baxandall, *Giotto and the Orators*, Oxford, 1971
6 Florence, Galleria degli Uffizi

Manuscripts, Humanism and Patronage in Renaissance Florence
1 Rome, Biblioteca Apostolica Vaticana, Urb. Lat. 1 and 2
2 Wolfenbüttel, Herzog August Bibliothek, Cod. Guelf. 39 Aug. 4
3 Lyon, Bibliothèque Municipale, MS 5123 and Le Havre, Musées des Beaux-Arts André Malreaux
4 Florence, Biblioteca Medicea Laurenziana, MS Plut. 15,17

Chapter 16
1 London, National Gallery
2 Paris, Musée du Louvre
3 Milan, Pinacoteca di Brera
4 Florence, Galleria degli Uffizi
5 London, British Library
6 London, British Library, Add. MS 34294
7 London, British Library, Add. MS 20927
8 National Gallery, London
9 Paris, Musée du Louvre
10 London, Royal Academy
11 Florence, Galleria degli Uffizi

12 Dresden, Gemäldegal.
13 Duke of Sutherland Collection, on loan to the National Gallery of Scotland

Chapter 17
1 Baltimore, Walters Gallery
2 Madrid, Museo del Prado
3 Munich, Alte Pinakothek
4 London, National Gallery
5 Florence, Galleria degli Uffizi
6 Bruges, Groeningemus
7 Brussels, Musées Royaux des Beaux-Arts
8 Antwerp, Koninklijk Museum Voor Schone Kunsten
9 Washington, National Gallery of Art

Chapter 18
1 Madrid, Museo del Prado
2 Weimar, Stadtkirche
3 Colmar, Musée D'Unterlinden
4 Madrid, Museo del Prado
5 Berlin, Gemäldegal
6 London, Courtauld Institute of Art Gallery
7 Antwerp, Museum Meyer van den Bergh
8 Vienna, Albertina
9 Prague, National Gallery
10 Basle, Kunstmuseum
11 Leiden, Stedelijk Musuem
12 Windsor, Royal Collection
13 London, National Gallery and Apsley House
14 Edinburgh, National Gallery
15 New York, Metropolitan Museum

Chapter 19
1 Venice, Gallerie dell'Accademia
2 Venice, Gallerie dell'Accademia
3 Venice, Gallerie dell'Accademia
4 Venice, Gallerie dell'Accademia
5 Venice, Gallerie dell'Accademia
6 Venice, Gallerie dell'Accademia

From Counter-Reformation to Baroque: Aspects of the Arts in Rome
1 See G. Paleotti, *Discorso delle immagini sacre e profane*, 1582
2 Paris, Musée du Louvre
3 Berlin, Dahlem Museum, lost during the Second World War
4 Rome, Vatican Museum
5 F. M. Torrigio, *Le Sacre Grotte*, 1618

Chapter 20
1 London, Victoria and Albert Museum
2 Vienna, Kunsthistorisches Museum
3 Florence, Galleria degli Uffizi
4 Rome, Vatican Museum
5 Paris, Musée du Louvre
6 Valletta, Oratory of St John
7 Messina, Museo Regionale
8 London, Marlborough House
9 London, Royal Collection
10 Florence, Galleria degli Uffizi
11 Lincolnshire, England, Burghley House
12 Lyon, Musée des Beaux-Arts

13 Private collection
14 Berlin, Gemäldegal
15 Munich, Alte Pinakothek
16 London, National Gallery
17 Frankfurt, Städelsches Kunstinstitut und Städtisches Galerie
18 Dresden, Gemäldegal
19 London, National Gallery
20 Amsterdam, Rijksmuseum
21 Royal Collection
22 Paris, Musée du Louvre and Copenhagen, Statens Museum for Kunst
23 Madrid, El Escorial
24 Toledo, San Tomé
25 Toledo, Museo de Santa Cruz
26 New York, Metropolitan Museum
27 Naples, Museo Nazionale di Capodimonte
28 Edinburgh, National Gallery of Scotland
29 Madrid, Museo del Prado
30 Madrid, Museo del Prado
31 Madrid, Museo del Prado
32 London, National Gallery
33 London, National Gallery
34 Madrid, Museo del Prado
35 Paris, Musée du Louvre

Rubens and the Theatre of the Counter-Reformation
1 London, National Gallery
2 London, National Gallery
3 London, National Gallery

Chapter 21
1 Los Angeles, Getty Museum
2 Paris, Musée du Louvre
3 Paris, Musée du Louvre
4 London, National Gallery
5 Paris, Musée du Louvre
6 Paris, Musée du Louvre
7 Paris, Musée du Louvre and London, National Gallery
8 Paris, Musée du Louvre
9 Rome, Vatican Museum
10 Duke of Rutland, Belvoir Castle and Duke of Sutherland, National Gallery of Scotland
11 London, Dulwich Picture Gallery
12 London, National Gallery
13 Washington, National Gallery
14 Karlruhe, Kunsthalle
15 Marseilles, Musée des Beaux-Arts
16 Brussels, Musée Royaux
17 Saint Sulpice, Paris

Chapter 22
1 London, Tate Britain, Clore Gallery
2 Pennsylvania, USA; Washington DC, The Phillips Collection
3 London, British Museum, Department of Prints and Drawings
4 1831, London, National Gallery
5 1830, London, Tate Britain
6 1879, New York, Metropolitan Museum

Permission, Prohibition, Patronage and Methodism
1 John Fletcher, *Last Check to Antinomianism* (London, 1775)
2 H. Honour, 'John Jackson R.A.', *The Connoisseurs' Year Book*, 1957

Chapter 23
1 Connecticut, New Haven, Yale University Art Gallery
2 Connecticut, New Haven, Yale University Art Gallery
3 Illinois, Chicago, R. H. Love Galleries
4 New York, Kinderhook, Columbia County Historical Society
5 New York, Albany Institute of History and Art
6 Washington DC, National Gallery of Art
7 Columbia County Historical Society
8 Washington DC, Smithsonian, National Museum of American Art
9 Washington DC, Corcoran Gallery of Art
10 New York, Metropolitan Museum,
11 San Francisco, Fine Arts Museum
12 Pennsylvania, Nazareth, Moravian Historical Society
13 New Mexico, Santa Fe, Museum of New Mexico
14 T. Dwight, *Travels in New England and New York*, I, 1821
15 Horace Bushnell, *Dogma and Spirit*, 1848
16 Letter from Magoon to Matthew Vassar, 30 May, 1864; *Magoon Papers*, Vassar College Library, Poughkeepsie, New York
17 *Magoon Papers*, Vassar College Library, Poughkeepsie, New York
18 Philadelphia, Philadelphia Museum of Art

Religious Folk Art
1 Brussels, Musées des Beaux-Arts
2 Mexico, New Mexico State University Art Gallery
3 New York, Metropolitan Museum of Art
4 Pennsylvania, Philadelphia, Pennsylvania Academy of Fine Arts
5 Florence, Brancacci Chapel
6 Massachusetts, North Grafton, Willard House and Clock Museum

Chapter 24
1 Staatliche Museen zu Berlin, Nationalgalerie
2 Dresden, Gemäldegal
3 Berlin, Nationalgalerie
4 New York, Utica
5 Venice, Galleria d'Arte Moderna
6 London, Tate Britain
7 Manchester, Manchester Art Gallery
8 London, Tate Britain
9 Port Sunlight, Lady Lever Gallery
10 Altarpieces for Keble College, Oxford, 1853–56, and St Paul's Cathedral, London, 1904, and a smaller version in Manchester Art Gallery
11 London, Tate Britain

Chapter 25
1 Paris, Musée du Louvre
2 St Germain-en-Laye, Musée Departemental Maurice Denis
3 Edinburgh, National Gallery
4 Florida, West Palm Beach, Norton Museum of Art
5 Boston, Museum of Fine Arts, 1897
6 Amsterdam, Van Gogh Museum
7 Paris, Musée d'Orsay

Chapter 26
1 Vienna, Leopold Museum
2 New York, Solomon R. Guggenheim Museum
3 Moscow, The State Tretyakov Gallery
4 London, Tate Modern
5 Published posthumously in 1987
6 New York, Museum of Modern Art
7 Oslo, National Gallery
8 Chicago, Art Institute
9 Nice, Cimiez Musée

Jewish Art, Christian Themes
1 Hamburger Kunsthalle
2 Moscow, The State Tretyakov Gallery
3 Warsaw, National Museum
4 Location unknown
5 Illinois, The Art Institute of Chicago

Chapter 27
1 Barcelona, Museo Picasso
2 Madrid, Centro de Arte Reina Sofia
3 Prado, Madrid
4 New York, Museum of Modern Art
5 Dallas, Museum of Fine Arts
6 Washington, National Gallery
7 New York, Whitney Museum
8 Private Collection
9 T. J. Clark, 'Arguments About Modernism: A Reply to Michael Fried', in F. Frascina, ed., *Pollock and After: The Critical Debate. Second Edition*, 1985
10 L'Art Brut, I, 1964

Chapter 28
1 Stuttgart, Staatsgalerie
2 Cologne, Wallraf-Richartz Museum
3 San Francisco, Lincoln Park
4 London, Tate Britain
5 London, Tate Britain
6 London, Tate Britain
7 Venice, LXVII Biennale

The Millennium and Beyond
1 Mark Angus, Trevor Appleston, Armando Ara, Philip Archer, Oliver Barratt, Elaine Bennet, Roland Biermann, George Blaiklock, Adam Boulter, Dunan Bullen, Simon Burdar, Matthew Burrows, Aileen Campbell, Andrew Carnegie, Mark Cazalet, Paul Clowney, Julie Cook, Tom Denny, Alan Everett, Rose Finn-Kelcey, Alan Flood, Tom Gidley, Richard Gilbert, Joy Girvin, Chris Gollon, Michael Gough, Kate Green, Robert Hardy, Claude Heath, Paul Hobbs, Kaori Homa, Margarete Horner, Polly Hope, Ghislaine Howard, Gemma Iles, Philip Jackson, Victoria Jones, John Keane, Diana Roe Kendall, John Kirby, Natasha Kissell, Jean Lamb, Jake Leber, Gillian Lever, Edward Litchfield, Ernesto Lozada-Usuriaga, Charlie Mackesy, John Maddison, Carol Marples, Henry Martin, Jenny Martin, Paul Martin, Louise McClary, Iain McKillop, Charlie Millar, Garry Fabian Miller, Richard Miller, Tessa Milward, Carla Moss, Nicholas Mynheer, Jennie Pedley, Bill Penney, Adele Prince, Jonathan Rabagliati, Michael Radcliffe, Hephzibah Rendle-Short, Kate Rose, Martin Rose, Jill Sim, Peter Smith, Rosalind Stoddart, Gigi Sudbury, Ian Thompson, Roger Wagner, David Ward, Penny Warden, Alison Watt, Richard Kenton Webb, Cynthia Whelan, Noel White, Peter White, Willie Williams, Kate Wilson, Tom Wood, David Wynne, Emily Young.

Chapter 29
1 Martina Hamilton and Associates Inc., New York

Chapter 30
1 Lindisfarne Priory, Holy Island, north-east England
2 Installed in St Paul's Cathedral, London, 2004
3 San Diego Museum of Man, Balboa Park
4 White Cube Gallery, London

Chapter 31
1 Tom Faulkner, reviewing his *New York Stations of the Cross* in *Art and Christianity* 45, January 2006

Christianity and Contemporary Art in North America
1 See www.CIVA.org
2 Members include: Lynn Aldrich, Chris Anderson, Sandra Bowden, Tanja Butler, Dan Callis, Guy Chase, Tyrus Clutter, Roger Feldman, Christine Forsythe, Donald Forsythe, Makoto Fujimura, Kate Hammett, Tim Hawkinson, Bruce Herman, Edward Knippers, Tim Lowly, Mary McCleary, Albert Pedulla, Catherine Prescott, Theodore Prescott, Tim Rollins, Joel Sheesley, Melissa Weinman, Patty Wickman and George Wingate.
3 2 Corinthians 13:14
4 Matthew Barney, James Lee Byars, Stephen De Staebler, Howard Finster, Eric Fischl, Dan Flavin, Robert Gober, James Hampton, Keith Haring, Tim Hawkinson, Christian Jankowski, Jasper Johns, Tobi Kahn, Vitaly Komar and Alex Melamid, William de Kooning, Jeff Koons, Robert Longo, Robert Mapplethorpe, Kerry James Marshall, Paul Pfeiffer, Robert Rauschenberg, Tim Rollins, Thomas Roma, David Salle, Julian Schnable, George Segal, Andres Serrano, Cindy Sherman, Kiki Smith, James Turrell, Bill Viola, Andy Warhol and Joel-Peter Witkin.
5 These would include: Wayne Adams, Julie Allen, Claudia Alvarez, John Bauer, Dayton Castelman, Brent Dickinson, Erica Downer, David Johanson, Greg King, Scott Kolbo, Hannah LaBorie, Allison Luce, Summer Merritt, Libby Pace, Chelsea Guest Perez, Heidi Petersen, Kathryn Romaine, John Silvis and Kelly Vanderbrug.

Glossary

Antependium	altar frontal
Autocephalous	self-governing, a church with its own head
Baldacchino	canopy that serves as a mark of honour towards that which it covers, often supported by four barley-twist columns recalling that which covered the Tabernacle in the Temple of Jerusalem
Caroline Minuscule	a multi-purpose script devised in the late eighth century by Carolingian scribes to promote regional cultural homogeneity
Cathechumen	baptismal candidate
Champlevé	fields of enamel recessed into a base plate
Ciboria	altar canopies
Cloisonné	fields of enamel separated by gold wires soldered onto a base plate
Deeisis	Christ flanked by the intercessory figures of the Virgin Mary and St John the Baptist
Diptych	two panels hinged together
Doom	Last Judgement
Dormition of the Virgin	'falling asleep', known in the Byzantine iconic tradition as the 'Koimesis'
Écorché	flayed figures, with the underlying skeletal and muscular structures revealed
Gesso	plasterwork, usually a ground upon which gold leaf was laid
Iconostasis	chancel screen bearing icons, in the Orthodox tradition
Koimesis	*see* Dormition of the Virgin
Majolica	tin-glazed earthenware
Mandorla	a burst of glory, usually almond-shaped, which is usually found containing the figure of the deified Christ
Manuscript	handwritten scroll, book or document
Nimbus	halo, a burst of glory behind the head, indicating sanctity; round indicates deceased, and square, living
Palimpsest	reused, erased and overwritten manuscript
Predella	small panels of scenes at the foot of an altarpiece
Reredos	panel behind an altar
Retable	panel behind an altar
Stuccowork	raised, modelled plasterwork
Tondo	roundel
Uncial	a formal, rounded book script used during Late Antiquity and the Early Middle Ages for high-grade biblical and liturgical books

435

Bibliography

Introduction and General

D. Apostolos-Cappadona, *Dictionary of Christian Art* (New York, 1994)

M. Austin, *Explorations in Art, Theology and Imagination* (London and Oakville, CT, 2005)

Sister W. Beckett, *On Art and the Sacred* (London, 1992)

H. Brigstocke, ed., *The Oxford Companion to Western Art* (Oxford, 2001)

Y. Christie *et al.*, eds, *Art in the Christian World, 300–1500* (London, 1982)

A. Grabar, *Christian Iconography* (Princeton, 1968; reptd London, 1980)

R. Holman, *The Art of the Sublime: Principles of Christian Art and Architecture* (Aldershot, 2006)

Index of Christian Art Online (Princeton, 2003)

R. Loverance, *British Museum, Christian Art* (London, 2007)

D. Morgan, *Visual Piety, A History and Theory of Popular Religious Images* (Berkeley and Los Angeles, 1998)

P. and L. Murray, *Oxford Dictionary of Christian Art* (Oxford, 2004)

G. Schiller, transl. J. Seligman, *Iconography of Christian Art* (London, 1971)

G. Schiller, *Iconography of Christian Art* (Greenwich, CT, 1968)

R. K. Seasoltz, *The Sense of the Sacred: Theological Foundations of Christian Architecture and Art* (London, 2005)

J. Speake, *The Dent Dictionary of Symbols in Christian Art* (London, 1994)

R. Williams, *Grace and Necessity: Reflection on Art and Love* (London, 2005)

B. Williamson, *Christian Art: A Very Short Introduction* (Oxford, 2004)

Chapter 1

J. Beckwith, *Early Christian and Byzantine Art* (2nd edn., Harmondsworth, 1979)

A. Cameron, *The Later Roman Empire* (London, 1993)

M. Gough, *The Origins of Christian Art* (London, 1973)

M. Henig, ed., *A Handbook of Roman Art. A Survey of the Visual Arts of the Roman World* (Oxford, 1983)

S. MacCormack, *Art and Ceremony in Late Antiquity* (Berkeley, Los Angeles and London, 1981)

F. Mancinelli, *Catacombs and Basilicas. Early Christians in Rome* (Florence, 1981)

A. Nestori, *Repertorio topografico delle pitture delle catacombe romane* (Rome, 1975)

M. Schapiro, *Late Antique, Early Christian and Medieval Art* (London, 1980)

E. M. Smallwood, *The Jews under Roman Rule* (Leiden, 1976)

J. Wilpert, *Le pitture delle catacombe romane* (Rome, 1903)

Chapter 2

M. Biddle, *The Tomb of Christ* (Stroud, 1999)

J. Elsner, *Art and the Roman Viewer. The Transformation of Art from the Pagan World to Christianity* (Cambridge, 1995)

J. Elsner, *Imperial Rome and Christian Triumph* (Oxford, 1998)

R. Harries, *The Passion in Art* (Aldershot, 2004)

E. Hartley, J. Hawkes, M. Henig and F. Mee, eds, *Constantine the Great, York's Roman Emperor*, Yorkshire Museum exhibition catalogue (York, 2006)

K. Weitzmann, *Late Antique and Early Christian Book Illumination* (London, 1977)

K. Weitzmann, ed., *Age of Spirituality. Late Antique and Early Christian Art, Third to Seventh Century*, Metropolitan Museum of Art exhibition catalogue (New York, 1979)

K. Weitzmann and H. L. Kessler, *The Cotton Genesis* (Princeton, 1986)

Chapter 3

J. Curran, *Pagan City and Christian Capital. Rome in the Fourth Century* (Oxford, 2000)

I. della Portella, *Subterranean Rome* (Cologne, 2000)

R. Krautheimer, W. Frankl, S. Corbett and A Frazer, *Corpus Basilicarum Cristianorum Romae*, 4 vols (Vatican, 1937–77)

R. Krautheimer, *Rome: Profile of a City 312–1308* (Princeton, 1980)

R. Krautheimer, *Three Christian Capitals* (Princeton, 1983)

R. Markus, *Gregory the Great and His World* (Cambridge, 1997)

W. Oakeshott, *The Mosaics of Rome from the Third to the Fourteenth Centuries* (London, 1967)

Chapter 4

L. Avrin, *Scribes, Script and Books* (London and Chicago, 1991)

International Seminar on Jewish Art, *Scripture and Picture: The Bible in Jewish, Christian and Islamic Art* (Jerusalem, 1999)

B. Kuhnel, ed., *The Real and Ideal Jerusalem in Jewish, Christian and Islamic Art* (Jerusalem, 1998)

G. E. Marrison and V. Nersessian, *The Christian Orient* (London, 1989)

T. F. Mathews and R. S. Wieck, *Treasures in Heaven. Armenian Illuminated Manuscripts*, Pierpont Morgan Library exhibition catalogue (New York, 1994)

B. Narkes, *Armenian Art Treasures of Jerusalem* (London, 1980)

S. der Nersessian, *Armenian Art* (London, 1978)

V. Nersessian, *Armenian Illuminated Gospelbooks* (London, 1987)

V. Nersessian, *Treasures from the Ark. 1700 Years of Armenian Christian Art*, British Library exhibition catalogue (London, 2001)

M. Piccirillo, *The Mosaics of Jordan* (Amman, 1993)

J. Ward-Perkins, *Justinianic Mosaic Pavements in Cyrenaican Churches* (Rome, 1980)

Chapter 5

A. Badawry, *Coptic Art and Archaeology* (Cambridge, Mass., 1978)

G. Gabra, *Cairo: the Coptic Museum and Old Churches* (Cairo, 1993)

E. Hein, *Ethiopia, Christian Africa* (Ratingen, 1999)

G. Mann, ed., *Art of Ethiopia*, Sam Fogg exhibition catalogue (London, 2005)

V. Nersessian, *Treasures from the Ark, 1700 Years of Armenian Christian Art* (London, 2001).

R. Wieck, ed., *Treasures in Heaven: Armenian Art, Religion and Society*, exhibition catalogue, Pierpont Morgan Library (New York, 1994)

Chapter 6

J. J. G. Alexander, *Medieval Illuminators and Their Methods of Work* (New Haven, 1992)

C. de Hamel, *A History of Illuminated Manuscripts* (Oxford, 1986)

C. Nordenfalk, *Early Medieval Book Illumination* (New York, 1988)

O. Pächt, *Book Illumination in the Middle Ages: An Introduction* (London, 1986)

J. Pelikan, *Mary Through the Centuries: Her Place in the History of Culture* (New Haven, 1996)

M. C. Ross, *Catalogue of the Byzantine and Early Medieval Antiquities in the Dumbarton Oaks Collection* (Washington D.C., 1962)

M. Spiro, *Critical Corpus of the Mosaic Pavements on the Greek Mainland, 4th–6th Centuries* (New York, 1978)

K. Weitzmann, *Late Antique and Early Christian Book Illumination* (London, 1977)

D. H. Wright, *The Vatican Virgil* (Berkeley, 1993)

Chapter 7

D. Buckton, ed., *Byzantium. Treasures of Byzantine Art and Culture*, British Museum exhibition catalogue (London, 1994)

P. Hetherington, *Byzantium* (London, 1983)

E. Kitzinger, *The Place of Book Illumination in Byzantine Art* (Princeton, 1975)

R. Loverance, *Byzantium* (London, 1988)

J. Lowden, *Early Christian and Byzantine Art* (London, 1997)

L. Rodley, *Byzantine Art and Architecture: an Introduction* (Cambridge, 1994)

S. Runciman, *Byzantine Style and Civilization* (Harmondsworth, 1975)

L. Safran, ed., *Heaven on Earth: Art and the Church in Byzantium* (University Park, PA, 1998).

D. Talbot Rice, *Art of the Byzantine Era* (London, 1963; 1977)

Chapter 8

R. W. Bulliet, *Conversion to Islam in the Medieval Period* (Cambridge, Mass., 1979)

F. Déroche and F. Richard, *Scribes et manuscrits du Moyen-Orient* (Paris, 1997)

R. Walker, *Views of Transition: Liturgy and Illumination in Medieval Spain* (London and Toronto, 1998)

Christian Art in Muslim Contexts

S. Bloom and J. Blair, *Islam: a Thousand Years of Faith and Power* (New Haven and London, 2002)

S. Bloom and J. Blair, eds, *Cosmophilia: Islamic Art from the David Collection, Copenhagen* (Chestnut Hill, Mass., 2006)

Chapter 9

J. J. G. Alexander, *Insular Manuscripts, 6th to the 9th Century* (London, 1978)

M. P. Brown, *Guide to Western Historical Scripts from Antiquity to 1600* (London and Toronto, 1990; revd edn, p/b 1994; 1999)

M. P. Brown, *The Lindisfarne Gospels: Society, Spirituality and the Scribe* (London and Toronto 2003)

M. P. Brown, *How Christianity Came to Britain and Ireland* (Oxford, 2006)

M. P. Brown, *Manuscripts from the Anglo-Saxon Age* (London, 2006)

D. Ganz, 'Roman Manuscripts in Francia and Anglo-Saxon England', in *Roma fra Oriente e Occidente, Settimane di studio del centro italiano di studi sull'alto medioevo* 49 (Spoleto, 2002)

J. Graham-Campbell and D. Kidd, eds, *The Vikings*, exhibition catalogue, BM and Metropolitan Museum (London and New York, 1980)

G. Henderson, *From Durrow to Kells, the Insular Gospel books 650–800* (London, 1987)

F. Henry, *Early Christian Irish Art* (Dublin, 1954)

C. Nordenfalk, *Early Medieval Book Illumination* (New York, 1988)

M. Ryan, ed., *Treasures of Irish Art*, exhibition catalogue, Metropolitan Museum (New York, 1977)

L. Webster and J. M. Backhouse, eds, *The Making of England: Anglo-Saxon Art and Culture AD 600–900*, BM / BL exhibition catalogue (London, 1991)

L. Webster and M. P. Brown, eds, *The Transformation of the Roman World AD 400–900* (London, 1997)

Chapter 10

R. Deshman, 'The Exalted Servant: The Ruler Theology of the Prayerbook of Charles the Bald', *Viator* 11 (1980), pp.385–417

W. Diebold, *Word and Image: A History of Early Medieval Art* (Boulder, 2000)

H. Kessler, *The Illustrated Bibles from Tours* (Princeton, 1977)

H. Mayr-Harting, *Ottonian Book Illumination: An Historical Study*, 2 vols (London, 1991)

R. McKitterick, ed., *Carolingian Culture: Emulation and Innovation* (Cambridge, 1994)

F. Mütherich, F. and J. Gaehde, *Carolingian Painting* (London, 1976)

K. Van der Horst *et al.*, eds, *The Utrecht Psalter in Medieval Art* (MS 't Goy, 1996)

Words Passed Down

Paul E. Dutton and Herbert L. Kessler, *The Poetry and Paintings in the First Bible of Charles the Bald* (Ann Arbor, 1997)

Herbert L. Kessler, *Spiritual Seeing: Picturing God's Invisibility in Medieval Art* (Philadelphia, 2000)

437

Chapter 11

M. P. Brown, *Manuscripts from the Anglo-Saxon Age* (London and Toronto, 2006)

E. Temple, *Anglo-Saxon Manuscripts, 900–1066* (London, 1976)

D. H. Turner, J. M. Backhouse and L. Webster, eds, *The Golden Age of Anglo-Saxon Art, 966–1066*, BM / BL exhibition catalogue (London, 1984)

D. M. Wilson, *Anglo-Saxon Art* (London, 1984)

Chapter 12

J. J. G. Alexander, *Norman Illumination at Mont St Michel, 966–1100* (Oxford, 1970)

A. Andersson, *The Art of Scandinavia* (Feltham, 1970)

A. Chastel, *French Art: Prehistory to the Middle Ages* (Paris, 1994)

M. Durliat, *La sculpture romane de la route de Saint-Jacques* (Mont de Marsan, 1990)

R. G. Gameson, *The Manuscripts of Early Norman England, c. 1066–1130* (Oxford, 1999)

C. M. Kauffmann, *Romanesque Manuscripts, 1066–1190* (London, 1975)

C. Rudolph, *Pilgrimage to the End of the World: The Road to Santiago de Compostela* (Chicago, 2004)

H. Swarzenski, *Monuments of Romanesque Art. The Art of Church Treasures in North-Western Europe* (London, 1954; 1974)

E. Vergnole, *l'art monumental de la France romane* (London, 2000)

I. Villela-Petit, *l'art gothique international* (Paris, 2004)

G. Zarnecki *et al.*, eds, *English Romanesque Art 1066–1200*, Hayward Gallery exhibition catalogue (London, 1984)

Monastic Aesthetics and the Rise of Gothic Art

C. Rudolph, *Artistic Change at St-Denis: Abbot Suger's Program and the Early Twelfth-Century Controversy over Art* (Princeton, 1990)

C. Rudolph, *The 'Things of Greater Importance': Bernard of Clairvaux's Apologia and the Medieval Attitude Toward Art* (Philadelphia, 1990)

C. Rudolph, *Violence and Daily Life: Reading, Art, and Polemics in the Cîteaux Moralia in Job* (Princeton, 1997)

C. Rudolph, ed., *A Companion to Medieval Art: Romanesque & Gothic in Northern Europe* (Oxford, 2007)

Chapter 13

J. J. G. Alexander, *Medieval Illuminators and Their Methods of Work* (New Haven, 1992)

J. J. G. Alexander and P. Binski, eds, *Age of Chivalry: Art in Plantagenet England, 1200–1400*, exhibition catalogue, Royal Academy (London, 1987)

F. Avril *et al.*, eds, *L'art au temps des rois maudits: Philippe le Bel et ses fils, 1285–1328*, exhibition catalogue, musées nationaux (Paris, 1998)

J. M. de Azcárate, *Arte gótico en España* (Madrid, 1990)

M. P. Brown, *Understanding Illuminated Manuscripts: a Glossary of Technical Terms* (London and Malibu, 1994)

G. Buzwell, *Saints in Medieval Manuscripts* (London, 2005)

M. Camille, *The Gothic Idol* (Cambridge, 1989)

M. Camille, *Image on the Edge: Margins of Medieval Art* (London, 1992)

C. de Hamel, *A History of Illuminated Manuscripts* (Oxford, 1986)

C. de Hamel, *Scribes and Illuminators* (London, 1992)

E. Duffy, *Marking the hours: English people and their prayers 1240–1570* (New Haven and London, 2006)

G. Fischer, *Figurenportale in Deutschland 1350–1530* (Frankfurt and New York, 1989)

R. Gottfried, *The Isenheim Altar* (Edinburgh, 1997)

R. Ivančević, *Art Treasures of Croatia* (Zagreb, 1993)

E. Mâle, transl. D. Nussey, *The Gothic Image: Religious Art in France of the Thirteenth Century* (London and Glasgow, 1961)

R. Marks and P. Williamson, eds, *Gothic: Art for England, 1400–1547*, V&A exhibition catalogue (London, 2003)

R. Mellinkoff, *Outcasts: Signs of Otherness in Northern European Art of the Late Middle Ages*, 2 vols (Berkeley, Los Angeles and Oxford, 1993)

W. Neumeister, *Gothic Art in Bohemia* (Oxford, 1977)

Medieval Stained Glass

V. Raguin, *The History of Stained Glass* (London, 2003)

Chapter 14

M. Baxandall, *Giotto and the Orators* (Oxford, 1971)

Sister W. Beckett, *The Art of Faith: A Lent and Easter Journey Through Duccio's Maestà* (Chawton, 2007)

J. Cannon and B. Williamson, eds, *Art, Politics and Civic Religion in Central Italy* (Aldershot, 2000)

H. Flora, *Cimabue and early Italian devotional painting* (New York, 2006)

A. Ladis, ed., *The Arena Chapel and the Genius of Giotto* (New York, 1998)

J. White, *Art and Architecture in Italy, 1250–1400* (New Haven and London, 1993)

Christian Art and the Italian City-State

A. Ladis, *Studies in Italian Art* (London, 2001)

Chapter 15

H. N. Abrams, ed., *The Vatican Collections: the Papacy and Art*, exhibition catalogue, Metropolitan Museum (New York, 1982)

J. H. Beck, *From Duccio to Raphael: Connoisseurship in Crisis* (Florence, 2006)

A. Cole, *Art of the Italian Renaissance Courts* (Upper Saddle River, NJ, 1995)

G. Holmes, *The Florentine Enlightenment 1400–50* (London, 1969)

A. L. Jenkens, ed., *Renaissance Siena: Art in Context* (Kirksville, MO, 2006)

L. B. Kanter *et al.*, *Painting and Illumination in Early Renaissance Florence 1300–1450*, exhibition catalogue, Metropolitan Museum (New York, 1994)

D. Kent, *Cosimo de' Medici and the Florentine Renaissance* (New Haven and London 2000)

P. L. Rubin and A. Wright, *Renaissance Florence: The Art of the 1470s*, exhibition catalogue, National Gallery (London, 1999)

Manuscripts, Humanism and Patronage in Renaissance Florence

F. Ames-Lewis, *The Library and Manuscripts of Piero di Cosimo de' Medici* (New York & London, 1984)

E. Callmann, *Apollonio di Giovanni* (Oxford, 1974)

C. Csapodi and K. Csapodi-Gárdonyi, *Biblioteca Corviniana: The Library of King Matthias Corvinus of Hungary* (Shannon, 1969)

M. Levi D'Ancona, *Miniatura e Miniatori a Firenze dal XIV al XVI Secolo* (Florence, 1962)

M. Evans, 'Italian Manuscript Illumination 1460–1560', in T. Kren (ed.), *Renaissance Painting in Manuscripts*, exhibition catalogue, J. Paul Getty Museum, Pierpont Morgan Library, British Library (Los Angeles, New York and London, 1983), p.90

M. Evans, 'La miniature del Rinascimento a Firenze', in A. M. Piazzoni (ed.), *La Bibbia di Federico da Montefeltro*, vol. 1 (Modena, 2005), pp.61–92

A. Garzelli and A. C. de la Mare, *Miniatura Fiorentina del Rinacimento 1440–1525. Un Primo Censimento*, 2 vols (Florence, 1985)

A. C. de la Mare, 'Cosimo and his Books', in F. Ames-Lewis (ed.), *Cosimo 'il Vecchio' de' Medici, 1389–1464* (Oxford, 1992), pp.115–56

O. Pächt, *Book Illumination in the Middle Ages* (Oxford, 1984)

Vespasiano da Bisticci (ed. and trans. W. G. Waters and E. Waters), *The Vespasiano Memoirs* (London, 1926)

Chapter 16

Jonathan J.G. Alexander, ed., *The Painted Page: Italian Renaissance Book Illumination 1450–1550*, exhibition catalogue, Royal Academy and Pierpont Morgan Library, (London and New York, 1994)

D. A. Brown, *Leonardo da Vinci: Art and Devotion in the Madonnas of his Pupils* (Milan, 2003)

D. Franklin, ed., *Leonardo da Vinci, Michelangelo and the Renaissance in Florence*, exhibition catalogue, Nat. Gal. of Art, Ottawa (Ottawa and New Haven, 2005)

Richard A. Goldthwaite, *Wealth and the Demand for Art in Italy 1300–1600* (Baltimore and London 1993)

M. B. Hall, ed., *Rome* (Cambridge, 2005)

M. B. Hall, *Michelangelo's Last Judgement* (Cambridge, 2005)

F. Hartt and D. G. Wilkins, *History of Italian Renaissance Art* (Harlow, 2007)

R. Toman, ed., *The Art of the Italian Renaissance* (Cologne, 2005)

Giorgio Vasari, *Lives of the Artists*, ed. M. Aronberg Lavin (Mineolo, NY, 2005)

W. Wray, ed., *Leonardo da Vinci, in His Own Words* (London, 2005)

Brazen Images and Sounding Brass

C. Avery and A Radcliffe, eds, *Giambologna, 1529–1608: Sculptor to the Medici*, Arts Council exhibition catalogue (London, 1978)

V. J. Avery, *The Early Works of Alessandro Vittoria (c. 1540–70)* (Cambridge, 1996)

Chapter 17

L. Campbell, *The Fifteenth-Century Netherlandish Schools* (London, 1998)

L. Campbell, *Renaissance Portraits: European Portrait-Painting in the 14th, 15th and 16th Centuries* (New Haven and London, 1990)

C. Harbison, *The Art of the Northern Renaissance* (London, 1995)

T. Kren and S. McKendrick, eds, *Flemish Illuminated Manuscripts, 1400–1550*, exhibition catalogue, Royal Academy and J. Paul Getty Museum (London and Malibu, 2003)

J. Snyder, *Northern Renaissance Art* (New York, 1985)

Chapter 18

S. Blick and R. Tekippe, *Art and Architecture of Late Medieval Pilgrimage in Northern Europe and the British Isles* (Leiden, 2005)

P. F. Cuneo, *Art and Politics in Early Modern Germany* (Leiden, 1998)

E. Duffy, *The Stripping of the Altars: Traditional Religion in England, c. 1400–1580* (2nd edn, New Haven and London, 2005)

P. W. Parshall and L. B. Parshall, *Art and the Reformation: an Annotated Bibliography* (Boston, Mass., 1986)

D. H. Price, *Albrecht Dürer's Renaissance: Humanism, Reformation and the Art of Faith* (Ann Arbor, 2003)

The Dispute on Images During the Reformation

P. M. Jones and T. Worcester, From Rome to Eternity: Catholicism and the Arts in Italy, c. 1550–1650 (Boston, 2002)

Chapter 19

W. L. Barcham, *The Religious Paintings of Giambattista Tiepolo* (Oxford, 1989)

P. F. Brown, *The Renaissance in Venice* (London, 1997)

J. Martineau and A. Robinson, eds, *The Glory of Venice: Art in the eighteenth century*, exhibition catalogue, Royal Academy and Nat. Gal. of Art, Washington, D.C. (London and New Haven, 1994)

G. Romanelli, ed., *Venice: Art and Architecture* (Cologne, 1997)

M. Varia, *Venice, City of Art* (London, 2006)

From Counter-Reformation to Baroque

M. C. Abromson, *Painting in Rome during the papacy of Clement VIII (1592–1605): a documented study* (New York, 1981)

R. Wittkower, *Bernini: the sculptor of the Roman Baroque* (London, 1997)

Chapter 20

J. Boyd and P. Esler, *Visuality and the Biblical Text* (Florence, 2004)

J. I. Durham, *The Biblical Rembrandt: Human Painter in a Landscape of Faith* (Macon, GA, 2004)

W. A. Dyrness, *Reformed theology and visual culture : the Protestant imagination from Calvin to Edwards* (Cambridge, 2004)

S. F. Ostrow, *Art and Sprituality in Counter-Reformation Rome* (Cambridge, 1996)

G. Parry, *The Arts of the Anglican Counter-Reformation: Glory, Laud and Honour* (Woodbridge, 2006)

J. Roberts, *Holbein* (revd edn, London, 2005)

439

Rubens and the Theatre of Counter-Reformation

D. Jaffé, ed., *Rubens, a Master in the Making*, exhibition catalogue, National Gallery (London, 2005)

Chapter 21

R. Kasl and S. L. Stratton, *Painting in Spain in the Age of Enlightenment: Goya and his Contemporaries*, exhibition catalogue, Indianapolis Museum of Art (Indianapolis, 1997)

G. Mauner, *et al.*, eds., *Paris, Center of Artistic Enlightenment* (University Park, PA, 1988)

D. Roberts, *Art and Enlightenment: Aesthetic Theory after Adorno* (Lincoln, Nebraska, 1991)

The Rise of the Study of the History of Christian Art

N. Netzer and V. Reinburg, *Fragmented Devotion: Medieval Objects from the Schnütgen Museum, Cologne*, exhibition catalogue, McMullen Museum (Boston, 2000)

V. Raguin, *Catholic Collecting* (Worcester, MA, 2006)

Chapter 22

D. Bindman, *William Blake* (London, 2000)

E. Lorenz, *Neoclassicism and Romanticism, 1750–1850: sources and documents* (London, 1970)

R. Rosen, *Romanticism and Realism* (New York, 1984)

W. Vaughan, *et al.*, eds, *Samuel Palmer*, BM exhibition catalogue (London, 2005)

Permission, Prohibition, Patronage and Methodism

S. P. Casteras, *James Smetham* (London, 1985)

F. H. Everson, *This is Methodism* (London, 1957)

P. Forsaith, *A Brand Plucked as from the Burning* (Oxford, 2004)

D. M. Rosman, *Evangelicals and Culture* (London, 1984)

R. Woollen, *Catalogue of the Methodist Church Collection of Modern Christian Art* (Oxford, 2003)

Chapter 23

J. Davis, *The Landscape of Belief: Encountering the Holy Land in Nineteenth-Century American Art and Culture* (Princeton, 1996)

J. Dillenberger, *The Visual Arts and Christianity in America. The Colonial Period through the Nineteenth Century* (Chico, CA, 1984)

G. Gunn, *The Bible and American Arts and Letters* (Philadelphia & Chico, CA, 1983)

N. Harris, *The Artist in American Society: the Formative Years 1790–1860* (New York, 1966)

B. Novak, *American Painting of the Nineteenth Century: Realism, Idealism and the American Experience* (New York, 1969)

B. Novak, *Nature and Culture: American Landscape and Painting 1825–75* (New York, 1980)

S. Promey, *Spiritual Spectacles: Vision and Image in mid-nineteenth-century Shakerism* (Bloomington, 1993)

Religious Folk Art

S. D. Brenton and P. Benes, *The Art of Family: Genealogical Artifacts in New England* (Boston, Mass., 2002)

A. Frankenstein, *Angels Over the Altar: Christian Folk Art in Hawaii and the South Seas* (Honolulu, 1961)

J. Kallir, *The Folk Art Tradition: Native Painting in Europe and the United States*, exhibition catalogue, Galerie St. Etienne (New York, 1981)

E. Netto Calil Zarur and C. Muir Lovell, *Art and Faith in Mexico: The Nineteenth-century Retablo Tradition* (Albuquerque, 2001)

Chapter 24

M. B. Frank, *German Romantic Painting Redefined: Nazarene Tradition and the Narratives of Romanticism* (Aldershot, 2001)

E. Prettejohn, *The Pre-Raphaelites* (London, 2000)

P. Stansky, *Redesigning the World: William Morris, the 1880s and the Arts and Crafts* (Princeton, NJ, 1985)

Chapter 25

A. Boime, *Art in an Age of Counter-Revolution, 1815–1948* (Chicago, 2004)

R. Meier, *Recent American Synagogue Architecture* (New York, 1963)

D. Morgan, ed., *Icons of American Protestantism: the Art of Warner Sallman* (New Haven, 1996)

A. Sturgis, R. Christiansen, L. Oliver *et al.*, *Rebels and Martyrs. The Image of the Artist in the Nineteenth Century* (London: National Gallery exhibition catalogue, 2006)

J.C. Taylor, *America as Art* (Washington, 1976)

J.C. Taylor, *The Fine Arts in America* (Chicago, 1979)

Chapter 26

M. Bushart, *Der Geist der Gotik und die expressionistische Kunst: Kunstgeschichte und Kunsttheorie 1911–25* (Munich, 1990)

J. and J. Dillenberger, *Perceptions of the Spirit in Twentieth-Century American Art*, exhibition catalogue, Indianapolis Museum of Art (Indianapolis, 1977)

H. Fischer and S. Rainbird, eds, *Kandinsky. The Path to Abstraction*, exhibition catalogue, Tate Gallery (London, 2006)

K.C. Lindsay and P. Vergo, eds, *Kandinsky, Complete Writings on Art*, 2 vols (London, 1982)

J. Romaine, 'Vincent van Gogh: Between Mythology and Art', *Art Journal of the College Art Association* (New York, 1998)

Jewish Artists, Christian Themes

Z. Amishai-Maisels, 'The Jewish Jesus', in *Journal of Jewish Art 9* (1982), pp.84–104

A. Barzel, *Israele Arte e Vita 1906–2006*, exhibition catalogue (Milan, 2006)

E. D. Bilski, *Berlin Metropolis: Jews and the New Culture, 1890–1918* (Berkeley, 2000)

N. Guralnik, *In the Flower of Youth: Maurycy Gottlieb 1856–79*, exhibition catalogue (Tel Aviv, 1991)

V. B. Mann and E. D. Bilski, *The Jewish Museum New York* (London, 1993)

N. N. Perez, *Corpus Christi: Les représentations du Christ en Photographie 1886–2002* (Paris and Jerusalem, 2002)

Chapter 27

N. Bourriaud, *Relational Aesthetics* (Dijon, 2002)

M. Duchamp, *Have You Seen the Horizon Lately?* (Oxford, 1997)

H. Flora and S. Yun Kang, *This Anguished World of Shadows: Georges Rouault's Miserere Et Guerre* (New York, 2006)

J. Jenkins, ed., *In the Spirit of Fluxus* (Minneapolis, 1983)

R. A. Lofthouse, *Vitalism in Modern Art, c. 1900–50: Otto Dix, Stanley Spencer, Max Beckmann and Jacob Epstein* (Lewiston, Lampeter, 2005)

R. Nathanson, *Georges Rouault 1871–1958: paintings and the fourteen aquatints for 'Les fleurs du mal'* (London, 1972)

The Episcopal Church of the USA and Visual Arts: www.ecva.org

Fellowship of Quakers in the Arts: www.quaker.org/fqa

Chapter 28

F. Frascina, ed., *Pollock and After: The Critical Debate, Second Edition* (London and New York, 1985)

R. Giles, *Repitching the Tent* (revd edn, Norwich, 2004)

M. Hammer, *Bacon and Sutherland* (New Haven, 2005)

I. Sandler, *Art of the Postmodern Era: from the late 1960s to the early 1990s* (New York, 1996)

R. S. Vosko, *God's House is Our House; Re-imagining the Environment for Worship* (Collegeville, Minnesota, 2006)

The Millennium and Beyond

C. Baile de Laperrière, *Who's Who in Art* (Calne, Wilts., 2006)

T. Devonshire Jones, ed., *Presence: Images of Christ for the Third Millennium*, exhibition catalogue, Bible Lands (London, 2004)

Chapter 29

M. Arnold, *Women and Art in South Africa* (Cape Town, 1996)

G. Nasfeter, *Lichtpyramide: A catalogue of Art as a Document of an Ecumenical Adventure* (Berlin, 2005)

S. Williamson and J. Ashraf, *Art in South Africa, the Future Present* (Cape Town, 1996)

Asian Christian Arts Association: www.asianchristianart.org

Zimbabwe Christian Art, exhibition catalogue, Anglican Cathedral, Harare (Harare, 1986)

Chapter 30

N. Bustard, ed., *It was Good: Making Art to the Glory of God* (Baltimore, MD, 2000)

B. Spackman, *A Profound Weakness: Christians and Kitsch* (Carlisle, 2005)

G. Wolfe, *Intruding Upon the Timeless: Meditations on Art, Faith and Mystery* (Baltimore, MD, 2004)

Image: a Journal of the Arts and Religion: www.imagejournal.org

The Scribe Speaks

www.saintjohnsbible.org

Chapter 31

C. Deacy, *Faith in Film* (Aldershot, 2005)

W. A. Dyrness, *Visual Faith: Art, Theology, and Worship in Dialogue (Engaging Culture)* (Grand Rapids, MI, 2001)

J. Elkins, *On the Strange Place of Religion in Contemporary Art* (London and New York, 2004)

G. Howes, *The Art of the Sacred* (London, 2006)

D. Johnson Fleming, *Each With His Own Brush: Contemporary Christian Art in Asia and Africa* (New York, 1938)

R. K. Johnson, *Reel Spirituality: Theology and Film in Dialogue (Engaging Culture)* (Grand Rapids, MI, 2006)

C. McDonnell, *Material Christianity: Religion and Popular Culture in America* (New Haven, 1995)

T. Prescott, ed., *A Broken Beauty* (Grand Rapids, MI, 2005)

C. Townsend, *The Art of Bill Viola* (London, 2004)

S. Turner, *Imagine: a Vision for Christians in the Arts* (Leicester, 2001)

Art and Christianity Enquiry: www.ace.org

Christianity and Contemporary Art in North America

J. Romaine, *Objects of Grace: Conversations on Creativity and Faith* (Baltimore, 2002)

Christians in the Visual Arts: www.CIVA.org

441

Index

444

Picture Acknowledgements

447

448